First Amendment Law in Louisiana

First Amendment Law in Louisiana

edited by

William R. Davie

T. Michael Maher

2015
University of Louisiana at Lafayette Press

© 2015 by University of Louisiana at Lafayette Press
All rights reserved
ISBN (paper): 978-1-935754-65-7

University of Louisiana at Lafayette Press
P.O. Box 40831
Lafayette, LA 70504-0831
http://ulpress.org

Library of Congress Cataloging-in-Publication Data:

First Amendment law in Louisiana / edited by William R. Davie, T. Michael Maher.
    pages cm
  Includes bibliographical references and index.
  ISBN 978-1-935754-65-7 (alk. paper)
  1. Freedom of expression--Louisiana. 2. Freedom of religion--Louisiana. 3. Civil rights--Louisiana. 4. Constitutional law--Louisiana. 5. United States. Constitution. 1st Amendment. I. Davie, William R., 1952- editor. II. Maher, T. Michael, editor.
  KFL412.R45F57 2015
  342.7308'509753--dc23
                            2015016619

Front and back covers: The Louisiana Supreme Court building on Royal Street in New Orleans is fronted by a statue of Edward Douglas White, Jr., a native of Thibodaux, Louisiana, who served as the ninth Chief Justice of the United States. *Photos by T. Michael Maher.*

Contents

Foreword..6
William R. Davie and T. Michael Maher, Univ. of Louisiana at Lafayette

1   The law and legal system of Louisiana...8
    Pearson Cross, Univ. of Louisiana at Lafayette

2   Freedom of expression..26
    Rick A. Swanson, Univ. of Louisiana at Lafayette

3   Religious liberty...44
    Rick A. Swanson, Univ. of Louisiana at Lafayette

4   Defamation...61
    William R. Davie with Rick A. Swanson, Univ. of Louisiana at Lafayette

5   Privacy and the right to be left alone...84
    Amy Gajda, Tulane University Law School

6   Student rights of expression..104
    Joe Mirando, Southeastern Louisiana University

7   Courts and media...121
    S. L. Alexander, Loyola University

8   Access to public documents and meetings..145
    James Stewart, Nicholls State University

9   Obscenity..168
    William R. Davie, Univ. of Louisiana at Lafayette

10   Intellectual property...191
    Steven J. Dick, Univ. of Louisiana at Lafayette

11   Commercial expression..215
    Rick J. Norman, McNeese State University

12   Digital media..240
    Ashley Packard, University of Houston - Clear Lake

Glossary..263

Index of Court Cases...275

Index...283

Foreword

By William R. Davie and T. Michael Maher, Univ. of Louisiana at Lafayette

This book is about the First Amendment's robust career in Louisiana, which has a legal tradition unlike that of any other state. As explained in our opening chapter, Louisiana's legal heritage derives from both continental law and common law. This gives our body of laws a hybrid vigor that serves as a better model for understanding freedom of expression in politics and business around the world.

Although *First Amendment Law in Louisiana* was chiefly written for a college student readership, practicing attorneys and the general public will find this book's chapters invaluable to understanding the legal principles and precedents behind many of the communication issues of the day. For example, here are some recent news stories whose underlying issues are explained in this book:

- Gov. Bobby Jindal's top aides communicated with personal email accounts beyond the reach of public records laws (Deslatte, 2012), a tactic repeated in 2015 by Secretary of State and presidential hopeful Hillary Clinton (Schmidt & Chozick, 2015). Chapter 8 of this book explains the legal thought behind requiring policy makers to keep their policy deliberations on the record and accessible to the public.

- The Covington City Council, which had virtually banned door-to-door sales, dropped the ban after a city attorney said the ban violated the First Amendment (State roundup, 2014). Chapter 11 explains that while commercial speech is more tightly regulated than political speech, legitimate commercial messages should not be restricted by government.

- An attorney for a Baton Rouge pizzeria sent a cease and desist order to Lafayette's Dean-O's Pizza, over its advertising of a boudin pizza, which the Baton Rouge vendor had trademarked (Carter, 2013). Chapter 10 explains the nuances of copyright and trademark law.

- A Baton Rouge judge sent sheriff's deputies to seize records related to the LSU Board of Supervisors' 2014 search for a new president/chancellor, records the board had refused to give the Baton Rouge *Advocate* (Hasten, 2014). Chapter 8 gives the reader background in why the public should have access to documents related to the governance of public institutions.

We could offer many more examples of First Amendment issues, and many more seem likely to develop in the near future: personal flying drones with video cameras raise new privacy issues; social media offer new venues for threatening messages; new hand-held police radar provides a powerful tool for both law enforcement and privacy invasion; digital media give advertisers rich databases about our personal lives and likes.

Technology and culture will continue to provide challenges to our First Amendment freedoms. And as they do, this book will continue to provide readers with the legal principles that undergird *First Amendment Law in Louisiana*.

This book owes much to an extraordinary group of contributing authors, who include distinguished practitioners of law and professors of political science, journalism and mass communication. We salute their excellent contributions, without which this book would not be possible. We are grateful for the guidance and editorial expertise offered by the University of Louisiana Press, and the special assistance of James Wilson.

Works Cited

Carter, S. (2013, June 17). Legal matters: The name game. *The Independent*. Retrieved from http://theind.com/article-13941-legal-matters-the-name-game.html

Deslatte, M. (2012, Dec. 11). Jindal aides use personal email to strategize. *The Daily Advertiser*, p. A2.

Hasten, M. (2014, Sept. 11). Judge orders seizure of LSU records. *The Daily Advertiser*, p. B1.

Schmidt, M., & Chozick, A. (2015, March 4). Using Private Email, Clinton Thwarted Records Requests. *The New York Times*, p. A1.

State roundup (2014, Aug. 22). *The Daily Advertiser*, p. A 12.

Dedication

We dedicate this book to Ashley Packard, who wrote Chapter 12 as she was dying of cancer, and who lost that battle in November 2014. Ashley is the former student of both editors, who remember her fondly as being brilliant and personable. She never mentioned her health issues during the process of writing and editing this book. We deeply regret her passing and wish to honor her memory with this dedication.

Chapter 1
The Law and Legal System of Louisiana
By Pearson Cross, University of Louisiana at Lafayette

Learning Objectives
In this chapter, readers will:
- identify the broad ideals underlying western systems of justice, including Louisiana
- demonstrate an understanding of how judicial principles are reflected in the operation of federal and state courts
- appreciate the principle of judicial review in defining the operation of the court under common law systems of jurisprudence
- become familiar with the four-tiered court system in Louisiana
- contrast the principle of jurisprudence constante found in the civil law system with the civil law common law principles of stare decisis
- develop a nuanced understanding of the cultural heritage that gave rise to Louisiana's mixed system of laws and legal administration
- discern the federal appellate jurisdiction from the state system of courts

Governments in Western industrial democracies are founded on the broad ideals of liberty, equality, and justice. They were created to protect fundamental rights that are understood as inherent in each person, including the right to self-expression, the right to order one's life as he or she wishes (individualism), and the right to own and dispose of property (capitalism). For example, under the framework of law and rights contained in the United States Constitution, free expression is protected and limits are placed on the power of government to regulate public and private opinion. Yet, our free society produces conflict as citizens use the great liberties given them to express themselves and pursue their various interests. To resolve these conflicts governmental institutions act as impartial referees, seeking to mitigate conflict by promoting just solutions that respect the rights of people and organizations while limiting damage to the system itself. As conflicts are successfully resolved through the use of public institutions, citizens become more supportive of government, which, in turn, increases the public perception of governmental legitimacy. Although governments mitigate conflict through equitable representation, efficient administration and well-written legislation, a comprehensive and well-developed system of laws and courts has been created to address specific conflicts arising from relations between citizens, between citizens and organizations, and between citizens and the state.

This chapter will focus on the system of laws and courts that has been created in Louisiana to address legal conflicts and serve the public. The justice system in Louisiana is unlike that of any other state, although it shares many features. The main reason for Louisiana's unique system of law and courts is its French and Spanish heritage, which has provided the state with a code-of-law system that is sometimes called "Napoleonic" or "continental" law. Louisiana has a mixed legal system that contains elements drawn from both continental law (French, Spanish) and "common law" (English) sources. It is the intermixture of these two heritages that creates a unique setting for the settling of legal conflict in Louisiana.

The subjects and controversies examined in the following chapters occur within the legal framework and setting that is the subject matter of this present chapter. Grasping the intricacies of First Amendment law in Louisiana will require the student to understand the different types of law that underlie the system: fundamental law (constitutions), written law (codes, legislation), and judge-made law (case law); the court system at the federal and state level; the officials and individuals who work in and use the justice system (judges, lawyers, district attorneys, individual citizens); and finally, the various organizations (bar, law schools, journals) that staff, study, document, and influence the system. This large area of study is too broad for this introductory chapter, which will focus on the different types of law, the history of law and courts in Louisiana, judicial elections, and (briefly) the effect of the Voting Rights Act on judicial districts in the state. This chapter provides maps illustrating the Louisiana and national court systems and a research section for those interested in learning more about Louisiana courts, its laws, and system of jurisprudence.

THE FEDERAL SETTING

Although we are focused on First Amendment law in Louisiana, Louisiana is part of a federal system of government. In a federal system, power is divided between federal and state governments, with rights and responsibilities broadly specified by the constitution and legislation. The most fundamental source of law in the federal system is the United States Constitution, which reflects the will of the people as ratified in 1787, and amended twenty-seven times since. The "Supremacy Clause" in the Constitution establishes a hierarchy of law in the United States. Under this hierarchy, constitutional provisions, laws passed by Congress, and decisions of the federal court system are supreme and supersede any provisions in state constitutions and state law. Whenever there is a conflict between federal and state law, federal law must win out.[1]

While the supremacy clause creates the conditions for an extremely powerful and overweening federal government, in fact, the federal government has limited authority and *jurisdiction* compared to state government. Jurisdiction means legitimate oversight or control over a certain area of human endeavor. State governments are understood to possess "police powers," which means they have the legitimate authority to regulate behavior for the individual and common good, excepting those areas specifically set aside by the state or federal bill of rights. In contrast, the power of the federal government is quite limited in most areas relative to state power, although the struggle for power between national and state governments is an omnipresent part of American life. Ultimately, when there is a conflict between the laws of the nation and a state government, it is authoritatively addressed by the federal court system in exercise of its power of judicial review.[2]

Judicial review is the power to say what is, and what is not, in keeping with the law. Thus, the federal courts can strike down laws passed by Congress, actions of federal officials, administrative regulations, decisions of lower courts, and state laws that are in violation of federal law or the United States Constitution. State courts also possess the power of judicial review and can strike down the actions of legislatures when they violate the constitution, local governments when they violate state law or invade citizens' rights, and the actions of companies or business corporations when they transgress on the rights of citizens or employees. Thus, the power of judicial review is shared by state courts, which may rule on the basis of the state constitution and laws passed by state legislatures, as well as on the basis of the federal constitution.[3]

The Federal Court System

The Supreme Court is established in Article III of the United States Constitution. Section 1 of that Article gives federal judges lifetime tenure during good behavior and forbids punishing justices for their opinions. Section 2 delimits the extent of judicial power, mandates trial by jury, sets the Supreme Court's jurisdiction, and provides for trials in the state where the crime occurred.[4] Congress spent most of the second half of its initial session working on what became the Judiciary Act of 1789, which gave shape to the federal court system by creating a circuit and district court in each state. Although the Supreme Court is one of the three co-equal branches of the national government (along with the president and Congress), the framers of the Constitution gave Congress the power to shape the lower levels of the federal judiciary, or as they put it, to "ordain and establish" inferior courts. Since the founding period, Congress has passed a number of laws affecting the courts, including changing the number of judges, creating new courts and districts, and limiting legal jurisdiction in some areas while clarifying the judicial responsibility in others.

In order to check further the judiciary's power, the framers gave the president the power to nominate judges, subject to approval by the Senate. Taken together, both Congress and the president exercise controls that limit the power of the judicial branch. The Senate approves or denies appointments to the federal bench, while Congress as a whole determines the size and sweep of the court's jurisdiction, except where it is established in the Constitution. The president selects and appoints all the judges for the federal courts, subject to approval by the Senate. Should Congress disagree with a ruling of the federal courts, it is free to pass legislation, which is binding on the federal judiciary, unless, of course, that legislation violates the Constitution. Finally, like the president, federal judges can be removed through impeachment, which proceeds much as it does for presidential impeachments: The House of Representatives brings charges and the Senate sits as Jury, presided over by the Chief Justice of the United States.

While the number of active judges at any one time varies with the ebb and flow of death, retirement, appointment, and confirmation, there are positions for 874 judges serving in all the federal courts. Nine justices serve on the Supreme Court, 179 judges serve on the 13 circuit courts of appeals, and 677 justices serve on the 94 district courts.[5] Eleven of the appeals courts serve a geographical area, while the other two are based in Washington, D.C. One of the Washington-based courts focuses on hearing cases arising from the operation of federal agencies, while the other, established in 1982, has a unique nationwide jurisdiction over international trade, patents, government contracts, and other areas.

Judges placed on the federal district courts are appointed and vetted in much the same manner as Supreme Court justices and appellate court judges, albeit with less controversy and publicity. Louisiana is divided into three geographic districts for federal purposes, the Western, the Middle, and the Eastern. The Western District is the largest with forty-two parishes, covering all of north, central, and southwest Louisiana. The Middle District contains the nine parishes of West and East Feliciana, Pointe Coupee, Iberville, West Baton Rouge, East Baton Rouge, Ascension, Livingston, and St. Helena. The Eastern District contains the thirteen parishes of Tangipahoa, Washington, St. Tammany, St. John the Baptist, Assumption, St. James, Orleans, St. Bernard, St. Charles, Terrebonne, Lafourche, Jefferson, and Plaquemines.

LOUISIANA: THE STATE CONTEXT

Law in Louisiana operates in a context unique among the fifty states. At the most basic level, law emerges organically from the cultural, historical, and documentary sources of a people (Algero, 2007). In the case of Louisiana, the initial settlement of the territory by France, and its subsequent possession by Spain, followed in 1803 by the United States, has had an extraordinary and long-lasting effect on the sources of law, legal procedure, and the practice of law. Perhaps most importantly, the French and Spanish brought with them a "civil code," which is one of the distinguishing features of "continental jurisprudence." Reliance on a code of laws created *in toto* by a law-making body distinguishes Louisiana from the rest of the American states, which operate based on a "common law" system with roots in English practice.[6] In the paragraphs that follow, we will examine the sources of law in Louisiana, focusing particularly on the codification of the Louisiana Civil Code in 1808 with subsequent revisions in 1825 and 1870. We will also distinguish the practice of law under the civil code from the practice of law under the common law system, focusing particularly on the role of precedent in each system. The evidence presented supports the contention that Louisiana is a "mixed jurisdiction," containing both substantive and procedural elements of the civil and the common law systems (Tetley, 2000).[7]

Aside from the United States Constitution, the most fundamental source of law in Louisiana is the state constitution ratified in 1974.[8] Article V of the Louisiana Constitution establishes the court system and delimits the jurisdiction of the various state and local courts. It also provides for judicial selection, including qualifications, and has provisions relating to grand juries, juvenile justice, compensation, mayoral and justice of the peace courts, retirement, and a judiciary commission. In addition, it describes the other principal actors in the legal system, including district attorneys, sheriffs, clerks of court, coroners, and jurors.

In its scope and reach, Article V of the Louisiana Constitution is much more comprehensive than its counterpart Article III of the United States Constitution, which left vast powers in Congress's hands to shape the federal courts. In Louisiana, change to any part of the system of justice mentioned above requires a constitutional amendment passed by both houses of the legislature, followed by a statewide referendum requiring the support of a majority of voters. Simply put, change to the legal system is harder to effect in Louisiana because more of it has been placed in the constitution than has been the case at the national level.

Apart from the provisions in the constitution, the most fundamental source of law in Louisiana is the civil code, which is a "codification" of the civil law.[9] The term "civil law" comes from "Jus Civile, the law of the *cives*, or citizens of the city of Rome" (Pascal, 1999). In historical terms, the civil law was established in Louisiana during the Crozat administration (1712-1717), whose charter "provided that the edicts and ordinances of the custom of Paris were to be in effect in the territory" (Fontenot, 2003, p. 1150). Procedure used in civil cases was based on the "four titles of the Custom of Paris" related to "real actions, actions generally, arrests and executions, and the seizure and sale of movables" (McMahon, 1960, pp. 3-4). However, this law rarely came into use as there were few cases and even fewer lawyers during the early days of settlement. What really established the civil law and code in Louisiana was the transfer of power from France to Spain in 1762 under the secret Treaty of Fontainebleau. Don Alejandro O'Reilly, who arrived to take possession of the hitherto French colony, established courts and instituted a code of law based on the one the Spanish had created to govern their far-flung empire. This code was, in turn, based on a much more complete version of the civil code then in use in Spain.[10]

Although France reassumed possession of Louisiana a month prior to its sale to the United States in 1803, no attempt was made in this brief period to return Louisiana to French law. After obtaining the Louisiana territory, Congress was slow to make any major substantive changes in the law governing the territories. In the first two years of possession, Congress passed three acts concerning Louisiana. The first one left unchanged all of the laws currently in effect, while the other two reorganized state government along the contours of the American system of common law, including the writ of *habeas corpus* and provision for trial by jury, respectively (McMahon, 1960: 3-4).

The Legislative Council of the Territory of Orleans, which was given the power to legislate for Louisiana, adopted something known as the "Practice Act" of 1805. It is this act that was to become the root of the civil code in Louisiana, although it has changed somewhat over the years. There has been significant disagreement among scholars over the Practice Act's influences. Some argue that the act merely summarized the Spanish procedure extant in the colony at the time, while others contend that it was a "refinement and simplification of contemporary American chancery practice" (McMahon, 1960, p. 7). As is typical in disputes of this sort, there is evidence to support both sides. It is clear that the Practice Act was based on Spanish practice at the time, but also included English terms for various procedural aspects of the law, and an admixture of common law practices, including jury trials and the testimony of witnesses in open court. When Louisiana was admitted to the Union in 1812, it adopted a system of courts based on

> ### The U. S. Court of Appeals for the Fifth Circuit
>
> The federal circuit courts of appeal are quite powerful in terms of the nation's rule of law. Because the U.S. Supreme Court chooses to hear fewer than one hundred cases of more than ten thousand appeals submitted to it each year, the final ruling of these intermediate courts are left standing in the vast majority of federal cases.
>
> The term "circuit court" harkens back to a time when poor roads and available judges challenged the nation's federal legal system. Circuit judges traveled on horseback around a region of courthouses to try civil and criminal cases. Nine circuits were designated by Congress in 1891 to hold jurisdiction over federal trials and appeals. Twenty years later the circuit courts dispensed with original trial jurisdiction, which meant they only would hear appeals to lower court rulings. These appellate courts would determine if a reversible error had occurred in a decision based on questions of law, but not on the factual record established at trial.
>
> The U. S. Court of Appeals for the Fifth Circuit was created to hear appeals from six states: Texas, Louisiana, Mississippi, Alabama, Georgia and Florida. It was divided in half in 1981, and the eastern-most states formed a new Eleventh Circuit with its courthouse located in Atlanta. The Fifth Circuit encompasses Texas, Louisiana, and Mississippi, and its courthouse is in New Orleans at the John Minor Wisdom United States Court of Appeals Building. The building's namesake was a federal judge.
>
> During the civil rights movement of the 1960s, the Fifth Circuit heard appeals to important and controversial decisions whereby litigants wanted to secure voting rights for African Americans, and the desegregation of public schools in the South. Judge John Minor Wisdom was one of four judges who served to address these rights in his decisions along with Judges Elbert Tuttle, Richard Rives, and John Brown. Today the Fifth Circuit also addresses controversial questions of racial equality, including affirmative action policies used for student admissions at public universities.

the American judiciary of the Supreme Court, district courts, and justice of the peace courts, but retained the code under which the Spanish had governed.

Perhaps the clearest evidence for the varied sources of fundamental law in Louisiana is found in the notes accompanying the Code of Practice of 1825, which was a revision of the Practice Code of 1805. Prompted by a legislative request, a new procedural code was submitted to the Legislature in 1823 and went into effect in 1825. The adopted "Code of Practice" contained 1,155 articles numbered consecutively and divided into titles, chapters, and sections. It has been called a "mixture of French, Spanish, and Roman law elements, together with common law elements of English origin" (McMahon, 1960, p. 11). Interestingly, the three-person team (redactors) who put the code together listed the sources of the most important articles contained in the code. Their notes are summarized in Table A, next page. Their sources appear as source notes revealing that the majority of the code's provisions were Spanish, followed by French, with some English and Roman referents. In contrast, the English or Anglo-American influence was felt predominantly in the area of judicial administration (composition of courts, functions of judicial officers, etc.).

During the period between the Code of 1825 and the production of a new code in 1870, the influence of Anglo-American procedure grew stronger, as French and Spanish speakers and readers became less common. Despite these changes, the Louisiana Civil Code of 1870 was, in large part, the Code of 1825, excluding the sections regulating unfree-labor. The code was revised again during Reconstruction. One of the main purposes of the revision was to remove all references to slavery and servitude from the code, prompted no doubt in part by the demography of the Louisiana State Legislature, which, for the first time, contained significant numbers of African Americans

(Yiannopoulos, 1992). Also included in the revised code was all the legislation affecting procedure passed by the legislature between 1825 and 1870. Although there was a failed attempt at major code revision in 1913, the Code of 1870 continued largely un-amended until 1961, when two major changes were made: first, the numbering of articles changed from consecutive to split numbering to allow for continuous revision; and second, the redactor's comments were included in the code itself along with cases of relevance.[11] At this point it may be worthwhile to focus on the Civil Code in more detail, showing how it operates, and also how it differs from the common law tradition.

Louisiana's Civil Law System

As noted above, a civil law system usually, but not always, operates with a written "code" that is a nearly comprehensive statement of what the law is, separated into a number of sections, headings, and topics. Thus, in a system with a written code, the specifics of individual cases or areas arising under the law are abstracted or "codified" into their more general properties. As general statements of what the law is, they can then be applied to future cases. In practice, a judge reviewing a case requiring the disposition of a person's property following his or her death would consult the code to see what the law says about the correct way to dispose of the property, i.e. who gets what. Then using the principles outlined in the code, the judge would rule based on the individual case. In making this ruling, the judge would not be bound to consult and conform to decisions in previous cases, as common law judges typically are. Conversely, the judge is not unlikely to consult similar cases and see if there exists something called a "*jurisprudence constante*," which is a French term for "line of prior, consistent decisions" on a topic that "may be persuasive evidence of the proper interpretation of the law" (Algero, 2005). The judge in the civil law case then might take note of this line of interpretation and decide the case in question along the same line, but he or she is in no way obligated to do so, or even to point out that his or her application of the code in the case at hand departs from previous decisions.[12]

Article I of the Louisiana Civil Code identifies the sources of law in Louisiana as legislation and custom. Legislation, in this case, refers to anything already in the code or as Article 2 puts it, "a solemn expression of legislative will." This allows for legislation expanding or altering the code. Article 3 defines *custom* as "practice repeated for a long time and generally accepted as having acquired the force of law." Yet, "custom may not abrogate legislation," and is not to be balanced against existing legislation. In the

---

Table A. Sources of Louisiana Civil Code

Compiled in 1823 by L. Moreau Lislet, Edward Livingston and Pierre Derbigny, legislatively appointed editors/revisers of the Louisiana Civil Code of 1808.

Source	Number of References
Roman law	11
Spanish Law	63
Practice Act of 1805*	45
Louisiana statues	69
Civil Code of 1808 (Code Napoleon)	26

*based on Spanish law.

Source: Henry G. McMahon. The Louisiana code of Civil Procedure, *Louisiana Law Review*, 21 La. L. Rev. (1960)

absence of legislation and custom, Article 4 requires the courts to "proceed according to equity," which is defined as resorting to "justice, reason, and prevailing usages." There is nothing in the code referring to precedent as established in prior judicial decisions, or specifying what impact previous cases should have on future ones, beyond the idea of custom.

Despite this lack of support for precedent in both the civil code and legislation, the Louisiana Supreme Court indicated in *Ardoin v. Hartford* (1980) that a court should consider prior decisions as "secondary information . . . which may or may not reflect the meaning of the laws for contemporary purposes" (Algero, 2005).[13] And, despite rather frequent disclaimers about the relevance of prior cases for decisions in a civil law system, Louisiana judges "rarely write opinions without mentioning prior decisions," and particularly without mentioning decisions made by the Louisiana Supreme Court where they apply (Algero, 2012). Under the Constitution, the Louisiana Supreme Court is given "general supervisory jurisdiction over all other courts" in the Louisiana system, which means that its decisions in particular areas are, for all intents and purposes, definitive, even if not actually recognized by the code in this manner.[14] Hence, although the power of precedent is not recognized in the Louisiana system, the role of the Supreme Court in the system itself, along with the concept of jurisprudence constante, inclines judges to consider previous cases in their decision-making process. A further element that increases the likelihood that judges will consider legal precedent is that most judges have received their training in schools of law where they were immersed in common law techniques and history.

Common Law System

In a common law system, which characterizes every state other than Louisiana, precedent is an exceedingly important part of how cases are decided. The term for precedent in common law cases is "Stare decisis et quieta non movere" (usually shortened to stare decisis), which translates as "to stand by things decided and not disturb settled law" (Algero, 2012). How a system based on stare decisis operates is that previous decisions indicate future rulings. That is, an early or authoritative ruling in a particular case and area of the law sets a precedent that guides future cases in this area. Thus, when a judge considers a case, he or she refers back to a similar case in the past. As judges do this, they create a body of "judge-made law," that is, references to a number of cases that are called "leading" or "ruling" cases in each area of the law. This is the essence of the common law system. It is based on judge-made law, interpreting the fundamental constitutional and legislative law and setting precedents that later courts cite and follow. The train of precedents revealing judicial thought and history are wound into the opinion that is rendered by the court in a common law jurisdiction. A departure from precedent is similarly accompanied by a supportive web of cases and interpretations. In this way, law evolves in a common law system out of the cases that come before the court.

The concept of stare decisis, or binding precedent, is essential for a system of laws based on the idea that decisions in a previous case should rule or control a current one. Without following precedents, there would be no way to predict the outcome of any particular case, which would then depend entirely on the judge and the circumstances of the case. This would be chaotic, to say the least, as well as inequitable and unjust in the long run. Thus, common law is based on precedent; and, while not without its problems, precedent allows litigants and functionaries (e.g. lawyers) to be able to predict probable outcomes of particular cases based on previous decisions. To put it in more general terms, in the common law approach the judge extracts rules of general applicability out of the specificity of each case, whereas in the civil law approach, the judge applies the existing general rule to the specific case under examination. Thus, the civil law system works from generality (code) to specifics (cases), while the common law system works from specifics (cases) to generalities (rules).[15] In practice, however, there are a number of similarities between a common law syatem and a civil law system.[16]

Reconciling the Systems

Louisiana's system of law, courts, and judges is more accurately referred to as a "mixed" system rather than a pure form of either civil or common law. At base, both systems emerge from the Western law family and share the social objectives of individualism, liberalism, and personal rights (Pascal, 1999). And, given its long exposure to Anglo-American forms of law, the Louisiana system admits to a good bit of what Henry McMahon calls "interstitial seepage" (1960). This is to say that Anglo forms have insinuated themselves in and between the provisions of positive civil law both substantively and procedurally. In some areas, commercial law for example, Anglo-American practice has predominated, as the civil code has not been expanded to encompass the enormous variety of economic activities characterizing modern society.[17] Additionally, Louisiana judges possess the power of judicial review and may overturn acts of lower courts, officials, and laws that they find not to be in keeping with the fundamental law. In fact, in *Johnson v. St. Paul Mercury Insurance Co.* (1970),[18] the Louisiana Supreme Court held that in the absence of statutory authority or guidance, "the law is what this court has announced it to be" (p. 218), a statement which would seem to be the very antithesis of a civil law system (Algero, 2005). As noted, the state supreme court's supervisory role over the entire system gives its decisions a great deal of weight when other courts consider similar questions. Also, judges in Louisiana are elected, which is a departure from the civil law tradition in which judges are trained in special schools and appointed to the bench based on merit and qualification.

Judge James Dennis, who has served as both a Louisiana and federal judge, points to three factors that incline the Louisiana civil law system towards greater accommodation with the common law system: First, because of the lack of judges fluent in both French and Spanish, the majority of law reviews and texts that judges consult are English language journals, which mostly focus on common law. Second, attorneys are trained to be conversant in common law systems in law schools, which focus most of their curriculum on common law practice. Finally, the recruitment system in Louisiana (election) works to draft strong personalities who want to "leave their mark" on the law, quite unlike their civil law contemporaries (Dennis, 1993). Strong personalities find fulfillment in common law techniques, where judges can "expand contract and manipulate the 'ratio decidinde' of a previously decided case. . . ."[19] For reasons then of language, law school curricula, and judicial ambition, it is best to describe Louisiana as a mixed system of civil and common law traditions.

THE HISTORICAL LOUISIANA COURT SYSTEM

Prior to its possession by Spain, French Louisiana dispensed justice by a Superior Council whose members sat "*en banc.*" As the territory gained more residents, the "appointment of inferior judges and courts were authorized" to better serve far-flung residents (Fontenot, 2003). However, when Governor O'Reilly took control of Louisiana as Spain's representative, he dissolved the Superior Council and established the "Cabildo" form of government. Under this Spanish system, there was relatively little separation between justice and administration. The municipal magistrates in Louisiana were called the Alcaldes, who "sat as individual judges" with "both criminal and civil jurisdiction." Outside New Orleans, army officers had the authority to hear civil cases and administer justice in criminal cases. Governor O'Reilly abolished all French law in 1769 and replaced it with a compilation known as the "Code O'Reilly," which was a combination of other codes, including the "Laws of the Indies, the Siete Partidas, and the Code Noir." Although France repossessed Louisiana for just a month prior to its sale to the United States, Napoleon's emissary to Louisiana, Pierre de Laussat, "issued an order abolishing the Cabildo," and thereby "abolished the entire court system." Thus it was that the United States received Louisiana without any courts or system of justice in place whatsoever (Fontenot, 2003, pp. 1155-57).

William Claiborne, appointed governor of Louisiana by his cousin, Thomas Jefferson, was given the power to establish a court system in the territory, and on December 30, 1803, Claiborne "established a Court of Pleas" as well as a "Governor's Court" to deal with civil matters. Shortly after this time, the civil law of the territory was gathered into the Digest or "Practice Code" discussed above. Interestingly, criminal law in Louisiana was Anglo-American from the start, as "Jefferson instructed Claiborne to impose common law concepts of penal law and to reflect the mandate of the U.S. Constitution" with its focus on rights. Claiborne's temporary system remained in effect until 1805 when the "legislative council created a new judiciary composed of a Superior court of original and appellate jurisdiction and a system of county courts" (Fontenot, 2003, p. 1159).

Seeking admission to the Union in 1812, Louisiana modeled its constitution on the Kentucky Constitution of 1799. The court system established by this first constitution created a three- to five-person supreme court depending on need, with seven district courts of general jurisdiction, courts in each parish, and justices of the peace. The Supreme Court of Louisiana was a true "circuit" court and traveled to Opelousas, Alexandria, Natchitoches, Donaldsonville, Rapides, Pointe Coupee, and Monroe (Labbe, 1995).[20] The new court sat for the first time on March 1, 1813, at Government House in New Orleans. The Judiciary Act of 1813 set the size of the bench to three members and gave the court rule-making authority over the lower courts. It also required that justices be "learned in law."

The Constitution of 1845 reformed the court by providing for a chief justice and three associate justices who were elected for eight-year terms. It also stripped the legislature of the power to establish inferior courts, leaving only a supreme court, district courts, and justices of the peace in place.[21] The Constitution of 1852 added another associate justice and changed the length of the judge's term in office to ten years. In a departure from previous practice, the Constitution of 1879 changed the Supreme Court's method of selection to appointment.[22] In addition, the Constitution of 1879 created intermediate appellate courts and gave them the power to hear civil appeals amounting to less than $2,000.[23] Perhaps most importantly, Article 88 of the same constitution gave the supreme court the power to "control and supervise the lower courts and to issue various remedial writs for this purpose, such as certiorari, quo warranto, mandamus, and prohibition" (Labbe, 1995, p. 7).[24] Further changes to the court brought by later constitutional amendments are addressed below.

THE LOUISIANA COURT SYSTEM TODAY

As our discussion has indicated, the court system in Louisiana and the body of law on which its rulings are based has changed considerably over the years, in structure if not in function. The evolution of the system of courts and law continues to the present day. Currently, the Louisiana court system has four *tiers* or *layers*. At the bottom are the minor or inferior courts, which include justice of the peace courts and the small-claims courts. Also at this level are the nearly fifty mayor's courts and parish courts. The second rung is occupied by the forty-three district or "trial" courts and includes some specialized drug courts and family courts.[25] The third rung belongs to the five courts of appeal. At the top is the supreme court with supervisory authority over the entire system, including all 380 justices working at different levels in the system.[26] The next section will sketch out the current court system in Louisiana, detailing its structure, demography, and jurisdiction beginning with the supreme court.

The Supreme Court of Louisiana has seven justices. The justice with the most seniority on the court is selected as the chief justice. Justices are elected for ten-year terms in districts that are not geographically equal but are roughly equal in population.[27]

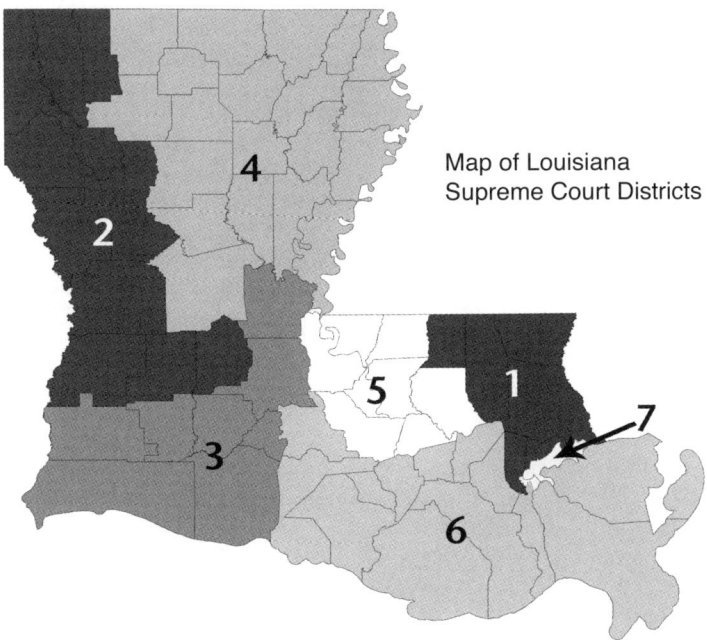

Map of Louisiana Supreme Court Districts

Justices are not term limited, although they cannot seek reelection once they reach the age of seventy. The Supreme Court districts (see map above), and indeed, all judicial districts in Louisiana, are drawn by the state legislature, which redistricts once every ten years following the U.S. Census. Districts may also be altered on other occasions, usually as a result of court challenges, constitutional amendments, or national laws.[28]

Louisiana is one of only six states that elect all their judges at the district level and above in partisan elections.[29] This preference for partisan elections aligns with selection processes for other positions in state government, as the South is more typically committed to partisan elections, owing perhaps to its legacy of racial division and single-party dominance. Prior to a court challenge, judges were elected in district elections using the *at-large* method of selection. In this method, voters choose from a number of judges running in the same election. Those candidates receiving the most votes are placed on the bench. However, at-large elections in districts with racial minorities and race-line voting have been shown to be prejudicial to minorities by electing fewer judges than might be elected using "single-member election" districts.

In 1986, a suit was filed in Louisiana contending that the "at-large system violates the United States Voting Rights Act and the United States Constitution by denying blacks equal representation." This suit requested that all elections be enjoined until after the issue was resolved. At the time of the suit only "5 of the 178 state judges" at the supreme court, appellate court, and district court level were black.[30] The Bush administration argued, "judges elected by the people and accountable to the people in every sense are representatives" and hence should be protected under the Voting Rights Act.[31] Ultimately, the court ruled that Section 2 of the Voting Rights Act did apply to state and local judges, a decision that affected thirty-nine states and as many as 6,375 judges, at least potentially.[32] Despite this ruling, judicial redistricting has been less regular and less uniform than districting in other types of districts such as, for example, congressional districts, where a strict one-man, one-vote standard is maintained.

> ### Supreme Controversy
> The judicial system in Louisiana is presided over by one chief justice and six associate justices. The chief justice has authority over the supreme court's administration, which in addition to judicial review of lower court decisions involves temporary judicial appointments, punishing lawyers for misconduct, and hearing appeals from prisoners on death row. Who serves in the role of chief justice should be a matter of simple arithmetic, as the associate justice with the longest tenure ascends to that office. But the change of command became a matter of controversy in 2012.
>
> Chief Justice "Kitty" Kimball of Ventress, La., was the first Louisiana woman to take the oath of office as chief justice following sixteen years of service as an associate justice (1992-2008). Chief Justice Kimball announced her retirement after four years in the head office following a stroke. Two associate justices soon claimed it as their right to succeed her as presiding officer of the court based on differing interpretations of the tenure requirement.
>
> Associate Justice Bernette J. Johnson, the first African American woman on the bench, reported the longest tenure as associate justice; however, she came to the court following a federal consent decree designed to increase minority representation in the judiciary. The decree temporarily expanded the bench from seven to eight justices in order to remedy racial discrimination. Associate Justice Jeffrey P. Victory of Shreveport based his claim on his election as one of the traditional seven justices of the court.
>
> Chief Justice Kimball announced that her court would reach a decision on the two competing claims regarding her successor before she retired, but Assoc. Justice Johnson took exception to this plan of action. She filed a discrimination suit in federal court with support of the U.S. Justice Department and the NAACP Legal Defense and Educational Fund. A federal judge agreed with Justice Johnson's analysis of her tenure claim, and asked that the Supreme Court of Louisiana proceed accordingly. The court followed the judge's ruling and Associate Justice Bernette Johnsonand Associate Justice Bernette Johnson was sworn in as the first African American chief justice of Louisiana on February 28, 2013.

In an effort to more fairly represent minorities, and perhaps to avoid court challenges to the entire electoral system, the legislature created a number of majority-minority sub-districts at both the district and appeals level. These districts have been quite successful at electing minorities to the bench in Louisiana. Currently, 21 percent of the Louisiana judiciary at the district level is African American, which, while somewhat less than the percentage of African Americans in the population as a whole (32.4), is still sharply higher than the level of justices prior to the creation of sub-districts. The Louisiana judiciary is still largely a male preserve at the district level, with females making up only 23 percent of district court judges. From a partisan point of view, 64 percent of justices are Democratic while 31 percent are Republican and nearly 5 percent are identified as *other* or *no-party*. This contrasts with registration statistics indicating that only 48 percent of the Louisiana electorate is registered with the Democratic Party. In contrast, the percentage of Republican judges (31 percent) at the district level corresponds closely with the statewide percentage of registered Republican voters at 28 percent.[33]

Although the Louisiana Supreme Court has appellate authority over every type of case arising in the Louisiana judicial system, its "original" jurisdiction is limited to disciplinary cases against lawyers and judges. It has appellate jurisdiction over cases involving the death penalty.[34] All other cases reach the court by appeal, chiefly through the granting of "*cert*" (certiorari), which in its Latin roots means to inform or advise. Appeals to higher courts arise from decisions in lower courts that are contested. If litigants on either side of a case heard in a lower court feel that the case has been decided incorrectly, they are, in most cases, granted the right to appeal to a higher court. The higher court reviews the case to make sure that the criminal or civil procedures were correctly followed and that the facts supporting the decision were correct.[35] The supreme court will grant certiorari or its willingness to review a case in which it feels that its entrance into the matter is required. Certiorari is typically granted at times when a decision of a lower court conflicts with that of an upper court; when there are significant unresolved issues of law or a legal question that needs addressing authoritatively; when the decision of the lower court is one that is no longer in line with current jurisprudence in the area; when there has been a mistake in constitutional interpretation; and when there has been a stark departure from good courtroom management or judgment.[36]

The Louisiana Constitution also gives the supreme court general supervisory jurisdiction over all other courts, along with the power to select a judicial administrator and other personnel. The Louisiana Legislature has been historically reluctant to give the courts the necessary tools for self-regulation and control. However, Justice John Fournet did "persuade the legislature in 1938 to fund the hiring of law clerks as a means of speeding up" the work facing the court. Later, as chief justice, Fournet helped to create the Judicial Council and was instrumental in supporting a constitutional amendment providing the courts with a judicial administrator to help with management of the entire system (Billings, 2013, p. 464).

Indeed, management was sorely needed by the supreme court, which had staggered under the weight of administering the system, as well as a huge number of appeals. According to figures provided by Dr. Ron Labbe, during the "1955 to 1956 term, each [supreme court] justice wrote seven opinions, worked on thirty-six others, and . . . participated in the disposition of fifty-one cases" all within a five-week cycle. This workload was clearly straining the court to the breaking point and limiting the attractiveness of the judiciary as a career (Labbe, 1995, p. 10). The solution was the expansion of the responsibilities of the courts of appeal. The number of appeals accepted by the supreme court declined precipitously after the full expansion of the duties of the appeals courts in 1982. Today the workload of the supreme court is much more reasonable in relation

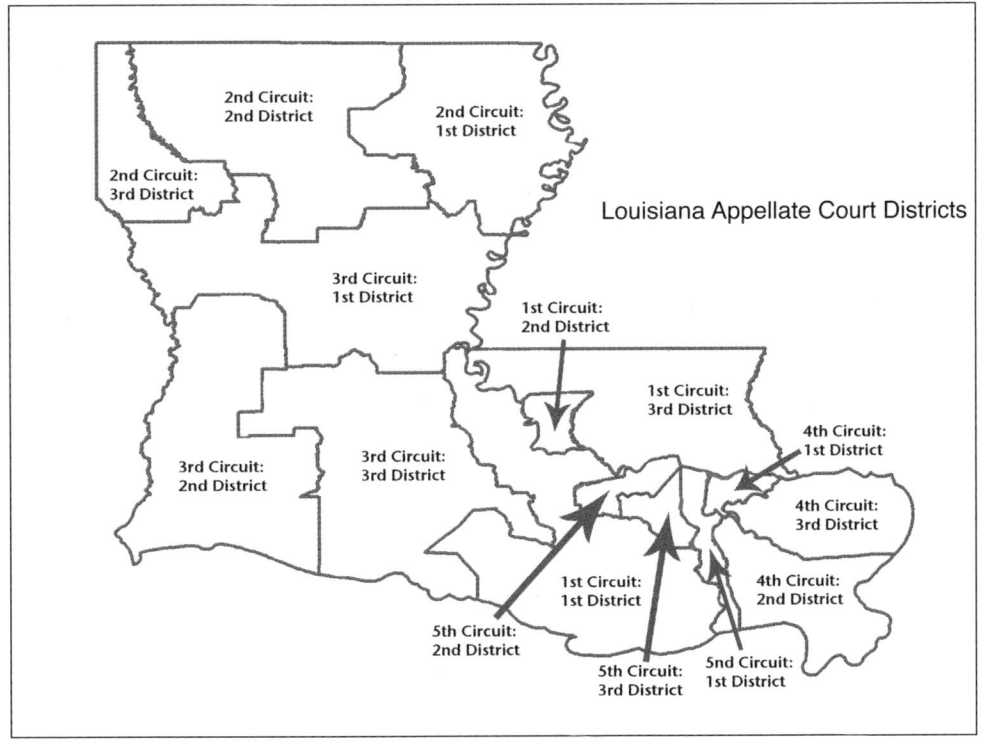

to the rest of the court system. For example, in 2011, 2,852 cases were filed with the supreme court and the court disposed of 2,916 cases (some from previous terms). Of those cases reaching the court by writ, 946 were civil and 581 were criminal, excluding *pro se* writs presented by prisoners. In comparison there were 7,949 filings with the five Louisiana Courts of Appeal, and 787,104 filings in the district courts. Filings in city and parish courts amounted to 972,559.[37]

The courts of appeal were established in the Constitution of 1879 with six courts, authorized to hear civil appeals of more than $100 but less than $1,000. Criticism of their expense relative to their work led to five of the six courts being abolished in the Constitution of 1898. Only the Court of Appeal for Orleans was continued, yet the problem of an overloaded docket that the appeals court offered help with did not disappear. As a result, in 1906 the constitution was amended to add two more courts of appeal and from that point on, the history of the Louisiana's appellate courts is, in large part, a history of gradual expansion of their scope and duties. Despite their expansion the appeals courts did not initially undertake the work expected of them as their jurisdiction was limited to civil jurisdiction until 1982. Criminal appeals prior to the 1982 changes were made to the supreme court, clogging that court's docket with cases best heard at a lower level. For example, in 1976 there were 1,729 cases appealed to the supreme court "of which 1,339 were applications for discretionary writs and 390 were mandatory appeals..." In that year, criminal cases "constituted 47% of the writ applications [and] . . . 76% of the appeals." In sum, "criminal cases accounted for 77 percent of opinions actually rendered by the court in 1976" (Labbe, 1995, p. 11). The vast number of criminal appeals sent directly to the supreme court meant that justices spent the majority of their time on matters that, in a well-organized court system, are best left to the appellate courts.

In recognition of the oppressive and restrictive caseload placed on the supreme court's docket, political pressure grew in the legislature for changing the system of criminal appeals. This pressure was relieved by the adoption of constitutional amendments in 1982, which transferred criminal cases to the appellate courts, relieving the supreme court of all its obligatory criminal duties with the exception of death penalty cases. At the same time, a fifth circuit court was added along with additional justices to accommodate the extra workload placed on the circuit court. Today, as the map (following page) illustrates, the courts of appeal have five circuits, based in Baton Rouge (1st), Shreveport, (2nd), Lake Charles (3rd), New Orleans (4th), and Gretna (5th), with fifty-six total judges.

The appeals court has jurisdiction over all civil matters, all family and juvenile courts, and all criminal cases occurring in the district courts, except those cases that are referred directly to the supreme court (death penalty). In civil cases, the court's jurisdiction extends to questions of law and fact, while in the area of criminal law; the court's jurisdiction extends only to questions of law.[38] Each court has a chief judge based on length of service (seniority) on the court. In judging a case, the appeals court does not empanel a jury, but instead sits with three judges, two of whom are required for a judgment to be rendered. In important or controversial cases, the entire court may sit "*en banc*," but this is quite unusual. Judges for the circuit courts of appeal are elected in districts drawn for that purpose. The constitution mandates that each circuit be "divided into at least three districts" with "at least one judge . . . elected from each." They serve for ten years and may be reelected up to the seventy-year-old age limit.

Below the courts of appeal are forty-three district courts, which are the "workhorses" of the Louisiana court system and the only courts that empanel juries.

Nearly every case of any consequence originates in a district court and the vast majority of these cases are disposed of at the district level without appeal to other courts. In 2011, there were 300,590 cases filed with the district courts, of which 141,047 were civil (46.9%) and 158,743 (52.1%) were criminal. Less than one percent of these cases resulted in a jury trial.[39] This caseload dwarfs the Louisiana Supreme Court that, in

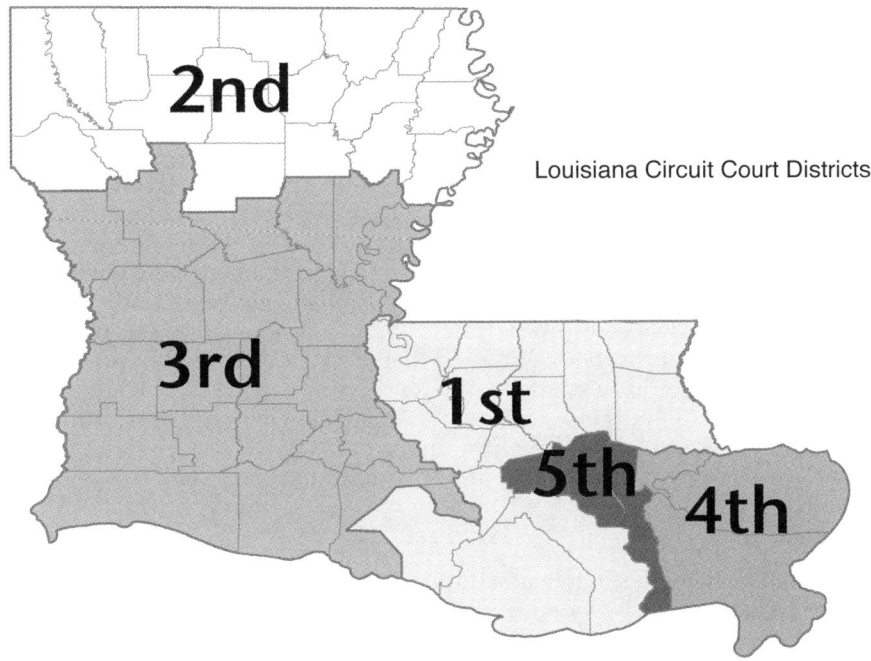

Louisiana Circuit Court Districts

comparison, disposed of 2,916 cases in 2011, while the five appellate courts combined had 7,949 cases filed in 2011. The district courts have original jurisdiction of "all civil and criminal matters" and "felony cases," the "right to office or other public position," and "civil or political right," as well as "probate and succession."[40] The district courts also have appellate jurisdiction over the mayor's and parish courts, where they can review, and if necessary, retry a case originating in one of the inferior courts (Labbe, 1995: 7).[41] Each district court elects a chief judge. Qualifications for a position on the bench are, generally, the same for all Louisiana judges in district, appeals, and supreme court: judges must have been admitted to the practice of law in Louisiana for either eight years (district) or 10 years (appeals, supreme); they must have lived in their district for at least one year prior to the election; and they cannot practice law once elected.[42] District courts vary widely in the number of justices assigned to them, from the several districts (including the 11th District in Sabine) with one judge to the 24th District in Jefferson Parish with sixteen. Currently, there are 247 district court judges.

Operating beneath the district courts is a number of minor or "inferior" courts. These courts are generally of limited jurisdiction and may be staffed by lawyers or non-fulltime judges, some of whom may practice law depending on the court, although the city and parish courts are required to meet the same judicial standards as the other Louisiana courts. As a rule of thumb, cases arising in inferior courts are not felonies and are limited in terms of monetary awards. Currently the jurisdiction of the city courts in civil cases ranges from $5,000 to $25,000. In some cases, inferior courts may exercise concurrent jurisdiction with the district court in the area (e.g., drug courts). City judges, in contrast, spend the majority of their time on juvenile and traffic cases. In 2011, for example, there were 458,864 traffic cases filed with minor courts. This number exceeds the number of civil and criminal cases filed with the district courts combined. In addition to city and parish courts, there are a great many mayor's and justice of the peace courts operating in Louisiana.[44] Current estimates suggest that there are approximately 250 mayor's courts and more than 380 justices of the peace, performing minor functions like marriages, issuing peace bonds, and the like.

Conclusion

This chapter has established the federal and state systems for courts and the administration of justice, focusing particularly on the sources of law both federal and in Louisiana. We've also described the federal and state court systems and pointed out the very real differences between the operation and staffing of the two systems. We have examined in some detail the origin and development of the Louisiana mixed system of justice, with contributions from both continental and Anglo sources. We analyzed how a court system based on a code differs from a common law system, focusing particularly on the role of precedent in both systems. Finally, we covered the Louisiana court system, focusing particularly on the four different levels of courts, the administration of justice, the supervision of the system itself, and the election of judges. In the chapters that follow this one, readers will see how the court system addresses First Amendment questions arising under Louisiana law and constitutional government.

Research

Readers are encouraged to pursue questions of interest raised by this chapter. Sources of relevance may be found in the "References" section at the end of the book. The sources that were vital to this research were the law journals of Louisiana, including the *Louisiana Law Review*, the *Tulane Law Review*, and the *Loyola Law Review*. These journals may be found in the libraries of Louisiana's great universities. A great source of information about the Louisiana justice system is the Louisiana Supreme Court's Web site at www.lasc.org. Statistics and information about elections may be found on the secretary of state's Web site at sitewww.sos.la.gov.

Footnotes

1 "This Constitution, and the Laws of the United States which shall be made in pursuance thereof . . . shall be the supreme law of the land; and the judges in every state shall be bound thereby, anything in the constitution or laws of any state to the contrary notwithstanding." Article VI, Clause 2, United States Constitution.

2 Although not mentioned in the United States Constitution, judicial review was alluded to by Alexander Hamilton in the *Federalist Papers* (No. 78) and announced by Chief Justice John Marshall in *Marbury v. Madison*, an 1803 case that ruled on the constitutionality of the Judiciary Act passed by Congress in its first session. In his decision Marshall famously stated: "It is emphatically the province and duty of the Judicial Department to say what the law is. Those who apply the rule to particular cases must, of necessity, expound and interpret that rule. If two laws conflict with each other, the Courts must decide on the operation of each." For a good short explanation see Ginsburg, (1997).

3 State courts can and do base their opinions on the American Constitution but it is more common to refer to a provision in the state constitution. In the prior instance a court's rulings are subject to review by federal courts.

4 United States Constitution, Article III. It should be noted as well that the Bill of Rights ratified in 1791 contains five amendments that limit and clarify the power of the judiciary and protect citizens from unjust courts. The Amendments are IV-VIII.

5 There is also a Court of International Trade with nine justices and a distinct jurisdiction.

6 Several other states retain slight vestiges of civil law practices reflecting their Spanish heritage. These states are those in the southwestern United States, including New Mexico, California, and Texas.

7 Other mixed systems include Quebec, Puerto Rico, Scotland, South Africa, and Egypt.

8 Louisiana has had more constitutions than any other state. The 1974 Constitution is the eleventh in the series. And, at this writing, voices are calling for a new constitutional convention.

9 To "codify" something means to make it general and applicable to a number of cases.

10 An excellent short discussion of the early years in Louisiana judicial history may be found in Fontenot, 2003.

11 Including comments in the code is a departure for Louisiana Civil Procedure and an acknowledgement of the increasing importance of precedent in modern Louisiana jurisprudence.

12 In practice, however, judges in the civil law tradition do pay attention to preceding cases.

13 *Ardoin v. Hartford Accident and Indemnity Company*, November 6, 1980. 360 So. 2d 1331, 1339.

14 Louisiana Constitution, Article V., Section 5.

15 For a number of differences between the two traditions see William Tetley's authoritative discussion (Tetley, 2000).

16 For an impassioned defense of the superior merits of the civil as opposed to common law system, see Pascal, 1999.

17 In fact, in the revision of 1825, commercial law was excluded, resulting in the fait accompli of common law describing the majority of commercial transactions.

18 236 So. 2d 216-226 (1970).

19 Ratio decidinde refers to the rationale for a decision or the legal principle underlying a decision.

20 The Louisiana Supreme Court discontinued its circuit in 1898. Also, see Billings, 2013.

21 At the time of this change, there were forty-six parish courts in Louisiana.

22 Becoming elective in 1904.
23 Although this was insufficient to deal with the increasingly heavy workload that the Supreme Court was facing, it was the first step towards alleviating a serious problem in the system.
24 Curiously, the "absence of criminal jurisdiction in the supreme court under the Constitution of 1812 meant that the decisions of the district courts in criminal cases were not appealable to any court." This practice continued until 1843 when the Legislature recognized the "folly of allowing . . . trial courts to serve as the courts of last resort in criminal cases. . . ." (Labbe, 1995).
25 In 2011, Louisiana maintained foty-seven adult and juvenile drug courts. Supreme Court, Annual Report, 2011.
26 http://www.lasc.org/about_the_court/faq
27 Article V, Sections 3 and 4. *Chisom v. Roemer*, (1991).
28 Louisiana State Constitution, Article V; Sections 1, 3, 4, 6, 23(b). However, as of this writing judicial districts have not been reshaped since the mid-1990s owing to a series of court decisions that distinguished "judging" from representation and hence made the "one-man, one-vote" rule of *Baker v. Carr* (1962) less applicable.
29 From American Bar Association, "Fact Sheet." Oddly, judgeships at the three different court levels were made elective at different times. The trial courts were made elective in 1868, the courts of appeal in 1879, and the Supreme Court in 1904. (Labbe, 1995: 14).
30 *Chisom v. Roemer*, (1991). Reported in *The New York Times*, August 12, 1988.
31 *Chicago Tribune*, April 23, 1991.
32 "Court Says Rights Law Applies In Judge Elections," *Chicago Tribune*, June 21, 1991.
33 Elected officials database and voter registration statistics maintained by the Louisiana Secretary of State (www.sos.la.gov). Other data drawn from http://quickfacts.census.gov. An interview with Louisiana Legislative Demographer Dr. William Blair provided some of the information on redistricting used in this chapter.
34 This means that these cases cannot be appealed to other courts. Disciplinary cases begin at the supreme court and death penalty cases proceed directly there, bypassing the Court of Appeals. Louisiana Constitution, Section 5(B), (C).
35 In fact, Supreme Court Objective 1.1 is "To provide a reasonable opportunity for litigants to seek review in the Supreme Court of decisions made by lower tribunals." "Justice at Work," Published by the Louisiana Supreme Court, 2010-11 (http://www.lasc.org/press_room/publications.asp). The question of whether only the law can be examined or whether the facts of the case can be reexamined as well is an important one. In Louisiana, unlike some other states, the appellate courts can review the facts on certain types of cases. In civil cases the court's jurisdiction extends to both law and facts while in criminal matters, its jurisdiction extends only to questions of law.
36 List from Louisiana Supreme Court's Web site: http://www.lasc.org/about_the_court/faq.asp
37 "Statistical Overview," *Supreme Court of Louisiana, Annual Report 2011*.
38 Louisiana Constitution, Art. V, Sections 8-10.
39 Less than .064 percent in criminal cases and .0019 percent in civil cases. Statistics taken from the *Supreme Court of Louisiana: Annual Report 2011*, "Statistical Overview," p.13. Typically a deal is struck in a criminal trial where a "plea" is arranged prior to trial and settling the case to the satisfaction of the contending parties, or the state and the citizen(s). Known as a "plea bargain," this technique relieves the court of what would be an enormous increase in workload and expense were every case to require a jury. The practice of plea bargaining has been criticized by some who feel that it allows criminals to escape condign punishment and by others who feel that it pressures the innocent to take a lesser penalty to avoid the possibility of a harsh punishment.
40 Art. V, Section 16, (A), (B).

41 Ibid., Art. V, Sections 17 and 24.
42 Louisiana Constitution, Art. V, Section 16.
43 Attached to the courts are "court commissioners" who are "legally trained officers of the court who perform limited . . . and quasi-judicial functions . . . including family, probate, criminal and juvenile matters." They may be found in both state and federal courts. (Harges, 2007, p. 7).
44 The latter without much supervision.

REFERENCES

Algero, M.G. (2005). Symposium on the Bicentennial of the French Civil Code: The Value of Precedent in Louisiana: A Contemporary Examination. *Loyola Law Review, 51*, 87.101.

Algero, M.G. (2005). The Sources of Law and the Value of Precedent: A Comparative and Empirical Study of a Civil Law State in a Common Law Nation. *Louisiana Law Review, 65*, 775-789.

Algero, M.G. (2012). Considering Precedent in Louisiana: Balancing the Value of Predictable and Certain Interpretation with the Tradition of Flexibility and Adaptability. *Loyola Law Review, 58*, 113-133.

Billings, W. M. (1997). The Supreme Court of Louisiana and Its Chief Justices. *The Louisiana Courts and Judiciary*. Baton Rouge: LGS, Inc.

Billings, W. M. (2013). The Supreme Court of Louisiana at 200. *Louisiana Bar Journal, 60*, 462-465.

Dennis, J. L. (1993). Interpretation and Application of the Civil Code and the Evaluation of Judicial Precedent. *Louisiana Law Review, 54*, 1-17.

Dennis, J. L. (2001). Judicial Power and the Administrative State. *Louisiana Law Review, 62*, 59-96.

Dennis, J. L. (2003). Capitant Lecture: Introduction: The role of the Louisiana Judge. *Louisiana Law Reviee, 63*, 1003-1017.

Fontenot, H. W. (2003). The Louisiana Judicial System and the Fusion of Cultures. *Louisiana Law Review, 63*, 1149-1160.

Ginsburg, R.B. (1997). An Overview of Court Review for Constitutionality in the United States. *Louisiana Law Review, 57*, 1019-1027.

Harges, B. M. (2007). Appropriate Dispute Resolution inside the State Courts: A Closer Look at the Power, Duties, and Responsibilities of Court Commissioners and Hearing Officers in Domestic Cases. *Loyola Journal of Public Interest Law, 7*, No. 1.

Hood, J. T. (1961). History of the Courts of Appeal in Louisiana. *Louisiana Law Review, 21*, 531-552.

Karlan, P. S. (2009). Electing Judges, Judging Elections, and the Lessons of Caperton. *Harvard Law Review, 123*, 80-103.

Labbe, R. M. (1982). The Judiciary. In James Bolner, (Ed.), *Louisiana Politics: Festival in a Labyrinth*. (89-122). Baton Rouge: Louisiana State University Press.

Labbe, R. M. (1995). Two Centuries of the Louisiana Judiciary. *Guide to the Louisiana Judiciary*. Baton Rouge: Louisiana Governmental Studies, Inc.

McMahon. H. G. (1960) The Louisiana Code of Civil Procedure. *Louisiana Law Review, 21*, 1-52.

Pascal, R. A. (1999). Louisiana Civil Law and Its Study. *Louisiana Law Review, 60*, 1-12.

Tetley, W. (2000). Mixed Jurisdictions: Common Law v. Civil Law (Codified and Uncodified). *Louisiana Law Review, 60*, 677-738.

Wickham, M. T. (1992). Mapping the Morass: Application of Section 2 of the Voting Rights Act to Judicial Elections. *William and Mary Law Review, 33*, 1251-1293.

Yiannopoulos, A. N. (1992). Two Critical Years in the life of the Louisiana Civil Code: 1870 and 1913. *Louisiana Law Review, 53*, 5-33.

Yiannopoulos, A. N. (2008). The Civil Codes of Louisiana. *Civil Law Commentaries, 1*, 1-23.

Chapter 2
Freedom of Expression
By Rick A. Swanson, University of Louisiana at Lafayette

Learning Objectives
In this chapter, readers will:
- recognize values commonly offered in support of free expression
- be able to trace a brief history of the First Amendment's development
- weigh the absolutist versus balancing approaches to freedom of expression issues
- be able to order a three-tiered analysis of content-based regulation
- see how time, place, and manner affect freedom of expression on public property
- contrast the free-expression components of Louisiana's Constitution with the U.S. First Amendment
- discover where Louisiana free speech law both follows and differs from federal free speech law

FREE SPEECH PHILOSOPHY

From ancient philosophers to contemporary times, writers have argued that freedom of expression is valuable and worthy of protection. Among the most common reasons given for freedom of expression are that it is an essential means of obtaining truth; it is necessary for democratic self-governance; it serves as a check against oppressive government; and it functions as a means for individual self-actualization and as a social safety valve. It also establishes the foundation for freedom of religion, which will be discussed at length in the subsequent chapter.

The ideas of English political philosopher John Locke arguably made the greatest impact on the political thought of the early Americans more than any other thinker. His social contract theory, found in his *Second Treatise on Government* published in 1690, became the philosophical foundation for the existence of the United States of America as a separate and independent nation. Thomas Jefferson borrowed wholesale from Locke's theory when he drafted the U.S. Declaration of Independence, and the final language in the Declaration matches step-for-step the essence of Locke's social contract theory:

> All men are created equal, that they are endowed by their Creator with certain unalienable Rights, that among these are Life, Liberty and the pursuit of Happiness — That to secure these rights, Governments are instituted among Men, deriving their just powers from the consent of the governed — That whenever any Form of Government becomes destructive of these ends, it is the Right of the People to alter or to abolish it. (U.S. Declaration of Independence, 1776).

The Declaration then explains how the King of England has violated the rights of the American colonists, thus justifying their refusal to bow to the crown of England and create their own government instead.

One early British thinker to defend the freedom of speech was the writer, poet and philosopher John Milton, best known for his epic poem *Paradise Lost*. In his pamphlet, *Areopagitica*, in 1644, he argued that the freedom to print without government license is necessary if one hopes to discover truth through exploring the competition of ideas. This means that all positions of an idea—all sides and all viewpoints—should be heard in order for the people to make a genuinely informed judgment about which ideas are best, or even true.

This argument was supported by the English political philosopher John Stuart Mill in his work *On Liberty* (1869), and also later by U.S. Supreme Court Justice Oliver Wendell Holmes. In his dissent in *Abrams v. U.S.* (1926), Holmes argued that all viewpoints must be left to compete freely in the marketplace of ideas:

> (W)hen men have realized that time has upset many fighting faiths, they may come to believe even more than they believe the very foundations of their own conduct that the ultimate good desired is better reached by free trade in ideas—that the best test of truth is the power of the thought to get itself accepted in the competition of the market, and that truth is the only ground upon which their wishes safely can be carried out. That at any rate is the theory of our Constitution (p. 630).

Freedom of expression is also seen as a necessary means for democracy to function. One writer who is known for expounding this idea is Alexander Meiklejohn, who defined the terms of self-governance in his 1948 work *Free Speech and its Relation to Self-Government*. The term *democracy*, in fact, comes from the Greek, and literally means "rule by the people." In order for the people to be self-governed, they must be able to debate amongst themselves who should lead, what the laws should be, how the current rulers are doing, and which rulers should be elected or removed from office.

Without obtaining as much information as possible on an issue and without the freedom to engage in debate, how can people effectively govern themselves? For example, imagine a classroom where the teacher decides to leave the classroom for a time and asks the students to take charge in her absence. The teacher tells the class "you can govern yourselves however you want while I'm gone, except you cannot communicate with each other in any way." Obviously, it would be impossible for the students to figure out how to conduct the class without the ability to communicate with each other and discuss how they should govern themselves.

Both Mill and Meiklejohn are known for advocating another purpose for the freedom of speech. If someone were to ask you what is the most important part of your personal identity—that is, what makes you unique as a human being—what would you say? You probably would not describe your favorite color or favorite food, but instead would talk about personal and deeply cherished beliefs, such as your political views, religious beliefs, or the moral principles that you follow. The inability to express those deeply held beliefs would deny you the ability to express your individuality. Thus, the freedom to seek out possible options for one's identity, and then the ability to choose and express those beliefs and opinions, are essential to individual freedom and autonomy. The denial of the ability to express one's individual identity would enforce conformity to the point where we would appear to be little more than clones. Thus, freedom of expression is essential to our very humanity.

The right to express one's identity also includes the corresponding right not to be forced to express a belief that one disagrees with, and thereby violate one's religious or moral conscience. For example, in *West Virginia State Board of Education v. Barnet* (1942), the U.S. Supreme Court reasoned that public school children should not be punished for refusing to repeat the pledge of allegiance to the U.S. flag. After noting the political compulsion enforced by fascist regimes, the Court concluded: "Those who begin coercive elimination of dissent soon find themselves exterminating dissenters. Compulsory unification of opinion achieves only the unanimity of the graveyard" (p. 641). The Barnett decision famously concluded, "If there is any fixed star in our constitutional constellation, it is that no official, high or petty, can prescribe what shall be orthodox in politics, nationalism, religion, or other matters of opinion or force citizens to confess by word or act their faith therein" (p. 642). Similarly, the U.S. Supreme Court held in *Santa Fe Independent School District v. Doe* (2000) that public-school children should not be forced to listen to or participate in a religious exercise, such as a prayer, that offends their own religious conscience.

Stifling freedom of expression may pose harmful consequences for civil society. Legal scholar Thomas Emerson wrote a 1963 *Yale Law Journal* article titled "Toward a

General Theory of the First Amendment," wherein he argued that the ability to express oneself freely serves as a social safety valve. What does this mean? Imagine a pressure cooker on top of a stove. The lid of the pressure cooker is clamped down so that steam cannot escape. As the steam pressure builds up, the pressure must be released or else the pot will explode. In order to prevent such an explosion from occurring, there is a release valve attached to the lid of the pot. Steam naturally escapes through this safety valve, thus relieving some of the pressure. Likewise, the nature of human beings is such that they sometimes build up anger and frustration with their political rulers. Their freedom of expression allows people to vent their frustration and anger about issues and events, whether it take place through writing a letter to an elected official or by shouting protests at a street rally. If people are forbidden this freedom—if they are threatened with punishment for peacefully expressing their anger—then their frustrations will build up and possibly explode into aggressive acts, sometimes even causing violence. Emerson argued that the ability to freely express one's frustrations serves as an emotional catharsis, thereby channeling one's frustrations and energy lawfully rather than violently.

One more key purpose of the freedom of expression—and in particular the freedom of the press—that is often suggested by journalists is that the news media serve as a watchdog on behalf of the public. In literal terms, a watchdog guards its human owner, barking in order to warn its master when danger is approaching, such as an intruder. Figuratively speaking, the news media guard the public's interests by keeping a careful, watchful eye on government's rulers, or other intruders, and then they warn the public when there is cause for concern. This watchdog function is performed by reporting on abuse of power or other wrongdoing by government officials and corporate bosses, such as fraud, wastefulness, or other scandals. Justice Hugo Black perhaps best described this role for journalists in his concurrence in *New York Times v. U.S.* (1971):

> In the First Amendment the Founding Fathers gave the free press the protection it must have to fulfill its essential role in our democracy. The press was to serve the governed, not the governors. The Government's power to censor the press was abolished so that the press would remain forever free to censure the Government. The press was protected so that it could bare the secrets of government and inform the people. (p. 717)

FEDERAL FREEDOM OF SPEECH LAW

The philosophical foundations of free speech law just described manifest themselves via concrete law in slightly different ways at the state and federal levels within the United States. At the same time, much (though certainly not all) of Louisiana free speech law simply parallels federal free speech law. Thus, it is necessary to first extensively describe federal free speech law so that one can then examine the similarities and differences between federal free speech law and free speech law in Louisiana.

Origin of the Federal Free Speech Clause

In the United States, the public's yearning for the freedom of speech and press began to take root during the colonial period. At that time, the British government suppressed political criticism of its colonial rule. One way the appointed colonial rulers did this was through prior restraint on publication. A prior restraint occurs when the government is able to stop communication before it happens (as opposed to punishing a communicator afterward).

Prior restraints were accomplished through printing licenses. Printing presses were rare at the time, and in order to operate a printing press, one needed a license from the government. If printers criticized the government, they were at risk of losing their printing license or worse. Thus, to maintain their business, printers would censor their publications prior to the final printing in order to avoid offending the regime, which would place in jeopardy their livelihoods and liberty.

A second way the British colonial magistrates suppressed freedoms of speech and press was by prosecuting a crime that was known as seditious libel. Anyone who insulted the government, or chose to criticize particular government rulers, would be subject to prosecution. Basically, insulting the government would be committing a treasonous act, and thus could be punished by a fine or imprisonment.

Although some people favored authoritarian rule over speech and the press, when it came time to add a bill of rights to the U.S. Constitution, concerns about protecting free speech were on the minds of many early Americans. The U.S. Constitution was ratified in 1789, and only two years later, in 1791, the Bill of Rights was added. These first ten amendments to the U.S. Constitution contain a list of core political and religious rights, as well as protection for those individuals accused of crimes involving those rights. The First Amendment contains five basic democratic freedoms—religion, speech, press, assembly, and petition:

> Congress shall make no law respecting an establishment of religion, or prohibiting the free exercise thereof; or abridging the freedom of speech, or of the press; or the right of the people peaceably to assemble, and to petition the Government for a redress of grievances.

There is disagreement about the precise nature of the protection that early Americans intended to give to their freedoms of speech and the press. Most scholars, however, believe that the free speech and free press clauses were intended to accomplish a few key objectives. First, these clauses were intended to protect unpopular ideas from official government suppression. Understand that if the American founders wanted to protect only popular ideas, there would be no need for any constitutional clauses protecting either freedom of speech or the press. A democratically elected legislature chosen by the majority of the people will never be inclined to ban ideas that are popular and supported by a majority of their constituents. Thus, the very reason for having expressly stated constitutional protections for the freedom of speech and the press is to protect unpopular and offensive ideas from being punished by government.

The consensus among constitutional historians is that the ratifiers of the First Amendment believed it would protect unpopular ideas from punishment in two key ways: by prohibiting prior restraints such as publishing licenses, and by eliminating the crime of seditious libel—both of which were taken up by the U.S. Supreme Court in what are considered to be landmark constitutional rulings.

The U.S. Supreme Court case of *Near v. Minnesota* (1931), ruled that the early Americans who adopted the First Amendment intended that prior restraints of the press should be prohibited in general, with few exceptions. "In determining the extent of the constitutional protection [of the Free Press Clause], it has been generally, if not universally, considered that it is the chief purpose of the guaranty to prevent previous restraints upon publication" (p. 713).

One famous application of the presumption against prior restraints occurred in *New York Times v. U.S.* (1971). There, the Court held that the U.S. government could not prevent newspapers from publishing confidential military reports that would be embarrassing to the government. Although the justices could not agree on a single legal standard to apply, a majority seemed to agree that the articles' publication should not be prevented absent a clear showing that it would directly harm national security.

The landmark decision of *New York Times v. Sullivan* (1964) explained how allowing individuals to be punished for speech critical of government was inconsistent with the basic intent of the First Amendment. In what has come to be called the "chilling effect," the Court noted that either the crime of seditious libel or civil lawsuits by public officials for defamation would severely hinder the freedom of speech. People would be afraid to say things for fear their statements might be viewed as critical of government.

Thus, many people would choose to say nothing rather than risk punishment or prosecution. This worry could create a chilling effect on freedom of expression, contrary to the core purpose of the First Amendment. The Court noted the First Amendment's intent was to enforce the "profound national commitment to the principle that debate on public issues should be uninhibited, robust, and wide-open, and that it may well include vehement, caustic, and sometimes unpleasantly sharp attacks on government and public officials" (p. 270). To protect this public discourse, the Court ruled that public officials must overcome a high hurdle in order to sue for defamation. The public official must show that the defendant either knew what was said was false, or acted in reckless disregard of whether or not the communication was true or false.

Incorporation Doctrine

Originally, the First Amendment limited only the powers of the U.S. government. The First Amendment speaks to the acts of Congress, so individual states could limit speech however they wished, except to the degree their own particular state constitutions prevented them from doing so. This power, however, was federalized in the twentieth century. The U.S. Supreme Court ruled that the Fourteenth Amendment, which was ratified in 1868, and which limits the powers of state governments, was also intended to apply some of the Bill of Rights to the state governments. This concept is known as the *incorporation doctrine*, meaning that the Fourteenth Amendment incorporates (includes) some of the Bill of Rights and thus limits the powers of the state governments to act in opposition.

Rather than stating that all of the Bill of Rights would apply to the state governments via the Fourteenth Amendment, the U.S. Supreme Court chose to apply sections of the Bill of Rights one at a time through individual rulings. The clauses of the First Amendment were selectively incorporated by the following cases: the Establishment Clause (which provides that Congress shall make no law respecting an establishment of religion) was incorporated in *Everson v. Board of Education* (1947); the Free Exercise Clause (which says Congress shall not prohibit the free exercise of religion) in *Cantwell v. Connecticut* (1940); the Free Speech Clause (which declares Congress shall not abridge the freedom of speech) in *Gitlow v. New York* (1925); the Free Press Clause (which says Congress shall not abridge the freedom of the press) in *Near v. Minnesota* (1931); the Free Assembly Clause (which says Congress shall not abridge the right of the people peaceably to assemble) in *DeJonge v. Oregon* (1937); and the Petition Clause (which declares Congress shall not abridge the right of the people to petition the government for a redress of grievances) in *Edwards v. South Carolina* (1963). Today all of the clauses in the federal First Amendment limit the powers of state governments.

Federal Protection for Free Expression

The protections listed in the First Amendment are stated in very broad terms, and its sweeping generality raises at least two important questions. First, are protections for free speech absolute or qualified? Second, what types of speech are protected as "free speech"? The views of leading justices on the U.S. Supreme Court and certain opinions found in landmark cases go a long way to answer our questions regarding the kinds of freedom that are protected in terms of expression and to what extent.

Different justices on the U.S. Supreme Court have disagreed over the years about whether the freedom of speech is absolute or qualified. Justices Hugo Black and William O. Douglas both believed in an absolutist approach to the freedom of speech. They argued that the phrase "Congress shall make no law abridging the freedom of speech" should be strictly, literally construed as no law. This would mean that government could never pass laws restricting speech in any way, regardless of whether the expression was viewed as threatening, obscene, defamatory, or any other type of harmful speech.

> ### Development of the First Amendment
>
> The U. S. Constitution was ratified without a bill of rights, but with the promise that there would be added amendments to assure Americans the freedom fought for in the War of Independence was protected. On June 8, 1789, James Madison, now a member of the new U. S. House of Representatives, proposed amendments to be inserted into the text of the Constitution. Borrowing from ideas and language from prior thinkers and documents, such as Locke's *Second Treatise on Government* and the Virginia Declaration of Rights, Madison formally submitted to the U. S. Congress several proposed additions to Article I, Section 9's limitations on the powers of Congress. Some of these proposed changes eventually evolved into the First Amendment. Madison's proposal read:
>
>> *The civil rights of none shall be abridged on account of religious belief or worship, nor shall any national religion be established, nor shall the full and equal rights of conscience be in any manner, or on any pretext, infringed.*
>>
>> *The people shall not be deprived or abridged of their right to speak, to write, or to publish their sentiments; and the freedom of the press, as one of the great bulwarks of liberty, shall be inviolable.*
>>
>> *The people shall not be restrained from peaceably assembling and consulting for their common good; nor from applying to the Legislature by petitions, or remonstrances, for redress of their grievances (U. S. House Record, June 8, 1789).*
>
> The House revised Madison's wording and passed seventeen proposed amendments, two of which read:
>
>> Article 3. *Congress shall make no law establishing religion, or prohibiting the free exercise thereof, nor shall the rights of conscience be infringed.*
>>
>> Article 4. *The freedom of speech, and of the press, and the right of the people peaceably to assemble and consult for their common good, and to apply to the government for redress of grievances, shall not be infringed.*
>
> When the House sent its proposals to the Senate, it modified and passed twelve of the seventeen proposed amendments. After language differences between the House and Senate versions were reconciled, those twelve were sent onto the states for consideration. Religious liberty and the several rights involving free expression had been combined into the third proposed amendment on the list. The states ratified all but the first two proposed amendments, and thus what had been the third proposed amendment moved up into its final, permanent position as the First Amendment to the U. S. Constitution.

The views of Black and Douglas, however, were always in the small minority on the U.S. Supreme Court. The majority adopted what is called the preferred position, balancing the competing interests of the individual versus the interests of the government/society. The balance is weighted in favor of freedom of expression, particularly if there is any indication of prior restraint or censorship. The Court has held, however, that the weight given to each side's interests differs depending on the type of speech in question. Essentially, the Court places different types of speech into one of three possible categories of content: types of speech where the content receives nearly absolute protection, areas where the content receives strong (but not absolute) protection, and those types of speech where the content receives little or no First Amendment protection.

Political and Religious Speech

Political speech is considered to be at the very heart of the First Amendment's protection, and thus receives nearly absolute Constitutional protection. The same is true of religious speech, which will be discussed in the next chapter. The Supreme Court has concluded that these types of speech involve the core purposes of the freedom of expression. This distinction was illustrated by the landmark Supreme Court case of *Texas v. Johnson* (1989). The state of Texas prosecuted Johnson for burning a U.S. flag near the site of the Republican National Convention as part of a political protest against President Reagan's policies. He was officially charged with the crime of desecration of a venerated object, which essentially meant that Johnson was convicted of disrespecting a symbol of transcendent importance.

When Johnson's case reached the high court, however, the majority of justices held that the Texas statute was unconstitutional because the First Amendment protects political expression no matter how unpopular, including the extremely unpopular (and to some people, intolerable) expression of desecrating the U.S. flag. The Court declared "If there is a bedrock principle underlying the First Amendment, it is that the government may not prohibit the expression of an idea simply because society finds the idea itself offensive or disagreeable" (p. 414).

Commercial Speech

A second category of speech receiving strong, but somewhat lower, level of protection is commercial speech. The best example of this type of commercial content is solicitation and promotion by businesses and corporations. Business advertising and other types of expression designed to generate commerce have some leeway, but are less protected than political speech or private conversations. For example, individuals are free to lie about their personal beliefs, but in the context of their business may not display false advertising or commit other types of commercial fraud. Advertisers can be compelled to add communication to their commercial messages if the government believes that a matter of health, safety, or financial security is involved.

The limits on freedom for commercial speech can even compel business people to disclose certain kinds of information and not remain silent as individuals sometimes can. Government cannot force individuals to publicly reveal their views on politics or religion, but businesses can be required to label their products with safety warnings, ingredients, nutrition labels, or other consumer information. There are exceptions, when government has gone too far in regulating commercial speech. For example, in *44 Liquormart, Inc., v. Rhode Island* (1996), the state of Rhode Island outlawed all advertising of alcohol prices. The Supreme Court struck down the law, ruling that government may not ban truthful, non-misleading business advertising that serves to provide information, such as product prices, to consumers..

Symbolic Expression

Within the middle category of speech that receives an intermediate level of First Amendment protection is another type of speech referred to as symbolic speech. This is expression in the form of conduct that communicates a message. A law regulating this type of speech needs to be justified only by some "important" or "substantial" government interest. The Court has reached a number of contrasting decisions when this type of nonverbal speech was involved. For example, in *Tinker v. Des Moines* (1969) the Court held that a public high school could not prohibit students from silently wearing black armbands as a form of political protest. The Court also held, as earlier noted, that a state may not ban the public burning of the American flag as a form of political protest

(*Texas v. Johnson*, 1989). But the Court did uphold a Congressional ban on the public burning of draft registration cards as a form of political protest (*U.S. v. O'Brien*, 1968). It also upheld a local ban on nudity by dancers in adult nightclubs, despite the claim by the club that the dancing was a form of "erotic expression" (*Erie v. Pap's A. M.*, 2000).

Unprotected Speech

Expressions without particular value that tend to incite harmful acts of aggression or offend sexual morals comprise a third category of speech without Constitutional protection. The Court has justified this approach by explaining that some types of communication have little if anything to do with the values behind the freedom of expression. Various Supreme Court cases over the decades have found that several types of speech meet these criteria and thus receive little or no protection from the First Amendment. Such types of speech include true threats (*Virginia v. Black*, 2003); advocating imminent lawless acts of violence (*Brandenburg v. Ohio*, 1969); provoking someone to react violently through the use of "fighting words" (*Chaplinsky v. New Hampshire*, 1942); extreme forms of pornography that meet the legal definition of "obscenity" (*Miller v. California*, 1973); any type of child pornography (*New York v. Ferber*, 1982); and injuring someone's reputation by falsely defaming them (*New York Times v. Sullivan*, 1964); (*Gertz v. Welch*, 1973).

Over the past two decades, the Court has been asked several times to expand its list of unprotected speech to include content that depicts acts of violence, hate, and aggression. In every instance, the majority of justices have declined to do so. No matter how controversial the subject matter, the Court extends Constitutional protection to speech that is hateful toward individuals due to their race, sex, or religion (*R. A. V. v. City of St. Paul*, 2003), films depicting intentionally brutal and gruesome animal cruelty (*U.S. v. Stevens*, 2010); and the portrayal of extremely graphic violence in video games (*Brown v. Entertainment Merchants Association*, 2011).

Time, Place, and Manner Regulations

In addition to this three-tiered framework for protecting speech in various degrees depending on its content, the Supreme Court also applies a separate analysis for laws that regulate speech not based on its content, but because of the location and means of communication. The high court has said that laws regulating the time, place, and manner of speech on government property are subject to different levels of legal scrutiny depending on the nature of that property.

Under this framework, all public property is divided into three types. Government property that has historically been open to use by the public for open discourse is defined as a traditional public forum. For example, the Supreme Court noted in *Frisby v. Schultz* (1988) that public parks, streets, and sidewalks have been used as public forums from "time immemorial" (since before recorded history).

The second type of venue is public property that the government has intentionally opened up as a forum for free discussion within certain limits. This type of property is called a designated public forum. In *Widmar v. Vincent* (1981), the University of Missouri at Kansas City had allowed more than one hundred student groups to use its campus facilities except "for purposes of religious worship or religious teaching." A religious student group challenged the policy by filing suit against UMKC. The Supreme Court ruled that by allowing student organizations access to its buildings and grounds, UMKC had created a limited public forum. The First Amendment thus prohibited UMKC from discriminating against religious organizations that wanted to use the forum. Several subsequent Supreme Court cases have reiterated the principle that once a public school creates a limited public forum, the school must allow both secular and religious speakers equal access to the forum. See *Lamb's Chapel v. Center Moriches Union Free School District* (1993); *Rosenberger v. Rector and Visitors of the University of Virginia* (1995); and *Good News Club v. Milford Central School* (2001).

All other types of government property by default fall into the third category of public property: they are simply not public forms. A military base, for example, is not a public forum as held by *Greer v. Spock* (1976), nor is a prison (*Adderly v. Florida*, 1966), nor a public transit system (*Lehman v. City of Shaker Heights*, 1974), nor a public airport terminal (*ISKCON v. Lee*, 1992).

Time, place, or manner regulations in either a traditional public forum or a designated public forum are subject to legal analysis under the standard of judicial review that is called strict scrutiny. Although the Supreme Court has described this standard of judicial review in a variety of ways, the simplest way to define this level of scrutiny is to state that the law must be "narrowly drawn to further a compelling state interest" (*ISKCON v. Lee*, 1992). This essentially means that the government seeking to justify the law must show that there is some overridingly important reason for regulating the speech in question, and that the law must be carefully written so that it regulates no more speech than is absolutely necessary to achieve that specific purpose.

On the other hand, speech regulations involving government property that is not a public forum need only be reasonable in their terms, and not an effort to suppress the speaker's point of view. The Court has stated that time, place, and manner regulations include zoning ordinances. For example, in *Renton v. Playtime Theatres* (1986), the Court held that adult theatres could be prohibited within one thousand feet of any residential zone, church, park, or school, due to the harmful "secondary effects" of such theatres, such as the negative impact on children and the contribution such theatres make to neighborhood blight.

Federal Public Forum Law and Civil Rights in Louisiana

During the peak of the Civil Rights Movement in the early 1960s, Louisiana had a series of prominent cases reach the Supreme Court involving arrests of civil rights protestors. In *Garner v. Louisiana* (1961) and *Taylor v. Louisiana* (1962), the Court ruled that blacks peacefully sitting at a "whites only" lunch counter or in a "whites only" bus depot could not be charged with violating Louisiana's "breach of the peace" statute. Although these cases involved private property, shortly after these cases were decided two other cases arose that involved civil rights protests on public property, thus implicating the public forum doctrine.

In *Cox v. Louisiana* (1965), a group of civil rights protestors sang, cheered, and clapped on the sidewalk in front of a public courthouse in order to peacefully protest segregated businesses across the street from them. They were arrested for "breach of the peace" and "obstructing public passages." On the first count, the Court noted that there was no evidence of any breach of the peace. Moreover, state courts had interpreted "breach of the peace" as meaning "to agitate, to arouse from a state of repose, to molest, to interrupt, to hinder, to disquiet." The U.S. Supreme Court held that these vague terms were overbroad, and so such an interpretation and application of Louisiana's breach of the peace statutes violated the First Amendment.

On the obstructing public passages count, the Court ruled that although the state has a right to protect the smooth flow of automobile or pedestrian traffic, in this case the police and city officials had granted parade permits to other groups but had arbitrarily denied civil rights protesters such permits. Such discrimination against the exercise of speech and assembly rights violated both the First and Fourteenth Amendments.

The next year, in *Brown v. Louisiana* (1966), the Court similarly overturned the "breach of the peace" convictions of several blacks who were sitting or standing quietly in a public library reserved for "whites only." The Court noted that, given the fact there was no evidence of a breach of the peace or any attempt to incite one, the convictions violated the defendants' rights to speech, assembly, and redress of grievances.

Other Free Expression Concepts

The Supreme Court has also struck down federal regulations that are vague due to the chilling effect such laws have on freedom of expression. For example, in *Reno v. ACLU* (1997), the Court overturned a congressional ban prohibiting "indecent" speech on the internet. "The vagueness of such a regulation raises special First Amendment concerns because of its obvious chilling effect on free speech... The severity of criminal sanctions may well cause speakers to remain silent rather than communicate even arguably unlawful words, ideas, and images" (pp. 871-872).

The Court also will strike down laws it considers to be overbroad. In *Airport Commissioners v. Jews for Jesus* (1987), it struck down a public airport regulation prohibiting all First Amendment activities. "Under the First Amendment overbreadth doctrine," the Court reasoned, "an individual whose own speech or conduct may be prohibited is permitted to challenge a statute on its face because it also threatens others not before the court—those who desire to engage in legally protected expression but who may refrain from doing so rather than risk prosecution" (p. 574). On a related note, the public use of vulgar words is protected as free speech (*Cohen v. California*, 1971). The Court explained that all words—including the most vulgar terms—are chosen to convey both substantive and emotional meanings; and thus the elimination of any words from the public vocabulary would restrict the speaker's ability to convey ideas.

One exception to the principles of vagueness and vulgarity is the regulations that the broadcast media face from the Federal Communications Commission. In *FCC v. Pacifica* (1978), the Court held that "indecent" speech on radio and television at certain hours of the day is unprotected and may be punished by the federal government. The Court reasoned that the broadcast channels differ from other forms of media because the transmission of their electromagnetic signals physically invades homes and automobiles, and so the government has an increased interest in protecting the public's interest. Because children also have easier access to the broadcast media, harmful exposure to even a single expletive or nude image is considered worthy of government restriction. Thus, the government has a greater interest in ensuring that holders of broadcast licenses operate in the public interest, convenience, and necessity.

The Supreme Court also created particular rules for free expression in a context where some special relationship exists between the government and the individuals involved. Such situations include communication by prison inmates (*Turner v. Safley*, 1987), publications by public high school students (*Hazelwood School District v. Kuhlmeier*, 1988), and the words of public employees (*Garcetti v. Ceballos*, 2006). In these contexts, the government has more leeway in controlling communication than it would otherwise, given the government's heightened interests at stake due to its additional responsibility for oversight in these situations.

The First Amendment addresses other freedom of expression issues as well. For example, in *Boy Scouts of America v. Dale* (2000) the U.S. Supreme Court ruled that the First Amendment protects a right of association. Under this right, private groups may exclude people from membership if the speech or conduct of those individuals would interfere with the "expressive message" of the organization. Also, in *Richmond Newspapers v. Virginia* (1980), the U.S. Supreme Court ruled that the public, including the news media, has an implicit but qualified "right of access" or a "right to gather information" under the First Amendment. This includes the right to observe criminal trials unless the trial must be closed to the public to achieve a fair trial for the defendant.

Note that under the entire First Amendment framework discussed here, only *government* restrictions on speech are limited by the First Amendment. By definition, the amendments in the Bill of Rights are limitations on the powers of government, not private entities. Thus, private individuals, private schools, or private businesses generally may regulate speech on their property without being limited by the First Amendment. For example, owners of private homes may kick party guests out of their homes simply because of the guests' political or religious views. The First Amendment does not apply in that instance.

FREE SPEECH IN LOUISIANA

Now that we have described federal free speech law in detail, we can examine the ways in which Lousiana law follows federal law in this regard, and the ways in which Louisiana pursues its own independent legal path when it comes to the freedom of speech.

Development of the Louisiana State Constitution

Louisiana became a state by act of Congress and entered the union on the last day of April in 1812. Its first state constitution approved that same year clearly envisioned freedom of expression; however, it also included an abuse clause to discourage harmful speech. Article VI declared:

> Section 21. Printing presses shall be free to every person who undertakes to examine the proceedings of the Legislature, or any branch of the government, and no law shall ever be made to restrain the right thereof. The free communication of thoughts and opinions is one of the invaluable rights of man, and every citizen may freely speak, write and print on any subject, being responsible for the abuse of that liberty.

The state constitution was re-drafted three times before the Civil War, and again in 1861 when Louisiana seceded from the United States and joined the Confederate States of America. In 1879, a fifth state constitution was drafted. Louisiana rewrote its state charter on four more occasions:1898, 1913, 1921, and finally in 1974. The language that now guides freedom of expression, religion, and assembly is found in Article 1, Sections 7-9, which corresponds to the First Amendment of the U.S. Constitution:

> Section 7. No law shall curtail or restrain the freedom of speech or of the press. Every person may speak, write, and publish his sentiments on any subject, but is responsible for abuse of that freedom.
> Section 8. No law shall be enacted respecting an establishment of religion or prohibiting the free exercise thereof.
> Section 9. No law shall impair the right of any person to assemble peaceably or to petition government for a redress of grievances.

Lockstep Interpretation of the Louisiana Constitution

In *Robbins v. Pruneyard Shopping Center* (1980), the U.S. Supreme Court announced that state courts are free to give broader protection to rights in their state constitutions than the protection for rights found in the U.S. Bill of Rights. Some states, such as California, have chosen to take this route, and interpret the freedom of expression in their own bills of rights in unique and different ways, separate and apart from how the federal courts protect freedom of expression under the First Amendment. Many other states, however, follow what is sometimes called the lockstep doctrine. Under this doctrine, a state court will interpret a right found in its state constitution to be precisely in parallel with how the federal courts, especially the U.S. Supreme Court, interpret the corresponding right in the U.S. Constitution. For the most part, Louisiana follows the lockstep doctrine with a few exceptions.

Although Louisiana cases interpreting Article 1, Sections 7-9 of the Louisiana Constitution do not expressly use the term "lockstep doctrine," a number of decision reflect this philosophy. For example, in *Finkelstein v. Barthelemy* (1990), an assistant city attorney was fired when he voiced opposition to a tax increase proposed by the city's administration. He argued the politically based firing violated both his free speech rights and his equal protection rights. The Louisiana Court of Appeal declared, "Since Article I, Sections 3 and 7 of the Louisiana Constitution are similar in nature to the First and Fourteenth Amendments of the United States Constitution we look to the federal courts for guidance" (pp. 1100-1101). The court then ruled against the attorney based on U.S. Supreme Court precedents that declared the free-speech rights of high-level public employees in discretionary policy-making positions are outweighed by the government's interest in effective and efficient operation of government policy.

An even clearer statement came from the Louisiana Supreme Court in the case of *In re Ridenhour* (2004), which evaluated whether news reporters may keep the identity of their sources confidential. After quoting portions of the federal First Amendment and Article 1, Section 7 of the Louisiana Constitution, the court declared, "For purposes of this issue we will consider the two constitutions together. The information is either protected by both or not protected by either." The court then directly followed the U.S. Supreme Court precedent of *Branzburg v. Hayes* (1972) in holding that reporters have a limited free press right to withhold the identity of their sources under certain conditions. Similarly, in *State v. Franzone* (1980), the Louisiana Supreme Court ruled unconstitutional a state law that punished property owners who knowingly rented their property to anyone who was going to use the property for obscene practices. After discussing *Near v. Minnesota* (1930) and other U.S. Supreme Court precedents that ruled the federal First Amendment prevents such prior restraints, the Louisiana Supreme Court declared, "We are satisfied that our state constitution's guarantee of these liberties was designed to serve the same purpose and provides at least coextensive protection" (p. 411).

Even without such clear statements, when interpreting Article I, Sections 7-9, Louisiana courts mirror federal court rulings interpreting First Amendment rights. This can be seen in Louisiana court holdings on various types of free expression issues. In *Louisiana Life v. McNamara* (1987), the Louisiana Court of Appeal struck down a state law that taxed magazines but exempted newspapers from the tax. The court directly followed several U.S. Supreme Court precedents in simultaneously interpreting both the federal First Amendment and Article I, Section 7 of the Louisiana Constitution. The Louisiana Court of Appeal held that the state government may not tax publishers without an overriding reason to do so, nor may such a tax discriminate among different types of publishers. Likewise, in *State v. Fulton* (1976), the Louisiana Supreme Court ruled Article I, Section 7 of the Louisiana Constitution prohibited a state law mandating that political flyers contain the author's identification. In reaching this conclusion, the court simply looked to interpretations of the federal First Amendment by the U.S. Supreme Court, the Louisiana Supreme Court, and the courts of other states. Also, in interpreting the rights to speech, petition, and assembly in the Louisiana Constitution in *Godwin v. East Baton Rouge Parish School Board* (1981), the Louisiana Supreme Court simply looked to federal precedent interpreting the federal First Amendment. The court then held a school board policy prohibiting signs at school board meetings was a reasonable time, place, or manner regulation.

Moreover, in *Louisiana Republican Party v. Foster* (1996), the Louisiana Supreme Court looked extensively to federal precedents interpreting the First Amendment to determine whether a state law directing how the Republican Party elects its state central committee violated sections 7 and 9 of Article I of the Louisiana Constitution. Mike Foster had been a Democratic Louisiana state senator but switched party affiliation from Democratic to Republican in order to run for Louisiana governor in 1994. He successfully campaigned as an outsider who would bring reform to the system. After winning the election, he and his supporters battled the leaders of the Louisiana Republican Party for control of the party. Toward this goal, Foster's supporters in the state capitol passed legislation that mandated how the Louisiana Republican Party State Central Committee members were chosen. The Louisiana Republican Party filed a lawsuit challenging the law. The court declared that the state had no compelling interest that overrode the state party's right to freedom of association. In short, the summary of free expression law discussed earlier follows closely Louisiana jurisprudence under Article I, Sections 7-9 of the Louisiana Constitution.

Independent Louisiana Free Expression Law

Despite the fact that much free-expression law in Louisiana matches federal interpretation of the First Amendment, one free-expression component of the Louisiana Constitution differs significantly from the federal First Amendment. Recall that Article I, Section 7 of the Louisiana Constitution states: "No law shall curtail or restrain the freedom of speech or of the press. Every person may speak, write, and publish his sentiments on any subject, but is responsible for abuse of that freedom." The "abuse of freedom" clause in the second sentence of Section 7 has no counterpart in the federal First Amendment. To fully understand how Louisiana courts have interpreted and applied this section, one must first understand how the Louisiana legal system uniquely differs from that of the other forty-nine states.

In the Anglo-Saxon legal system, which originated in England and now includes the United States as well, courts generally had authority to make law on their own in the absence of other applicable law. As noted in the previous chapter, the body of decisions that such courts have made are collectively known as the common law. Under the common law, historically many broad areas of law have been created in part or whole by the courts. The U.S. Supreme Court has ruled that while states have such power, the Constitution does not empower federal courts to create a federal common law, nor has Congress ever given the federal courts such authority. Thus, within the United States, the fifty state-court systems have exclusive domain to create a common law system unique to each state.

Unlike the other forty-nine states, however, Louisiana has chosen not to create a common law system. Instead, Louisiana has kept the civil law system that it inherited from when it was governed by France, but it has also incorporated elements of the common law system so that it is best described as a mixed system. Under this mixed system, and according to the very first sentence of the Louisiana Civil Code: "Art. 1. Sources of law. The sources of law are legislation and custom." These provisions of the Civil Code mean that because only legislation and custom can have the force of law, Louisiana courts may not create bodies of law on their own as courts in common law states sometimes choose to do.

In common law jurisdictions, courts have traditionally been responsible for creating most tort law. Tort law involves non-criminal wrongs, such as negligence. Besides physical torts such as negligence that results in bodily harm, there are non-physical torts as well, including defamation (falsely injuring someone's reputation), invasion of privacy, and the intentional infliction of emotional distress. Because each of these three torts is based on expressive activity, the common law involving these three torts involves First Amendment issues. The U.S. Supreme Court therefore has ruled that state common law expressive torts are subject to some First Amendment limitations, but beyond those constraints states are free to define their common law expressive torts as they choose.

Because Louisiana follows the civil law, Louisiana courts have had to rely on legislation as a legal foundation for recognizing expressive torts. Primarily, Louisiana Civil Code Article 2315 states in part: "Liability for acts causing damages. A. Every act whatever of man that causes damage to another obliges him by whose fault it happened to repair it." Acting under this express legislative authority, the Louisiana Supreme Court has created and applied the expressive torts of defamation, invasion of privacy, and intentional infliction of emotional distress.

For example, in *Costello v. Hardy*, (2004) the Louisiana Supreme Court cited Article 2315 as giving the court authority to apply the law of defamation in order to remedy harm to someone's reputation. The court explained that it "borrowed from the common law" to determine defamation law concepts, and applied the standard common law definition: "words which tend to harm the reputation of another so as to lower the person in the estimation of the community, to deter others from associating or dealing with the person, or otherwise expose a person to contempt or ridicule" (p. 140). In *Costello* the court then declared that accusing an attorney of legal malpractice would tend to hurt that lawyer's reputation.

In *Jaubert v. Crowley Post Signal* (1979), the Louisiana Supreme Court decided to recognize the tort of invasion of privacy. The court noted that the "abuse of freedom" phrase in Article I, Section 7 of the 1974 Louisiana Constitution was retained from earlier constitutions to allow lawsuits for expressive torts under Article 2315 of the Louisiana Civil Code. Adopting the common law definitions, the court then announced that four different types of invasion of privacy will exist within Louisiana: "the appropriation of an individual's name or likeness, for the use or benefit of the defendant"; "when the defendant unreasonably intrudes upon the plaintiff's physical solitude or seclusion"; "publicity which unreasonably places the plaintiff in a false light before the public"; and "unreasonable public disclosure of embarrassing private facts" (p. 1388). In *Jaubert*, the court ruled that an unauthorized picture of a house in the local newspaper as part of a photo display of city scenes did not invade the homeowner's privacy in any of the four possible ways.

In *White v. Monsanto* (1991), the Louisiana Supreme Court decided that the "fault-reparation principles" of Article 2315 of the Civil Code allowed the court to recognize liability for the tort of "intentional infliction of emotional distress." Looking to the common law for "practical guidance" on defining the tort, the court declared that "one who by extreme and outrageous conduct intentionally causes severe emotional distress to another is subject to liability for such emotional distress" (p. 1209). The court held, though, that a single minute-long outburst of vulgar insults directed by a supervisor towards an employee did not meet this standard. In this case, as was the situations involving defamation and invasion of privacy, the "abuse of freedom" clause of Article I, Section 7 of the Louisiana Constitution, coupled with Louisiana Civil Code section 2315, allowed the Louisiana Supreme Court to recognize expressive torts that do not exist under federal law.

Louisiana free expression law differs from federal law not only when the state constitutional language differs from analogous federal constitutional language, but also when state statutory language differs from analogous federal statutory language. For example, in circumstances leading to *Keller v. Aymond* (1998), plaintiffs' conversations were recorded without their knowledge or legal authorization. Transcripts of the recordings were given to newspapers that then published excerpts from the transcripts. The plaintiffs filed suit against the newspapers for violation of the Louisiana Electronic Surveillance Act, which criminalizes unauthorized recordings and also provides for civil lawsuits against parties who "use" or "disclose" such recordings. The newspapers argued that they should be protected by the freedom of speech such that they can be held liable only if they "willfully" (i.e. knowingly or intentionally) used or disclosed illegal recordings, as is required by the counterpart federal statute that outlaws wiretapping. The trial court granted summary judgment to the newspapers and the plaintiffs appealed.

The Louisiana Court of Appeal reversed the trial court. Citing the "abuse of freedom" clause in Article I, Section 7 of the Louisiana Constitution, along with the plaintiff's right of privacy protected by both the state and federal constitutions, the Louisiana Court of Appeal first reasoned that "the press cannot escape the prohibitions of the Louisiana Electronic Surveillance Act under the guise of constitutional protection" because the press has "no right of access to private telephone conversations between individual citizens" (p. 1230). The court then noted that the state statute does not have the same language as the federal wiretapping statute. Unlike the federal statute, the state statute holds a publisher liable for "use" or "disclosure" of illegally obtained conversations regardless whether the publisher knew the recordings were illegal. The court thus concluded that under the state statute, publishers are civilly liable for disclosing the contents of illegally obtained conversations.

Jurisprudence Constante

As has been discussed, in issues involving free speech and religious liberty, Louisiana courts follow the lockstep doctrine in areas where the state constitution's language matches that of the federal Constitution. When the wording differs, however, or when state courts are otherwise given the authority to create and apply independent state law, Louisiana courts have often done so, such as by deciding to recognize the expressive torts. These policies are unlikely to change given another unique aspect of Louisiana's civil code tradition.

As a civil law state, Louisiana formally recognizes only two types of law. Recall that the very first article of the Louisiana Civil Code states in its entirety: "The sources of law are legislation and custom" (Civil Code, Art. I). Thus, as the Louisiana Supreme Court has explained, because individual court decisions are neither legislation nor custom, "prior holdings by this court are persuasive, not authoritative, expressions of the law . . . one of the fundamental rules of the civil law tradition is that a tribunal is never bound by the decisions which it formerly rendered: it can always change its mind" (*Doerr v. Mobil Oil Corp.* 2000, p. 129). This practice differs from that of common law states or at the federal level, where the principle of stare decisis (Latin for "let the decision stand") requires that even a single court decision is generally binding on future decisions by that same court in all but exceptional circumstances.

Although individual court cases need not be followed by the Louisiana Supreme Court, a long tradition of similar court rulings can become "custom" and therefore be authoritative law. Article 3 of the Civil Code states in part: "Custom results from practice repeated for a long time and generally accepted as having acquired the force of law." As explained by the Louisiana Supreme Court in *Doerr*, "it is only when courts consistently recognize a long-standing rule of law outside of legislative expression that the rule of law will become part of Louisiana's custom under Civil Code article 3" (p. 129). This principle, which applies when a history of similar court rulings can become legally authoritative "custom" under the civil code, is called jurisprudence constante. "A long line of cases following the same reasoning within this state forms jurisprudence constante. . . . When a series of decisions form a constant stream of uniform and homogenous rulings having the same reasoning, jurisprudence constante applies and operates with considerable persuasive authority." (*Doerr v. Mobil Oil Corp*, 2000, p. 128).

All the Louisiana court interpretations of freedom of expression in the Louisiana state constitution discussed earlier have been applied for many years. That is, both the lockstep doctrine (which applies when the state and federal constitutional language is identical) and independent state constitutional interpretation (which applies when the state constitutional language differs or where federal constitutional law authorizes state rights to vary) have been consistently applied in long series of cases over several decades now. Under the principle of jurisprudence constante, then, the legal principles regarding the lockstep doctrine, as well as the independent state constitutional interpretations discussed earlier, have all become "custom" under Article 3 of the Civil Code. This means that Louisiana courts would be very unlikely to depart radically from the past, such as by no longer following the lockstep doctrine on most issues of free speech or religious liberty, or by (for example) no longer recognizing the expressive torts within Louisiana. In short, the Louisiana court holdings discussed in this chapter are likely to remain authoritative law for the foreseeable future.

Conclusion

There are several important values behind the freedom of speech. Free expression is a means of attaining truth, achieving democracy, serving as a social safety valve, promoting self-actualization, and checking government. The intended purposes of the federal First Amendment were to protect offensive and unpopular speech, to prohibit prior restraints on speech such as publishing licenses, and to abolish the crime of seditious libel. Although free-expression rights could be interpreted in an absolute manner, the U.S. Supreme Court and Louisiana courts apply a balancing approach, whereby the interests of the individual wishing to speak are weighed against the interests of the state and society. Under this approach, political and religious expression both receive nearly absolute protection, commercial and symbolic speech receive strong protection, and other types of speech—such as threats, the advocacy of violence, fighting words, defamation, or obscenity—receive little or no constitutional protection. Free expression on government property that is a traditional or designated public forum is strongly protected, whereas speech on other types of government property is only moderately protected. Private entities regulating speech on their own private property are not subject to any of the constraints of the federal First Amendment or Article I, Section 7 of the Louisiana Constitution.

Most of the language of the Louisiana Constitution's protection for free expression and religious liberty matches the language of the federal First Amendment. Louisiana courts mostly follow the lockstep doctrine by interpreting the free-expression rights in the Louisiana Constitution to be equivalent to the rights in the federal First Amendment. The U.S. Supreme Court has said, however, that the federal First Amendment allows state legislatures and state courts some flexibility to define state rights differently. Also, the "abuse of freedom" language in Article I, Section 7 of the Louisiana Constitution differs from the federal First Amendment and thus supports differing interpretations of free expression rights in some instances. Acting on these legal authorizations, Louisiana has created free-expression and religious-liberty law that differs from federal law. As examples in the area of free expression, Louisiana courts have created the expressive torts of defamation, invasion of privacy, and intentional infliction of emotional distress, and the Louisiana legislature has provided broader criminal and civil liability for publishers of illegally obtained private conservations. Examples of independent Louisiana law in the area of religious liberty will be discussed in the subsequent chapter. All these differing rights are subject to future legal development by the Louisiana legislature and by Louisiana courts, but judicial doctrines are unlikely to substantially change due to the civil law principle of jurisprudence constante.

REFERENCES

Emerson, T. (1963). Toward a general theory of the First Amendment, 72 *Yale Law Journal* 877-956.

Locke, J. (1690). Second treatise on government. Retrieved from http://www.gutenberg.org/files/7370/7370-h/7370-

Meiklejohn, A. (1948). *Free speech and its relation to self-government.* Retrieved from http://uwdc.library.wisc.edu/collections/UW/MeikFreeSp

Mill, J. S. (1860). *On liberty.* Retrieved from http://www.constitution.org/jsm/liberty.htm

Milton, J. (1644). *Areopagitica.* Retrieved from http://www.gutenberg.org/ebooks/608

Stephens, J. F. (1887). *Digest of the criminal law,* 4th ed. Retrieved from https://archive.org/details/adigestcriminal02stepgoog

CASES CITED

Abrams v. United States, 250 U.S. 616 (1926).
Adderly v. Florida, 385 U.S. 39 (1966).
Airport Commissioners v. Jews for Jesus, 482 U.S. 569 (1987).
Boy Scouts of America v. Dale, 530 U.S. 640 (2000).
Brandenburg v. Ohio, 395 U.S. 444 (1969).
Branzburg v. Hayes, 408 U.S. 665 (1972).
Brown v. Entertainment Merchants Association, 564 U.S. (2011).
Brown v. Louisiana, 383 U.S. 131 (1966).
Cantwell v. Connecticut, 310 U.S. 296 (1940).
Chaplinsky v. New Hampshire, 315 U.S. 568 (1942).
Cohen v. California, 403 U.S. 15 (1971).
Costello v. Hardy, 864 So. 2d 129 (La. 2004).
Cox v. Louisiana, 379 U.S. 436 (1965).
DeJonge v. Oregon, 299 U.S. 353 (1937).
Doerr v. Mobile Oil Corp., 774 So. 2d 119 (La. 2000).
Edwards v. South Carolina, 372 U.S. 229 (1963).
Erie v. Pap's A. M., 529 U.S. 277 (2000).
Everson v. Board of Education, 330 U.S. 1 (1947)
FCC v. Pacifica, 438 U.S. 726 (1978).
Finkelstein v. Barthelemy, 565 So. 2d. 1098 (La. Crt. App. 1990).
Frisby v. Schultz, 487 U.S. 474 (1988)
Garcetti v. Ceballos, 547 U.S. 410 (2006).
Garner v. Louisiana, 368 U.S. 157 (1961).
Gertz v. Welch, 418 U.S. 323 (1974).
Gitlow v. New York, 268 U.S. 652 (1925).
Godwin v. East Baton Rouge Parish School Board, 408 So. 2d 1214 (La. 1981).
Good News Club v. Milford Central School, 533 U.S. 98 (2001).
Greer v. Spock, 424 U.S. 828 (1976).
Hazelwood School District v. Kuhlmeier, 484 U.S. 260 (1988).
In re Ridenhour, 520 So. 2d 322 (La. 2004).
ISKCON v. Lee, 505 U.S. 672 (1992).
Jaubert v. Crowley Post Signal, 375 So. 2d 1386 (La. 1979).
Keller v. Aymond, 722 So. 2d 1224 (La. Crt. App. 1998).
Lamb's Chapel v. Center Moriches Union Free School District, 508 U.S. 384 (1993).
Lehman v. City of Shaker Heights, 418 U.S. 298 (1974).
Louisiana Life v. McNamara, 504 So. 2d 900 (La. 1987).
Louisiana Republican Party v. Foster, 674 So. 2d 225 (La. 1996).
Miller v. California, 413 U.S. 15 (1973).

Near v. Minnesota, 283 U.S. 697 (1931)
New York v. Ferber, 458 U.S. 747 (1982).
New York Times v. Sullivan, 376 U.S. 254 (1964)
New York Times v. U.S., 403 U.S. 713 (1971).
R. A. V. v. City of St. Paul, 505 U.S. 377 (1992)
Reno v. ACLU, 521 U.S. 844 (1997).
Renton v. Playtime Theatres, 475 U.S. 41 (1986).
Richmond Newspapers v. Virginia, 448 U.S. 555 (1980).
Robbins v. Pruneyard Shopping Center, 447 U.S. 74 (1980)
Rosenberger v. Rector and Visitors of the University of Virginia, 515 U.S. 819 (1995).
Santa Fe Independent School District v. Doe, 530 U.S. 290 (2000).
State v. Birdsong, 422 So. 2d 1135 (La. 1982).
State v. Franzone, 384 So. 2d 409 (La. 1980).
State v. Fulton, 337 So. 2d 866 (La. 1976).
Taylor v. Louisiana, 370 U.S. 154 (1962).
Texas v. Johnson, 491 U.S. 397 (1989).
Tinker v. Des Moines, 393 U.S. 503 (1969).
Turner v. Safley, 482 U.S. 78 (1987).
U.S. v. O'Brien, 391 U.S. 367 (1968).
U.S. v. Stevens, 559 U.S. 460 (2010).
Virginia v. Black, 538 U.S. 343 (2003).
West Virginia State Board of Education v. Barnett, 319 U.S. 624 (1942).
White v. Monsanto, 585 So. 2d 1205 (La. 1991).
Whitney v. California, 274 U.S. 357 (1926).
Widmar v. Vincent, 454 U.S. 263 (1981).
44 Liquormart, Inc. v. Rhode Island, 517 U.S. 484 (1996).

FOR FURTHER READING

Collins, R. K. L., & Chaltain, S. (2011). *We must not be afraid to be free: Stories of free expression in America.* (New York: Oxford University Press).

Kidd, T. S. (2012). *God of liberty: A religious history of the American revolution* (New York: Basic Books).

Martin, R. (2001). *The free and open press: The founding of American democratic press liberty, 1640-1800.* (New York: NYU Press).

Schauer, F. (1982). *Free speech: A philosophical enquiry* (1982). (New York: Cambridge University Press).

Volokh, E. (2007). *The First Amendment: Problems, cases, and policy arguments* (3d ed.) (New York: Foundation Press).

Chapter 3
Religious Liberty
By Rick A. Swanson, University of Louisiana at Lafayette

Learning Objectives
In this chapter, readers will:
- be able to understand the rationale for separation of church and state
- learn about the Supreme Court's interpretation of the Free Exercise and Establishment Clauses
- see how First Amendment rights affect tax-supported funding for religious groups, government-sponsored prayer, and religious displays on public property
- understand how the lockstep doctrine affects religious liberty through Louisiana's response to federal legislation and precedents
- differentiate the rights of free expression and religious liberty in Louisiana from federal law based on the state legislature and court actions
- be able to describe how the common law stands in contrast with the civil law system in terms of religious liberty in Louisiana

ORIGINS OF RELIGIOUS LIBERTY

Throughout human history, governments have refused to tolerate freedom for political expression, believing that such public criticism would threaten, challenge, and ultimately undermine the legitimacy of their reign. Rulers felt their thrones needed safeguards at home to survive open vocal challenge, and found religious reasons to preserve their rule. In ancient Europe, emperors and monarchs claimed their authority to rule was derived from heavenly powers. In England this theory eventually became known as the "divine right of kings," which rulers based on the Bible: "There is no authority except that which God has established. The authorities that exist have been established by God" (Romans, 13:1). The advantage of this theory for the monarch was that no one had a "right" to disagree with God's authority, and so no one could question or criticize the king or queen's rule either.

One of the leading proponents of this divine right theory was political thinker Robert Filmer, (1680). Using the scriptures, he reasoned in *Patriarcha* that God gave the first human, Adam, dominion over the Earth, and the occupants of the throne who followed Adam were actually his direct blood descendants—so they inherited a god-given absolute right to rule over others. With the rise of the Enlightenment, however, political thinkers began to question, challenge, and eventually dismiss the divine right of kings.

English philosopher John Locke held an important position in shaping early American political thought, and in his *Second Treatise on Government* (1690) systematically rebutted Filmer's arguments. He offered an alternative explanation for the origin of government: the ideal that all humans are born with equal natural rights, including life, liberty, and property. Only when individuals come together for the mutual protection of those rights and consent to be governed, can their resulting government claim legitimate authority. Thus, in Locke's view, government requires freedom of political speech, which is essential to forming such a "civil society."

Locke wrote other works that widely influenced Americans' conceptions of the freedom of speech and religious liberty. Of particular significance is Locke's *Letter Concerning Toleration*, published in 1689. He argued that earthly civil governments oversee an entirely different sphere of human existence than does religion. Neither sphere should govern the other, he reasoned, nor should civil government persecute, rather than tolerate, people of various religious faiths. However, even in his *Letter Concerning Toleration* Locke made a notable exception for atheists. Because atheists are unbounded by religious oaths, Locke believed they were not to be trusted as members of civil society.

Locke was not the first thinker to recognize government and religion as distinctly different realms of human life. Indeed, leading Christian theologians planted the first seeds of this philosophy at the dawn of Christianity. Ecclesiastical scholar Augustine argued in the early fifth century that the earthly "City of Man" was temporal and flawed but the heavenly "City of God" was perfect and eternal. Then in the early thirteenth century, Italian theologian Thomas Aquinas articulated a clear distinction between "human law" and the "eternal" and "divine" laws of nature.

Fathers of the Protestant Reformation, Martin Luther (the founder of Lutheranism) and John Calvin both distinguished between the worldly and heavenly realms of law. Calvin, whose theology formed the foundation of several Protestant denominations, argued for separation in his *Institutes on the Christian Religion*: "But he who knows to distinguish between the body and the soul, between the present fleeting life and that which is future and eternal, will have no difficulty in understanding that the spiritual kingdom of Christ and civil government are things very widely separated" (Chapter 20, Section 1 of the Fourth Book). Thus, by the time Locke explained his theories on separation, he was building upon the philosophical foundations laid by several major thinkers (See *Two Treatises on Government* and *Letter Concerning Toleration*).

RELIGIOUS LIBERTY IN AMERICA

Before the nation's founding, most American colonies had established official religions, but not all. Two notable exceptions were the colonies of Rhode Island, which was organized by Roger Williams, and Pennsylvania, founded by William Penn. They based their colonial governments on the principles of religious freedom and tolerance. Because most of the colonies were English, though, they had typically established the Anglican Church (The Church of England) as the official religion. By the time American Independence was declared, the new states kept their official religions, which began to change following the writings of one influential Virginian.

The Virginia Act for Establishing Religious Freedom

In 1779, Thomas Jefferson, then governor of Virginia, proposed an Act for Establishing Religious Freedom. This law would undo any official state support for religion in Virginia, and thus would disestablish the Anglican Church as the official state religion. Baptists, Methodists, Presbyterians, Catholics, Jews, Deists, and other non-Anglican groups supported the proposal. There were those who wished to maintain state support for the Anglican Church, however, and under the powerful leadership of Patrick Henry they were able to block Jefferson's proposal.

In 1784, Henry proposed his own bill that would have provided state tax money to subsidize the salaries of Christian ministers in the state. Henry believed state support of religion was necessary for the maintenance of public morality. In response, James Madison wrote and distributed his now-famous *Memorial and Remonstrance against Religious Assessments* (1785). Among his several points, he argued that state-sanctioned churches of any kind violate the freedom of conscience, corrupt religion, and result in persecution or worse. Henry, then governor of Virginia, saw his proposal blocked by popular opposition that favored separation of church and state. Finally, Madison, Jefferson, and their supporters enacted a version of the bill Jefferson had originally proposed in 1779. The Virginia Statute for Religious Freedom established the basis for the wall of separation:

> Be it enacted by the General Assembly, That no man shall be compelled to frequent or support any religious worship, place or ministry whatsoever, nor shall be enforced, restrained, molested or burdened in his body or goods, nor shall otherwise suffer on account of his religious opinions or belief; but that all men shall be free to profess, and by argument to main-

tain, their opinion in matters of religion, and that the same shall in no wise diminish, enlarge, or affect their civil capacities (Section 2).

The 1786 Virginia Statute for Religious Freedom was one of the most important precursors to the religion clauses in the federal First Amendment.

Jefferson's thoughts about separation were inspired by Locke, Rousseau and others who knew well the problems caused by religious entanglement in government. His fellow Virginian, James Madison, convincingly argued that state-sanctioned churches tended to corrupt the purity of religious institutions, people, and teachings: "During almost fifteen centuries has the legal establishment of Christianity been on trial. What have been its fruits? More or less in all places, pride and indolence in the Clergy, ignorance and servility in the laity, in both, superstition, bigotry and persecution" (Madison, 1785, see section 7). By the time the U.S. Constitution was written in 1787 and ratified in 1789, the states were in a gradual but ongoing process of disestablishing their state religions, which was almost completed by the end of the century. Only three states (Connecticut, New Hampshire, and Massachusetts) took until the 1800s to do so.

The framers of the U.S. Constitution agreed that the U.S. government should not be given any power to legislate in the area of religion. Although the Constitution did not create any national religious establishment, no general right of religious liberty was listed in its seven articles either. Two years after the ratification of the Constitution, the Bill of Rights was added in 1791. The religion clauses of the First Amendment state, "Congress shall make no law respecting an Establishment of Religion, or prohibiting the Free Exercise thereof." Jefferson later authored an iconic phrase describing the First Amendment's religion clauses as a "wall of separation between church and state" (Thomas Jefferson, Letter to the Danbury Baptists, Jan. 1, 1802). Although other major thinkers at the time, such as Madison, had used similar terms, Jefferson's particular wording produced our most commonly used expression, "the separation of church and state," to describe the relationship between government and religion in the United States.

The Free Exercise Clause

The Free Exercise Clause protects both religious belief and, to a lesser degree, religious practice. The Supreme Court first interpreted the meaning of the Free Exercise Clause in *Reynolds v. U.S.* (1878). Congress had outlawed polygamy in the Utah territory and George Reynolds, a Mormon polygamist, was convicted of violating the law. Reynolds argued his religion required him to be a polygamist, and thus the law violated his religious liberty. The Supreme Court declared that the Free Exercise Clause absolutely protects belief, but not actions such as polygamy that are "a violation of social duties or subversive of good order" (p. 164).

By the 1960s, the high court protected the Free Exercise of worship by applying a balancing test. The Court struck down laws that burdened someone's religious practices unless the government could show a "compelling state interest" for the intrusion. In *Sherbert v. Verner* (1963), the Court ruled against the state of South Carolina for refusing to provide unemployment compensation to a Seventh-Day Adventist—a textile mill worker, Adell Sherbert—who had been fired for refusing to work on Saturday, her religious Sabbath. In *Wisconsin v. Yoder* (1972), the Court held that the state of Wisconsin could not punish Amish parents for refusing to send their children to public school for an additional two years of education beyond the Amish education that ended at the age of fourteen. In neither of these cases could the state supply a sufficiently compelling reason to impose the law based on the circumstances in question.

Within two decades, however, the Court's analysis changed. In *Employment Division v. Smith* (1990), the Court declared that the Free Exercise Clause does not provide a right to any religious exemptions from a "valid and neutral law of general applicability." (p. 879). This controversial ruling motivated Congress to pass the Religious Freedom

Restoration Act (RFRA) the following year. This law basically reinstated the compelling interest test of Sherbert and Yoder. The Supreme Court later held that Congress does not have the Constitutional authority to apply this act to state laws, although the RFRA certainly applies to federal law. Then, in *Church of Lukumi Babalu Aye v. City of Hialeah* (1993), the Court clarified its reasoning that the compelling interest test still applies in the narrow occasion where a law specifically regulates an action only when it is done with a religious motivation. In *Church of Lukumi*, the city of Hialeah, Florida, could not offer a compelling reason for prohibiting the killing of animals as part of a religious ritual, while at the same time allowing their killing for other reasons such as food production, sport hunting, vermin extermination, or euthanasia.

Even though the Free Exercise Clause is the only Constitutional provision that expressly protects religious practice, the Free Exercise and Free Speech Clauses taken together protect religious beliefs and their expression. The Supreme Court has declared that rights to religious expression are equivalent to rights of non-religious speech under the Free Speech Clause. In other words, the Free Exercise Clause does in some circumstances give special protection to religious *practices*, but it does not afford additional protection to religious *belief* or *expression* beyond what is given by the Free Speech Clause. As a result, religious groups and individuals for years have worked toward expanding equivalent religious expression rights under both clauses.

Three landmark cases illustrate how the Supreme Court has protected religious expression on free-speech grounds. In *Cantwell v. Connecticut* (1940), a family of Jehovah's Witnesses was arrested for spreading their message door-to-door without a village license to do so. The U.S. Supreme Court declared that the First Amendment prohibits government from requiring a license for people wishing to verbally share their message with those who are willing to listen. In *West Virginia State Board of Education v. Barnette* (1942), public school students were expelled and their parents threatened with prosecution after the children refused to say the Pledge of Allegiance on religious grounds. The high court famously declared "If there is any fixed star in our constitutional constellation, it is that no official, high or petty, can prescribe what shall be orthodox in politics, nationalism, religion, or other matters of opinion or force citizens to confess by word or act their faith therein" (p. 642). Four decades later, a minister was prohibited from passing out religious literature in the Los Angeles International Airport by an airport regulation that prohibited "all First Amendment activities." The Court in *Board of Airport Commissioners v. Jews for Jesus* (1982) struck down that regulation as constitutionally vague and overbroad.

The Establishment Clause

There was general agreement at the time of the ratification of the First Amendment that the U.S. Congress should not and could not declare any official religion or establish a national church. Beyond that agreement, however, there was and still is a lack of consensus over the precise meaning of the Establishment Clause, which remains a challenge today. In principle, three issues have regularly arisen where the Establishment Clause is pivotal in the decision: tax-supported funding of religion, school-sponsored prayers and religious teachings, and religious displays on public property.

Government Funding of Religion

The first case to consider the meaning of the Establishment Clause was *Everson v. Board of Education* (1947), which struggled with the question of government financial assistance to religion. After reviewing the history of the First Amendment, the U.S. Supreme Court defined the Establishment Clause and concluded with Jefferson's metaphor:

> The 'establishment of religion' clause of the First Amendment means at least this: Neither a state nor the Federal Government can set up a church. Neither can pass laws, which aid one religion, aid all religions, or prefer one religion to another. Neither can force nor influence a person to go to or to remain away from church against his will or force him to profess a belief or disbelief in any religion. No person can be punished for entertaining or professing religious beliefs or disbeliefs, for church attendance or non-attendance. No tax in any amount, large or small, can be levied to support any religious activities or institutions, whatever they may be called, or whatever from they may adopt to teach or practice religion. Neither a state nor the Federal Government can, openly or secretly, participate in the affairs of any religious organizations or groups and vice versa. In the words of Jefferson, the clause against establishment of religion by law was intended to erect 'a wall of separation between Church and State' (p. 15-16).

Applying that standard, the Court in *Everson* approved a state program that used taxpayer money to pay for busing students to private religious schools, given that equal taxpayer funding was provided for busing students to public schools. Thus, religion was not being favored, nor was it being discriminated against, and the money was merely part of a general government program that applied to all children regardless of their religion.

Later the Court adopted a detailed standard for the Establishment Clause that was to determine when a law had gone too far. In *Lemon v. Kurtzman* (1971), three criteria were created for what became known as the "Lemon Test": "First, the statute must have a secular legislative purpose; second, its principal or primary effect must be one that neither advances nor inhibits religion; finally, the statute must not foster 'an excessive government entanglement with religion'" (pp. 612-613). Applying this test, a unanimous decision in *Lemon* struck down a state program to fund teacher salaries, textbooks, and educational supplies at religious schools. The Court held that extensive government monitoring and judgments would be needed to ensure state funds were used only for "secular" activities in such schools as opposed to "religious" activities. Thus, the Court ruled that this would excessively entangle the state with religion.

Although the Court in some cases since *Lemon* has ruled against indirect taxpayer funding of religious entities, its recent decisions tend to prefer the neutrality principle found in *Everson* rather than the Lemon test. In *Zelman v. Simmons-Harris* (2002), for example, the Supreme Court upheld a state program in which parents could choose to take a taxpayer-provided voucher and equally apply it toward their child's tuition at a public school, private nonreligious school, or private religious school. Citing precedents where government money did eventually flow to private religious schools, the Court declared "where a government aid program is neutral with respect to religion, and provides assistance directly to a broad class of citizens who, in turn, direct government aid to religious schools wholly as a result of their own genuine and independent private choice, the program is not readily subject to challenge under the Establishment Clause" (p. 652).

Government-Sponsored Prayers and Religious Teachings

The second type of issue involving the Establishment Clause is government sponsorship of religious prayer and religious teachings. The Court first considered this issue in *Engel v. Vitale* (1962), in which a New York state law required that a prayer written by the New York Board of Regents be read by school officials at the start of each public school day. The Court struck down the law, stating that the Establishment Clause prohibited public officials from promoting religious belief as part of school activities.

Only a year later, the Court similarly ruled in *Abington Township v. Schempp* (1963) that the same rationale applied even where the school officials had not composed the prayer (in this case, it was the Lord's Prayer taken from the New Testament). The Court explained that there was no secular purpose to the law, and the practice had the primary effect of promoting religion, thus violating the Establishment Clause.

Since *Abington*, the Court has continued to strike down government-sponsored religious activities in public schools. These include a state-required "moment of silence" in public schools for the purpose of silent prayer (*Wallace v. Jaffree* 1985), and a prayer by a rabbi chosen by a public middle school principal for the graduation ceremony (*Lee v. Weisman*, 1992). In *Santa Fe Independent School District v. Doe* (2000), the Court ruled unconstitutional an "invocation" using the loudspeaker system at a public high school's football games where many students such as players, cheerleaders, and band members were required to attend. Quoting *Lee*, the Court declared, "at a minimum, the Constitution guarantees that government may not coerce anyone to support or participate in religion or its exercise" (p. 302). Hence this standard is often referred to as the *coercion* test.

Creationism

In addition to sponsoring religious prayers, governments have tried to teach public school students religious views about the role of God in creation. Charles Darwin's theory of evolution explained the appearance of humanity in a way contrary to the creation story in the book of Genesis. Christians who believe in a literal interpretation of the Bible subsequently attacked the theory of evolution, and some have preferred the teaching of "creationism." Creationism is the belief that humans were created fully formed in a single moment by a supreme being, rather than evolving over millions of years from primates, as evolution claims. Disliking the fact that evolution was taught in public schools as a valid scientific theory, Biblical literalists lobbied a few states to outlaw the teaching of evolution in the early twentieth century. This dispute led to the famous "Scopes Monkey Trial" in 1925, where a Tennessee high school science teacher was convicted for violating a state law prohibiting the teaching of evolution in any of the state's public schools.

Only a handful of states ever formally outlawed the teaching of evolution, but after the Scopes trial the theory of evolution all but disappeared from school textbooks, as textbook publishers became afraid to cover evolution for fear of losing sales (Scott, 2004). Tougher science education standards caused by the cold war and space race with the Soviet Union reintroduced the teaching of evolution into public school classrooms. The Supreme Court in *Epperson v. Arkansas* (1968) finally ruled that anti-evolution statutes violate the Establishment Clause because the "effort was confined to an attempt to blot out a particular theory because of its supposed conflict with the Biblical account, literally read" (p. 109).

After *Epperson*, Biblical fundamentalists adopted a new strategy to see that creationism was taught alongside evolution in the science classrooms of public schools. In line with this strategy, the Louisiana Legislature in 1982 passed a law requiring that "creation science" be taught in public school classrooms whenever evolution is taught. A challenge to the law reached the Supreme Court in *Edwards v. Aguillard* (1987). Applying the *Lemon* test, the high court ruled the statute violated the Establishment Clause because there was no valid secular purpose behind the law. Instead, "The preeminent purpose of the Louisiana Legislature was clearly to advance the religious viewpoint that a supernatural being created humankind" (p. 591).

Religious Displays on Public Property

The third type of situation commonly involving the Establishment Clause is religious displays on government property. *Stone v. Graham* (1980) addressed a Kentucky statute that required the Ten Commandments to be posted in every public school classroom in the state. The Supreme Court held the statute violated the first prong of the *Lemon* test, because the "plainly religious" purpose of the statute was "to induce the schoolchildren to read, meditate upon, perhaps to venerate and obey, the Commandments" (p. 42).

Lynch v. Donnelly (1984) involved a town that maintained a tradition of erecting a

Lane v. Sabine Parish School Board

As has been seen, Supreme Court precedents interpreting the Establishment Clause make clear that a public school would be forbidden from opening official school events with prayers, hanging a large picture of Jesus above the school entranceway, declaring on the school's web site "We believe that: God exists," displaying Bible verses throughout hallways and on the school's outdoor video marquee, and hanging posters in school hallways urging students to "Pray," "Believe," and "Worship." Nor may public school teachers routinely lead students in Christian prayers and openly disparage other faiths. Yet all these things are what a federal lawsuit with the backing of the American Civil Liberties Union alleges occurred in northwestern Louisiana. Sharon and Scott Lane filed court documents in 2014 alleging that their son C. C., a Buddhist of Thai descent who attended the sixth grade in Negreet High School in Sabine Parish, had become the "target of proselytization and harassment by faculty and administration" in Sabine Parish (McGaughy, 2014).

The lawsuit made numerous other allegations, many of which were focused on C. C.'s science class. C. C. was called "stupid" in front of other students for not believing in God, and the teacher nodded in agreement. Students were asked on a test to identify the "Lord" as creator, and the teacher scolded C. C. in front of the class for not writing in "Lord" as the answer. Other students were granted bonus points for citing Bible verses on tests. The teacher dismissed evolution as "impossible," and "a theory stupid people made up because they don't want to believe in God," despite coverage of evolution in the class textbook. The lawsuit goes on to allege that when the Lanes complained to Sara Ebarb, the Sabine Parish superintendent, of this Christian indoctrination, Ebarb defended the teacher. Ebarb told the Lanes "this is the Bible Belt" and so they should tolerate being proselytized and should not be offended. Ebarb also asked if C. C. could change his faith, and referred to their son's Thai heritage by suggesting he might be happier if he was transferred to a school where "there are more Asians." Ebarb then wrote a letter to the principal approving the religious practices at Negreet High School, which the principal read over the school public-address system. In response, the Lanes moved C. C. to a different school and filed a lawsuit against the religious practices in the Sabine Parish public schools.

After reading the court documents of this case, CBS legal analyst Andrew Cohen observed, "This is not a case about a few student-led prayers at graduation or a Christmas display. . . . This is a case that digs down to the foundation of the wall that is supposed to separate church and state" (Cohen, 2014, para. 2). Charles Haynes, a senior scholar at the Freedom Forum's First Amendment Center added, "I can honestly say that the allegations in the case are among the most serious I have ever seen" (Cohen, 2014, para. 5). In March 2014, a federal district court approved a consent decree between the parties, wherein the school board agreed to cease all its problematic practices and to train staff on First Amendment law and the effects of religious discrimination on students.

What made the Sabine Parish case stand out were the allegations of complicit behavior involving faculty and administrators. In most cases involving school districts where administrators and teachers appear to be favoring one religion, the violations of the Establishment Clause are not so egregious. "If these allegations are true, many administrators (including the top administrator for the district) and many teachers have been complicit in doing nothing less than converting a public school into a Christian school in flagrant violation of the law" (Cohen, 2014, para. 15). The point is that academic freedom in public schools does allow teaching *about* religion in an objective manner. It is only when teachers and principals decide to promote one religion over other faiths that the Establishment Clause has been violated in public schools.

crèche, or Nativity scene, every Christmas. The Court upheld the display, ruling that the secular purpose was to acknowledge the origin of the holiday, and that any benefit to religion was only "incidental." Later, however, in *County of Allegheny v. ACLU* (1989), the Court ruled unconstitutional a crèche located in the central atrium of a courthouse and that contained the words "Glory to God in the Highest!" The Court distinguished the case from *Lynch*, noting that the courthouse crèche had no secular elements blended with the religious elements. Thus, the county had "chosen to celebrate Christmas in a way that has the effect of endorsing a patently Christian message" (p. 601). This standard is thus commonly referred to as the *endorsement test*.

Two cases decided on the very same day in 2005 made the standard for religious displays on government property unclear. In *McCreary County v. ACLU* (2005), the U.S. Supreme Court considered the constitutional validity of posting the Ten Commandments on the inside walls of a courthouse; and in *Van Orden v. Perry* (2005) the high court considered the constitutionality of a six-foot-high monument of the Ten Commandments on the grounds of a state capitol. The Court actually ruled both ways—finding that the monument was permissible, but the wall postings crossed the line. In *McCreary County*, a five-justice majority ruled that government may not favor religion over non-religion, and that framing the Ten Commandments on the wall had the purpose of favoring religion. In *Van Orden*, there was no majority opinion, but the four justices in the plurality opinion decided that the monument simply honored the tradition that religion played in American life, a familiar feature of buildings for all branches of government. After detailing this acknowledgement, the four justices voted to affirm the monument as constitutional. Concurring Justice Stephen Breyer, who provided the necessary fifth vote, cited no particular legal test in reaching his decision, but summarily concluded that the monument did not violate the purposes of the First Amendment.

As has been seen, the Supreme Court has at times preferred various different legal tests to analyze the Establishment Clause. These include five judicial approaches. First is the three-pronged *Lemon test*, which requires that the law have a secular purpose, but does not have the primary effect of hindering or advancing religion, nor may the law excessively entangle government with religion. The neutrality test requires that government treat religion and non-religion equally. The coercion test forbids government from coercing people into participation in a religious belief or practice. The endorsement test prohibits government from endorsing religion. Finally, the Court looks to U.S. history and legal tradition for guidance regarding the degree to which government can become involved with religion.

It remains unclear precisely which one of these tests, or perhaps combination of these tests, best explains the meaning of the Establishment Clause. Besides policy disagreement with the Court's rulings among legal scholars and much of the public, the lack of clear guidance on the meaning of the Establishment Clause is another reason that the Court's rulings in this controversial area have been harshly criticized.

Theories of the Establishment Clause

Regardless of how the Supreme Court interprets the Establishment Clause, the manner in which it *should* be interpreted has been the topic of strident, often heated debate pitting competing theories against each other over the past several decades. At one end of the spectrum are those who argue that there should be absolutely no connection between government and religion, such that no public support is ever provided to religious entities, even indirectly. This view essentially holds that government must sometimes discriminate against religious individuals. Under this approach, were a state to create a taxpayer-funded private school tuition voucher plan, tuition vouchers would be given to the parents of children who attend private nonreligious schools, but not to parents whose children attend private religious schools. This approach is called either *strict separationism* or simply *separationism*. The decision reached in *Lemon v. Kurtzman*

(1971), where public funding for private school textbooks and personnel was held to be unconstitutional, is a good example of this approach.

A slightly less restrictive approach maintains that government should always treat religion and non-religion equally. Thus, a private school tuition voucher would have to provide equal vouchers to parents regardless of whether their children attend religious or secular schools. This approach goes by the term of *non-preferentialism*, and the decision reached in *Zelman v. Simmons-Harris* (2002) stands as the case in point of this approach. In that ruling, the Court applied a "private choice test" affirming voucher programs that have a secular purpose and are neutral with respect to religion. That is, the voucher program would be available to all parents without regard to their religion or which private or parochial schools their children attend.

A different approach to the Free Exercise Clause argues that government should be able to accommodate churches and sects by making it easier for their followers to engage in religious practices. Officially recognized public holidays for Hannukah or Easter would be examples of this approach, which is typically called *accommodationism*. The ruling in *Marsh v. Chambers* (1983), whereby the Court upheld legislative invocations by a state-paid chaplain as consistent with historical tradition, is an example of this approach.

Finally, an approach even more favorable to religion would allow government to overtly favor religion over non-religion, and perhaps even favor some particular beliefs such as monotheism, over others. This approach is called *preferentialism*. Justice Scalia's dissenting opinion in *McCreary County v. ACLU* (2005) is an example of this view. In that case, he disagreed with the majority's decision to disallow the posting of the Ten Commandments on the wall of a public building. He examined the historical traditions of this country, and found that government within the United States had long been able to publicly acknowledge a general belief in monotheism—the existence of a single supreme being. Thus, Justice Scalia would have allowed the posting of the Ten Commandments because he believed the Establishment Clause allows government to disregard both polytheists (those who believe in more than one god) and atheists (those who believe there is no god).

Federal Statutes

Besides the constitutional protections for religious liberty at the federal level, several congressional acts address religious liberty as well. The federal Religious Freedom Restoration Act (RFRA) was passed after the Supreme Court's decision in *Employment Division v. Smith* (1990), discussed earlier. Recall that in that decision, the Court declared that religiously neutral laws do not violate the First Amendment's Free Exercise Clause even if the law violates a religious believer's conscience or practice. Believing the Court was not giving enough protection to religious liberty, Congress passed this law to allow, under some circumstances, religious exemption to religiously neutral laws. Specifically, 42 U.S. Code, Section 2000bb-1 establishes the limits:

> Government may substantially burden a person's exercise of religion only if it demonstrates that application of the burden to the person—
> (1) is in furtherance of a compelling governmental interest; and
> (2) is the least restrictive means of furthering that compelling governmental interest.

This law thus codifies the "strict scrutiny" test discussed in the overview chapter on free speech. In other words, no religious exemption will be given to a neutral law if government can show the law promotes a public purpose of utmost importance, and there is no other way to achieve that purpose without necessarily interfering with religious practice. For example, in *Gonzales v. O Centro Espirita Beneficente Uniao do Vegetal* (2006), the Supreme Court ruled that the federal government could not show any compelling reason for criminalizing a church's sacramental use of a hallucinogenic tea.

The Religious Freedom Restoration Act uses the broad term "government," and is intended to apply both to federal and state laws, but in *City of Boerne v. Flores* (1997), the Supreme Court declared that Congress did not have constitutional authority to apply this religious exemption to state laws. Since the *Flores* decision, RFRA only provides for religious exemptions to federal law. Congress responded to *Flores*, however, by using its constitutional authority under the Spending Clause and the Commerce Clause to devise a more limited religious exemption to state laws. This later statute is called the Religious Land Use and Institutionalized Persons Act (RLUIPA), and is directed at property uses. It states in part, "No government shall impose or implement a land use regulation in a manner that imposes a substantial burden on the religious exercise of a person, including a religious assembly or institution" (See U.S. Code section 2000cc). In practice, this section most commonly applies to churches that object to zoning ordinances. RLUIPA also protects prisoners from indoctrination or restrictions on their chosen belief systems. "No government shall impose a substantial burden on the religious exercise of a person residing in or confined to an institution" (Sec. 2000cc-1, RLUIPA).

Regardless of the context, though, both these sections of RLUIPA (cited above) additionally declare that government may impose a substantial burden on one's religious exercise if the burden "(**A**) is in furtherance of a compelling governmental interest; and (**B**) is the least restrictive means of furthering that compelling governmental interest." Note that this is the same strict scrutiny test used in RFRA. Both these sections of the law further declare that they apply only when federal funds or interstate commerce is involved, which means when "the substantial burden is imposed in a program or activity that receives federal financial assistance," or when "the substantial burden affects, or removal of that substantial burden would affect, commerce with foreign nations, among the several States, or with Indian tribes." In other words, state and local governments must comply with RLUIPA as a condition of accepting federal money, or when their actions interfere with the types of commerce that are under federal oversight. In this way, Congress has made sure it can lawfully apply the narrow exemptions of this national law to the states.

Employment discrimination is addressed in a federal statute known as Title VII of the Civil Rights Act of 1964, more commonly referred to as Title VII. It prohibits several types of employment discrimination, including discrimination based on religion. Title VII treats religion differently in several ways, however, from other types of discrimination. First, it declares that its prohibitions generally do not apply to religious organizations that wish to hire employees on the basis of religion (Section 2000e-1(a) of Title VII). The religious exemption goes further and allows all employers to hire on the basis of religion if the employer can show that religion is a "bona fide occupational qualification reasonably necessary to the normal operation of that particular business or enterprise" (Sec. 2000e-2(e)(1)). Another section similarly allows educational institutions to hire on the basis of religion if they are supported or managed in part by a particular faith, or if the school's curriculum "is directed toward the propagation of a particular religion" (Sec. 2000e-2(e)(2)).

Moreover, Title VII prohibits an employer from firing an employee for religious reasons "unless an employer demonstrates that he is unable to reasonably accommodate to an employee's or prospective employee's religious observance or practice without undue hardship on the conduct of the employer's business" (Section 2000e(j)). In other words, employers have an affirmative legal duty to adjust their business operations to a limited degree around an employee's religious faith or practice, as long as that limited accommodation is reasonable—that is, unless the accommodation would impose undue hardship on the employer. But when does hardship on an employer become "undue"? The Supreme Court declared in *Trans World Airlines v. Hardison* (1977) that any hardship that is "more than a de minimis cost" (p. 84) is undue. This opinion means that any business adjustment that is more than minimal in nature would impose too much hardship on the employer. In practical effect then, employers must make only a slight accommodation to employees' faith and practices, and any demand beyond that de minimis sacrifice would be deemed "unreasonable" under Title VII. In such a situation, if employees persist with a religious practice that interferes with their employer's business, the employer may fire them without violating Title VII.

RELIGIOUS LIBERTY IN LOUISIANA

There were no general rights of religious liberty in the first Louisiana Constitution. Article II of that Constitution, which defined the qualifications for the legislative branch, forbade ministers from public office: "Section 22. No person while he continues to exercise the functions of a clergyman, priest or teacher of any religious persuasion, society or sect, shall be eligible to the general assembly, or to any office of profit or trust under this State." Article III, which defined the executive branch, similarly forbade any religious minister from serving as governor. It also exempted men from militia service if such combat duty would violate their religious conscience, provided they pay a fee:

> Sect. 6th. No member of Congress, or person holding any office under the United States, or minister of any religious society, shall be eligible to the office of Governor. . . . Sect. 22nd. The free white men of this State, shall be armed and disciplined for its defence [sic]; but those who belong to religious societies, whose tenets forbid them to carry arms, shall not be compelled so to do, but shall pay an equivalent for personal service.

Louisiana adopted its fifth state constitution in 1879, and its authors reworded Article 4 so that it more closely resembled the First Amendment's protection of religious liberty: "No laws shall be passed respecting an establishment of religion or prohibiting the free exercise thereof, or abridging the freedom of speech, or of the press . . ." Yet Article 51, whose articles defined the composition and powers of the legislative branch, contained a prohibition on the state funding of any particular religious group:

> Art. 51. No money Shall ever be taken from the public treasury, directly or indirectly, in aid of any church, sect or denomination of religion, or in aid of any priest, preacher, minister or teacher thereof, as such, and no preference shall ever be given to, nor any discrimination made against, any church, sect or creed of religion, or any form of religious faith or worship.

The Current State Constitution

Louisiana rewrote its state charter on four more occasions: in 1898, 1913, 1921, and finally 1974. The language that now primarily guides religious liberty is found in Article 1, Section 8, which states "No law shall be enacted respecting an establishment of religion or prohibiting the free exercise thereof." In addition, Article 1, Section 12, outlaws religious bias in areas of public access: "In access to public areas, accommodations, and facilities, every person shall be free from discrimination based on . . . religion." Although Article I, Section 12, prohibits some types of discrimination based on religion, Louisiana courts generally look to the provisions in Article 1, Section 8, in determining the general rights of religious liberty within the state.

Probably because the religious liberty language of Article I, Section 8, of the Louisiana Constitution is nearly identical to the religion clauses of the federal First Amendment, Louisiana courts have basically applied the "lockstep doctrine," discussed in this book's second chapter. In other words, although in decisions interpreting Article I, Section 8, of the Louisiana Constitution, Louisiana courts have not expressly used the term "lockstep doctrine," they have simply recognized the same meaning as the U.S. Constitution: "The First Amendment of the United States Constitution and Article I, Sect. 8, of the Louisiana Constitution both guarantee religious freedom" *Roppolo v. Moore* (1994, p. 210). In *Roppolo*, the Louisiana Supreme Court declared that Louisiana would not recognize the tort of clergy malpractice, a cause of action that no other state had adopted either.

Louisiana Religious Liberty Law

As is the situation with free expression in Louisiana, religious liberty differs from federal law in situations wherein the U.S. Supreme Court has said the U.S. Constitution allows states the flexibility to differ from federal law. As one example, the U.S. Supreme Court has declared in several cases that states must avoid taking sides in ecclesiastical or theological disputes involving either doctrine or practice within religious organizations. Those same Supreme Court cases, however, have also made it clear that state courts are free to apply their own "neutral principles" regarding state-created property, contract, and corporation law when adjudicating financial and property disputes within a religious organization. In a property dispute between two churches or between two groups within a religious organization, state civil courts may look to general state-law principles of contract and property law. This would allow state courts to review church deeds, organizational charters, or the constitutions and by-laws of religious organizations in order to determine the contractual intent of the parties, just as contracts in any circumstance would be interpreted.

The ruling in *Fluker Community Church v. Hitchens* (1982) exemplifies how Louisiana applies its "neutral principles" approach to church property disputes. There, a majority of members of the local church, the Fluker Community Church, voted to leave their denomination, the African Methodist Episcopal Church (A.M.E.). Both the local church and the affiliated denomination claimed title to a parcel of local property, referred to as "Tract A." The Louisiana Supreme Court first took note that it was prohibited by the First Amendment from deciding the case based on religious beliefs, doctrines, or practice. Then, using the general principles of state property and contract law, the court ruled in favor of the larger denomination: "Applying the neutral principles which are evoked by our examination of the documents in purely secular terms, we conclude that it was the intention of the parties, agreed upon before the dispute arose, that Tract A may not be alienated without A.M.E.'s consent, and will be considered abandoned to A.M.E. upon Fluker's disbanding as an A.M.E. society" (p. 448).

Louisiana religious liberty also differs from federal law because the Louisiana Legislature has given special protection to religious liberty beyond that provided by the First Amendment. Recall that the U.S. Supreme Court's decision in *Robbins v. Pruneyard Shopping Center* (1980) gave states the freedom to grant more rights under state law than the First Amendment provides. Also recall that the U.S. Supreme Court in *Employment Division v. Smith* (1990) declared the Free Exercise Clause does not provide any religious exemption from laws of general applicability, even if the law requires one to violate one's religious beliefs or practices. After the U.S. Supreme Court's decision in *Employment Division v. Smith*, many states enacted laws that increased protection for the free exercise of religion by allowing some type of religious exemption to state law. Louisiana is one of those states.

The 2010 Louisiana Preservation of Religious Freedom Act requires a version of the compelling interest test be applied in Louisiana similar to the rule that was applied in the U.S. Supreme Court's *Sherbert* and *Yoder* cases, discussed earlier in this chapter. The key provision of the statute reads:

> Government shall not substantially burden a person's exercise of religion, even if the burden results from a facially neutral rule or a rule of general applicability, unless it demonstrates that application of the burden to the person is both:
> 1. In furtherance of a compelling governmental interest.
> 2. The least restrictive means of furthering that compelling governmental interest. LRS 13: 5233

The Louisiana Preservation of Religious Freedom Act has yet to be interpreted in court, but it could result in the expansion of religious rights that would become broader than those allowed under the Free Exercise Clause. By the power of this statute, religious exemptions to otherwise generally applicable laws might be granted. Louisiana churches might receive exemptions from zoning ordinances, health care workers at public hospitals might be able to refuse to provide contraception or abortions, and employers and landlords might avoid application of state civil rights laws that protect employees or tenants. In other potential applications, prison inmates might receive special exemptions from the prison's food or clothing policies, public school teachers may be able to refuse to teach evolution, and religious groups might be able to legally use controlled substances. Indeed, given the number of state laws combined with the number of possible religious objections to those laws, the legal exemptions that could be granted are potentially limitless.

Another unusual feature of religious law in the state is the Louisiana Science Education Act, adopted in 2008 by the state legislature. Its core provisions allow teachers, with permission of the State Board of Elementary and Secondary Education and the local school board, to promote "critical thinking skills, logical analysis, and open and objective discussion of scientific theories being studied including, but they are not limited to, evolution, the origins of life, global warming, and human cloning" (LRS 17: 285.1(B)(1)). Its stated goal is to help students "understand, analyze, critique, and objectively review scientific theories" (LRS 17: 285.1(B)(2)), in an "objective manner" LRS 17: 285.1(C). Section (D) of the law promises that it "shall not be construed to promote any religious doctrine, promote discrimination for or against a particular set of religious beliefs, or promote discrimination for or against religion or non-religion."

This law understandably has been controversial and has received international news coverage as a result of its religious implications. Despite the language of section (D) of the Act, which expressly prohibits instruction in religious doctrine, opponents have argued that the law allows for anti-science skepticism and opens the door to non-scientific ("pseudo-scientific") religious concepts such as creationism in the science classroom. Calls to repeal the act have come from a number of quarters, including scientific professional organizations, a petition of seventy Nobel-Prize-winning scientists, and from technology firms and higher education leaders who claim they are having trouble attracting scientific researchers to the state. The Society for Integrative and Comparative Biology (SICB), one of the oldest and most prestigious international professional organizations for biologists, has declared a boycott of the state. After the SICB cancelled a convention in New Orleans, Orleans Parish expressly prohibited the teaching of creationism within Orleans Parish and then symbolically voted to repeal the Act. As a result, the SICB has stated it will continue to boycott the rest of the state except Orleans Parish. Attempts by opponents to convince the state legislature to repeal the Act have failed three years in a row (2011-2013), but by increasingly narrow margins. Whether the Act will actually have the educational consequences feared by opponents is debatable, and so far no court has evaluated the constitutional implications of the Act. Thus, the full educational, political, and legal consequences of the Act remains to be seen.

Another law involving religious liberty was enacted by the Louisiana legislature in 2013. To facilitate private prayer on public school grounds, Section A of LRS 17: 2115.11 states, "school authorities may permits students to gather for prayer in a classroom, auditorium, or other space that is not in use at any time before the school day begins when the school is open and students are allowed on campus, at any time after the school day ends provided that at least one student club or organization is meeting at that time, or at any non-instructional time during the school day." Section B of the statute allows school employees to attend these meetings if they are not working, as well as parents and invited members of the community, so long as they adhere to school procedures for the approval of visitors on campus. Critics of the statute claimed it was unnecessary, but proponents argued the law clarifies the rights of public school students to engage in private prayer on school grounds. The statute has not yet been interpreted by a court.

One other development in Louisiana law tangentially related to religious liberty is the recent ruling in *Louisiana Federation of Teachers v. State of Louisiana* (2013). In that case, the Louisiana Supreme Court considered several procedurally based constitutional challenges to a state law that would have allowed public taxpayer funding to be used to partially fund elementary and high school tuition for students attending private schools of their choice, including religious schools. The court struck down the school voucher plan on the challenged grounds. The Louisiana legislature has since funded the program through other means, however, thus providing taxpayer dollars in some cases to parents of children attending private religious schools. This revised program has not yet been challenged in court, but would arguably be constitutional under the U.S. Supreme Court's neutral and independent choice analysis in *Zelman v. Simmons-Harris* (2002).

Other than the ways Louisiana law differs from federal protections for religious liberty, at least two Louisiana anti-discrimination statutes address religious liberty by largely paralleling the federal statutory prohibitions against religious discrimination. Louisiana has created and authorized the Louisiana Human Rights Commission (Title 51, Section 2233) to enforce state anti-discrimination statutes and to cooperate with the federal Equal Employment Opportunity Commission (EEOC) by enforcing U.S. anti-discrimination statutes (LRS 51:2235), including Title VII's prohibition on employment discrimination based on religion. Local parishes and municipalities are also empowered to prohibit discrimination based on religion if they so choose (LRS 5:2236). Religious discrimination is also prohibited statewide in services provided by public accommodations (LRS 51:2247) and by financial institutions (LRS 51:2254).

A different section of the Louisiana Revised Statutes constitutes the Louisiana Employment Discrimination Law, which essentially parallels federal Title VII by prohibiting several types of employment discrimination, including religious discrimination (LRS 23:332), and yet exempts religious organizations from the prohibition against religious discrimination (LRS 23:302). Also, like the federal Title VII counterpart, it allows employment discrimination based on religion when the employer can show religion is a "bona fide occupational qualification reasonably necessary for the normal operation of that particular business or enterprise" (Section 23:332(H)(1)).

CONCLUSION

Regarding the first sixteen words of the First Amendment, "Congress shall make no law regarding the establishment of religion or prohibiting the free exercise thereof," there are important reasons for minimizing the involvement between government and religion. This separation of church and state helps protect religious minorities from persecution, helps prevent the corruption of religious institutions, leaders, and teachings by government influences, and helps limit the possibility of religious civil wars. The First Amendment requires neutrality when government involves itself with religion. The Free Exercise Clause absolutely protects all religious beliefs, and requires that people of all religions, regardless of the practices that their faith requires or prohibits, obey religiously neutral laws. If a law discriminates on the basis of religion, however, the government must show some compelling reason for singling out a particular religious practice for regulation. Louisiana's Preservation of Religious Freedom Act provides for broader protection of Free Exercise rights within the state, such that government must show a compelling reason why religious exemptions should not be allowed when religiously neutral laws are applied. This particular statute has yet to be interpreted by courts, though.

The Establishment Clause prevents government from declaring any official religion. It also requires that government treat religious and nonreligious entities—such as schools receiving funding or individuals receiving government benefits—equally. Government must not sponsor religious activities in a way that coerces individuals to participate in the activity. If government displays religious items on public property, it must do so in a way that does not give the appearance of endorsing the religious message. The U.S. Supreme Court's interpretation of the religion clauses has been controversial and shifting, and in the case of the Establishment Clause, at times unclear. Given the highly divided nature of the Court in these areas, these interpretations could easily change in the future. Within Louisiana, the state supreme court has struck down the state's private-school voucher program on non-religious grounds, but the program has since been modified and is now in operation. This revised voucher program, as well as the Louisiana Science Education Act, and the statute allowing public school students to engage in private prayer on school grounds, all remain to be legally evaluated by courts.

REFERENCES

Aquinas, T. (ca. 1265-1274). *Summa Theologica*. Retrieved from http://www.ccel.org/ccel/aquinas/summa.html.

Augustine (ca. 413-430). *City of God*. Retrieved from http://www.ccel.org/ccel/schaff/npnf102.

Calvin, J. (1536). *Institutes of the Christian Religion*. Retrieved from http://www.ccel.org/ccel/calvin/institutes/.

Cohen, A. (2014, Jan. 28). The Public School Where Prayer Is Everywhere. *The Atlantic*. Retrieved from http://www.theatlantic.com/education/archive/2014/01/the-public-school-where-prayer-is-everywhere/283384/.

Filmer, R. (1680). *Patriarcha*. Retrieved from http://www.constitution.org/eng/patriarcha.htm.

Jefferson, T. (1802). Letter to the Danbury Baptists. Retrieved from http://www.loc.gov/loc/lcib/9806/danpre.html.

Locke, J. (1689). Letter Concerning Toleration. Retrieved from http://www.constitution.org/jl/tolerati.htm.

Locke, J. (1690). *First Treatise on Government*. Retrieved from http://oll.libertyfund.org/simple.php?id=222.

Locke, J. (1690). *Second Treatise on Government*. Retrieved from http://www.gutenberg.org files/7370/7370-h/7370-.

Luther, M. (1520). Address to the Christian Nobility. Retrieved from http://www.bartleby.com/36/5/2.html.

Madison, J. (1785). Memorial and Remonstrance against Religious Assessments. Retrieved from http://religiousfreedom.lib.virginia.edu/sacred/madison_m&r_1785.html

McGaughy, L. (2014, 29 Jan.). ACLU, parents of Buddhist student in N. La. sue Christian educators for religious harassment. Nola.com. Retrieved from http://www.nola.com/crime/baton-rouge/index.ssf/2014/01/buddhist_christian_louisiana_sabine_aclu.html.

Scott, E. C. (2004). *Evolution vs. creationism: An introduction*. Westport, Conn.: Greenwood Press.

CASES CITED

Abington Township v. Schempp, 374 U.S. 203 (1963).
Board of Airport Commissioners v. Jews for Jesus, Inc., 482 U.S. 569 (1987).
Cantwell v. Connecticut, 310 U.S. 296 (1940).
County of Allegheny v. ACLU, 492 U.S. 573 (1989).
Church of Lukumi Babalu Aye v. City of Hialeah, 508 U.S. 520 (1993).
Edwards v. Aguillard, 482 U.S. 578 (1987).
Employment Division v. Smith, 494 U.S. 872 (1990).
Engel v. Vitale, 370 U.S. 421 (1962).
Epperson v. Arkansas, 393 U.S. 97 (1968).
Everson v. Board of Education, 330 U.S. 1 (1947).
Fluker Community Church v. Hitchens, 419 So. 2d 445 (La.1982).
Lee v. Weisman, 505 U.S. 577 (1992).
Lemon v. Kurtzman, 403 U.S. 602 (1971).
Louisiana Federation of Teachers v. State of Louisiana, 118 So. 3d 1033 (2013).
Lynch v. Donnelly, 465 U.S. 668 (1984).
Marsh v. Chambers, 463 U.S. 783 (1983).
McCreary County v. ACLU, 545 U.S. 844 (2005).
Reynolds v. U.S., 98 U.S. 145 (1878).
Robbins v. Pruneyard Shopping Center, 447 U.S. 74 (1980).

Roppolo v. Moore, 644 So. 2d 206 (La. Crt. App. 1994).
Santa Fe Independent School District v. Doe, 530 U.S. 290 (2000).
Sherbert v. Verner, 374 U.S. 398 (1963).
Stone v. Graham, 449 U.S. 39 (1980).
Van Orden v. Perry, 545 U.S. 677 (2005).
Wallace v. Jaffree, 472 U.S. 38 (1985).
West Virginia State Board of Education v. Barnette, 319 U.S. 624 (1942).
Wisconsin v. Yoder, 406 U.S. 205 (1972).
Zelman v. Simmons-Harris, 536 U.S. 639 (2002).

Chapter 4
Defamation Law
By William R. Davie, with Rick A. Swanson, University of Louisiana at Lafayette

Learning Objectives
In this chapter, readers will:
- see how words injuring someone's reputation were judged over time
- distinguish defamation lawsuits from criminal libel prosecutions
- recognize the elements of per se defamation and differentiate it from defamation per quod by implication or innuendo
- inventory the plaintiff's defamation elements and defenses against them
- differentiate expressions that are privileged conditionally or absolutely
- weigh the standards of fault required of public and private plaintiffs
- compare Louisiana Supreme Court decisions with federal landmarks

Louisiana law recognizes the invasion of the personal interest in reputation as either a crime against society or a personal offense that would distort one's good name. As a result, wrongful terms harming reputation give rise to both civil lawsuits and criminal prosecutions in Louisiana. The emphasis in both the civil tort and the crime of libel is placed on the social harms inflicted, including the loss of friendly relations and business associates. Case law in Louisiana often cites the key elements of defamation found in the American Law Institute's Restatement (Second) of Torts (1977) that requires a showing of (1) a false and defaming expression about another; (2) an unprivileged publication to a third party; (3) fault by the speaker at the level of negligence or higher; and (4) a consequential injury. This chapter covers the cases and the statutes that define both the tort and the crime. The law's interest in reputation is almost as old as civilization itself, but the penalties given to punish offenders have changed dramatically over time, so we begin by tracing the historic roots of defamation.

HISTORY

From ancient times both the scriptures and the law promised severe penalties for harming your neighbor's good name. The Twelve Tables of Roman law decreed slanderers should be pummeled to death with a club for the offense. For the Hebrews, bearing false witness was forbidden in the Ninth Commandment, but the specific warning against slander was fearsome in Psalms (101:5), "Whoso privily slandereth his neighbor, him will I cut off. . . ." Proverbs also warned against despicable conversation, "He that uttereth a slander is a fool. . . ." (10:18). The New Testament scriptures admonished Christians to "speak not evil one of another . . ." in James (4:11), and in Titus (3:2), "put them in mind to speak evil of no man. . . ." The offense of harming reputation eventually led to religious punishment.

Under Salic law (also called Frankish law) that governed areas of central Europe in the sixth through the ninth centuries, offenders would be given the choice of paying a fine known as a "wergild" according to social class. Christianity took root in Europe and Great Britain, and Archbishop Stephen Langton in 1222 declared those guilty of slander were to be excommunicated: "Furthermore, we excommunicate all those who for lucre, hate, favour, or any other cause maliciously impute a crime whereby anyone is defamed among good and grave persons. . . ." (Plunknett, 2001, p. 484).

Defamation was wrong even if the charges were true under British common law. Magistrates held to the wisdom of the infamous Star Chamber (a secretive and powerful royal court during the fifteenth through seventeenth centuries), "the greater the truth, the greater the libel," given that seditious allegations might provoke an insurrection against the rule of the governors. Legal historians have observed that the safety of magistrates came first because defaming words could cause "not only the breach of the peace but also the scandal of the government" (Freund, 1904, p. 506). *De Scandalis Magnatum*, a British law issued in 1275, made it a crime to defame the royal authority (kings and magnates), and that included more severe punishments, the loss of ears for spoken words or amputating the right hand for written statements. Smith (1988) found that it was seditious libel—words of treason—that was necessarily prosecuted to preserve the throne's rule. If you insulted the government, or if you chose to criticize particular government rulers, you were subject to prosecution. Basically, by insulting the government, you would be committing a treasonous act, and this act could be punished by a fine or imprisonment.

The crime of seditious libel was created by the English common law case of *De Libellis Famosis*, in which a writer was found guilty in 1606 of publishing a poem ridiculing the Archbishop of Canterbury, the head of the Church of England (Smith, p. 60). The crime of seditious libel was authoritatively defined in 1887 by James Fitzjames Stephens, a judge on England's High Court, in his *Digest of the Criminal Law*:

> A seditious intention is an intention to bring into hatred or contempt, or to excite disaffection against the person of, His Majesty, his heirs or successors, or the government and constitution of the United Kingdom . . . or to incite any person to commit any crime in disturbance of the peace, or to raise discontent or disaffection amongst His Majesty's subjects, or to promote feelings of ill-will and hostility between different classes of such subjects (Stephens, 1887, p. 66).

Colonial Americans were angered by the way the British government censored political speech through the licensing of publishers and through prosecuting the crime of seditious libel. The most famous of these prosecutions occurred in 1735 in New York City, when a German immigrant printer named John Peter Zenger was jailed for eight months for his published attacks on the royal governor.

Zenger printed *The New-York Weekly Journal* with articles from contributing political writers, not Zenger himself. He was jailed, nonetheless, for libeling Gov. William Cosby through his newspaper's columns. The royal governor notoriously seized salaries and offices from the colonists for his personal and political gain. Zenger was brought to trial for seditious libel, and his attorney Andrew Hamilton successfully defended him with a clever strategy relying on the jury's zeal for truth and liberty. Hamilton's soaring rhetoric framed the jury's decision not in terms of guilt or innocence but in the ideal of freedom:

> It is not the cause of one poor printer, nor of New York alone, which you are now trying. No! It may in its consequence affect every free man that lives under a British government on the main of America. It is the best cause. It is the cause of liberty. And I make no doubt but your upright conduct this day will not only entitle you to the love and esteem of your fellow citizens, but every man who prefers freedom to a life of slavery will bless and honor you as men who have baffled the attempt of tyranny, and by an impartial and uncorrupt verdict have laid a noble foundation for securing to ourselves, our posterity, and our neighbors, that to which nature and the laws of our country have given us a right to liberty of both exposing and opposing arbitrary power (in these parts of the world at least) by speaking and writing truth (Lindner, 2001).

Zenger was acquitted and the news rapidly spread across the colonies through multiple printings of a popular account of the trial. Five decades later, colonists aware of Zenger's lesson sheltered freedom of the press through the First Amendment.

Competing Values

Louisiana's Constitution proclaims, "the press shall be free. Every citizen may freely speak, write, and publish his sentiments on all subjects; being responsible for an abuse of that liberty" (La. Const. Art. 4, 1879). Note well that the same article ensuring freedom of expression in Louisiana also warns against abusing it. The remedy for curing abuse is found in the state civil code, which declares every personal act causing harm shall be repaired by whoever is found to be at fault. Civil Code Article 2315 defines the grounds for lawsuits: "Liability for acts causing damages. Every act whatever of man that causes damage to another obliges him by whose fault it happened to repair it."

Under the common law, verbal harms were identified by the term *slander*, and if printed were defined as *libel*. The distinction hinged on the notion that if defamation were spread in writing, it would reach more people and consequently cause greater damage. In instances whereby Louisiana courts recognized this distinction, slander was defined as "oral expressions or transitory gestures" (*Boone v. Reese Services, Inc.*, 2004). However, in his research, Cox found that Louisiana's "civilian heritage makes no libel-slander distinction based on the oral or written form of defamation; all defamation is treated alike" (1967, p. 88). Weiss and Forsyth confirmed the fact that state courts rarely distinguish between libel and slander, and they prefer the term *defamation* for lawsuits of this sort (p. 674). The emphasis is placed on the elements of defamation rather than the medium of expression, and that means the plaintiff at the very least must show publication, identification, defamation, and injury.

Publication

Laws against defamation cover more than mere spoken or written words, which the term *publication* might imply. Defamation includes photographs, recordings, drawings, letters, and any other forms of communication. What the plaintiff must show is that these expressions produced injurious falsehoods against his or her good name. The specific legal element referred to as *publication* means that a false statement of fact was spoken, printed, broadcast, downloaded, recorded, or republished by someone other than the subject of the abuse. It is the conveyance of a defamatory message to a third person, and not the fact that it was spoken, written, or printed, that actually fulfills the element of publication.

If the speaker communicates only to the person being insulted, there has been no publication. For example, if an employer walks into someone's office, shuts the door, and falsely accuses that employee of embezzlement, there is no defamation because no third person heard the statement. If, however, the same boss walks up to an employee in a cubicle surrounded by other office workers and shouts the same accusations of embezzlement, there *is* publication—even if only one other person heard the accusation.

Following the rise of social media, defamation claims have reached the courts even for text messages as brief as 140 characters or less described by the contrived term of "twibel," libel by means of Twitter. The controversial comments of celebrity rocker Courtney Love, who took issue with both her seamstress and a former attorney, brought to popular attention this defamation this sort of tort (Peterson, 2014). Twibel is covered more fully in the digital media chapter, of this book but this form of defamation does raise an interesting point regarding its harms and liability.

Twitter's followers are encouraged to "re-tweet" by copying tweets and sending the message to others. If the content is defamatory, the rule holds that the "bearer of tales is as liable as the teller of tales," which includes re-tweeting offensive content for others to see. The law sees no right of recovery, however, if it is the offended party repeating the message in order to recover damages. In Louisiana, the injured person or group has one year from the point of the publication or republication of a defamation to file suit and seek recovery, whether it is by tweeting, re-tweeting, or any other form of communication.

Identification

Identification, the second element of defamation, means the harmed party is known by some means. The legal requirement of identification specifies only that the offensive communication is "of and concerning" the plaintiff and not someone else, even if no name has been published. *The Louisiana Weekly*, for example, described a local retail merchant, the New Orleans Clothing Store's manager as a "sharp-dealing" shopkeeper in its news report of a fracas with one of the store's customers. Based on the article's omission of the plaintiff's name, the newspaper argued that it actually did not identify the store manager, Carl Naihaus, and therefore could not have defamed him. It made no difference, the court held, and sustained damages in his favor because readers easily recognized the plaintiff as the proprietor of the New Orleans Clothing Store, and his business suffered as a result (*Naihaus v. Louisiana Weekly Publishing Co.*, 1932).

Besides identification by implication, identification also can be made by photograph, also without a name attached to it. This case in point came in *Mulina v. Item Co., Inc.* (1950), which involved a newspaper photograph under the headline proclaiming, "Milk War Indictees Photographed Despite Their Threats" (p. 562). Washington Parish Sheriff Mulina sued because he was shown in the picture but had not been personally indicted for any of the alleged crimes during the milk strike. The Louisiana Supreme Court held that the photo and text were not defamatory because Mulina was separated from the indictees by a vertical line down the photo and was described as standing among "other figures" (p. 562).

This identification requirement also prevents friends and family members who are upset with controversial news reports from recovering damages in a libel suit. A young, unmarried woman who jumped to her death from a burning building in New Orleans was falsely reported to be pregnant at the time, and her parents sought recovery in damages but were denied standing on her behalf (*McBeth v. United Press International*, 1974) because the story was not "of and concerning" them. In a northern Louisiana case, the children of a married couple wrongly identified on television as brother and sister were not allowed to recover for damages either for a report about their deceased parents (*Johnson v. KTBS, Inc.*, 2004) for the same reason.

Because of the identification requirement, the court must decide who actually has the right to sue for defamation, and precisely how the offending communication identified them. A business might have grounds to sue on behalf of its leading executives if there is some identifiable association. A non-profit corporation such as a church could be linked to its minister in the public's eyes, and be given standing to sue after defamatory charges reach the public. In 1986, a confrontation between two prominent Pentecostal ministers created a stir in Louisiana once accusations of sexual impropriety were reported. Rev. Jimmy Swaggart accused Rev. Marvin Gorman of immorality and demanded that the minister confess to his sins before the Assemblies of God (*Gorman v. Swaggart*, 1988). The court chose to give standing to Gorman's religious corporation, Marvin Gorman Ministries (MGM), to file a defamation claim against Swaggart based on his role as the spokesman.

There are cases in which restaurant owners and clothing retailers also are given standing to sue for defamation in order to recover damages for their business's reputation (See *Shylock, Inc. v. Covenant Broadcasting Corporation of Louisiana*, 1977; *Mashburn v. Collin*, 1976; *Naihaus v. Louisiana Weekly Publishing Co.*, 1932). In other cases, Louisiana courts found the relationship between the plaintiff and the business too tenuous to establish a link of identification necessary for standing. In *McConathy v. Ungar* (2000), for example, an insurance agent was upset about pointed criticisms claiming that his company's policies were worthless, but he was not allowed to recover damages for his reputation.

Defamation of an entire profession is not likely to give any single member the legal grounds to sue. Thomson Newspapers was taken to court by a physician who felt he was defamed by a report that obstetricians had "butchered" pregnant women by doctors recommending "C-sections" instead of opting for natural birth delivery. The court found that report to lack identifying elements with the specific doctor's complaint. Likewise, the shareholders of a corporation owning the Catfish Cabin of Monroe did not meet the identification standard to sue over an email alleging that "someone intentionally poisoned the food" there (*Catfish Cabin of Monroe, Inc., v. State Farm Fire and Cas. Co.*, 2002).

In cases where single members of larger groups feel they have been defamed, the question does in fact depend on identification. In *Bujol v. Ward* (2001), half the members of Jefferson Parish Sheriff's Street Crimes Unit were refused standing to sue in response to the defamatory remarks made during a campaign by one parish council candidate, who singled out no one particular officer for the alleged abuse of excessive force, hostility, or mistreatment of minorities. The court in *Bujol v. Ward* (2001) held that groups larger than twenty-five do not have standing to sue for defamation unless names or other forms of identification target the individual with some certainty. The guiding principle holds the injury must touch one individual reputation and that reputation must belong to the plaintiff.

Defamation and Injury

Defamation deals not just with bruised feelings or a sudden loss of pride, but the assertion of a false fact that has the lasting impact of lowering individual standing in the eyes of friends and relations. Court complaints filed for name-calling, hyperbole, and private insults do not warrant recovery unless third parties heard or saw a sincere statement of fact. The injury element means substantive harm has been inflicted to reputation; the soft abrasion of an obnoxious epithet or a hurled insult is insufficient. Injured plaintiffs eventually have to show how personal careers or social relations were seriously damaged.

When is a statement considered harmful to reputation? Louisiana is not a common law state, but it has adopted the general common law terms for this tort:

> Defamatory words are, by definition, words which tend to harm the reputation of another so as to lower the person in the estimation of the community, to deter others from associating or dealing with the person, or otherwise expose a person to contempt or ridicule. . . . Words which convey an element of personal disgrace, dishonesty, or disrepute are defamatory *Costello v. Hardy* (2004).

The question is, who makes up the "community" that might lose respect for the harmed individual? Under the common law, the entire community need not lose respect, nor even a majority of the community. On the other hand, it takes more than just one person or a few people who might disassociate with the individual whose reputation was wronged. Whether words are defamatory is determined by whether "a substantial and respectable minority" of the community would lower their esteem for the defamed individual. For example, even though today many Americans see nothing wrong with couples' having sexual relations before marriage, a religious group in the community might condemn it as immoral. Thus, a false allegation that "he had sex with his girlfriend" could be deemed defamatory if those words diminished the person's reputation among this substantial and respectable minority.

Defamation Per Se

It is true that some harmful statements will satisfy the general definition of defamation just given, but there are certain types of harm clearer to see than others. Louisiana is a *per se* state, which means that it holds certain false accusations as presumptively injurious. Categories in which courts do not require plaintiffs to show proof of damages to substantiate claims of harm include charges of professional deficiency, criminal behavior, sexual immorality, or of harboring a vile disease. These charges automatically have the impact of exposing a person to "hatred, contempt, or ridicule" (LSA-R.S. 14:47). It is easy to see how after someone charges you with a serious criminal act, sexual misconduct or deviance, endangering others with a loathsome disease, professional incompetence or misconduct, your professional relationships and social standing would suffer.

A defamation claim arising from an accusation of professional misconduct was argued in *Costello v. Hardy* (2004). Josephine Costello was an aggrieved mother who sought to receive $25,000 a year from her deceased son's estate. Just before his imminent death, her son had asked his lawyer, Ashton Hardy, to revise his will in order to entitle his mother. When the will was not amended prior to her son's passing, Ms. Costello sued the attorney for legal malpractice. Hardy in turn sued her for defamation, "the invasion of a person's interest in his or her reputation and good name," because her words caused him "an element of personal disgrace, dishonesty, or disrepute" (pp. 139-140). Hardy was awarded damages, but it was reversed on appeal due to a lack of fault on Ms. Costello's part.

An offhanded remark that suggests criminal behavior, however, is *per se* defamation. For example, in *Allen v. Thompson Newspapers* (2005), an extra-marital affair involved a doctor in Lafayette who later accused his ex-lover of stalking him. The philandering physician had been charged with attempted murder for injecting her with the AIDS virus, and was sued for defamation. Louisiana jurisprudence recognizes a presumption of liability in such cases of libel. "If the words are defamatory on their face—defamatory per se—falsity and malice are presumed and the defendant has the burden of rebutting the presumption" (*Martin v. Markley*, 1942). Because stalking is a crime in Louisiana, calling a person a stalker amounts to defamation per se.

Published jests are not considered to be per se defamation, however. When a speaker made fun of a Cajun lawyer's accent, poked fun at his non-standard use of grammar, and even chose to describe him as a "coonass," it failed to warrant recovery (*Tate v. Bradley*, 1987).

Defamation by Implication

True statements can be suggestive, and quite capable of legal action if the words are "susceptible of a defamatory meaning" (*Costello v. Hardy*, 2004, p. 140). Courts in the state have struggled with how to address claims of defamation by implication, which in other states is usually described as "libel per quod," but Louisiana considers the claim to be a question of law and not one of fact to decide. The words can be true, but the impression conveyed by them can be decidedly false. For example, imagine a situation wherein a university president is shown in a photograph on the front page of the campus newspaper walking hand-in-hand with an attractive woman, though not his wife. The caption reads, "University president leaves party holding hands with a pretty but unsteady young lady." Those facts may be true, but the impression conveyed is defamatory. The president advises the newspaper that the girl happened to be his daughter, who was having trouble walking in high heels on a slippery surface and needed his hand for balance. In Louisiana, this would be an example of defamation by implication or innuendo.

The Louisiana Supreme Court resolved a dispute in 1981 between a high-ranking state official and a daily newspaper over the question of defamation by implication. In *Schaefer v. Lynch* (1981), the *New Orleans States-Item* was sued for a story by Bill Lynch about Roy B. Schaefer Jr., who at the time was serving as director of the Louisiana State Employees Retirement System. Schaefer maintained that Bill Lynch's report of his use of bank loans for a restaurant business was factually accurate but had "libelous imputations," which injured his reputation. He felt that the reporter made it seem as if he had "used his official position to influence lending institutions for the benefit of his investment in the Beef Corral restaurant" (p. 187). And one affidavit filed for Schaefer even claimed that Lynch told someone he wanted to run Schaefer "out of state government if it was the last thing he did" (p. 188). The court held there was no libel by innuendo because Lynch was only covering public issues related to Schaefer's office. The public nature of the issues and official were constitutionally protected and did not sustain damages for defamation.

In 1993, another case of defamation by implication came before the state supreme court. In *Sassone v. Elder* (1993), an investigative reporter, Bill Elder, was brought to court because of his New Orleans TV coverage of what he saw as a suspicious land deal. A group of attorneys were advising potential heirs to some property that it was worth a fortune in mineral rights and convinced them to pay fees to support a class action lawsuit and recover the land. Elder's news reports strongly implied that the lawyers were engaged in a scheme to fraudulently misrepresent the value of the land in order to take the plaintiffs' money.

Even though the court expressed concern over Elder's reporting, it also noted how "adequate protection of freedom of the press requires that the alleged implication (of defamation) is the *principal* inference" (p. 354) particularly when a public figure or matter of public concern is involved. In this case, there were different interpretations of the TV news reports, so that not everyone understood the reports to be defamatory. The ruling held that Elder's accounts were within his privilege to report on matters of "public or general concern," and the "derogatory expressions" relating to the plaintiffs were protected (p. 356).

The Louisiana Supreme Court later expanded its protection of public commentary to lawsuits based on implication and innuendo in the case of a television news interview. In *Fitzgerald v. Tucker* (1999), a substance abuse counselor sued a member of the state board in charge of certification for suggesting to a TV reporter that she was not professionally certified. The ruling held that defamation by implication is actionable only when the communication is about private people and private affairs (p. 717).

FEDERAL DEFAMATION LAW

There is no cause of action for defamation at the federal level, either by statute or by case law. Because defamation involves expression, however, the U.S. Supreme Court has ruled that the Free Speech Clause of the First Amendment places certain boundaries on how states may define defamation. In terms of civil lawsuits, the degree of fault on the part of the defendant is an automatic presumption under the common law, but after a landmark ruling by the U.S. Supreme Court in 1964, the law of libel took a dramatic shift toward protecting media defendants. If a celebrity or government officer believes public commentary or criticism tarnishes their reputation, they must meet the liability standard of *actual malice*. This new standard of fault for defamation is defined in a landmark decision stemming from the civil rights protests of the 1960s.

The *New York Times* Standard

Before 1964, libel law was solely the province of state governments, and under the common law libel leaned heavily toward the defamed plaintiff by presuming both the offensive words to be false and their author to be at fault. During the civil rights era of the 1960s, a newspaper advertisement/editorial or "advertorial" provoked a lawsuit that rewrote those premises. The full-page paid advertorial in the *New York Times* titled "Heed Their Rising Voices" cost $4,800 to publish, was ten paragraphs in length, and charged Alabama state police were directing an "unprecedented wave of terror" at "southern negro students." The police were "armed with shotguns and tear gas ringed the historically black Alabama State College Campus . . . their dining hall was padlocked in an attempt to starve them into submission" (*New York Times*, 1960).

L. B. Sulllivan, the fire and police commissioner of Montgomery, Alabama, disputed those published claims. If such police tactics were under his orders, it would amount to "grave misconduct" and "improper actions" on his part. Sullivan asked *The New York*

Times for a retraction, which expressed puzzlement about why he thought it was about him. Sullivan's attorneys then sued for defamation in Alabama district court. Trial witnesses testified that even though Sullivan's name was not published, they assumed the police orders came from him. Sullivan won a $500,000 libel judgment against the *New York Times* that was affirmed up through the Alabama Supreme Court, which did not consider the mistaken claims to be constitutionally protected. The U. S. Supreme Court took a different approach after it granted certiorari to the newspaper.

In writing for a unanimous court, Assoc. Justice William Brennan concluded that Sullivan's case must be judged in light of the First Amendment's requirement that "debate on public issues should be uninhibited, robust, and wide open, and that it may well include vehement, caustic, and sometimes unpleasantly sharp attacks on government and public officials" (p. 270). The ruling held that there will be no "damages for a defamatory falsehood relating to his official conduct unless he proves that the statement was made with 'actual malice'—that is, with knowledge that it was false or with reckless disregard of whether it was false or not" (pp. 279-280). Alabama-born Justice Hugo L. Black concluded that this standard was necessary because "state libel laws threaten the very existence of an American press virile enough to publish unpopular views on public affairs and bold enough to criticize the conduct of public officials" (p. 294). The decision has resonated ever since.

Not only did *New York Times v. Sullivan* "federalize" the tort of defamation and raise the proof of fault required of public officials, it also raised questions concerning what type of public persons were covered, and how the law would define fault for private individuals, including those who thrust themselves into the public arena. The news media wanted to be clear about how libel law would affect their reporting when covering controversial issues of public importance, especially when powerful reputations are at stake.

Actual Malice in Louisiana

Two Louisiana cases just so happen to be instructive based on national precedent: *Garrison v. Louisiana* (1964) and *St. Amant v. Thomson* (1968) served to define the standard of actual malice for defendants. In *Garrison*, District Attorney James Garrison prosecuted denizens of the "clip joints of Canal Street," but found his office lacking in support and funding for this crusade. Eight judges of the Criminal District Court of Orleans Parish refused to render all the resources Garrison had demanded to prosecute vice in the French Quarter. In response, the prosecutor held a press conference and took pains to color the criminal tribunal as a group of self-indulgent magistrates more inclined to appropriate vacation time than monies needed to clean up crime along Louisiana's river gateway.

Following this public challenge, police arrested Garrison and charged him with criminal libel. He was convicted, but appealed his case up through the Louisiana Supreme Court, all to no avail. When the U. S. Supreme Court granted his case certiorari, the timing worked well in his favor. The *New York Times* standard of fault required a showing of actual malice that was not in evidence. Garrison's $1,000 fine and conviction were overturned because his words were not spoken with a "high degree of awareness of their probably falsity" (p. 74). Proof was needed that the prosecutor either failed to check on his facts that were reasonably suspect, or held in his possession evidence that would exonerate the judges whom he had so loudly criticized. The Supreme Court ruled in Garrison's favor because Louisiana "incorporates constitutionally invalid standards in the context of criticism of the official conduct of public officials" (p. 77).

Please note that *Garrison* was a *criminal* libel case, and most states no longer enforce defamation as a crime. Louisiana glories in its unique heritage, and although criminal defamation is not entirely unique, it is becoming less common among the states. Colorado struck down its criminal libel law in 2013, but Louisiana R.S. 14:47 specifies the offense:

> Defamation is the malicious publication or expression in any manner, to anyone other than the party defamed, of anything which tends:
> 1. To expose any person to hatred, contempt, or ridicule, or to deprive him of the benefit of public confidence or social intercourse; or
> 2. To expose the memory of one deceased to hatred, contempt, or ridicule; or
> 3. To injure any person, corporation, or association of persons in his or their business or occupation.
>
> Whoever commits the crime of defamation shall be fined not more than five hundred dollars, or imprisoned for not more than six months, or both.

In terms of fault, Louisiana's criminal defamation statute specifies "where a nonprivileged defamatory publication or expression is false it is presumed to be malicious unless a justifiable motive for making it is shown" (R.S.14: 48).

It is worth noting other provisions of Louisiana's criminal defamation statute have proved to be more problematic. One provision prohibits speaking ill of the dead by exposing "the memory of one deceased to hatred, contempt, or ridicule" (R.S. 14:47, 2). The defamation of the dead provision is a crime against the state because those who are deceased have no right of legal recovery unless it is shown that their family survivors suffered some reputational injury due to the defamation. Under the common law, however, there could be no defamation of deceased individuals.

This rationale was accepted in *Gugliuzza v. K.C.M.C.* (1992). There, a widow brought suit against a Shreveport television station following the murder of her husband. The TV report claimed her husband's murder was possibly linked to a gambling debt and that organized crime might have been involved in the killing. The *Gugliuzza* decision held that the statute failed to create a cause of action for the widow's recovery despite the anguish that she had suffered over the news coverage because "once a person is dead, there is no extant reputation to injure or for the law to protect" (pp. 791-92).

Parts of the criminal libel statute also address standards of fault and privilege. Fault in this sense means the communicator acted with intent; in the crime of defamation that would mean a presumption of malice unless a justifiable motive is identified. Louisiana's criminal libel law declares, "where such a publication or expression is true, actual malice must be proved in order to convict the offender" (R.S. 14:48). Because *New York Times v. Sullivan* (1964) defined actual malice as knowledge of falsity or reckless disregard for the truth, it is hard to see how this provision could effectively fit the Supreme Court's definition.

The reasoning behind the actual-malice standard of *New York Times v. Sullivan* was elaborated in *St. Amant v. Thompson* (1968). This Louisiana case involved a political candidate, St. Amant, who was sued following the broadcast of his campaign speech in Baton Rouge. Deputy Sheriff Herman Thompson objected to the manner in which candidate St. Amant described Thompson's handling of a safe full of money. Deputy Thompson sued for defamation and won a $5,000 judgment. The U. S. Supreme Court stated that Thompson's evidence of actual malice on the part of St. Amant did not meet the *New York Times* test.

St. Amant relied on a sworn affidavit containing the testimony of a local union member, whom St. Amant honestly believed was recounting Deputy Thompson's handling of the safe. Citing its earlier opinion in *Garrison* (p. 64), the Court repeated the necessity of showing a "high degree of awareness of . . . probable falsity" necessary to meet the standard. "Recklessness may be found where there are obvious reasons to doubt the veracity of the informant or the accuracy of his reports" (p. 732). Failure to probe does not in itself establish bad faith. "Reckless conduct is not measured by whether a reasonably prudent man would have published, or would have investigated before publishing. There must be sufficient evidence to permit the conclusion that the defendant in fact entertained serious doubts as to the truth of his publication" (p. 727). The phrase "entertained serious doubts" serves to illustrate what the high court would consider to be

> ### A Little Trouble in Big Mamou
>
> Citizens who strongly feel that justice should be served by all police officers in uniform may become upset if they believe that justice is deferred for some due to favoritism. In April 2009, Bobby Simmons, a former police officer, contacted the *Ville Platte Gazette* via e-mail. Simmons wrote about local Mamou police chief, Greg Dupuis, and his encounter with state police because of his role in a drunk driving case involving another police officer. Simmons wanted to know why there was no news coverage of Dupuis's activities. Simmons's message asked, "who was the Mamou police officer (female) that was arrested for DUI, what happened to the arrest of Greg Dupuis last night or early morning by LSP. Why is there no story on Greg locing the state police out of the room at Mamou PD because they would not release his officer [sic]" (*Simmons v. Mamou*, 2012).
>
> Following the rumors that spread throughout the community of Mamou, Chief Dupuis obtained a subpoena to search the newspaper's email records in order to discover who exactly sent that inquiry to the *Gazette*. After detecting the anonymous source, the chief quickly had Simmons jailed on charges of criminal libel. You will recall that in the *Garrison* case, the U. S. Supreme Court held that Louisiana's criminal defamation statute was deficient in its requirement of the fault necessary to convict speakers who make false statements about public officials, even though they honestly believe them to be accurate. Accordingly, Simmons was not convicted of the crime of libel because he did not know that his accusation was false, nor did he act in reckless disregard of its truth or falseness.
>
> U. S. District Judge Elizabeth Enry Foote wrote stirringly in favor of the First Amendment. "There can be no doubt that the freedom to criticize public officials, including police officers, is unequivocally protected by our Constitution" (pp. 15-16). Besides exoneration, there was some good news for Simmons, because the federal judge's ruling allowed him to proceed with a lawsuit against the city of Mamou for unlawful arrest, violation of due process, and infringement of his constitutional rights.

evidence of reckless falsity. The Court also sought to clarify when "good faith" is not in evidence. "Professions of good faith will be unlikely to prove persuasive, for example, where a story is fabricated by the defendant, is the product of his imagination, or is based wholly on an unverified anonymous telephone call" (p. 727).

Who is a Public Official?

Besides the issue of fault, there is the question of who exactly is a public official, and what definition should be used to clarify that distinction. The New England libel case of *Rosenblatt v. Baer* (1966) dismissed a public official's title in his defamation lawsuit against a newspaper columnist. Baer was a county recreation supervisor in New Hampshire who sued Rosenblatt for writing about alleged financial impropriety in his department. The supervisor won his case at the state level, but the U. S. Supreme Court refused to accept the statutory language that New Hampshire preferred to define a public official. The high court instead ruled that it must be someone "among the hierarchy of government employees who have, or appear to the public to have, substantial responsibility for or control over the conduct of government affairs" (p. 85). In short, a public official for the purposes of defamation claims either appears to control or has substantial responsibility over governmental affairs.

Public Figures

If identifying a public official can be a challenging task, consider the difficulty in defining a *public figure* in court. Journalists cover newsworthy figures who hold no public office but who attract media attention through their talent or celebrity. Presuming their prominence affords them greater access to a media platform, should the law apply a higher standard of fault when they file a lawsuit to seek court-ordered recovery for defamation? The U. S. Supreme Court merged two cases in 1967 based on a "justified and important interest" in the personal affairs of the popular plaintiffs. The companion cases of *Curtis Publishing Co. v. Butts* and *Associated Press v. Walker* (1967) dealt with a former coach and prominent athletic director in the Southeast Conference, Wally Butts of the University of Georgia, and a retired U. S. Army commander in Texas, Gen. Edwin Walker.

In the first case, a national news magazine fell for a sensational story told by an insurance salesman by the name of George Burnett, who was accidentally patched into a phone conversation between University of Georgia Athletics Director Wally Butts and University of Alabama Coach Paul "Bear" Bryant before their respective teams would compete in a college football game. Burnett heard them sharing details about their players and thought that this constituted a "fix" that would predetermine the game's winner. *The Saturday Evening Post* remarkably developed this sensational story using Burnett as its only source. In the aftermath of this alleged football scandal, Butts sued the *Saturday Evening Post*, which used as its defense against defamation a claim of *substantial truth*. A story need not be precisely accurate in every detail in order to be protected speech in the eyes of the court, only that it be considered substantially true. The *Post* reported Athletic Director Butts and Coach Bryant had a phone conversation that was overheard—that much was true—but the Court found no substantial truth to the charge they had conspired to corrupt the game.

In the companion case, Gen. Walker's complaint stemmed from a wire story taken from eyewitness accounts of a student riot that erupted at the University of Mississippi on September 30, 1962. That was the day an African American student, James Meredith, enrolled at the once all-white institution. The Associated Press mistakenly reported that General Walker led a charge against U. S. marshals who were implementing the federal desegregation order on Meredith's behalf. This was a fast-breaking news story though, and not a magazine piece.

Because of their prominence, neither Walker nor Butts could recover damages from the Associated Press and Curtis Publishing Co. unless they met the standard required in *New York Times v. Sullivan*. The Supreme Court held there was a difference between the two men based on the reasoning that Athletic Director Butts was a public figure for all purposes, while General Walker had temporarily thrust himself into public prominence. Walker thus was considered a *limited-purpose* public figure (to be defined more fully later). In both cases, the men had sufficient means through other media to expose the errors against them (p. 164). In the case of the Associated Press covering the civil rights disturbances, the Court felt that there was insufficient evidence of actual malice given the imperatives of breaking news coverage. The *Saturday Evening Post*, on the other hand, was relying on a single source with a known criminal background for its story, and with no comparable deadline pressure, thus placing it outside the standards of professional journalism. Citing *Garrison v. Louisiana* (1964), the Court held that actual malice should be required of public figures with access to media.

The landmark decision of *New York Times v. Sullivan* concerned public officials, and the *Butts* and *Walker* ruling pertained to public figures. But what happens to *private figures* that are the subject of news coverage that injures their reputation? *Rosenbloom v. Metromedia, Inc.* (1971) focused the Supreme Court's attention on that question. There, a radio report in Philadelphia described the police arrest of George Rosenbloom, who was labeled a "smut merchant," charged with obscenity and yet was later exonerated. He sued the broadcast station's owner, Metromedia, Inc., and won a $25,000 judgment for defamation. Rosenbloom was not viewed as either a public official or public figure, and so the standard of fault he faced would not necessarily carry the same burden—or would it? The Supreme Court reached a vote in the broadcaster's favor by requiring the actual malice test of Rosenbloom. The radio story was about an issue of public interest, even though the plaintiff was neither a public official nor a public figure. The news media celebrated the decision since it seemed to extend the actual malice standard to all sorts of news coverage and would afford more freedom to report while covering private figures.

In 1974, the Court took a step back from Rosenbloom and modified its opinion about private figures. Elmer Gertz was a Chicago attorney who represented a family in court whose teenage son had been gunned down by police. A conservative magazine, *American Opinion*, charged that Gertz was not just interested in recovering damages in a wrongful death case, but was part of a larger Communist conspiracy seeking to undermine the Chicago police force. The magazine article called Gertz a Leninist and member of the Red Guild, and published a picture with a caption saying Gertz was harassing the police. Gertz sued for libel, but lost his case in an Illinois court that applied the actual malice standard to the erroneous reporting.

In *Gertz v. Welch*, the Supreme Court first clarified the definition of who is a public figure: "Those who, by reason of the notoriety of their achievements or the vigor and success with which they seek the public's attention, are properly classed as public figures and those who hold governmental office may recover for injury to reputation only on clear and convincing proof that the defamatory falsehood was made with knowledge of its falsity or with reckless disregard for the truth" (p. 342). The Court then made a distinction between types of public figures, explaining that some public figures "have assumed roles of especial prominence in the affairs of society. Some occupy positions of such pervasive power and influence that they are deemed public figures for all purposes. More commonly, those classed as public figures have thrust themselves to the forefront of particular public controversies in order to influence the resolution of the issues involved" (p. 345). In other words, the Court distinguished between public figures for all purposes, and public figures for a limited purpose. If one is generally famous, that plaintiff must meet the *New York Times* standard regardless the nature of the defamatory statement. If, however, one is publicly known due to active involvement only in some specific public issue, then that plaintiff must meet the *New York Times* standard only if the defamation involves that limited public purpose.

Did Gertz's involvement in a family lawsuit against a police officer make him a public figure either for all purposes or for a limited purpose? The case undoubtedly dealt with a public controversy that attracted popular media coverage—a police shooting—but Gertz had not sought extraordinary publicity. He had not publicly discussed either the criminal or civil litigation, and "he plainly did not thrust himself into the vortex of this public issue, nor did he engage the public's attention in an attempt to influence its outcome" (p. 352). The Supreme Court consequently held that he was a private figure and deserved a new trial (one at which he ultimately prevailed).

The Court declared that when a private figure is a plaintiff in a defamation suit, the jury is not allowed to impose liability without fault or presume damages without proof of injury. Other than that though it is up to the individual states to decide just how much fault a private person will have to show, so long as it was something more than strict liability. Writing for a 5-4 majority, Justice Lewis Powell declared, "so long as they do not impose liability without fault, the States may define for themselves the appropriate standard of liability for a publisher or a broadcaster of defamatory falsehood injurious to a private individual" (p. 346).

The Louisiana Supreme Court adopted the standards of *Gertz* and *Sullivan* in *Kidder v. Anderson* (1978). Newspaper reporter Bob Anderson accused acting Baton Rouge police chief Howard Kidder of taking kickbacks and favors from gamblers and barroom owners. Kidder sued Anderson for defamation. Kidder won his defamation suit at the trial level, but the state supreme court held that he had not satisfied the standards set out in *New York Times v. Sullivan* (1964) and *Gertz v. Welch* (1974). Kidder needed to prove the defendant acted with knowing or reckless falsity, and would have to do so with "clear and convincing proof," rather than just a "preponderance of the evidence" (p. 1308). The burden of proof was set one step below the criminal standard of *beyond a reasonable doubt*, but higher than the civil standard of *preponderance of evidence* that simply means the facts weigh more in favor of the plaintiff than they do in favor of the defendant. (That is, the plaintiff's version of facts is more likely than true than not, meaning the defendant is liable.)

Louisiana continued to refine the elements of defamation by finding that good faith and a lack of malice would remove liability in *Neuberger, Coerver & Goins v. The Times Picayune Pub. Co.* (1992). This dispute arose after the New Orleans daily newspaper published a series of reports alleging accounting irregularities took place in the financial records provided by Neuberger et al.'s firm for Slidell Memorial Hospital. A staff writer for the *Times-Picayune* erred in her research and reported that the accounting firm failed to account for overdrafts. However, the newspaper corrected its error once it became aware of it. The *Times Picayune*'s request for a summary judgment dismissing the lawsuit was affirmed when the court ruled that the newspaper "acted in good faith and without malice" in preparing the reports about the accounting firm (p. 1184).

Clarifying Fault versus Falsity

After *Gertz*, courts recognized two types of public figures: *all-purpose public figures* such as celebrities, and *limited-purpose public figures* who thrust themselves into the vortex of a particular issue. In either situation, though, *Gertz* made clear the burden is on the plaintiff to show fault by the defendant when the allegations involve a matter of public concern. *Gertz* underscores the importance of distinguishing fact from opinion in defamation cases because it is the false facts, and not opinions (mere evaluative judgments), that are the substance of defamation claims. The decision also links punitive damages—the highest award in some cases—to proof of actual malice.

Louisiana jurisprudence has the potential for confusing readers in terms of assessing fault by sometimes linking the term "malice" to evidence of ill will or hostility, and other times relating it to knowledge of falsity. The restatement of torts compares it to a "lack of reasonable belief in the truth," akin to negligence (Church et al., p. 694). This lack of reasonable belief falls short of the reckless disregard or knowledge of falsity presumed by the actual malice standard, but the defendant's lack of belief in the truth of the defendant's statements must be shown by clear and convincing evidence in civil cases where public figures or public matters are involved in the state.

The U. S. Supreme Court shifted the focus from fault to falsity when it granted certiorari to a defamation dispute from Philadelphia. *Philadelphia Newspapers v. Hepps* (1986) concerned a plaintiff (Hepps) who, like Rosenbloom, was a private person and was the subject of a criminal investigation. *The Philadelphia Inquirer* reported that thrift stores operated by Hepps were linked to organized crime. The Court held that Hepps deserved no presumption of falsity in this news report of public interest, and that he would have to establish that error at trial. In Justice O'Connor's words, "at least where a newspaper publishes speech of public concern, a private-figure plaintiff cannot recover damages without also showing that the statements at issue are false. In order to ensure that true speech on matters of public concern is not deterred, the common-law presumption that defamatory speech is false cannot stand" (p. 767).

In short, although the term "malice" ordinarily in layperson's terms denotes hostility, in defamation law at the federal law, the term has a specific legal meaning that does not necessarily contain any ill will. The Supreme Court uses the terms "malice" or "actual malice" merely to indicate that a defamation defendant either knew an allegation was false, or made a statement with little or no regard for whether the statement was actually true or false. Although a statement made under such circumstances will often be made with a hostile intent as well, the *New York Times* standard looks only to the defendant's degree of knowledge, and not whether the defendant wanted to harm the plaintiff's reputation.

Private Persons—Private Matters

The law of libel makes a distinction for private persons litigating private matters. As has been seen, the Supreme Court has defined public officials and public figures, including both public figures for all purposes and public figures for a limited purpose. There is no separate legal definition of a "private figure." By default, if an individual is not a public official or a public figure—that is, if one does not meet the legal definitions of either a public official or a public figure—then that individual is simply a private figure. In the 1985 case of *Dun & Bradstreet, Inc. v. Greenmoss Builders, Inc.*, the Court's concern for protecting a private individual's reputation was a "strong and legitimate" duty of the law, particularly when only private issues were at stake. This case dealt with the credit records reported by Dun & Bradstreet, Inc., that erroneously indicated Greenmoss's business had declared bankruptcy. There were no public issues or public figures involved requiring First Amendment protection. "It is speech on matters of public concern that is at the heart of the First Amendment's protection," the Court held (pp. 758-759). In the realm of private matters concerning only private individuals, Louisiana law still looks favorably on the plaintiff and presumes that the defamation was false and the speaker was at fault.

Thus far we have discussed how the elements of defamation are defined by injury to reputation, by falsehoods, and by a level of fault that varies by the nature of the plaintiff's status as a public or private person. These elements can be ignored if the statements are true and/or the court finds that there is a privilege to speak on the subject because the communication is based on a valid interest or duty involved. There are other defenses that afford legal protection to expressions that, although they harm others, are still necessary.

DEFENSES OF LIBEL

A number of defenses can defeat accusations of defamation, but the most important one is the truth of the expression regarding the plaintiff, which is an absolute defense. If the defendant can substantiate the accuracy and validity of his or her expressions, then the communication is not actionable as either a crime or a libel tort, and the case should be dismissed. In Louisiana law, R.S. 13:3602 declares, "Whenever any civil suit for slander, defamation, or for a libel, shall be instituted in any court of this state, it shall be lawful for the defendant to plead in justification the truth of the slanderous, defamatory or libelous words or matter."

There also are times when unrestricted conversation and uninhibited exchanges are necessary in order to supervise, inspect, or protect private and public interests. This sort of conversation may be defamatory and false, and yet it is considered necessary communication. The legal freedom to make otherwise defamatory remarks without any restriction is called *absolute privilege*, but the same principle applies in certain circumstances whereby either a qualified or conditional privilege is given. Louisiana consequently defines at length its standards of conditional and absolute privilege in order to protect communication from defamation claims.

Absolute Privilege

Louisiana recognizes only a small category of situations whereby an absolute privilege exists. An absolute privilege attaches to judicial and legislative meetings where the public has an interest in robust debate over fiery issues of guilt, liability, or good governance. The broadcast media have an absolute privilege for statements made during broadcasts by individuals not affiliated with the media organization that transmits the broadcast. LRS 14:50 defines the privilege as follows:

> There shall be no prosecution for defamation in the following situations:
> 1. When a statement is made by a legislator or judge in the course of his official duties.
> 2. When a statement is made by a witness in a judicial proceeding, or in any other legal proceeding where testimony may be required by law, and such statement is reasonably believed by the witness to be relevant to the matter in controversy.
> 3. Against the owner, licensee or operator of a visual or sound broadcasting station or network of stations or the agents or employees thereof, when a statement is made or uttered over such station or network of stations by one other than such owner, licensee, operator, agents or employees.

Conditional or Qualified Privilege

Louisiana law affords a conditional privilege for other types of defamatory communication, so long as the expressions are made "(a) in good faith, (b) on any subject matter in which the personal communicating has an interest or in reference to which he has a duty, (c) to a person having a corresponding interest or duty" (*Toomer v. Breaux*, 1962; *Elmer v. Coplin*, 1986). In this sense, privilege is a defense to defamation claims because there are times when it is necessary to convey potentially damaging messages without suffering liability. Louisiana's criminal code, La. Rev. Stat. 14:49 specifies the qualified privilege:

> 1. Where the publication or expression is a fair and true report of any judicial, legislative, or other public or official proceeding, or of any statement, speech, argument, or debate in the course of the same.
> 2. Where the publication or expression is a comment made in the reasonable belief of its truth, upon,
> a. The conduct of a person in respect to public affairs; or
> b. A thing which the proprietor thereof offers or explains to the public.
> 3. Where the publication or expression is made to a person interested in the communication, by one who is also interested or who stands in such a relation to the former as to afford a reasonable ground for supposing his motive innocent.
> 4. Where the publication or expression is made by an attorney or party in a judicial proceeding.

In order to apply a conditional privilege to protect an offending statement, Louisiana looks at two factors. First, if the communication was made in good faith—the speaker believes the words to be true—and second, whether the speaker had a legitimate interest or duty to converse with a particular person on a subject that could possibly harm an individual's reputation. This requirement places idle gossip outside the legal protection, and yet allows law enforcement authorities to comment on investigations without fear of defamation claims. A conditional privilege would also apply, for example, to job references. If a prospective employer contacts a job applicant's past business associate to find out about his or her qualifications, those references are free to warn the potential new employer about any negative traits the job seeker has, without fear of a defamation lawsuit.

A Louisiana state police sting operation defined the line on privileged opinion when a police report on a raid at a bingo establishment was circulated in the press and provoked a lawsuit. Gordon "Tiny" Trentecosta of Chalmette and three Louisiana state police troopers were named in a department press release that accused Trentecosta of operating a "large scale illegal operation" (*Trentecosta v. Beck*, 1997, p. 556), which was a bingo hall in St. Bernard Parish. The legal issue turned on the police report's conditional privilege, which would be lost if someone receiving the report has no direct interest in the matter or if the comments contained in the report go too far. In the *Trentecosta* case the court found that the police comments contained in the report lost their qualified privilege because "if a person is cleared of the charges, an officer cannot add additional injurious statements that the officer had no reason to believe were true" (p. 564).

Since 1991, there is also a *fair report privilege* recognized in Louisiana for reporters who rely on press releases containing defamatory material. One case involves a Monroe television station that was sued for its broadcast of a police report detailing the arrest of a man in a movie theater supposedly for committing indecent behavior (*Thomas v. City of Monroe*, 2002). The reporter testified he had no reason to believe the police report was false, and the court dismissed the lawsuit because it ruled the broadcast journalist had a qualified privilege to report news taken from the police blotter.

The conditional privilege also came into play in *Kennedy v. Sheriff of East Baton Rouge* (2006) following the arrest of a college student at a Jack in the Box restaurant at midnight. Kennedy attempted to pay for his order with a one-hundred-dollar bill that one of the restaurant employees suspected was counterfeit. As a result, sheriff's deputies arrested and handcuffed him at the restaurant in the presence of his friends and took him to a sheriff's substation for further questioning. The money turned out not to be counterfeit, and Kennedy filed suit against both the Sheriff of East Baton Rouge Parish and Jack in the Box because the employee's words accusing him of criminal conduct were libelous per se.

Before the court reached the issue of a qualified privilege defense, it first had to decide what standard applies for the initial claim of defamation when a private plaintiff sues a private non-media defendant on a matter of public concern. Recall that when a private plaintiff proves communication is defamatory *per se* against a non-media defendant, falsity and fault generally are presumed and must be rebutted by the defendant (*Costello v. Hardy*, 2004, p. 129). The court in the *Kennedy* case, however, noted that the statements at issue here—alleged criminal wrongdoing—involved not a private matter but one of public concern. The court thus announced that when a private plaintiff sues a private non-media defendant for defamation involving an issue of public concern, the burden is on the plaintiff to show that the defendant lacked a reasonable belief in the truth of the statement. In other words, when a public issue is involved, a private plaintiff must show that the private non-media defendant acted negligently in failing to ascertain the truth or falseness of the matter asserted.

The court did not need to decide whether this initial element of negligence was met in this particular case, however, because it ruled that Jack in the Box could assert a qualified privilege as a defense. A qualified or conditional privilege exists in such situations because the justice system needs individuals to be free to report alleged wrongdoing to police officers without the fear of being sued for defamation when making honest mistakes. Because of the public interest in protecting reports of criminal action, the court decided that plaintiffs must be held to an even higher standard—the *New York Times* standard of actual malice—in proving liability on the part of defamation defendants. Applying the *New York Times* standard to the facts of the case, the court announced that Kennedy failed to show the Jack in the Box employees knew their allegations were either false or probably false, and thus the restaurant chain successfully asserted a qualified privilege as its defense.

Fair Comment and Criticism

Louisiana courts have borrowed heavily from the common law that maintains a harmful expression must be understood as an assertion of fact rather than mere opinion to be considered defmation. The published statement must allege some fact that, in theory at least, is capable of being proven either factually true or factually false. Thus, for example, mere evaluative opinions by food or film critics such as "this food tastes bad" or "this film is lousy" do not allege any particular fact. An allegation that "this food contains rat meat," however, asserts a fact that could be investigated so that the truth or falsity of the statement could be determined. Similarly, statements such as "I don't like that person" or "I wouldn't hire that person" or "that person is a bad person" do not allege any particular fact. On the other hand, stating "I wouldn't hire that person as a babysitter" arguably implies particular facts, and asserting "that person is a danger to children" definitely crosses the line from mere opinion to an allegation of a specific fact that could be objectively determined. Moreover, a speaker may not evade liability for defamation by hiding behind qualifying language such as "it's merely my opinion that doctor is incompetent." Because the content of the statement still alleges specific facts, it can be defamatory.

In cases whereby the decision turns on a constitutional privilege to voice an opinion, there have been efforts to establish a test distinguishing factual statements from comments (that is, mere opinions). In Louisiana, fair comments can be hyperbole, figures of speech, or other statements incapable of being proven either true or false. This privilege of fair comment, however, is a qualified one that follows the decision handed down in *Milkovich v. Lorain Journal* (1990), where a columnist claimed an Ohio coach was lying in court about a brawl at a wrestling match. The U. S. Supreme Court held that by couching his column in the frame of an opinion the writer did not sanitize or conceal his factual assertion of perjury. As a result, he received no shelter as a privileged opinion in the *Milkovich* ruling.

Journalists need the protection of privileged opinion, and another decision from an appellate court attempted to establish the test that would clarify when a statement represents a fact and when it represents an opinion. The 1985 case of *Ollman v. Evans* was about a university professor who sued two syndicated columnists that made disparaging comments about his professional qualifications. The decision distinguished between factual statements and opinions by requiring that four prongs be applied to the offending statement:

- First, the test of verifiability requires a statement be susceptible to verification as either fact or fiction.
- Second, the common meaning of the words should indicate whether it is an opinion or fact statement.
- Third, the journalistic context of the statements must be considered; and
- Fourth, the social context must be defined.

Opinion statements lose their legal protection if the court decides that they are based on false or incomplete facts, or if the opinions are based on erroneous assessments of accurate information. When it comes to separating facts from opinions, Louisiana provides constitutional protection for even the harshest opinions.

Often cited is the restaurant review case of *Mashburn v. Collin* (1977). A writer for the *New Orleans States Item* sampled a meal at the Maison de Mashburn and regarded the quality of the cuisine as suspect. His famous review read: "T'aint Creole, t'aint Cajun, t'aint French, t'aint country American, t'aint good" (p. 879), and the scathing comments in the review read: "I don't know how much real talent in cooking is hidden under the mélange of hideous sauces which make this food and the menu a travesty of pretentious amateurism but I find it all quite depressing." The newspaper won with its fair comment defense since the Louisiana court was mindful of the *Gertz* rationale, "however pernicious an opinion may seem, we depend for its correction not on the conscience of judges and juries but on the competition of other ideas" (pp. 339-40). The Louisiana Supreme Court held it was a matter of public interest for press reviews to be free to espouse criticisms absent a showing of reckless falsity. The offensive statements in question constituted mere opinion.

"Facts are stubborn things," as John Adams famously noted in his defense of British soldiers at the Boston Massacre trial. Although facts can be objectively verified, opinions rely on a subjective response as one heated broadcast in New Orleans showed. This broadcast was scrutinized when Louisiana's Fourth Circuit Court of Appeal relied on the fact versus opinion/comment test in *Wood v. Del Giorno* (2007). Bob Del Giorno, a New Orleans radio personality and avid sportsman, appeared as a guest on another radio talk show along with fellow guest Pinckney Wood, an animal rights advocate, to debate certain styles of hunting in the state. Del Giorno called Wood an "idiot," a "liar," and a "fraud" during their on-air discussion. Wood claimed that the Del Giorno's words were defamatory *per se* and injured his standing as an advocate and an educator.

Recall that in Louisiana, if a private plaintiff proves an offensive message is libelous on its face (per se) then the court can presume fault (malice) and falsity. The court concluded, however, that when the words are taken in context, the listeners would not take them to mean that Del Giorno was accusing Wood of fraud, but instead using hyperbole

---

"Veggie Libel"

As environmentalism became widespread in the 1970s and 1980s, part of this movement involved pursuing healthier food alternatives. This included plants grown without chemical pesticides, herbicides, fungicides, and fertilizers, animals raised without hormones or antibiotics, and food that does not contain a genetically modified organism (GMO). In reaction, the dominant, traditional agricultural industries in more than a dozen states persuaded their state legislatures to pass what are often called "veggie libel" laws. This slang term is perhaps confusing, because such laws apply equally to animal products as well as plant products. These statutes, analogous to defamation statutes protecting the reputations of persons, make defendants liable for disparaging food products. Other states are considering passing such legislation.

Louisiana passed a food disparagement law in 1991. L.R.S. 3:4503 states: "Any producer of perishable agricultural or aquacultural food products who suffers damage as a result of another person's disparagement of any such perishable agricultural or aquacultural food product has a cause of action for damages, and for any other appropriate relief in a court of competent jurisdiction." The statute defines "disparagement" in Section 4502(1):

> "Disparagement" means dissemination to the public in any manner of any false information that the disseminator knows or should have known to be false, and which states or implies that a perishable agricultural or aquacultural food product is not safe for consumption by the consuming public. Such information is presumed to be false when not based upon reasonable and reliable scientific inquiry, facts, or data.

Section 4504 then sets a one-year statute of limitations for civil actions filed under this section. Despite the number of states that have enacted such statutes, there have been extremely few cases brought as a result of these statutes, including no case yet in Louisiana. Moreover, of the cases that exist, no plaintiff has yet won, nor has any court yet decided the constitutionality of such a statute.

In short, although agricultural plaintiffs have so far been unable to successfully win cases for food disparagement, there have been very few cases filed under such statutes so far. And, given that no court has yet directly addressed the constitutionality of the specific language of these statutes, it remains to be seen how these statutes comport with the federal First Amendment's protections for free expression.

See also this book's chapter on commercial speech, for a discussion of *Texas Beef Group v. Winfrey* (1998), the unsuccessful attempt by Texas cattlemen to win a damage claim against television talk show host Oprah Winfrey, who made disparaging comments about beef.

rather than assertions of fact. In the court's judgment, Del Giorno was making "a purely subjective statement (that) can neither be true nor false," and so verification to determine the truth or falseness of the statements was unnecessary (and indeed impossible).

STRATEGIC LAWSUITS AGAINST PUBLIC PARTICIPATION

In the 1970s, corporations and industry groups began to regularly file lawsuits against public citizens who spoke out against commercial and industrial projects, often on the grounds that such projects were harmful to the environment. In these lawsuits, businesses typically claimed that the individual(s) had defamed the company. Although these lawsuits usually had no legal merit, they still forced individuals into lengthy and costly defenses against these lawsuits. For fear of being defendants in such lawsuits and hauled into court to defend themselves, individuals who otherwise would have been politically active in voicing their opinions on such public issues began to remain silent.

Legal commentators thus aptly named this type of lawsuit a *SLAPP: Strategic Lawsuit Against Public Participation*. Because of the growing public outcry against these legal acts of intimidation, states enacted statutes prohibiting SLAPPs and allowed muzzled activists and whistle-blowers to receive damages from those lawyers representing corporations or groups who file meritless defamation claims to silence critics.

Louisiana is one such state to enact an anti-SLAPP statute, which is found in La. Code. Civ. Proc. art. 971 (1999). The key provision is found in section A(1): "A cause of action against a person arising from any act of that person in furtherance of the person's right of petition or free speech under the United States or Louisiana Constitution in connection with a public issue shall be subject to a special motion to strike, unless the court determines that the plaintiff has established a probability of success on the claim." Section B allows the person to collect attorney's fees and costs. Thus, a SLAPP defendant in Louisiana can have a court dismiss the complaint and order the plaintiff to pay for his or her legal expenses.

DAMAGES

In those instances when the plaintiff wins his or her case, the court next turns to the question of damages. It is difficult to assess the loss of reputation in financial terms, but damages are estimated in a number of ways. There are damages to social reputation and damages based on professional losses, if the plaintiff can show how his or her business suffered out-of-pocket losses measured in terms of receipts and accounts. Standards of fault can relate to damages, which are measured in terms of *general* (also called *actual*), *special* (also called *pecuniary*) or *punitive* (also called *exemplary*) damages.

General or Actual

General damages are classified as compensatory, and are sometimes called *actual damages* because they represent the "actual" monetary loss that can be attributed to the defamation, even though this loss is intangible. Reputational harm is presumed unless the defendant offers evidence to show how poor the plaintiff's reputation was in the eyes of his or her community so that little injury was actually inflicted. The challenge of demonstrating subtle changes in one's social connections is another problem in defamation claims—there is no public shunning in modern times, and witnesses may have difficulty verifying how the offensive words influenced the attitudes and behavior of the friends and family of the plaintiff. Either way, the trier of fact—either judge or jury—must merely determine the amount of general damages the plaintiff should be awarded in order to compensate him or her for the actual loss to their reputation.

Pecuniary or Special

Special damages (also called *pecuniary damages*) are those that can be tied to a precise financial claim. Earnings or specific costs can be entered in evidence, for example, by businesses. In cases where there is a loss of business, however, defense attorneys can suggest that other factors in the market moved customers or clients away from the plaintiff that had nothing to do with the defaming words or expressions. Again, it would be up to the trier of fact (either judge or jury) to determine whether and how much money the business lost due to the defendant's statements.

Punitive or Exemplary

Defamed persons generally have a right to recover damages for all injuries suffered in their professional and personal lives. Many states have often allowed additional damages to be awarded to defamation plaintiffs in order to punish defamers and thereby deter them from making future defamatory statements. It should be noted that *Gertz* restricted the award of punitive damages to only those plaintiffs who could prove actual malice. In *Ciecierski v. Avondale Shipyards, Inc.* (1990), however, the court held that in Louisiana "state law does not allow the recovery of punitive damages in a libel or defamation action" (p. 835). This lawsuit was over the firing of an Avondale Shipyards employee and the offensive words used to explain his dismissal in a letter to U. S. Rep. Lindy Boggs. The court noted that for a brief period between 1976-1980, a statute allowed punitive damages and attorney fees in libel claims, but that type of recovery no longer exists in Louisiana since the statute was repealed.

CONCLUSION

Given the need for democracy to entertain robust and uninhibited debate on public policy and policy makers, freedom of expression is paramount. This freedom is tempered somewhat, however, in matters of reputation based on civil tort law and landmark cases interpreting or modifying that law. The elements of civil defamation include showing that someone has been falsely associated with a crime, immorality, incompetence, or other harm to their reputation without good reason or privilege for doing so on the part of the person making such injurious claims.

The injury inflicted and the question of whether or not the plaintiff is a public or private person plays a part in determining the level of liability. Louisiana is a civil law state, but generally follows federal case law in terms of requiring public figures and public officials show a higher standard of fault by defamation defendants. Even so, Louisiana agrees with the common law tradition that truth is a defense to defamation. When the plaintiff is a private person, and the matter is private, the burden of proving the truth of the statements is on the defendant. In that situation, the plaintiff must show the defendant was negligent—that is, the defendant made statements without any reasonable belief in their truth. When the plaintiff is a public official, public figure, or the media, or the issue involves a matter of public concern, the burden of proving the truth of the matter then falls on the plaintiff. In these cases, the plaintiff must show the defendant made the statements either knowing they were false or acting recklessly—that is, having no knowledge either way whether the statements were true or false yet making the assertions anyway.

A comparison of the perspectives of Louisiana and other states on defamation shows that even though the term "malice" is used to prove fault in the case of private plaintiffs suing over private defamatory matters, this standard is more akin to negligence than it is to hostility and ill will. "Actual malice"—the requirement that the plaintiff show the defendant acting knowing what they said is false or probably false—is typically the standard when the defamation lawsuit is brought by a public official, a public figure, or the issue involves a matter of public concern. In Louisiana, the prosecution of the crime of libel is also allowed, but it is seldom prosecuted and enforced. And, as in other torts, plaintiffs who have validated their case in court seek monetary compensation for the harm they have suffered, but this intangible injury to reputation is often hard to gauge in terms of damages.

REFERENCES

Church, J.M., Corbett, W.R., Richard, T.E., & White, J.V. (2008). Tort Law: The American and Louisiana Perspectives (Lake Mary, FL: Vanderplas Publishing). 687-703.

Cox, J.T. (1967). Defamation: A Compendium, 28:1 Louisiana Law Review. Retrieved from http://digitalcommons.law.lsu.edu/lalrev/vol28/iss1/5

Freund, E. (1904). The Police Power, Public Policy and Constitutional Rights, (Chicago: University of Chicago Press) p. 506.

Lindner, D. (2001). "The Trial of John Peter Zenger: An Account" Retrieved from http://law2.umkc.edu/faculty/projects/ftrials/zenger/zengeraccount.html

Peterson, K. (2014, Jan. 28). "S.D. Attorney Speaks Out On "Twible" Case Against Love" U-T San Diego

Retrieved from http://m.utsandiego.com/news/2014/jan/28/tp-sd-attorney-speaks-out-on-twible-caseagainst/

Plucknett, T., (2001). A Concise History of The Common Law, (Union, N.J.: The Lawbook Exchange, Inc. p. 484.

Rolph, D. (2008). Reputation, Celebrity and Defamation Law, (Burlington, VT: Ashgate, Pub., 2008), p. 50.

Roy, M.E. (2013). "Survey of Louisiana Employment Libel Law" in MLRC 50-State Survey: Employment Libel & Privacy Law 2013, Media Law Resource Center, Oxford University Press, 599-613.

Sack on Defamation: Libel, Slander & Related Problems (2010). Practising Law Institute Intellectual Property Law Library, 4th ed.

Smith, J.A. (1988). Printers and Press Freedom: The Ideology of Early American Journalism. New York, NY: Oxford University Press, Retrieved from http://books.google.com/books?id=mjzVBiWwSogC&pg=PA60&dq=De+Scandalis+Magnatum&hl=en&sa=X&ei=vsznUpaFD4WMyAHXh4D4CQ&ved=0CFMQ6AEwBg#v=onepage&q=De%20Scandalis%20Magnatum&f=false

Stephens, J. F. (1887). Digest of the Criminal Law, 4th ed. (New York, NY: McMillan & Co.) Retrieved from https://archive.org/details/adigestcriminal02stepgoog.

Weiss, J.M. & Forsyth, J.D. (2009). "Survey of Louisiana Libel Law" in Media Libel Law 2009-10, Media Law Resource Center, New York, NY: Oxford University Press, 673-707.

CASES CITED

Bujol v. Ward, 778 So. 2d 1175 (La. App. 5th Cir. 2001).
Catfish Cabin of Monroe, Inc. v. State Farm Fire and Cas. Co., 811 So. 2d 222 (La. App. 2d Cir. 2002).
Ciecierski v. Avondale Shipyards, Inc., 572 So. 2d 834, (1990).
Costello v. Hardy, 864 So. 2d 129 (La. 2004).
Curtis Publishing Co. v. Butts, 388 U. S. 130 (1967).
Dun & Bradstreet, Inc. v. Greenmoss Builders, Inc., 472U. S. 749, 758–59.
Elmer v. Coplin, 485 So. 2d 1717, 176 (La. App. 2nd Cir.), writ denied, 489 So. 2d 246 (1986).
Fitzgerald v. Tucker, 737 So. 2d 706 (1999).
Gertz v. Robert Welch, Inc., 418 U. S. 323 (1974).
Gorman v. Swaggart, 524 So. 2d 915 (La. App. 4th Cir. 1988).
Gugluzza v. K.C.M.C., Inc. 606 So. 2d 790, 791-92, 1992.
Johnson v. KTBS, Inc., 889 So. 2d 329. La. App. 2d Cir., 2004.
Kidder v. Anderson, 354 So. 2d 1306 (1978).
Kennedy v. Sheriff of East Baton Rouge, 935 So. 2d 669, La. 2006.
Martin v. Markley, 11 So. 2d 593 (1942).
Mashburn v. Collin, 341 So. 2d 1236, 2 Media L. Rep. 1555 (La. App. 1st Cir. 1976).

McBeth v. United Press International Inc., 505 F.2d 959, 1974.
McConathy v. Ungar, 765 So. 2d 12, 14, (2000).
Mulina v. Item Co., Inc. 47 So. Ed 560, 1950.
Naihaus v. Louisiana Weekly Publishing Co., 176 La. 240, 145 So. 527 (1932).
Neuberger, Coerver and Goins v. The Times Picayune Publishing Co., 597 So. 2d 1179 (La. App. 1st Cir. 1992).
Philadelphia Newspapers v. Hepps, 475 U. S. 767 (1986).
Rosenblatt v. Baer 383 U. S. 75 (1966).
Rosenbloom v. Metromedia, Inc., 403 U. S. 29, (1971).
Sassone v. Elder, 626 So. 2d 345 (1993). 601 So. 2d 792 (1992)
Shylock, Inc. v. Covenant Broadcasting Corporation of Louisiana, 352 So. 2d 379 (La. App. 4th Cir. 1977).
St. Amant v. Thompson, 390 U. S. 727 (1968).
Tate v. Bradley, 837 F.2d 206 (5th Cir. 1988).
Take v. Bradley, 679 F. Supp. 608 (W.D. Oa. 1987).
Thomas v. City of Monroe, 833 So. 2d 1282.
Trentecosta v. Beck, (1997) 703 So. 2d 552, 1997).
Toomer v. Breaux, 146 So. 2d 723, 725 (La.App. 3rd Cir., 1962).

FOR FURTHER READING

Anderson, D. (1984). Reputation, Compensation & Proof. 25 *William & Mary Law Review*, p. 742.

Crawford, W.E. (2009). *Louisiana Civil Law Treatise, Vol. 12, Tort Law*, 2nd ed. Egan, MN: Thomson Reuters.

Kelley, B.J. (2013). Tortious Tweets: A Practical Guide to Applying Traditional Defamation Law to Twibel Claims. 73 *Louisiana Law Review*, p. 559.

Konczal, M.A., & Flannery, G.V. (1989). *Defamation Law in Louisiana 1800-1988*. University Press of America.

Louisiana Press Association (2013). *A Law Guide for Louisiana's Newspapers.* Retrieved from http://www.lapress.com/2013lawguide.pdf

Pritchard, D. (2009). Rethinking Criminal Libel: An Empirical Study. 14 *Communication Law & Policy*, p. 303.

Walden, R. & Silver, D. (2009). Deciphering Dun & Bradstreet: Does the First Amendment Matter in Private Figure–Private Concern Defamation Cases? 14 *Communication Law & Policy*, p. 1.

Chapter 5
Privacy and the Right to be Left Alone
by Amy Gajda, Tulane University

Learning Objectives
In this chapter, readers will learn:
- the rationale for four separate torts in privacy law: misappropriation, intrusion, publication of private facts, and false light publicity
- the roots of privacy law from its inception in the state and the nation
- how Louisiana law uniquely established state standards to accompany the adopted torts of privacy law
- how photography and technology have played a role in increasing privacy invasions
- how courts define standards of reasonableness to determine areas of privacy invasion
- defenses in privacy suits, such as public documents laws and personal consent
- how the elements necessary to prove intrusion into seclusion are defined
- how to differentiate the false light tort from claims of defamation
- how public documents and records along with personal consent can be defenses against claims of privacy invasion

We begin this chapter with an example from the media: a television program titled *America's Funniest Home Videos*. That program is one of several so-called "reality" television programs in the United States that compile and show humorous or shocking videos of people doing laughable, ridiculous, and sometimes dangerous things. Some of these videos are cringe-worthy, not necessarily for the feats of daring that are shown, but for the embarrassing way in which people may be depicted: a man confidently jumping off a housetop into a wading pool to great injury, perhaps, or a drunk driver forgetting her ABCs or a novice singer shyly singing off-key for cameras that zoom too close to her darting eyes. Most of these videos, of course, were never meant for a national viewing audience or humorous commentary or resulting ridicule.

Such programs raise privacy issues. Put yourself in the shoes of a person featured in such a video, especially one that was taped without consent. The great embarrassment one would likely experience—the knowledge, for example, that he or she would not be able to face friends or colleagues without harassment or whispers—is the feeling of a loss of privacy. Such a feeling, as this chapter relates, can lead to litigation against those the plaintiff believes to be responsible.

Such cases, however, are not always successful. Privacy in a legal sense has elements that each plaintiff must prove to the satisfaction of a judge or jury before the plaintiff will be awarded damages—and overwhelming embarrassment or humiliation alone will not necessarily satisfy a claim because courts must balance competing interests, such as First Amendment freedom of expression and freedom of the press.

But cases founded in privacy can be successful. Just ask Umar Sharrif and Barry Martyn, two musicians who were featured on ABC's *America's Funniest Home Videos* in a clip that showed a stage collapse during one of their concerts, an accident that they did not find humorous. The musicians argued that the broadcast had invaded their privacy in four different ways under Louisiana law: first, that their images were used without permission commercially; second, that the embarrassing video intruded into what was their secluded space by broadcasting the accident to others; third, that the private fact of their actions during the stage collapse had been made public because an unauthorized camera had videotaped them; and finally, that by making the serious musicians look ridiculous, the video had placed them in a false light before the public.

Even though one might think that the plaintiffs could never win against a major media company with significant resources to defend itself, even though one might wonder how something that happened in public could ever be private, even though one might sense that the First Amendment would be a significant trump in such a case, a Louisiana appeals court found that the plaintiffs deserved at least a chance to prove to the satisfaction of a trial court that an invasion of privacy had occurred. It ruled that the musicians had all four potentially valid privacy-related claims: misappropriation, intrusion, publication of private facts, and false light. That case titled *Sharrif v. American Broadcasting Company* (1993) that is discussed more fully later in this chapter, also shows both the fickle nature of privacy (the trial court had initially ruled in favor of ABC) and, ultimately, its potential strength even in cases involving media powerhouses.

OVERVIEW OF PRIVACY LAW IN THE UNITED STATES

Many scholars believe that privacy law began with gusto in the United States shortly after an 1890 law review article by Samuel Warren and Louis Brandeis titled "The Right to Privacy" was published in the *Harvard Law Review* (Warren & Brandeis, 1890). In the article, the two authors argued that everyone's "right to be let alone" needed protection through a privacy tort, one they believed did not yet exist in United States jurisprudence. The two authors were inspired to write the piece because of what they perceived was an out-of-control media, one that they hoped could be halted through common law court rulings or legislation that gave plaintiffs the right to sue defendants for privacy invasions. It is probably not a coincidence that Samuel Warren and his family had been routine subjects of news coverage; his wife was the daughter of a United States Senator who soon would become Secretary of State under Grover Cleveland (Gajda, 2008).

Perhaps the most famous quote from "The Right to Privacy" is relevant even today as technology for invading privacy advances: "Instantaneous photographs and newspaper enterprise have invaded the sacred precincts of private and domestic life; and numerous mechanical devices threaten to make good the prediction that 'what is whispered in the closet shall be proclaimed from the house-tops'" (Warren & Brandeis, 1890, p. 195). As is apparent from language like "newspaper enterprise," Warren and Brandeis blamed much of the problem in the late 1800s on the business of news:

> Gossip is no longer the resource of the idle and of the vicious, but has become a trade, which is pursued with industry as well as effrontery. To satisfy a prurient taste the details of sexual relations are spread broadcast in the columns of the daily papers. To occupy the indolent, column upon column is filled with idle gossip, which can only be procured by intrusion upon the domestic circle (Warren & Brandeis, 1890, p. 196).

To combat these problems, Warren and Brandeis (1890) proposed a tort—a civil, not a criminal, wrong—that would allow plaintiffs to sue those who had invaded their privacy. The proposed tort anticipated varying levels of privacy depending upon the person involved and his or her location. Contrary to private persons who had considerable protection, especially if shielded from public view, non-private persons, including politicians, who had "renounced the right to live their lives screened from public observation" had a limited "private life" sphere because such persons would be "the subject of legitimate interest to their fellow citizens" (p. 215). Nevertheless, the two authors argued that even public figures deserved some level of privacy.

By 1890 at the very latest then, some legal observers in the United States had connected the very real potential for privacy invasions with what they perceived to be an out-of-control media corps, one that was a "blighting influence" on American culture and, in caring very little about individual privacy, had overstepped bounds "of propriety and of decency" (p. 196).

Warren and Brandeis's privacy tort took a while to catch on, however. The very first cases relating to their sort of privacy occurred early in the 1900s and involved photographs of people used without their permission in advertising. Plaintiffs would bring suit against the advertiser, arguing that their right to privacy had been invaded. When some plaintiffs failed to win their claims because judges hesitated to create new law out of nothing, legislatures stepped in to make things right and passed laws that those same judges would consequently enforce.

Two good examples of this reversal come from New York and Wisconsin. In New York, the state's highest court had refused protection for a girl whose photograph had been used without her permission to advertise flour (*Roberson v. Rochester Folding Box Co.*, 1902). The court, worried what effect a plaintiff's verdict would have on news media and believing that newspapers facing an adverse ruling might not be able to use photos of people to accompany newspaper stories, suggested that the New York legislature should change the law if it felt that the defense verdict was wrong. Soon after, New York lawmakers passed a statute that protected individuals from improper commercial use of their images. That statute is still on the books today (New York's Civil Rights Law, n.d.).

In 1950s Wisconsin, the legislature took similar action regarding another arguably more heinous form of privacy invasion. There, a bar owner had surprised women when he entered the bar's bathroom, took their photographs, and later showed the photos to other bar patrons (*Yoeckel v. Samonig*, 1956)—and the women brought suit for invasion of privacy. The Wisconsin Supreme Court rejected a privacy lawsuit springing from the owner's actions, however, and suggested that the legislature should change Wisconsin law if it felt such a change was warranted. The Wisconsin legislature accepted invasion of privacy as a viable tort cause of action shortly thereafter (Wis. Stat. Sec. 895.50)

In 1960, California law professor William Prosser read, analyzed, and categorized all privacy jurisprudence since the time of Warren and Brandeis. After looking through multiple court decisions from many jurisdictions, Prosser suggested in his own now-famous law review article, "Privacy" (1960), that four discrete categories had emerged: appropriation of the plaintiff's name or likeness for the defendant's advantage; intrusion upon the plaintiff's seclusion or solitude, or into his private affairs; public disclosure of embarrassing private facts about the plaintiff; and publicity that places the plaintiff in a false light in the public eye (p. 389).

Prosser defined each of his four categories more fully. *Wrongful appropriation* (often called "misappropriation" by today's courts and sometimes used interchangeably today with a parallel economic-harm based tort known as the "right of publicity") was described as the use without permission of the plaintiff's name or image in some way, usually as a part of an advertisement or some other commercial purpose (Prosser, 1960, p. 401). This privacy tort, of course, mimicked the facts of the early flour case from New York, and such a scenario would satisfy an appropriation claim as Prosser envisioned the tort.

Prosser (1960) described intrusions as those times in which the plaintiff rightly believed himself to be in a private space, only to be looked in upon by another, in a peeping tom-like scenario (p. 390). The prying, he explained, need not only involve in-person spying; Prosser suggested that anyone who looked into another's private papers, for example, would also be liable for intrusion into seclusion. He concluded that the tort was complete with the looking and, therefore, that the defendant's liability did not depend upon any publication of the information (pp. 391-92). An excellent example of an intrusion, as Prosser envisioned, would be the scenario in which the Wisconsin bar owner entered the private sphere of a bathroom stall where women were using the facilities.

Public disclosure of embarrassing facts about a plaintiff was meant to cover any resulting publication of private facts. In Prosser's analysis of existing cases, anyone who gave publicity to another's decidedly personal information would be liable for a privacy invasion as long as the information revealed was not newsworthy, meaning that newsworthy public figures would win such claims less often than private persons (Prosser, 1960, p. 392). Here, the bar owner's display of photographs of the women using the bar's bathroom might well be the basis for a public disclosure claim.

In all three of those privacy torts, truth was no defense. In other words, a defendant could use an actual photograph of a person or could peer in on someone or could publish truthful facts about him or her, and that defendant would still be liable for misappropriation, intrusion, and publication of private facts even though everything was, in fact, true.

The final category Prosser (1960) created was something he called *false light*, a privacy tort very similar to defamation (p. 398). This was the only one of the privacy torts that involved falsity. As in defamation, false light covered those times in which a publisher stated or printed something that was not factual (p. 400). Instead of looking to the reputational harm that the plaintiff may have suffered, as one would in defamation, however, the privacy tort covered the emotional harm resulting from such a false publication (pp. 400-01). Moreover, a false light claim would be viable for incorrect information that others would find merely "offensive," unlike defamation, which often required proof of certain economic damages for viability, such as a decrease in the plaintiff's business. To wrongly state that someone has won a medal of honor, for example, would likely not be defamatory because one's reputational status would not be negatively affected by such a misstatement. Yet it could be the basis for a false light claim since it could be argued that it would be "highly offensive" to have such a fantastic claim made about an individual if it was not true. False light complaints usually maintain that personal accounts are distorted, embellished, or completely fictionalized.

It is important to note that news media have the potential to be affected by all four torts as Prosser described them. First, media that used images of persons, particularly in advertising, had to consider the possibility of an appropriation lawsuit if they had not received permission in advance. Second, investigative journalistic work would sometimes involve intruding into another's seclusion. Third, the revelation of any of the information gathered in such a way had the potential to be a public disclosure of private facts. And finally, news media that reported something incorrectly, where others would find it highly offensive could be liable for a false light claim. Warren and Brandeis's proposed tort, it seemed, had indeed grown legs across the United States and had evolved to rein in journalism, perhaps even more firmly than the two authors had imagined. Yet there was more to come in the history of privacy jurisprudence.

In the 1970s, William Prosser helped draft the privacy portion of the Second Restatement of Torts (1977), an extensive encyclopedia-like publication used by lawyers and judges as highly persuasive authority in courts across the United States. Even today, if state legislatures or state courts have yet to accept a particular tort within a jurisdiction, they will often look to the Restatement for guidance as to how Restatement authors had defined the tort. A judge might also peruse the Restatement authors' helpful examples of sustainable and unsustainable claims, finding a plaintiff's complaint more viable if it parallels sustainable Restatement examples. The Restatement, then, has served to make law somewhat uniform across the states—and this is especially relevant in the privacy context, given that privacy is a relatively new concept in American law, one that developed significantly after the Restatement's publication. Here, then, is the way that the Restatement defines the four privacy torts (and, therefore, the way many jurisdictions across the United States define them):

> **Appropriation of Name or Likeness:** One who appropriates to his own use or benefit the name or likeness of another is subject to liability to the other for invasion of his privacy (Restatement (Second) of Torts, Sec. 652C, 1977).
>
> **Intrusion Upon Seclusion:** One who intentionally intrudes, physically or otherwise, upon the solitude or seclusion of another or his private affairs or concerns, is subject to liability to the other for invasion of his privacy, if the intrusion would be highly offensive to a reasonable person (Restatement (Second) of Torts, Sec. 652B, 1977).
>
> **Publicity Given to Private Life:** One who gives publicity to a matter concerning the private life of another is subject to liability to the other for invasion of his

privacy, if the matter publicized is of a kind that (a) would be highly offensive to a reasonable person, and (b) is not of legitimate concern to the public (Restatement (Second) of Torts, Sec. 652D, 1977).

Publicity Placing Person in False Light: One who gives publicity to a matter concerning another that places the other before the public in a false light is subject to liability to the other for invasion of his privacy, if (a) the false light in which the other was placed would be highly offensive to a reasonable person, and (b) the actor had knowledge of or acted in reckless disregard as to the falsity of the publicized matter and the false light in which the other would be placed (Restatement (Second) of Torts, Sec. 652E, 1977).

Following the definition of each privacy tort, the Restatement authors offer legal analysis and helpful examples that guide courts in deciding whether any given fact pattern would in fact be a viable invasion-of-privacy action. Important for this book, some language implicates news media either explicitly or implicitly. In Appropriation, for example, there is this explanation helpful to media, one that would decidedly allay the fears of the earlier New York court that had worried about the tort's impact on news media:

> It is only when the publicity is given for the purpose of appropriating to the defendant's benefit the commercial or other values associated with the name or the likeness that the right of privacy is invaded. The fact that the defendant is engaged in the business of publication, for example of a newspaper, out of which he makes or seeks to make a profit, is not enough to make the incidental publication a commercial use of the name or likeness. Thus a newspaper, although it is not a philanthropic institution, does not become liable under the rule stated in this Section to every person whose name or likeness it publishes. (Restatement 2d of Torts, Sec. 652C, 1977).

This example, then, helps guide courts to find no liability in cases within which newspapers use photographs of persons to illustrate news stories. A flour company would be liable for using a girl's photograph without permission in an advertisement, but a newspaper that published her photograph in a news story about the resulting lawsuit would not be. Many misappropriation cases, therefore, arise when a company uses a celebrity's image in advertising without that celebrity's permission. A classic example involves rock musician Don Henley. When Dillard's Department Store created an ad that used the phrase "Don's Henley" to advertise its three-button henley shirts, Don Henley successfully convinced a federal trial court in Texas that Dillard's had misappropriated his name and identity, even though he was not the man pictured in the ad and even though his exact name was not used (*Henley v. Dillard Department Stores*, 1999). Because the wordplay involving Don Henley's name in the ad caught the reader's eye and brought the singer Don Henley to mind, the court found that Dillard's had attempted to benefit financially from his name or likeness.

For Intrusion, there is this media-related example in the Restatement, involving what might be called tabloid journalism:

> A, a woman, is sick in a hospital with a rare disease that arouses public curiosity. B, a newspaper reporter, calls her on the telephone and asks for an interview, but she refuses to see him. B then goes to the hospital, enters A's room and over her objection takes her photograph. B has invaded A's privacy. (Restatement (Second) of Torts, Sec. 652B, 1977).

Investigative reporting raises intrusion-type privacy issues, and there have been a number of cases across the United States in which journalists fail to convince courts that the public's right to information should trump an individual's right to be protected from intrusion into seclusion. In California, for example, the state's highest court found that reporters filming the aftermath of an accident scene had intruded into a victim's seclusion by using a microphone that allowed them to overhear the victim's medical complaints and worries, and by accompanying the victim in the rescue helicopter on her way to the hospital without her explicit permission or, presumably, understanding (*Shulman v. Group W Productions. Inc.*, 1998).

For Publicity Given to Private Life, the Restatement authors offer multiple media-related examples and analysis, including this tabloid scenario:

> A gives birth to a child with two heads, which immediately dies. A reporter from B Newspaper asks A's permission to photograph the body of the child, which is refused. The reporter then bribes hospital attendants to permit him, against A's orders, to take the photograph, which is published in B Newspaper with an account of the facts, naming A. B has invaded A's privacy (Restatement (Second) of Torts, Sec. 652C, 1977).

Despite that particular Restatement plaintiff's victory on privacy grounds, because of significant First Amendment protections, many plaintiffs find it difficult to win publication-of-private-fact cases against media defendants. For example, the plaintiff who had been injured in the California accident and thereafter successfully sued for intrusion, failed to win her accompanying claim for publication of private facts based upon the resulting television broadcast of the video, both from the accident scene and inside the helicopter. The court found that the accident itself was newsworthy and, therefore, ruled that the public's interest in the accident and its aftermath was of greater importance than the individual victim's right to privacy. Not all plaintiffs are so unlucky, however; an Illinois court ruled in favor of a mother whose words spoken to the body of her dead son were published on the front page of the *Chicago Tribune* as a part of its series on young people and violence. The reporters had hospital permission to be on the premises but the mother testified that she had told them she did not wish to make a statement once her son had died (*Green v. Chicago Tribune Co.*, 1996). The appeals court sent the case back for trial but concerned *Chicago Tribune* attorneys settled the case soon after.

And, finally, for False Light, there is this media-based example from the Restatement:

> A is a war hero, distinguished for bravery in a famous battle. B makes and exhibits a motion picture concerning A's life, in which he inserts a detailed narrative of a fictitious private life attributed to A, including a nonexistent romance with a girl. B knows this matter to be false. Although A is not defamed by the motion picture, B is subject to liability to him for invasion of privacy (Restatement (Second) of Torts, Sec. 652E).

Note that such a report of a romance would likely not be harming to one's reputation and, therefore, not the basis for a viable defamation claim. Because many would find such a revelation to be "offensive," however, Restatement authors support the finding of a valid False Light claim. Across the United States in jurisdictions where False Light is an accepted cause of action, many defamation lawsuits include a related claim for False Light, if the incorrect information that is revealed is both damaging to reputation and offensive.

This history of privacy law in the United States—from Warren and Brandeis's "The Right to Privacy" to Prosser's "Privacy" to the Restatement sections on privacy—serves as a helpful foundation for a discussion of privacy law in Louisiana, a state in which all four privacy torts are accepted and a state that recognized the right to privacy long before Warren and Brandeis wrote their famous law review article.

Privacy Law In Louisiana

Even though the Louisiana Constitution of 1974 has a "Right to Privacy" provision, the Louisiana Supreme Court distinguished the private tort-based privacy action from the constitutional right of privacy action in *Jaubert v. Crowley Post-Signal, Inc.* (1979). Louisiana courts, therefore, apply the Louisiana Civil Code's all-encompassing tort provision, Article 2315, to Louisiana invasion-of-privacy actions. The tort provision states: "Every act whatever of man that causes damage to another obliges him by whose fault it happened to repair it" (Broyles, 2005, p. 854; La. Civ. Code Art. Art. 2315A). More specifically, in 1955, the Louisiana Supreme Court suggested that privacy in Louisiana meant "'the right to be let alone' and the right to live one's life in seclusion, without being subjected to unwarranted and undesired publicity" (*Hamilton v. Lumbermen's Mutual Casualty Co.*, 1955, p. 63). It is from that language of general tort wrong, and the more specific invasion-of-privacy wrong that the Louisiana privacy torts spring. As in other states, these torts often involve media—and a consideration of the media's vying rights. "Inherent [in privacy] is the paradox of the liberty of the press," a Louisiana appeals court wrote appropriately at the beginning of this century, "balanced against the private life of an ordinary citizen" (*Stern v. Doe*, 2001, p. 99).

It is of some note that the first privacy case in Louisiana courts was decided in 1811, almost eighty years before Warren and Brandeis wrote "The Right to Privacy," and that the case involved a media defendant. In *Denis v. Leclerc* (1811), the Louisiana court (Superior Court of the State of Louisiana, First District) suggested that it was "tortious" to publish a personal letter without the author's permission, especially (and note the privacy-sensitive language here) a letter "prepared for a lady to whom the plaintiff was paying his addresses," and one "written in mystery and confidence" (*Denis v. Leclerc*, 1811, p. 312). The defendant, a newspaper editor, had not published the full letter itself but had placed notice in the paper, suggesting that the letter was available for all interested parties to read at the newspaper offices. The court jailed the newspaper editor for ten days and fined him fifty dollars, finding that the defendant had published the information simply to "gratify [public] curiosity" (p. 318) and to inflict harm (p. 321). And the court specifically raised privacy concerns explicitly or implicitly in four scenarios that condemned an intruding press:

> A brother may correspond with his brother, and grieve with him on the distresses of the family, occasioned by the misconduct of their father, and devise the means of alleviating the consequences of it. With secrecy he may succeed: but if a gazetteer, in whose hands accident or knavery may place his letter, cannot be compelled to respect the privacy of these family secrets, the writer will innocently incur the odium of the conduct of the younger son of Noah.
> An injured wife may commit to paper, for the information of a parent, the cause of family disquietude; if the dishonest holder of a press, may give publicity to the complaint, adieu to all her hopes of domestic felicity.
> If a father remonstrate with a daughter on the errors of her conduct, the remedy which parental fondness and solicitude had prepared may, by the touch of a knavish printer, be turned into a deadly poison.
> A merchant may communicate to his friend the danger of his situation, solicit a timely relief, which will certainly avert his ruin, the indiscretion or malice of the messenger, may plunge him in the abyss, from which secrecy might have saved him (*Denis v. LeClerc*, 1811, p. 314).

It is somewhat of a mystery why Warren and Brandeis did not use this somewhat obvious Louisiana precedent in their media-centric law review article eighty years later, though legal research was certainly not as easy in the late 1800s as it is today.

In 1905, the Louisiana Supreme Court recognized a Warren-and-Brandeis-like right to privacy in *Itzkovitch v. Witaker* (1905, pp. 480-81). In that case the plaintiff kept a secondhand pawnshop, where the police believed thieves would conduct business and sell stolen items. The police arrested the plaintiff without informing him of the cause of arrest and brought him to the police inspector, who had photographs of the plaintiff taken. The plaintiff filed suit after the police inspector placed his photograph in the local police rogues' gallery and sent copies to various cities, which kept similar rogues' galleries. Though it did not specify the specific aspect of privacy law that had been violated, the court enjoined the police inspector's publication of the innocent man's photograph in the rogues' gallery. The court reasoned that "[t]here is a right in equity to protect a person from such an invasion of privacy rights" and that "every one who does not violate the law can insist upon being let alone (the right of privacy) . . . [a] right of privacy [that] is absolute" (pp. 480-81). Although this early court acknowledged that the right to privacy had some limits, it declined to discuss what those limits were.

Since *Itzkovitch*, the right to privacy has been defined by Louisiana jurisprudence both as "the right to be let alone" and "the right to an 'inviolate personality'" (as cited in *Jaubert v. Crowley Post-Signal, Inc.*, 1979, p. 1388; *Hamilton v. Lumbermen's Mutual Casualty Co.*, 1955). In 1979, the Louisiana Supreme Court recognized Prosser's four privacy torts, appropriation of name or likeness, intrusion into seclusion, public disclosure of private facts, and false light (*Jaubert v. Crowley Post-Signal, Inc.*, pp. 1388-89), even though it ultimately rejected the plaintiff homeowners' privacy claims against a newspaper that had published a photograph of their home with a disparaging caption; the state's high court reasoned that the right to privacy does not attach "to material in the public view" (p. 1391). In other words, as explained more fully below, in 1979, the court laid out the standard for privacy rights in Louisiana but ultimately found that the claim did not fit any of them.

In addition to recognizing the four Restatement privacy torts in that case, the Louisiana Supreme Court also set a more generalized standard for an invasion of privacy action, ruling that a claim is actionable "only when the defendant's conduct is unreasonable and seriously interferes with the plaintiff's privacy interest" (p. 1389). The court relied on a balancing test, which it explained in part that "[t]he reasonableness of the defendant's conduct is determined by balancing the conflicting interests at stake; the plaintiff's interest in protecting his privacy from serious invasions, and the defendant's interest in pursuing his course of conduct" (p. 1389). Two years later, the Louisiana Supreme Court elaborated on that reasonableness standard, explaining that a privacy claim is non-actionable, even though a privacy invasion has occurred, as long as "a defendant's action is authorized or justified by circumstance" (*Parish National Bank v. Lane*, 1981, pp. 1286-87).

Consistent with the requirement that a plaintiff's privacy be seriously invaded before a privacy claim is actionable and justifiable in Louisiana, a plaintiff must prove actual damages to recover for a privacy invasion (*Slocum v. Sears Roebuck & Co.*, 1989, p. 779). As one court explained, "Louisiana unlike common law does not award nominal damages for the mere invasion of a right, [if] no actual damage [has] resulted" (as cited in *Slocum*, 1989, p. 779). In *Slocum v. Sears Roebuck & Co.*, for example, a Louisiana appellate court held that parents could not recover from a department store for the appropriation of their child's name and likeness when the department store exhibited unauthorized displays of their child's photograph taken at the store's photography studio. The court found that while there was a technical violation of the child's privacy in the store's display of her photograph without consent, "fault alone does not produce recovery" (p. 779). The court reasoned that the privacy invasion was not serious enough to warrant recovery because the photograph of the child was "very pretty," the display was limited and did not identify the child, and the child was less than a year old when the photos were displayed. Thus, the parents could not recover because the privacy invasion was not serious enough to cause actual damages.

Limits on Privacy Law in Louisiana

Simply put, therefore, as regarding limits on Louisiana privacy law, a privacy claim is non-actionable when a fact-finder court or jury finds that the defendant has acted reasonably in invading the plaintiff's privacy (see *Parish Nat. Bank v. Lane*, 1981, p. 1287). That means that should a privacy breach be deemed insignificant by the fact finder, the plaintiff will not prevail.

There are other limitations for the plaintiff. In line with multiple other jurisdictions, for example, a plaintiff will not have a valid claim for invasion of privacy when he provides express or implied waiver (*Moore v. Cabiniss*, 1997, p. 1147) or "consents to the release of information" (*Tate v. Woman's Hospital Foundation*, 2011, p. 198). It is important to note that in Louisiana, however, consent does not always preclude the finding of an actionable privacy invasion. Prior to the Louisiana Supreme Court's adoption of Prosser's privacy torts in *Jaubert*, for example, a Louisiana appeals court held that a health studio had invaded a man's privacy when it used "before and after" photographs in advertisements ten years after the man was photographed with his consent (*McAndrews v. Roy*, 1961, p. 259). In line with Prosser's misappropriation privacy action, the man sued for embarrassment and humiliation resulting from the use of his photograph in an advertisement without his permission, explaining to the court that the beefier "after" photos made him the laughing stock at work (p. 257). The court reasoned that because the photographs had not been used for ten years, a period of time in which a person's physical appearance can greatly change, the health studio was required to obtain his renewed permission before using the photographs. Notably, the court refused to put the burden on the man to revoke the gratuitous authorization he gave ten years earlier.

Moreover, and as noted more extensively in other parts of this book, information that is a part of the public record can also be a limitation on a person's right to privacy because the Louisiana Constitution guarantees as fundamental the public's right to access public records (La. Const. Art. XII, Sec. 3). The Louisiana Public Records Act codifies the right, but provides for certain exceptions (La. Rev. Stat. Ann. Sec. 44-1) and limits them specifically to those enumerated in the Act or in the Louisiana Constitution (La. Rev. Stat. 44, Chap. 1., Part I, Sec. 4.1). In 1984, the Louisiana Supreme Court held that the public's right of access to a public record "must be construed liberally in favor of free and unrestricted access," that "access can be denied only when a law, specifically and unequivocally, provides otherwise" and that "doubt as to whether the public has the right of access to certain records . . . must be resolved in favor of the public's right to see" (*Title Research Corp. v. Rausch*, 1984, p. 936). This means, of course, that the more open and accessible the record, the less private the information contained in that record, and the lower the chance that a plaintiff will be able to sue successfully based upon the release of such information. Yet as explained in this chapter, as promisingly broad as that language sounds, media companies do not win all public record cases in Louisiana.

Similarity with the Common Law and the Privacy Torts

As suggested above in the discussion of the broad tort article in the Louisiana Code, Louisiana is a mixed law jurisdiction. This means that while it is a primarily civil law jurisdiction, or one that relies on statutory law as primary law, and jurisprudence as only secondary law, it also has adopted common law characteristics in order to facilitate Louisiana's place as a state within the rest of the common law United States. Therefore, although Louisiana law is primarily based on civil law doctrine, its privacy law resembles common law privacy and, since the four privacy torts were adopted in 1979, is heavily influenced by Prosser and the Restatement sections that define the privacy torts. The Louisiana Supreme Court, for example, explicitly relied on both Prosser and the Restatement in a publication of private facts case (*Roshto v. Hebert*, 1983). Other Louisiana cases in all four categories of privacy have similarly relied on the Restatement and Prosser's guidance. Some specific examples follow.

Misappropriation Overview

Misappropriation, as the reader will recall, is also known as appropriation and occasionally used interchangeably with the more commercially driven tort known as the right to publicity. It often arises in situations in which the defendant arguably has used another's identity without permission, as in the Don Henley case referenced earlier in this chapter. Because misappropriation is a privacy tort, courts, at least in principle, are supposed to focus on the emotional harm suffered by the plaintiff as opposed to any commercial damages caused by the misuse of the plaintiff's image. As shown by the Henley case, commercial interests certainly play a role in some cases, and courts will sometimes look to the dollar amount it would have taken to have a celebrity or even a non-celebrity agree to appear in an advertisement.

The basis for the misappropriation tort in Louisiana has an added layer of interest due to the nature and tradition of the civil law. While the Louisiana Supreme Court approved of a misappropriation privacy action in its explicit adoption of the four privacy torts in 1979, the pecuniary and commercial nature of a misappropriation privacy action departed in some sense from the traditional civilian doctrine that underlies the civil law. The civil law categorizes rights as real or personal. Real rights are rights that confer direct and immediate authority over anything and are good against the world, whereas personal rights are rights of one person, the obligee, to demand performance from another person, the obligor. Rights in property are an example of real rights; rights in contract are an example of personal rights. Misappropriation by its very nature seems to include both property—the right to one's identity in a commercial sense—and moral rights based upon the idea that all privacy rights stem from emotional harm. Nevertheless, all torts in Louisiana are considered personal rights.

In a 2012 case, for example, the plaintiff brought suit on behalf of his deceased mother, asserting an invasion of privacy misappropriation claim for the use of what he believed to be his mother's image in an airport mural; the court suggested that the image was "possibly" the deceased woman (*Tatum v. New Orleans Aviation Board*, 2012, p. 147). The court reasoned that as a personal right, the appropriation claim was personal to the plaintiff's mother in that the right belonged only to the person whose privacy was invaded. Therefore, the court awarded no damages to the plaintiff since only his deceased mother would have qualified for damages. The court also focused on the privacy foundation for the misappropriation tort and found that the plaintiff's mother had waived her right to privacy by taking part in jazz funerals and second lines on the streets of New Orleans, showing that she had "obviously excelled and enjoyed" her position in the "public arena" (p. 148).

Courts have also described misappropriation and right of publicity privacy actions as common law claims, thus ignoring the civil law analysis altogether. In *Prudhomme v. Procter & Gamble Co.* (1992), the United States District Court for the Eastern District of Louisiana labeled the Louisiana privacy law claims "common law right of privacy and publicity claims" (pp. 395-96). There, the plaintiff celebrity-chef Paul Prudhomme had brought a lawsuit raising various privacy causes of action regarding a coffee commercial that "depict[ed] an actor bearing a striking resemblance" to the plaintiff (p. 392). The court permitted the plaintiff's right of publicity claim to proceed, despite the defendant's argument that the right had not yet been recognized in Louisiana, reasoning that the plaintiff had made a good faith argument for extending the law on this subject (p. 396).

Misappropriation Case Example: *Tooley v. Canal Motors, Inc.*

Tooley v. Canal Motors, Inc. (1974), a case decided by an appellate court, is a good example of a Louisiana misappropriation case. It involves media and, like many misappropriation actions, arises from advertising and the use of a person's name without permission. It might be better to call the case "The Tale of the Two Tooleys."

In *Tooley*, a radio station in New Orleans began airing an advertisement for a car dealer that contained language describing the dealer's sales staff, likening some to chivalrous, attorney-like fighters: "The Canal Ford Knights don't sell cars," the announcer read, "they sell people. A Canal Ford City Knight is a combination of all professions. John Tooley, Jack Simmons and Ty Loup, like lawyers, express their ideas clearly" (*Tooley v. Canal Motors, Inc.*, 1974, p. 453). The ad then explained how other salespeople had characteristics that exemplified the best in other professions.

John Tooley was in fact the name of a man who sold cars at Canal Ford. Trouble was that this name was held not only by the John Tooley who sold cars, but also by a New Orleans attorney, John Tooley. Attorney Tooley explained that people who heard the ad—especially the suggestion that John Tooley expressed his ideas clearly, like a lawyer—began asking him if he had left the legal profession to become a car salesman or if he had taken a second job selling cars to help stave off a failing law practice. He asked that the ad be discontinued, but the ad continued its run in New Orleans.

John Tooley, the attorney, therefore, sued both the dealership and the radio station for invasion of privacy. He argued that the ad used his identity, his name, and had "mis[led] listeners into believing that John Tooley, the attorney, endorse[d] or participate[d] in the activities" of the dealership (p. 454). While the appeals court failed to mention misappropriation by name, the opinion explained that Tooley's claim was grounded in "the right to be let alone" and "the right to live one's life in seclusion without being subjected to unwarranted and undesired publicity" (p. 454). Attorney Tooley was successful in his privacy claim. Because he had put the defendants on notice of what he alleged to be an unauthorized use of his name, the court found a valid privacy invasion and ordered that the defendants pay Tooley $1,000 for his harm, along with all costs of the litigation.

It is interesting that the ad in question referred to what was apparently a completely different John Tooley, one who actually did sell cars at the dealership and one who, in fact, may have been as articulate as an attorney. Moreover, the court noted that there was no evidence that those who wrote the ad had known that an attorney with the same name was in practice in New Orleans. Here, however, the fact that a different John Tooley existed made little difference to the court, considering that attorney John Tooley had put the defendants on notice that he existed. "When this was made known to defendants," the court wrote, "it was unreasonable for them not to modify the advertisement so as to delete the portion which was in fact misleading the public to the detriment of the plaintiff" (p. 455). The fact that a listener would associate the car dealership and the attorney, then, was enough for a viable claim for invasion of privacy, whether or not car salesman John Tooley existed.

INTRUSION INTO SECLUSION OVERVIEW

Intrusion into seclusion is the privacy tort in which one peers into another's private affairs, be it with the use of binoculars or hidden cameras or computer hacking software. The tort is complete when the act of looking occurs; the defendant need not share what he saw or learned with anyone. This is, of course, in sharp contrast to the other privacy torts in which sharing of some kind is required. Louisiana, like all states, generally refuses to recognize a right to privacy for what takes place in public or what is already known by the public. In its adoption of the four privacy torts in 1979, the Louisiana Supreme Court defined the intrusion into seclusion privacy tort in a way that highlights that fundamental principle (*Jaubert v. Crowley Post-Signal, Inc.* 1979). Intrusion occurs "when the defendant unreasonably intrudes upon the plaintiff's physical solitude or seclusion" as long as the intruded-upon activity or situation is private and not a "public sight which any one is free to see" (p. 1388).

Some have suggested that Louisiana courts have construed facts more broadly in favor of plaintiffs and have found some arguably public settings secluded enough to support intrusion claims (*Szwak*, 2005). In a case involving the infamous "Girls Gone Wild" videotape series, one that features women who flash their breasts, the United States District Court for the Eastern District of Louisiana applied Louisiana law and found a genuine issue of material fact as to whether a "'party' on the second floor of a Bourbon Street bar" constituted a setting that was private and secluded enough to support a privacy claim. In the case, two women posed topless for a photograph with a famous rapper while at the party and filed an invasion of privacy action after the photograph ended up on the cover of a "Girls Gone Wild" video. The court reasoned that whether the party was public or private was a "close call" and required a jury determination (*Capdeboscq v. Francis*, 2004, as cited by Szwak, p. 261). The parties eventually settled, but the Louisiana court's decision directly conflicted with the reasoning of a California judgment that held that a party-goer, whose photograph was taken at a party open to the public and published in a magazine, did not have a "reasonable expectation of seclusion or solitude" that would support an intrusion into seclusion claim (*Prince v. Out Pub. Inc.*, 2002, as cited by Szwak, pp. 261-62). What is secluded enough to support an intrusion action, therefore is not always clear, and the layperson's definition for seclusion and its opposite may not align exactly with the legal one.

Intrusion Case Example: *Jaubert v. Crowley Post-Signal*

Because the definition for seclusion can vary with the precise facts, media have become especially wary of seclusion claims. As in the "Girls Gone Wild" example above, they can arise from photographs or videotape taken in what many might think was an obviously public setting. One might believe that a photograph of a house visible from the street would cause no privacy worries. But one would be wrong.

In *Jaubert v. Crowley Post-Signal* (1979), as noted above, the Louisiana Supreme Court accepted all four privacy torts. The case involved a house photo, and the lines of seclusion were surprisingly blurred. The Crowley, Louisiana, newspaper-defendant, the *Post-Signal*, published a photograph of the plaintiffs' home without the plaintiffs' permission and captioned it this way: "One of Crowley's stately homes, a bit weatherworn and unkempt, stands in the shadow of a spreading oak" (p. 1387). The photo of the house appeared on the front page and no other identifying information accompanied it. The couple that owned the home sued the newspaper for invasion of their privacy. The wife testified that she was "hurt and embarrassed" by the photograph, and the husband said that he had been repeatedly approached by those who had seen the photograph and knew that the house was his (p. 476). The newspaper, in turn, argued that the photograph was news and therefore protected, and could not possibly be the subject of an intrusion into seclusion claim.

The intermediate-level appeals court that heard the case ruled in favor of the couple, however. The court explained that the plaintiffs deserved protection against such unwarranted and undesired publicity. Moreover, any argument that the house itself was visible from the street lacked merit because, the court found, the intrusion itself was unreasonable. "Discovering during one's absence," the court wrote simply while quoting the similarly inclined trial court, "that his home has been given front page attention, without his permission, accompanied by a less than flattering caption, is an invasion of the right to privacy" (p. 478). The court explained that had the newspaper published the photograph without any commentary, privacy would likely not have been implicated, but a somewhat disparaging caption accompanying the photograph made the plaintiffs desire seclusion all the more—and gave them a valid claim.

But that was not the end of the case. The defendant newspaper appealed the appellate court decision to the state's highest court and won. The justices rejected the idea that a disparaging comment could cause a phoenix-like privacy right to rise from a photograph taken in an otherwise public place. "It is clear from the record," the justices wrote in an unanimous opinion, "that the Jauberts' home was plainly visible from the public street, and that passersby were presented with a view of the property which was identical to that published by the defendant" (*Jaubert*, 1979, p. 1391). Therefore, the court held that there was no intrusion into the plaintiffs' seclusion and no invasion of the right to privacy, slightly disparaging description or not.

The different outcomes, however, combined with the at least partially contradictory holding in the "Girls Gone Wild" case, are enough to put a media defendant on notice that courts can be fickle in deciding where to draw the line between what is private and what is public with regard to intrusion cases.

PUBLICATION OF PRIVATE FACTS OVERVIEW

The *Jaubert* decision specifically mentions intrusion, but it also has overtones of the Publication of Private Facts privacy tort. The publication tort arises when private information about someone is shared with others against the person's wishes; there is a special exception for newsworthy items, however.

Publication of private facts is defined in Louisiana as "unreasonable public disclosure of embarrassing private facts" and is also qualified by the court's adherence to the well-accepted rationale that it excludes information already made public (*Jaubert v. Crowley Post-Signal*, 1979, p. 1388) in line with the Restatement's assertion that "there is no liability for giving further publicity to what the plaintiff himself leaves open to the public eye" (p. 1391). In other words, had the Jaubert plaintiffs specifically brought a publication of private facts claim against the newspaper in addition to their intrusion claim, the argument would have been very similar to what they argued at trial: that it was nobody else's business how they kept their home. Therefore, the newspaper should be liable for publishing such private information. The Louisiana Supreme Court, however, likely would have responded in the way it did in the case, finding that newspapers deserved deference in determining news coverage that something as decidedly public and innocuous as a house could never be the basis for a valid publication of private facts case.

As noted earlier, publication of private facts is the privacy tort associated with the most significant First Amendment press freedoms, including its newsworthiness defense, and so it is particularly relevant in cases involving media. Not all publication of private facts cases involve traditional publishers, however. In a 1978 case, for example, the sued publisher was a business owner who had placed photographs in his business of a man who, the photos suggested, had been "caught in the act" of theft by a hidden camera (*Norris v. King*, 1978). The photographed man sued and the court found that the plaintiff's privacy had been invaded through such "harassing" behavior, likening it to the unreasonable interference with solitude that the court had found in the Case of the Two Tooleys (pp. 23, 25). The same appeals court, however, later ruled in favor of a newspaper that had published the name and address of a robbery shooting victim, even though the victim had argued that her right to privacy had been violated. The court rested its decision on the public nature of the crime, finding both that the information was not private because the crime happened in a public place (*Batts v. Capital City Press, Inc.*, 1985, p. 573), and that the news value in the coverage could help generate tips to a police hotline. Such varying decisions, however, show that even in privacy tort cases involving significant First Amendment values, media do not always win.

Publication of Private Facts Case Example: *Roshto v. Hebert*

In 1952, a court in Iberville Parish, Louisiana, convicted three brothers of cattle theft. Apparently the three had acted together and had stolen part of a neighbor's herd. The brothers were convicted of the crime, and each one of them served one year in prison and one year on probation. Thereafter, however, the three lived ordinary, crime-free lives—the court described them as "law-abiding citizens"—and each married and had children, none of whom apparently knew about their fathers' and uncles' criminal pasts (*Roshto v. Hebert*, 1983, p. 430).

Then, in 1983, *The Iberville South* republished one of its front pages from 1952 as a part of its "Page From Our Past" series—and this past page included the story of the brothers' cattle theft trial (p. 430). Alarmed, one of the brothers visited the newspaper offices on behalf of the three, and was assured by a newspaper representative that should similar pages ever be republished, the brothers' names would be removed. Four years later, however, the newspaper republished yet another front page, the one featuring the brothers as they headed to prison. The brothers, at least one of whom was a grandfather at the time, sued the newspaper for invasion of their right to privacy, specifically grounding their complaint in the publication of private facts tort. The case highlights the tension in many publication of private facts cases, one between an arguably interesting newspaper feature—here, a look back at a day in the history of the community through the eyes of its newspaper—and a group of rightfully embarrassed men who had righted their criminal wrongs and who wished to be known for the persons they had become, not the persons they had been twenty-five years ago.

The appeals court sided with the brothers (p. 929), referencing the court's reasoning in the *Jaubert* case. There, the court suggested, the house in question had been on public display. But the case involving the brothers was different because, in contrast, their criminal convictions were not publicly known in the same sense: "[A]lthough the convictions were matters of public record," the court reasoned, "they were twenty-five years old and not generally known to the current population of the community" (p. 930). The court therefore decided that the long-ago crime was within the brothers' zone of personal privacy and should not have been revealed by the newspaper. As for the argument that there was news value in the information, the court found that there had been no "independent reason" to publish the information, and the passage of so much time without new criminal behavior had, in effect, closed the once-open public record (p. 930). The court ordered that the newspaper pay each brother $35,000 and their court costs.

The Louisiana Supreme Court, however, reversed that judgment, finding in favor of the newspaper (*Roshto v. Hebert*, 1983). The justices disagreed that the passage of time should automatically change the nature of a public record from public to private, even one from twenty-five years before and even one regarding people who had otherwise behaved themselves appropriately. The court recognized that the newspaper may have been insensitive or careless when it republished a front page without looking into the persons who may be harmed upon republication, but it decided that such action could not lead to a viable right-to-privacy claim, noting especially that the act was non-malicious.

In holding that the republication of the article did not constitute invasion of privacy for publication of private facts, the court described the tort in line with the Restatement. It explained that invasion of privacy takes place "by giving publicity to a matter concerning the private life of another, when the publicized matter would be highly offensive to a reasonable person and is not of legitimate concern to the public" (p. 432). It also cited that section's Illustration 26 in explaining that lapse of time from original publication was a factor in determining whether the information was of public concern and, therefore, not viable. Moreover, the justices agreed with the newspaper that there was news value in past community news, and that the republication of a randomly selected front page containing information from years past was decidedly a matter of public concern.

But, important for media, the court did not absolve all journalistic inquiry into a person's criminal past. "[W]hen a person convicted of a crime has served his sentence, changed his name, moved to a faraway city, concealed his identity, and led an obscure, respectable, and useful life for 20 years," the court wrote, "a newspaper reporter who institutes an investigation of the little-known citizen's past history and reveals the conviction in a newspaper published in the citizen's new community (far from the site of the crime), the reporter possibly may be liable for . . . invasion of privacy . . . ." (p. 432). A lawyer would call that language "dicta," a word that means the court's thoughts on an issue that is not put squarely before it and, therefore, not binding. But it could, in fact, be of highly persuasive authority should a similar case ever come before a Louisiana judge.

> ### Eavesdropping Cops
>
> Secretly recording telephone conversations is a familiar practice for criminal investigations, but when does such police work violate personal privacy rights? During the 1960s, a Los Angeles bookmaker by the name of Charles Katz preferred a pay phone to run his gambling operation when FBI agents attached a listening device to the phone booth. Katz in court claimed that the federal agents had violated his Fourth Amendment rights. He won his case before the U.S. Supreme Court based on the reasoning that society expects that when one enters a phone booth and closes the door, the ensuing conversation is private and protected from unreasonable search and seizure. In *Katz v. United States* (1967) the Court held that a Fourth Amendment search takes place when police record a phone conversation in which there would be a "reasonable expectation of privacy" (p. 388).
>
> In a torts sense, the landmark decision was felt three decades later at the police department of Hammond, Louisiana, when officers not only recorded incoming phone calls of distressed residents, but also eavesdropped on each other's conversations. Sgt. Terry Zaffuto in 1997 called his wife, Susan, with the news that the Hammond Police Department was re-organizing its force to the disadvantage of a few superior officers. Ms. Zaffuto responded approvingly to the news her husband shared over the phone, but neither of the spouses knew that their conversation was secretly recorded and later would be re-played for other officers without their consent.
>
> The Zaffutos filed a privacy lawsuit against the police officer and another police employee who made and shared the recording, alleging that such actions represented an unreasonable disclosure of embarrassing private facts. The U.S. Fifth Circuit Court of Appeals agreed and ruled in the plaintiffs' favor. The decision turned not on a showing of malicious intent, but only used a simple balancing test instead that compared "the plaintiff's interest in protecting his privacy from serious invasions with the defendant's interest in pursuing his course of conduct" (*Zaffuto v. Hammond*, 2002, p. 491). The court awarded the Zaffutos just two dollars in damages, but confirmed that their right to privacy was more important than any reason give for police officers eavesdropping on the couple.

Courts today continue to struggle with line-drawing in cases like the brothers who were once cattle thieves, cases that pit plaintiffs' truthful but embarrassing personal information with media's argument that such information has news value. The United States Supreme Court has never decided precisely where to draw the line between what is news to the community and what is information that is too private to be shared.

False Light Overview

As noted previously, false light, which is the Restatement privacy tort that is most similar to defamation, requires that the published information be false. In 1979, the Louisiana Supreme Court described the false light privacy tort, in line with the Restatement, as "publicity which unreasonably places the plaintiff in a false light before the public" (*Jaubert v. Crowley Post-Signal, Inc.*, 1979, p. 1388). The court further noted that "[w]hile the publicity need not be defamatory in nature, but only objectionable to a reasonable person under the circumstances, it must contain either falsity or fiction" (p. 1388). Thus, Louisiana courts consider three elements in determining a false light action: the plaintiff's underlying privacy interest, the falsity of the information, and whether the defendant's conduct was in some way unreasonable (as cited in *Simpson v. Perry*, 2004, p. 16).

A Louisiana appellate court explained the equation more fully, writing "[i]f the publicity is an accurate portrayal of the public display, if the publicity is not unreasonable and false, then plaintiff has no actionable privacy interest, even if the publicity has caused embarrassment, offense, or damage" (*Easter Seal Society for Crippled Children and Adults of Louisiana., Inc. v. Playboy Enterprises., Inc.* 1988, p. 647). Moreover, Louisiana courts have found that "whether the publicity generated . . . was understood to portray plaintiffs in an objectionable way is a factual matter for determination by the trier of fact" (*Sharrif v. American Broadcasting Co.*, 1993, p. 771).

As noted elsewhere in this book, defamation, false light's counterpart, has been defined by the Louisiana Supreme Court, also in accordance with the Restatement, as having four elements: (1) a false and defamatory statement concerning another; (2) an unprivileged publication to a third party; (3) fault (negligence or greater) on the part of the publisher; and (4) resulting injury (see, for example, *Costello v. Hardy*, 2004, p. 139). Though defamation and false light claims have different purposes, Louisiana courts permit both claims to be brought together against a defendant for a single wrong (see *Smith v. Arkansas Louisiana Gas Co.*, 1994). Some courts have made traditional defamation defenses available to defendants of false light claims. In 1994, for example, an employee who was demoted for sexual harassment sued his employer for both defamation and false light for revealing this information to his co-workers. A jury ruled in favor of the plaintiff. A state appeals court reversed the jury decision, finding that the jury instructions had been inadequate because they failed to clearly explain that the qualified privilege available in the defamation claim was also available for the false light claim.

False light claims in Louisiana involving media include the case of a television station that broadcast a report on truancy featuring a student allegedly sent home because of improper paperwork (*Stern v. Doe*, 2001). After the station aired his processing at the truancy enforcement center, the student sued the television station for false light invasion of privacy. The television station won because the court found the situation was not offensive enough for a valid false light claim. In a different false light case, a father sued a television station that aired a report suggesting that he had walked out on his children (*Perere v. Louisiana Television Broadcasting Corp.*, 1988). An appeals court found for the defendant broadcaster, affirming the trial court's decision that the report was basically true even though the father paid child support. Sometimes false light claims have more nuance to them, as the following case illustrates.

False Light Case Example: *Easter Seal Society v. Playboy Enterprises*

False light claims, like defamation claims, can arise in situations where the underlying information may be true but is presented in a way that suggests to a reader or a viewer that the plaintiff endorses some activity that the plaintiff does not endorse. One could imagine, for example, a documentary on Internet pornographers that included generic video of a medical doctor working on a computer. If the doctor were not a pornographer, he would likely be able to argue successfully that the documentary had portrayed him in a false light and had also defamed him. In other words, even though the information reported was true in the sense that the doctor had, in fact, worked on a computer, the implication that he was a pornographer would be false. He would receive damages for the emotional harm springing from the false light in which he was placed, and damages for reputational harm based upon his defamation claim. Consider, however, how difficult it might be to draw the line in such cases. At what point does the use of old stock footage in a new media project malign a plaintiff by connecting him to the more offensive project?

That was the issue put before a Louisiana court in the case of *Easter Seal Society v. Playboy Enterprises* (1988). There, a number of volunteers had participated in a Mardi Gras parade reenactment, one videotaped for national broadcast during the Easter Seals Telethon. The volunteers knew that they were reenacting the parade for charitable purposes, and each participant refused monetary compensation. Later, the New Orleans PBS station that had sent its camerapersons to take video of the volunteers also used it in a series on Dixieland jazz. The video was then added to the station's film library.

Some time later, a producer called the PBS station, asking for generic Mardi Gras parade video footage that he wished to use in a film production. A station representative kindly turned over the stock video footage of the volunteers' parade reenactment—apparently without knowing that the producer's film was titled *Candy the Stripper*. Imagine the volunteers' surprise when they learned that the PBS parade video had been used in an adult film, interspersed with varying depictions of nudity and sex. The volunteers sued the filmmaker for false light, arguing that their involuntary appearance in *Candy the Stripper* "placed them in an objectionable false light before the public because the movie was a 'PLAYBOY movie,' which focused on sex and drugs" (*Easter Seal Society v. Playboy Enterprises*, 1988, p. 644) and, the plaintiffs argued, it implied that those depicted were perfectly fine with such a use.

Somewhat surprisingly, the volunteers lost. First, the court was uncomfortable with the notion that the parading volunteers could sue for privacy in what otherwise was a public spectacle that they knew would later be broadcast nationally. This shows that courts sometimes focus more than they should on the privacy part of a false light claim. One could very likely successfully sue for false light, for example, if one's photograph was taken in a public parade and later captioned with the phrase "Parading for Pornography."

However, and more in line with false light as it is defined in the Restatement, the court found that there was no suggestion or "innuendo connecting any [volunteers] with the subject matter of the [adult] film" (*Easter Seal Society v. Playboy Enterprises*, 1988, p. 648). The court found that the parade footage was a completely separate part of the film as distinguished from the sexual activity and, therefore, was not sufficiently intertwined to create a false impression of the volunteers in the mind of a viewer. In other words, the court found that the adult film's use of the clips did not constitute an inaccurate false portrayal constituting a false light claim because the group was, in fact, parading and the producers did not suggest anything more scandalous. "In this film," the court wrote, "the parade is no more than part of the New Orleans backdrop in the same way that many movies make use of a city or cities as settings and include shots of urban activity through which the film's characters pass" (p. 648). But such cases are not always decided in favor of the defendant. The more the plaintiff is cast in a light that makes others think he has done something he has not, something that others would find offensive, the more likely the plaintiff will succeed with a false light claim.

Departure from the Common Law

Interestingly, and as a final note, one point in which Louisiana courts depart from common law courts in other states is that corporate entities may have their very own right to privacy. A Louisiana appeals court in 1995 upheld a trial court's finding that a plaintiff corporation had a privacy right, supporting an injunction that would stop the defendant, a competitor of the plaintiff, from entering dumpsters used by the plaintiff and disseminating the sensitive information found there to news media (*Camp, Dresser & McKee, Inc. v. Steimle and Associates*, 1995). The court rejected the defendant's argument that a corporation, as a non-human, could not have a right to privacy or a reasonable expectation of privacy in its trash, and supported the injunction against the competitor's "unscrupulous behavior in the conduct of business" (p. 46). Following that court's lead, in 2010, the United States Bankruptcy Court for the Eastern District of Louisiana accepted a plaintiff corporation's asserted right to privacy in "its business information, privileged communications with legal counsel, and financial data," holding that the defendant was liable in tort for its repeated unauthorized access into the plaintiff-corporation's computer system (in re: *Thundervision, LLC*, 2010, at *16). The court reasoned that the conduct was "unreasonable, indefensible, and socially unacceptable . . . support[ing] a delictual cause of action" under the Louisiana Civil Code, specifically relying on Article 2315, for privacy invasion (in re: *Thundervision, LLC*, 2010, at *16).

Conclusion

Today, of course, everyone in Louisiana who has access to the Internet is a potential publisher with direct access to worldwide readers. And every individual Internet publisher faces the same legal scrutiny as did corporate media and other defendants in the privacy actions described above. Individuals are not immune from privacy law just because they are individuals or just because they have published others' private information not in hard copy but on the Internet. This is why an understanding of the law of privacy—and the other legal matters discussed in this book—is even more important today.

Let's say, for example, that a college entrepreneur posts a photograph of his former girlfriend to his company web site in an attempt to lure potential clients there. The photo is one he took while they were dating and contains partial nudity. The student captions the video something like "Hot babe ready to put out for everyone who buys anything from this website." In the same way that the defendant network ABC faced four privacy claims arising from the "funniest home video" in the *Sharrif* case described at the very beginning of this chapter, so too might the college-aged Internet publisher face those same four claims, even though he took the photograph himself. What actually matters is that the woman pictured did not give her permission. The former girlfriend could argue, for example, that he used her image for a business purpose without permission when he posted it on his website, thus potentially satisfying a misappropriation claim. She might also argue that, by posting the video, her former boyfriend had both intruded into her seclusion and had published private facts about her, both potentially viable privacy claims, especially if she did not reveal this particular image to the public. Finally, because the student suggested that his former girlfriend generally based her virtue upon a website purchase, a court could find that she had a valid false light claim.

And there would be little protection had the boyfriend instead published the same photograph on another's website anonymously. Courts today will more often order that an anonymous poster be revealed, if possible, as long as the plaintiff can prove with varying levels of certainty that an underlying cause of action exists, be it one based in privacy or defamation. Today, then, just as Warren and Brandeis once worried, it is entirely possible to shout, in effect, another's private secrets from the rooftops and share them with the world. But just as Warren and Brandeis had proposed, today it is possible for that publisher, be it media or be it an individual, to be brought to court on invasion of privacy grounds. A right to privacy, therefore, has a solid foundation in Louisiana and elsewhere today, one that has arguably existed for more than two hundred years, and those who study journalism or those who publish on websites, must take note of this.

REFERENCES

Broyles, P. N. (2005). *Intercontinental identity: The right to the identity in the Louisiana civil code.* 65 La. L. Rev. 823.
Gajda, A. (2008). *What if Samuel D. Warren hadn't married a senator's daughter?: Uncovering the press coverage that led to the "right to privacy."* 2008 Mich. St. L. Rev. 35.
Louisiana Civil Code Article 2315A.
Louisiana Constitution, Article XII, Sec. 3.
Louisiana Revised Statute Ann. Sec. 44:1.
Louisiana Revised Stat. 44, Chap. 1., Part 1, Sec. 4.1.
New York's Civil Rights Law, N.Y. CLS Civ. R. Sec. 51.
Prosser, W. L. (1960). Privacy. 48 Cal. L. Rev. 383.
Prosser, W. L. (1971). *Handbook of the law of torts.* St. Paul: West Pub. Co.
Restatement (Second) of Torts Sec. 652B (1977).
Restatement (Second) of Torts, Sec. 652C (1977).
Restatement (Second) of Torts, Sec. 652D (1977).
Restatement (Second) of Torts, Sec. 652E (1977).
Stone, Louisiana Law Treatise, 22-23, Vol. 12, Tort Doctrine (1977).
Superior Court of the State of Louisiana, First District.
Szwak, D.A. (2005). Privacy exposed. 59 Consumer Fin. L.Q.Rep. 261.
Warren, S. & Brandeis, L. (1890). The right to privacy. 4 Harv. L. Rev. 193.
Wisconsin Statute Sec. 895.50.

CASES CITED

Batts v. Capital City Press, Inc., 479 So. 2d 534 (La. Ct. App. 1985).
Batts v. Capital City Press, Inc., 501 So. 2d 302 (La. Ct. App. 1986).
Capdeboscq v. Francis, No. Civ. A.03-0556, 2004 WL 463316 (E.D. La. Mar. 10, 2004).
Camp, Dresser & McKee, Inc. v. Steimle and Associates, 652 So. 2d 44 (La. Ct. App. 1995).
Costello v. Hardy, 864 So. 2d 129 (La. 2004).
Denis v. LeClerc, 1 Mart. 297 (La. Super. Ct. 1811).
Easter Seal Society for Crippled Children and Adults of Louisiana, Inc. v. Playboy Enterprises, Inc., 530 So. 2d 643 (La. Ct. App. 1988).
Green v. Chicago Tribune Co., 675 N.E.2d 249 (Ill. Ct. App. 1996).
Hamilton v. Lumbermen's Mutual Casualty Co., 82 So. 2d 61 (La. Ct. App. 1955).
Henley v. Dillard Department Stores, 46 F. Supp. 2d 587 (N.D. Tex. 1999).
Itzkovitch v. Witaker, 115 La. 479 (1905).
Itzkovitch v. Witaker, 117 La. 708 (1906).
Jaubert v. Crowley Post-Signal, Inc., 375 So. 2d 1386 (La. 1979).
Joslyn Manufacturing Co. v. Koppers Co., Inc., 40 F.3d 750 (5th Cir. 1994).
Katz v. United States, 389 U.S. 347 (1967).
McAndrews v. Roy, 131 So. 2d 256 (La. Ct. App. 1961).
Moore v. Cabaniss, 669 So. 2d 1143 (La. Ct. App. 1997).
Norris v. King, 355 So. 2d (La. Ct. App. 1978).
Pack v. Wise, 155 So. 2d 909 (La. Ct. App. 1963).
Parish National Bank v. Lane, 397 So. 2d 1282 (La. 1981).
Perere v. Louisiana Television Broadcasting Corp., 721 So. 2d 1075 (La. Ct. App. 1998).
Perere v. Louisiana Television Broadcasting Corp., 812 So. 2d 673 (La. Ct. App. 2001).
Prince v. Out Publishing Inc., 2002 WL 7999 (2002).
Prudhomme v. Procter & Gamble Co., 800 F. Supp. 390 (E.D. La. 1992).
Roberson v. Rochester Folding Box Co., 64 N.E. 442 (N.Y. 1902).
Roshto v. Hebert, 439 So. 2d 428 (La. 1983).
Sharif v. American Broad Co., 613 So. 2d 768 (La. Ct. App. 1993).
Shulman v. Group W Productions, Inc., 955 P.2d 469 (Cal. 1998).

Simpson v. Perry, 887 So. 2d 14 (2004).
Slocum v. Sears Roebuck & Co., 542 So. 2d 777 (La. Ct. App. 1989).
Smith v. Arkansas Louisiana Gas Co., 645 So. 2d 785 (La. Ct. App. 1994).
Stern v. Doe, 806 So. 2d 98 (La. Ct. App. 2001).
Tate v. Woman's Hospital Foundation, 56 So.3d 194 (La. 2011).
Tatum v. New Orleans Aviation Board, 102 So.3d 144 (La. Ct. App. 2012).
Thundervision, LLC, No. 09-11145 A, 2010 WL 2219352, at * 16 (Bankr. E.D. La. June 1, 2010).
Title Research Corp. v. Rausch, 450 So. 2d 933 (La. 1984).
Tooley v. Canal Motors, Inc., 296 So. 2d 453 (La. Ct. App. 1974).
Yoeckel v. Samonig, 272 Wis. 430 (Wis. 1956).
Zaffuto v. City of Hammond, 308 F.3d 485, 486 (5th Cir. 2002).

Chapter 6
Student Rights of Expression
By Joe Mirando, Southeastern Louisiana University

Learning Objectives
In this chapter, readers will:
- understand how freedom of expression rights guaranteed to all American citizens are affected by conditions in the school environment
- draw distinctions between the rights of high school students and college students, and between the rights of students enrolled in private schools and enrolled in public schools
- identify the different situations and conditions when censorship is legally justified
- explain the special legal challenges involved with school broadcast productions and student online operations
- explain legal responsibilities associated with campus speech codes, as well as incitement and protest marches

Freedom of expression as a legal right for students has always been a touchy subject in American society. The First Amendment guarantees of freedom of speech, press, religion, assembly, and petition were meant to apply to all citizens of the United States. But the authoritarian nature of formal education, in particular the teacher-student relationship within the school environment, makes it difficult to assume that a student can expect to be treated with all the rights that all citizens are supposed to have.

During the course of the typical school day, regardless if it is occurring on a college campus or at a secondary school, maintaining order is considered essential to the educational process. In this context, the teacher or professor assumes the role of master or supervisor, and the responsibility for ensuring the success of the educational experience, or at least ensuring the student's safety, belongs to the teacher or professor. On the secondary school level today, and as time passes increasingly more and more on the college level, it is the teachers or professors who are the ones held accountable for the student's failure to understand the significance and application of the most basic concepts and even to later find a well-paying job. Meanwhile, the student's role is very rarely that of a collaborator or colleague despite the presence of a lot of well-intentioned modern scholarly literature encouraging teachers and professors to invite student involvement in lesson planning and make use of student feedback. Instead, throughout the history of public education in the United States, the student is the learner who is not necessarily required to believe what teachers or professors teach, but must at least become familiar with their lessons, respond when called upon to explain the lessons and not initiate discussion unless given permission.

On an extracurricular basis, teachers and professors, as well as other appointed school staff members, can utilize less rigid lesson planning, scheduling, and grading standards, allowing students more opportunities to demonstrate initiative, leadership, creativity, and innovation. But even in this non-traditional learning setup, authoritarian values are a key issue. On the secondary school level the presence of official school personnel is considered essential, and often their duties necessitate their being referred to as sponsors and moderators as well as coordinators and directors. On the college level, especially at institutions funded by the public, liability is such an important concern that a faculty or staff member who agrees to serve as an "adviser" for an extracurricular organization must seek to minimize the vulnerability of the school to lawsuits, even if it comes at the expense of the quality of the students' learning experience. Important questions in extracurricular situations revolve around whether the student participants were a captive audience, whether a public forum has been established, whether prior review of productions is warranted, as well as the propriety of facility use and accounting practices.

Even when formal class time has ended and there is no formal extracurricular activity that is taking place, questions involving school jurisdiction constantly pose a challenge to the entire educational system. Students' on-line behavior has risen to become a very serious recent concern, but jurisdictional issues involving questions of freedom of student expression existed long before the birth of the Internet. Ideas expressed far off campus and even inside the home frequently become the main topic of discussion in local communities and may test a school's authority.

Three of the most famous incidents in the history of student rights in the United States took place on college campuses in Louisiana, and the results of all three incidents underscore the difficulty inherent in the authoritarian nature of the American school. All three incidents involved censorship and became national news, and the actions of the school authorities involved were not inspiring moments.

In 1934 U.S. Senator Huey P. Long, the former governor of Louisiana, ordered Louisiana State University President James Monroe Smith to have copies of the student newspaper, *The Reveille*, reprinted because it contained criticism of Long (Garay, 2009). Louisiana State Police were told to confiscate the first printing, and President Smith had it replaced with new copies that did not contain the criticism. Smith then told staff members of *The Reveille* that they could not criticize the university or any of its supporters.

In response to Long and Smith's actions, the top four editors on the staff quit, and twenty-six staff members responded by signing a petition to have the editors reinstated. Smith suspended all students involved and told them that they would be reinstated if they signed a letter of apology. Seven of the students refused to apologize and were expelled.

About a quarter of a century later, violent disturbances took place over the course of a decade involving students enrolled at Grambling State University and Southern University. As pointed out by university Professor Thomas Aiello, the incidents at Grambling and Southern cannot be simply equated with the historic culture of protest and activism spawned by the student movement of the 1960s and early 1970s. Instead of marching for voting rights and speaking out against the Vietnam War, the Grambling and Southern students were protesting the very nature of black colleges as institutions set up to support class distinctions and racial segregation, and they directed their protests not at the white powers that be, but at the black officials who ran their universities (Aiello). Among several things, they demanded more student participation in policy making and representation on campus governance committees.

In 1961 Southern University students led by Rev. B. Elton Cox conducted a large-scale civil rights protest in Baton Rouge. Prior to the protest, twenty-three students were arrested for picketing at stores that had lunch counters that segregated their customers by race. Cox was arrested for his actions and convicted. His appeal to the Louisiana Supreme Court failed, but Cox prevailed in the U.S. Supreme Court. The high court, after viewing a film of the incident, ruled that the students did not act in a hostile manner under the direction of Cox, who was exonerated of the charges of disturbing the peace and obstructing public passages (*Cox v. Louisiana*, 1965).

In November 1972 at Grambling, students selected representatives to present their demands to Grambling President Ralph Waldo Emerson Jones. Tensions ran high as students conducted a boycott of classes, and the governor was asked to send in National Guard troops when events turned ugly, marked by crowds throwing rocks and glass objects, looting, firing guns, and flipping over an auto.

The leading students who organized the Grambling protest were suspended, and after a campus disciplinary hearing and an appeal to the Louisiana State Board of Education, their suspensions were upheld. They sued on First Amendment grounds in district court and failed to have their suspensions lifted. The case came to a close after they appealed to the U.S. Fifth Circuit Court of Appeals in New Orleans and failed again (*Jenkins v. Louisiana State Board of Education*, 1975). This appellate court ruled that their protest did not merit First Amendment protection because it provoked violence.

A little less than another quarter of a century later, students at Southeastern Louisiana University found themselves being censored on different terms. In 1993 the university's student newspaper, *The Lion's Roar*, published a factual news story that made the Student Government Association (SGA) president appear to be a weak politician and could damage his re-election campaign (*State of Louisiana v. Morice*, 1994). Members of the SGA president's fraternity reacted by stealing copies of the newspaper on behalf of the SGA president before students had the chance to pick them up from bins on campus.

Staff members of the newspaper continued their aggressive coverage and pursued theft charges against the fraternity members while university officials pressured them to relent to lessen harm to the university's image. The SGA president, who was also the student representative on the university's Board of Trustees, eventually lost his re-election bid. He, along with fraternity brothers, were arrested; however, the following year a Louisiana state district court ruled that the incident was nothing more than a "prank" because the theft involved a student publication distributed for free (*State of Louisiana v. Morice*, 1994). The results of the campus disciplinary proceedings were not released to the public by the university.

The stories of the Reveille Seven, the Grambling/Southern protests, and the Southeastern prank eventually did produce positive results. The seven LSU students, who were all journalism majors, were offered scholarships to attend the University of Missouri School of Journalism, and all but one eventually graduated. In 1941 the LSU Board of Supervisors passed a resolution to formally apologize to them and have their expulsions expunged from their student records. At Southern and Grambling, as with all universities in Louisiana, student representation on various campus committees is now assured, and even the state-wide supervisory boards for the universities have students as members who meet and discuss issues with the presidents of the universities. Southeastern students who were the top editors of their stolen newspaper were recognized for standing up for freedom of the press with special awards from the Student Press Law Center and the Southeast Journalism Conference, and all went on to work in the newspaper industry after graduation.

Technology has advanced, but freedom of expression for students enrolled in Louisiana schools and universities has remained an uncertain proposition. In a more recent incident that made national news in Fall 2013, a staff member of the school newspaper at Grambling State University was suspended for tweeting information with pictures that detailed inadequate health and safety conditions facing the university's football team (Sunne, 2013).

As seen in these and other incidents, the authoritarian nature of formal education in the United States is strongly supported by the lessons and traditions developed by educators involved in the teaching of journalism and mass communication in the United States. Ever since the late 1800s, teachers and professors have sought pedagogical models that place emphasis on simulating for students the same kind of experience they would likely encounter if they were working in a professional newsroom. In this setup editors and managers are in charge of enforcing standards, controlling workflow and ensuring that the process of producing a publication or on-air show proceeds in accordance with deadlines. This is why professional journalists, when asked later on to comment on the Reveille Seven or the Southeastern "prank," were divided on whether students' First Amendment rights were the main issue in these incidents or whether the students should have been punished for their actions.

These incidents are worthy of study because they involve all five of the classic violations of freedom of expression most often associated with corrupt government. First

Amendment scholars historically have debated what were the intentions of the founding fathers of the United States when they passed the Constitution, and how might they respond to modern challenges to freedom of expression that did not exist during the eighteenth century. However, there is little disagreement that the signers of the Constitution considered these five actions to be at odds with the ideals of the First Amendment:

1. Censorship. This is the suppression or removal of a person's spoken or written words after they were communicated, regardless of whether the words were generated in oral, printed, broadcast, or digital format. In a school environment it must be emphasized that censorship did not occur if a student's words were changed or deleted by another student serving in an editor or manager role. Thus, an article for the school newspaper revised by the editor, an on-air report cut by a program director, or a web page taken down by a webmaster does not constitute censorship when fellow students are making the decisions. These are examples of editing. Censorship occurs only when the decision to change or remove a student's words is made by a faculty member, who in a public school environment is acting as a government official and thus is in violation of the opening words of the First Amendment: "Congress shall make no law . . . ."

It must be noted that teachers and professors working in environments in which their classes are producing publications or broadcasts must exercise care in drawing distinctions between what is being evaluated as part of a lesson and what is to be published or aired. Teachers routinely cross out, correct, and move around words in what a student has written or spoken as part of the grading process, and this practice can be protected under the First Amendment as a form of academic freedom if students are still making the final decisions on what is published or aired regardless of how it is graded. Students who are officially employed to work for a student publication or other campus medium should check to see what is their status—registered student or government employee—in such items as the campus publication or media policy, student handbook, student code of conduct, or IF they should seek advice of the school attorney.

2. Prior Restraint. The words "censorship" and "prior restraint" are often used interchangeably, and this is unfortunate because it obscures important distinctions between these terms. Sometimes, censorship can take place in a manner that is wrong but may stem from good motivations—an overzealous teacher who simply desires to help a student avoid an embarrassing mistake, school staff members who think they are correcting an unintentional typo, or an administrator overly concerned with the consistency of how the institution communicates its values. However, prior restraint takes censorship to a new level in that a person's words are suppressed before they are ever communicated. It can be a much more serious matter because in order to carry out prior restraint, knowledge of what could be communicated is required, and a plan to prevent the communication would be needed.

Censorship involves removing the newspaper after it is circulated or cutting off the audio or video during mid-broadcast; prior restraint involves preventing the printing of the newspaper or stopping the show from going on the air. Other forms of prior restraint frequently involve the firing of editors and staff members, cutting funds, blocking access to websites, making equipment unavailable, and changing locks on office doors. These actions could be sanctioned by fellow students, which would make them permissible, but if they are carried out by administrators, faculty, and staff outside the context of a course assignment, a First Amendment violation is likely occurring.

3. Licensing. Early Americans were very aware of procedures whereby one needed to gain permission in order to speak or publish. Newspapers of the colonial era often bore the words, "Printed by authority" as a form of license in order to operate. Modern historians debate which publication qualifies to be considered the first newspaper in American history, and disagreement usually focuses on whether a paper known as *Publick Occurrences* can be considered the first because it was shut down after one issue in 1690 because the printer did not gain permission to publish, or whether another publication that did not appear until 1704, the *Boston Newsletter*, was the first because it did publish multiple issues, and to be able to do so permission had to be secured from the governor.

Professional training or a diploma has never been legally required to practice journalism in the United States, although some states provide paid journalists working for recognized news organizations the legal protection of a shield law for gathering information.

In the school environment licensing, most often comes in the form of special rules certifying that students are eligible to join the staff of a campus medium based on their classification, completion of a certain class, or having achieved a necessary grade point average. In addition, schools may have rules governing students' ability to produce "underground" newspapers, "pirate" broadcasts, or alternative websites. Such regulations can be problematic if certain political viewpoints are outlawed or favorable positioning is granted to one news medium but not another. School publications that refer to themselves as the official journal of the students of a specific school are usually acknowledging a formal identification with the school as just a symbolic gesture unless there is a definite school policy that outlines responsibilities related to distribution rights, branding, and staff membership.

4. Taxation. Early Americans were also very much aware of having to pay for the right to express themselves, and the anger colonials demonstrated over the British stamp acts is legendary. In the school environment, subsidies in the form of student fees to pay for production costs associated with student media amount to many of the same challenges that are similar to the setting up of licensing and other such certification procedures for access to this medium to express one's self. Other forms of taxation that can be problematic include items such as club dues and special event security fees.

5. Compelled Speech. In the typical school setting, students are very familiar with compelled speech. Whereas censorship and prior restraint most often occur in extreme situations, everyday classroom procedure may involve old-fashioned recitation or simply being required to respond to questions. The authority of the teacher and educational tradition give little cause for concern to such situations as a First Amendment issue, but these situations may establish a routine that becomes an expectation, as when administrators "encourage" school newspapers to print apologies or retractions, or when school boards "request" support for community-wide campaigns, or when a faculty member or coach makes a "plea" for devoting special attention to an event. Students who dare to say "no" to such a request to speak or write something can be faced with a predicament as dire as any situation in which their ability to write or say the same thing is suppressed.

As a final note on the applicability of freedom of expression in American education, it must be pointed out that First Amendment rights in schools and colleges are not just a matter of concern affecting students involved with their campus newspapers, yearbooks, magazines, radio stations, and television stations. The same challenges to freedom of expression face those students involved in producing plays for campus theatre, dance reviews, musical concerts, cheerleading routines, slogans for student government elections . . . even projects as simple as designing a T-shirt for a club, putting up flyers to promote a new class, and even texting, tweeting or posting on Facebook comments or descriptions of what happened on the campus quad that day. These challenges not only face students, but also any faculty or staff members who were involved in advising or setting policy for students.

BACKGROUND

Some constitutional scholars have argued that the First Amendment was written so simply—just forty-five words—to make sure there could be no misunderstanding that freedom of expression applies to every American, regardless of which Americans are expressing themselves. However, one of the early challenges that freedom of student expression faced as a legal concept was that formal education offered by schools and universities of America is nowhere directly addressed in the U. S. Constitution. It was left up to states to determine rules for formal education. As in most states, early formal education in Louisiana was dominated by individual tutors and small private schools. It was not until the adoption of the state constitution of 1845 that incentive was provided for establishing public schools in the state, and the appointment was made of the first official public school superintendent.

This is an important distinction because the First Amendment provides for protection of free expression from the government, not from individuals as in a private situation. Today, if an individual is prevented from taking a picture with a mobile phone by a police officer, a First Amendment right may have been violated. However, if another individual orders the person to stop taking pictures or even snatches away the phone, the charge of harassment or theft could be appropriate, but it is not a First Amendment violation. In the same manner, students enrolled in a private school under the supervision of a teacher engaging in such an action could probably not make a claim of a First Amendment violation and would more than likely be hard-pressed to show that their own actions were justified because they are students.

After public schools were created, the concept that came to dominate legal thinking was not a strict interpretation of the First Amendment, but a doctrine known as *in loco parentis*, a Latin phrase meaning, "in the place of a parent." The doctrine provides the reasoning that in the absence of the parent, the responsibility in all situations for making decisions for the good of the student lies in the hands of the teacher, or anyone appointed by school authorities. In regard to expressing ideas, *in loco parentis* has been often used as the justification for censorship, prior restraint, and compelled speech when students are involved. As early as 1859, this was the logic used to justify why an eleven-year-old student living in Vermont was beaten by his schoolmaster because the student spoke to the schoolmaster in what was considered a disrespectful manner even though the speech took place after school off campus (*Lander v. Seaver*, 1859). By the 1930s, in loco parentis was still very much in vogue, as the Reveille Seven found out very painfully.

It was in this legal environment that the U.S. Supreme Court took on its first case that directly involved students' freedom of expression. The students lost. In the 1940 case of *Minersville, Pa. v. Gobitis*, a seventh-grader and a fifth-grader refused to salute the flag and recite the Pledge of Allegiance as they were told to do by their father, who was acting upon a directive by leaders of their religious group, the Jehovah's Witnesses. Minersville had a school district policy making it a requirement for students to recite the Pledge of Allegiance, and the students were expelled for refusing to comply. The children's father took the matter to court and succeeded at the lower levels, but the Supreme Court ruled in an 8-1 decision that requiring the pledge was a reasonable form of compelled speech intended to instill in students a strong sense of allegiance to the United States. Alluding indirectly to the old constitutional question of state responsibility for formal education, the court ruled in its opinion that it would not serve as "the school board for the country" (*Minersville v. Gobitis*, 1940).

Students Become Recognized as Citizens

Just three years after *Gobitis*, a similar case of school children refusing to recite the Pledge of Allegiance made its way to the U.S. Supreme Court, but this time the students prevailed. In the 1943 case of *West Virginia v. Barnette*, two elementary school girls had refused to recite the pledge as directed by their father and by their background as Jehovah's Witnesses. During the three previous years the argument that the *Gobitis* decision was based largely on religious grounds had gained proponents, and even three of the Supreme Court justices who had a vote in the *Gobitis* decision publicly acknowledged their misgivings about their decision (Peterson, 2007). In *Barnette*, justices ruled in a 6-3 decision that refusal to recite the pledge was itself a form of free speech, and to require recitation of the pledge and/or a hand salute was unconstitutional.

The *Barnette* decision is also important in that it makes clear that violations of the

First Amendment in a public school are not permissible as state actions. The Fourteenth Amendment specifically refers to "equal protection" from government action, regardless of whether the government is a federal, state, or local unit. Even though the Fourteenth Amendment was passed in 1868, it was not until the 1925 case of *Gitlow v. New York* this principle was interpreted to mean the First Amendment's guarantee of free speech applied to the states as well as the federal government. *Barnette* showed that the First Amendment also applied to public schools through the Fourteenth Amendment (*Barnette v. West Virginia*, 1943).

Fourteen years after the *Barnette* decision, student freedom of expression rights received a boost from another Supreme Court decision, *Sweezy v. New Hampshire*. The decision in *Sweezy* is often not referred to as a student rights case because the decision involved a college professor who refused to answer questions about his lectures, and was charged with contempt by a state attorney general that was investigating allegations of subversive activities by the professor. Sweezy prevailed in the Supreme Court, and a statement on academic freedom by Chief Justice Earl Warren in support of *Sweezy* is frequently cited as championing student free expression. "Teachers and students must always remain free to inquire, to study and to evaluate, to gain new maturity and understanding; otherwise our civilization will stagnate and die" (*Sweezy v. New Hampshire*, 1957).

First Amendment scholars usually consider a 1969 Supreme Court decision, *Tinker v. Des Moines*, as the true beginning of student free expression in America. This time, instead of a situation involving compelled speech with overtones of religious freedom, censorship of students' political expression was the central issue. Three secondary school children wore black armbands to school as their way of symbolically protesting America's involvement in the Vietnam War. The students were told to remove their armbands and were suspended and sent home for having worn them. The students sued the school and proceeded to lose in lower courts mainly on the basis of the *in loco parentis* doctrine, but the Supreme Court agreed to take on the case and ruled in a 7–2 decision that the students' First Amendment right was violated.

The significance of the *Tinker* decision is twofold. First, by ruling in the students' favor, the Court set the precedent that students are full-fledged citizens in the eyes of the law, and thus in loco parentis was not an acceptable logic for the denial of students' civil rights for their own good: "It can hardly be argued that either students or teachers shed their constitutional rights to freedom of speech and expression at the schoolhouse gate" (*Tinker v. Des Moines*, 1969). The *Barnette* decision is generally accepted as the first time in American history that the country's highest court equated First Amendment rights with high school students, but Frank LoMonte, Adam Goldstein, and Michael Hiestand of the Student Press Law Center argue that it is the *Tinker* decision that is "the true landmark in defining students' free expression rights" (Student Press Law Center, p. 26). In *Barnette* it was found that school administrators could not force students to pledge their allegiance to the government, but it was in *Tinker* that the Court ruled that there was a limit as to what a school administrator could do to prevent students from expressing themselves in general.

Second, the *Tinker* decision provided a rationale for when censorship can be justified—only when a disruption is substantial and material. Somewhat similar to Oliver Wendell Holmes's "clear and present danger" reasoning, the *Tinker* standard for censorship makes clear that school officials cannot censor students simply because they disagree with their views or that their views may inspire arguments; to justify censorship, prior restraint or compelled speech, a school official, not the student, must present facts to show that a student's expression will create a disturbance that will halt learning and undermine the educational process (*Tinker*). Thus, students, just like any other citizens, have a legal right to express themselves peacefully, no matter if it is in school and during the school day. Students' views do not have to be approved in some formal manner by school administrators or faculty.

The *Tinker* decision ushered in an era during the 1970s when student free expression reached a high point. The *Tinker* standard was shown to apply to student media coverage, student government actions, student plays, glee club singing, cheerleading routines, and dress codes.

However, a 1974 book, *Captive Voices*, showed that despite the *Tinker* decision, censorship was still almost routine in American secondary schools. This development led that same year to the creation of an advocacy center for students based in Washington, D.C., the Student Press Law Center. The SPLC provides legal assistance to students who face unlawful censorship, and among its most valuable resources are its own website, splc.org, which provides students with free expert advice, a magazine, and a book the SPLC publishes, *Law of the Student Press*, that was in its 4th edition by 2013. Early on in its history, the SPLC made its mark with the 1977 case of *Gambino v. Fairfax*, in which the Fourth Circuit Court upheld the right of a student to publish a high school newspaper article on contraception and sexually active students. SPLC staff represented the student in this case, and the court ruled that because the newspaper was clearly a forum of expression, the students' First Amendment rights were guaranteed (*Gambino v. Fairfax*, 1977).

On the college level a similar trend of expansion of free expression rights took place. In 1971, the 26th Amendment to the U. S. Constitution was adopted, which gave voting rights in all elections to all citizens eighteen years old and older. Because nearly all college students are at least age eighteen, it could no longer be argued that students attending institutions of higher education were not adults or were not fully invested in the political process.

In 1972 the U. S. Supreme Court accepted its first-ever case involving college student expression. In *Healy v. James*, students organizing a chapter of the Students for Democratic Society were denied recognition because the group had been associated with civil disobedience and in some cases violent action on other campuses. Fresh off the *Tinker* decision, the Court ruled that to deny the students official status as a campus organization was a form of prior restraint. The threat of a substantial and material disruption caused by an SDS affiliation was not supported, and thus the denial of recognition amounted to a violation of the First Amendment (*Healy v. James*, 1972).

In 1973 the first case involving a student publication reached the U.S. Supreme Court, *Papish v. Board of Curators*. The publication was a college student newspaper at the University of Missouri. Controversy was at the heart of the dispute. The paper, *The Free Press Underground*, was not an official campus student publication; the student distributing it, Barbara Papish, was a graduate student who was on academic probation, and the issue of the paper in question contained a front page editorial cartoon depicting police officers raping the Statue of Liberty and the Goddess of Justice and an article inside the paper under the headline, "Motherfucker Acquitted." Papish was expelled for her actions. Basing its logic on the decisions in *Tinker* and *Healy*, the Court reversed lower court rulings and ruled that Papish's actions were a legitimate exercise of her First Amendment right in that they did not cause a disruption in university activities: ". . . The mere dissemination of ideas—no matter how offensive to good taste—on a state university campus may not be shut off in the name alone of 'conventions of decency'" (*Papish v. Board of Curators*, 1973).

In determining whether a disruption can necessitate censorship, prior restraint, or compelled speech, school officials usually must consider three aspects of any situation: 1) the age of the speaker and the audience, 2) the location of the speech, and 3) educators' responsibilities (Hopkins, 2014). The 26th Amendment and the *Healy* and *Papish* decisions make clear that administrators must meet a heavy burden to justify any restrictions placed on the free expression rights of college students.

An interesting decision by Louisiana courts based on actions in the late 1970s illustrates how educators' responsibilities in such disputes can serve to support the prohibition of censorship. In *Milliner v. Turner* (1983), three students at Southern University of New Orleans were found guilty of libel by a trial court for their articles that defamed two professors that appeared in the *SUNO Observer* newspaper. The professors also sued SUNO for not providing faculty supervision to the student newspaper in order to prevent the publishing of the defamatory statements. In 1983 a state appeals court decided to leave the libel judgment against the students intact but dismissed the professors' suit against SUNO on the basis that if SUNO did provide supervision, it would have been tantamount to censorship (*Milliner v. Turner*, 1983). Thus, the best protection for the university against the irresponsible actions of its students was to allow the students to have their First Amendment rights. *Milliner* shows that administrators and teachers who feel that it is always in the best interests of their schools to exercise strong control of their students' activities are using flawed logic.

Student Rights Begin to Erode

During the mid-1980s, the trend toward expansion of student free expression rights came to a halt as a highly influential presidential commission report, "A Nation at Risk: The Imperative for Educational Reform," turned into a landmark event in American history. Among the report's recommendations were a general scaling back on academic freedom and the strengthening of disciplinary measures. Few of the report's specific recommendations for reform eventually became enacted, but politically the report's influence is felt to this day.

Symbolic of this era was the adoption of the National Drinking Age Act, which set the minimum drinking age at twenty-one, and any states not in compliance with the act were punished by having their federal highway funds cut. A popular argument used at the time by students who opposed the Act was "If you're old enough to vote or die in a war, you should be old enough to drink a beer." While logically flawed, the argument underscored the loss of recognition that adulthood started at age eighteen, which an earlier generation had fought hard to achieve with the passage of the 26th Amendment.

In 1986 the first of what would turn out to be a series of exceptions to the *Tinker* Standard was generated in the case of *Bethel v. Fraser*. In this decision a student in charge of a high school classmate's campaign for Student Government Association president delivered a humorous speech at a school assembly that contained references to sexual behavior using words full of double meanings but not vulgar per se. The student was suspended, and when he sued for violation of his free speech rights, he prevailed at both the U.S. district and circuit court levels mainly on the basis that his speech was not disruptive. But the Supreme Court reversed, finding that censorship of students is allowed if the communication can be interpreted as lewd and offensive, regardless of whether it was disruptive (*Bethel v. Fraser*, 1986).

Just two years later the first case involving a student newspaper on the high school level was decided by the U.S. Supreme Court, *Hazelwood v. Kuhlmeier*. Again the *Tinker* standard's non-disruption rule was used by students to justify their actions, this time involving articles students wrote on teen pregnancy and children of divorced parents for their school newspaper, *Spectrum*, at Hazelwood East High School. The articles were journalistically strong in that they addressed very real concerns and were not laced with humor and poor taste as in *Bethel*, but the school principal prevented the articles from being published in the newspaper based on the reasoning that discussion of such controversial topics was not appropriate. The students sued, lost on the district level, but prevailed on the circuit level based on the *Tinker* standard. However, the Supreme Court ruled in a 5-3 decision against the students, reasoning that the *Tinker* standard did not apply and that the principal was justified in practicing censorship and prior restraint in this case (*Hazelwood v. Kuhlmeier*, 1988).

Not only was *Hazelwood* the first-ever decision by the high court to involve a high school newspaper, but also the case was the first to involve a school-sponsored publication on any level, and this aspect is the key to the Supreme Court's reasoning. The *Spec-

trum newspaper was produced as an official activity of a journalism class, and there was no attempt at the school to establish the paper as a public forum. In such a situation, the Court reasoned, it is possible the public could perceive the newspaper's production as being an official part of the curriculum. Thus censorship is acceptable for "legitimate pedagogical concerns," and it is a violation of the First Amendment only when it is conducted for "no valid educational purpose" (*Hazelwood v. Kuhlmeier*, 1988). Since the late 1980s, most cases that go to court involving student media and questions of student freedom of expression involve a determination of whether *Hazelwood* or the *Tinker* standard will be used to judge the merits of the arguments. The following three-part test developed by the Student Press Law Center (2013) is a good guide to understanding which standard will likely be used:

1) Can the publication be considered school-sponsored—has the school lent its name and resources to the publication? A "yes" answer to this question is support for use of the *Hazelwood* standard because school officials would have strong input into determining what is educational value. A "no" answer would support the *Tinker* standard because in such a setup students would be more likely to make most decisions.

2) Can the publication be described as a part of the school curriculum—was it created by the school to impart particular skills to students, and is it supervised by a faculty member, even if it is produced outside the classroom setting? A "yes" answer would be consistent with the *Hazelwood* standard because it would be assumed that the curriculum and the faculty member are focused on teaching a lesson. A "no" answer would be more consistent with the *Tinker* approach to learning by discovery and involvement.

3) Has the publication, by either school policy or practice, been created as a "public forum" or a "designated public forum" for student expression where students have been given the authority to make content decisions? A "yes" answer to this question would be the clearest endorsement of the *Tinker* standard since a policy or tradition in the school would indicate a school's commitment to student expression. A "no" answer would imply support for the Hazelwood standard restricting student freedom of expression.

Over the ensuing years articles published in *Journalism and Mass Communication Quarterly*, *Journalism and Mass Communication Educator*, *Student Press Law Center Reports*, and *Communication: Journalism Education Today* (C:JET) detailed the devastating effect the *Hazelwood* decision has had. Student rights groups have reacted by proposing state legislation protecting students' free expression, known as anti-*Hazelwood* laws. Such state laws stipulate that educational validity cannot be used as the legal logic in a First Amendment case within a state with such a law, and even though *Hazelwood* is a Supreme Court decision, such a state law is legally sound because it is intended to strengthen, not weaken, students' First Amendment protection (Hiestand, 2001).

California had such a law in place before *Hazelwood*, and since then Arkansas, Colorado, Iowa, Kansas, Massachusetts, and Oregon have enacted such laws. California has gone further with the adoption of the Journalism Student Protection Act of 2006 and the Journalism Teacher Protection Act of 2008, which make it illegal to discipline either a student for engaging in free speech activity, or a teacher for aiding a student engaging in free speech activity.

Louisiana is considered a *Hazelwood* state in that it has no such anti-*Hazelwood* law, and thus the valid educational reasoning will prevail in a student expression dispute. While some other states have at least attempted to pass such bills in their legislatures, the full Louisiana legislature has never considered such a law.

Despite anti-*Hazelwood* laws, the trend against student expression rights has continued. In 2007 the U.S. Supreme Court took on two school free-expression cases, and students lost in both. In *Harper v. Poway* (2007), a student was suspended for wearing a T-shirt containing a reference to the Bible intended as a demonstration of opposition to gay rights; he sued for a violation of his First Amendment rights, and the Court ruled the censorship was justified because the T-shirt was offensive. In *Morse v. Frederick* (2007), a student was suspended for holding a banner off-campus, "Bong Hits 4 Jesus," and the

Court ruled that censorship was justified because the banner could be seen as promoting drug abuse.

The effect of the *Hazelwood* decision has been felt on the college level. It was initially seen as a case confined to high school matters largely because of the public forum question, but in a footnote to the decision, the Court noted, "We need not now decide whether the same degree of deference is appropriate with respect to school-sponsored activities at the college and university level" (*Hazelwood v. Kuhlmeier*, p. 274, fn7). The *Hazelwood* logic has been used in two cases to reach U.S. circuit courts. In *Kincaid v. Gibson* (2001), the student yearbook at Eastern Kentucky University was censored, and after student staff members sued, a district court ruled in favor of the administration on the basis that *Hazelwood* gave the university the right to censor; however, the students appealed to the Sixth Circuit, which rejected the *Hazelwood* standard and ruled for the students.

Just four years after *Kincaid*, in *Hosty v. Carter* (2005), the student newspaper at Governor's State University was prevented from printing whole issues after previously publishing articles critical of the administration. Students sued to have this form of prior restraint declared a violation of their First Amendment rights and won on the district level, but in Seventh Circuit Court the administration prevailed on the court's reasoning that the *Hazelwood* standard could be applied on the college level.

It remains an open question as to whether or not the *Hazelwood* standard will be used if a college case does reach the Supreme Court in the future. As for schools in Louisiana, it is highly likely the *Hazelwood* standard will be used to determine the outcome if a high school case reaches the federal Fifth Circuit, but there has been little indication to show whether or not the judges will apply the *Hazelwood* standard if a lawsuit brought by college or university students reaches the circuit court level. In 2007 Grambling State University students chose to cease publication of their school newspaper, *The Gramblinite*, as a protest against their administration's assertion that university officials had the right to suspend the newspaper based on the *Hosty* decision (Taylor, 2007).

Dress Codes

Courts have shown an inclination to side with the decisions of school boards and PTAs that offer ample opportunities for parents to share in the decision on what clothing students can wear in school. In Louisiana, ample statutory law exists that has not been found in conflict with the First Amendment.

According to Louisiana state law, local school boards have the legal right to create dress codes and to set up rules for wearing required uniforms (La. Rev. Stat. Ann. §17:416.7). Directives on what not to wear and, in the case of required uniforms, what must be worn have been upheld as long as parents are given advance notice and as long as the directives are consistent with the educational mission of the school.

The decision in *Tinker* is one of the few rulings issued by the Supreme Court in a matter focusing on what a student can wear, although the black armbands the students were wearing that day amounted to political expression related to matters happening outside the school as opposed to an everyday dress code policy.

Just three years before the final *Tinker* ruling was issued, a similar case involving political expression, *Burnside v. Byars* (1966), was decided by the Fifth Circuit, which is the highest federal appeals court that rules on cases originating in Louisiana other than the U.S. Supreme Court. Mrs. Margaret Burnside was one of three parents whose children were students at Booker T. Washington High School in Philadelphia, Mississippi, and had been suspended for wearing "freedom buttons" that contained the words, "One Man One Vote" to protest racial segregation. The parents argued that their children's freedom of expression rights were abridged by the school's action, and they prevailed over the objections of school authorities who maintained that the buttons amounted to a disruptive action.

Thirty years after *Tinker*, another black armband case was reviewed by the federal district court of Louisiana, Western District. Jennifer Roe and three classmates at Parkway High School in Bossier City wore black ribbons on their arms as a form of protest against a uniform policy that was recently approved for the school. The principal told the students to remove the armbands because they were in violation of the uniform policy. According to the American Civil Liberties Union of Louisiana, the Parkway principal even told Roe and her parents that the *Tinker* decision was of no concern (ACLU). With the support of the ACLU, Roe sued for her right to wear the ribbon and prevailed.

Litigation was later brought against the Bossier Parish School Board over the legality of the uniform policy Roe and her classmates protested. This time the School Board prevailed in both the federal district and circuit court levels. The Fifth Circuit found the uniform policy was not a violation of students' First Amendment rights because it was "viewpoint-neutral," and was not intended to censor students' ability to express themselves through the clothing they wore (*Canady v. Bossier Parish School Board*, 2001).

In regard to recent controversies over male students wearing sagging pants, a non-Louisiana lower court ruling is instructive. In *Bivens v. Albuquerque Schools* (1995), a New Mexico court ruled that the wearing of sagging pants that may or may not bring one's underwear into view could be banned because it was more of a fashion statement instead of protected free speech.

However, the debate over dress codes and uniform policies continues. More recently, in the case of *Frudden v. Pilling* (2014), the Ninth Circuit ruled that forcing students attending a Nevada school to wear a school-approved motto is an unconstitutional form of compelled speech if the school dress code already makes exceptions for other recognized groups like the Boy Scouts.

Violence Concerns

The *Tinker* disruption standard and the *Bethel* offensive speech standard are usually cited as the starting points for legal consideration on the limits of student comments that refer to violent actions. However, because of heightened concerns stemming from high-profile violent incidents at Columbine, Colorado, and Newtown, Connecticut, even joking about violence has become a touchy subject in schools, and educators have adopted a "rather be safe than sorry" attitude. Students traveling on school trips see something of this attitude at airports with signs erected by Transportation Security Administration (TSA) warning against making humorous comments about bombs or weapons even though there are no federal laws making jokes illegal.

The key word in a situation involving students' comments on violence is *threat*; specifically, can the comments that are the cause for concern be clearly considered a credible threat? In order to meet this standard, courts usually rely on a judgment of whether a reasonable person would interpret the comments to be a legitimate threat or safety concern, and also decided whether the intent of the comments could be interpreted as threatening. As found by the Supreme Court in the *Brandenburg v. Ohio* (1969) case, citizens can be censored or punished for intentionally trying to incite "imminent lawless action."

The more recent concern related to violence and free expression is cyber-bullying. As defined by Louisiana state law, cyber-bullying is the sending of an electronic textual, visual, written, or oral communication with the malicious and willful intent to coerce, abuse, torment, or intimidate a person under age eighteen (La. Rev. Stat. Ann. §14:40.7). The communication must have been transmitted through a computer on-line network or Internet service, and it can include emails, chat rooms, electronic bulletin boards and text service. The law was amended to include among other things, blogs and social networking sites (La. Rev. Stat. Ann. §17:416.13).

Under state law, all Louisiana schools supported by public funds must have rules on the conditions and penalties involved with cyber-bullying. Schools are authorized to restrict electronic communication on-campus, but electronic communication that originates off-campus on a home computer on the student's own time may not necessarily be restricted.

Concern over a student's violent expression that was the subject of a 2004 case in Louisiana is worth close examination. In 1999, the same year that the massacre at Columbine High School occurred, a fourteen-year-old boy was at home when he crafted a drawing in a sketch pad of his school, East Ascension High School in Gonzales. The sketch contained images that made the school look like it was under armed attack, with profane words and disparaging remarks about the high school's principal. He showed it to his mother and his younger brother, and then placed the sketch pad in a closet in the family's home. Two years later the boy's younger brother found the same sketch pad and decided to use a blank page in the pad to draw a llama for his teacher. While riding on the school bus the younger brother allowed a fellow student to look through the pad. The student showed the pad to the bus driver and remarked, "They're going to blow up EAHS" (*Porter v. Ascension Parish Sch. Bd.*, 2004).

The boy who drew the sketch was by the time of the trial sixteen years old, and admitted that he drew it. When officials searched him, they found a half-inch blade in his wallet, a fake ID, and notebooks that had remarks about death, drugs, sex, and gangs in his book sack. He was arrested on a terrorism charge and jailed for four days in Donaldsonville, Louisiana. To avoid expulsion, his mother agreed to enroll the boy in an alternative school program.

His mother later sued the school board, arguing her son's First Amendment rights were violated, along with his Fourth and Eighth Amendment rights to freedom from unreasonable search and excessive punishment. The blade he had was a box cutter he used in his job at a local store, and he explained that the remarks on death were related to a school assignment and the gang remarks were symbols that depicted a group of students not considered a threat in the school. A federal district court ruled for the school board on all counts, and held that his drawing was not protected by the First Amendment. The Fifth Circuit affirmed the district court's ruling, but in reference to the First Amendment claim, the circuit court found that the drawing did not amount to a "true threat" because the drawing was not created on campus, and it was not intended to be brought to campus. Thus, an expressive action like a drawing that deals with violence is less likely to be considered a threat if it is brought to campus by someone who did not create the drawing. The circuit court ruled that it could not agree with the district court that a First Amendment violation did not occur, but because of the potential of violent actions, mistakes made in the name of safety in such uncertain situations are understandable, so school authorities deserve "qualified immunity" from being held responsible for denying freedom of expression to a student (*Porter v. Ascension Parish Sch. Bd.*, 2004).

Private Schools

By enrolling at a private school, students and/or their parents enter into a contractual agreement to abide by the rules of the private school. The obligation of legal contracts in Article I of the U.S. Constitution, not the First Amendment, is applicable in this situation. Thus, it is unconstitutional censorship when government does not allow citizens to express themselves, but it is not a First Amendment violation when parents agree, as in a private school arrangement, to suspend the free expression rights of their children. The situation is similar to when an editor of a newspaper changes the wording of a reporter's article or even decides to keep the article out of the newspaper; this action is called editing or editorial judgment and is not censorship. The best chances students have for legal recourse are on the occasions when their student publications or broadcast activities are hampered by the administrators of their private schools is to consult their schools' official guidelines for student publications and broadcast operations and/or seek official public forum status.

Broadcast

Like any professional or commercial radio or TV station, a student broadcast station must adhere to the terms of the station's Federal Communications Commission license. Students who organize a program or go on the air individually for a local radio or TV station or on a local access channel on a cable system are not necessarily engaged in public forum activities. The conditions set by the station or cable system take precedence, and these in turn are affected by the terms of FCC licenses and the federal Cable Acts.

SPEECH CODES AND ASSEMBLY

Usually the reasonableness of time, place, and manner restrictions are at issue when students organize free-speech activities of a non-journalistic nature, such as LSU's half-century-old free speech alley, or timely events, such as the student boycotts led by football players to protest university budget cuts at Grambling in Fall 2013. When controversies occur, according to the Foundation for Individual Rights in Education (FIRE), often the result is a situation whereby school officials are involved in unconstitutional viewpoint discrimination, and students are punished for speech that is not "politically correct" or just disagrees with the school's or college's official position.

A leading common law precedent in this area is a district court ruling, *Doe v. Michigan* (1989), which showed that when a school sets up a speech code, however well intentioned, it must not be overly broad (1989). A ban on hate speech in general will likely not pass constitutional muster, but codes banning harassment or supporting diversity mandates are legally stronger. An instructive Louisiana case in this area is *Sonnier v. Crain* (2010). In *Sonnier*, Southeastern Louisiana University's speech code restricted free speech activities to two hours per week with advance notice (time), at three pre-selected campus areas (place), required an application asking for personal identification information (manner), and charged a security fee for engaging in the speech activity. The U.S. Fifth Circuit found the first three restrictions acceptable but ruled that the fee was an unconstitutional violation of free speech.

In regard to activities of a school's extracurricular clubs, student organizations at public schools and colleges cannot be prohibited from using campus facilities for meetings if the school already allows non-school organizations to meet on the campus, as stipulated in the federal Equal Access Act of 1984. Access must be allowed for any groups regardless of the political or religious character if any non-school groups have already had access. In addition, the *Healy* decision shows that schools and universities have the ability to mandate rules for recognition of student organizations but cannot use the rules as a form of prior restraint. The limits of recognition and access were explored by the Louisiana Supreme Court in *Board of Supervisors of La. State Univ. v. Lewark* (1973). On the campus of LSU at New Orleans, now known as the University of New Orleans, two students formed a group known as the Revolutionary Communist Youth and were selling newspapers, newsletters, books, and pamphlets promoting communism. A university staff member told them to stop the sale of their publications, and the students sued, charging that their freedom of expression rights had been violated. The two students had never applied for official recognition as a campus organization and were the only members of the organization. On this basis the court ruled that prohibiting them from using campus facilities and selling their publications was not a violation of the students' constitutional rights.

CONCLUSION

The freedom of expression guaranteed to all American citizens is affected by conditions in schools, and has been substantiated by cases involving student speech, student newspapers, and student protests. The most important standard came from *Tinker v. Des Moines Independent School District* that placed the burden on the administration to show how the expression posed a substantial and material disruption to learning activities.

The 26th Amendment to the Constitution makes it clear that courts must draw a separation between the free speech rights of college students and the free speech rights of high school students. The *Hazelwood v. Kuhlmeier* decision, which relied on educators' determination of what are educational values, is the reigning standard in most cases involving high school students, but the *Tinker* standard is more often applied in cases involving college students and in states where the *Hazelwood* standard is not recognized.

Students enrolled in private schools do not have the same freedom of express rights as public schools students. Based on Article I of the Constitution, an individual school's policy will take precedence in most legal decision involving private school students.

Censorship may be legally justified in situations wherein a substantial disruption occurred (*Tinker*), when lewd and offensive speech was used (*Bethel*), when educational values are in question (*Hazelwood*), when a consistent anti-drug abuse message is not communicated (*Morse*).

Schools operating broadcast stations must be approved for a license from the Federal Communications Commission, and the stipulations contained in the license must be adhered to in the activities of the station.

Time, place, and manner restrictions are usually at the center of an issue when students engage in free speech activities of a non-journalistic nature. Campus speech codes contain these restrictions.

Students accused of inciting violence as part of a protest activity must exercise care to make sure their speech is not to be interpreted as a credible threat.

REFERENCES

Aiello, T. (2012), "Violence Is A Classroom: The 1972 Grambling and Southern Riots and the Trajectory of Black Southern Student Protest" in *Louisiana History*, Summer 2012, 53:3.

American Civil Liberties Union of Louisiana (1999), "ACLU Challenges Louisiana School's Ban on Armbands as Violation of Students' First Amendment Rights," press release, 1 November 1999, available at https://www.aclu.org/free-speech/aclu-challenges-louisiana-schools-ban-armbands-violation-students-first-amendment-rights.

Barnette v. West Virginia State Board of Education 319 U.S. 624 (1943).

Bethel School District v. Fraser, 106 S.Ct. 3159 (1986).

Bivens v. Albuquerque Schools, 899 F.Supp. 556 (D. N.M., 1995).

Board of Supervisors of La. State Univ. v. Lewark, 277 So. 2d 441 (1973).

Brandenburg v. Ohio, 395 U.S. 444, 447 (1969).

Burnside v. Byers, 363 F. 2d 744 (5th Circuit, 1966).

Canady v. Bossier Parish School Board, 249 F. 3d 437 (5th Circuit, 2001).

Cox v. Louisiana, 379 U.S. 536 (1965).

Doe v. University of Michigan, 721 F. Supp. 852 (E. D. Mich., 1989).

Frudden v. Pilling (9th Circuit, 2014) http://cdn.ca9.uscourts.gov/datastore/opinions/2014/02/14/ 1215403.pdf.

Gambino v. Fairfax, 564 F.2d 157 (1977).

Garay, R. (2009), *The Manship School*, Baton Rouge: LSU Press.

Harper v. Poway Unified School District, 127 S. Ct. 1484 (2007).

Hazelwood v. Kuhlmeier, 108 S.Ct. 562 (1988).

Healy v. James, 408 U.S. 169 (1972).

Hentoff, N. "They're Stealing the First Amendment," *Cherokee Herald*, 11 August 1993.

Hiestand, M. (2001), "Understanding anti-Hazelwood laws" in *Trends in High School Media*, January 2001, published by the National Scholastic Press Association and available at http://www.studentpress.org/nspa/trends/~law0101hs.html.

Hopkins, W., ed. (2014) *Communication and the Law*, Northport: Vision Press.

Hosty v. Carter, 412 F.3d 731 (7th Circuit, 2005).

Jenkins v. Louisiana State Board of Education, 506 F. 2d 992 (5th Circuit, 1975).

Kincaid v. Gibson, 236 F. 3d 342 (6th Circuit, 2001).

Lander v. Seaver 32 Vt. 114 (1859). Supreme Court Judge Clarence Thomas referred to this decision in a ruling in 2007.

La. Rev. Stat. Ann. §14:40.7(A).

La. Rev. Stat. Ann. §17:416.7(A).

La. Rev. Stat. Ann. §17:416.13(C)(1)(b).

Milliner v. Turner, 430 So. 2d 1300 (1983).

Minersville v. Gobitis, 310 U.S. 586 (1940).

Morse v. Frederick, 127 S.Ct. 2618 (2007).

Papish v. Board of Curators of the University of Missouri, 410 U.S. 667 (1973).

Peterson, G. (2007), Recollections of the *West Virginia State Board of Education v. Barnette*, St. John's Law Review, 81:4, pp. 9-10.

Porter v. Ascension Parish Sch. Bd., 393 F. 3d 608 (2004).

Sonnier v. Crain, 613 F. 3d 436 (5th Circuit, 2010).

State of Louisiana v. Morice (D, La., 21st Judicial District for Tangipahoa Parish, 1994).

Student Press Law Center (2013) *Law of the Student Press*, 4th ed., Arlington, Va.: Student Press Law Center.

Sunne, S. (2013) "Amid outcry, Grambling State University student newspaper editors' suspensions overturned," Student Press Law Center, http://www.splc.org/news/newsflash.asp?id=2623.

Sweezy v. New Hampshire, 354 U.S. 234, 250 (1957).

Taylor, J. (2007) "Grambling State student paper elects to shut down for fear of adviser termination," Student Press Law Center, http://www.splc.org/news/newsflash.asp?id=1415.

Tinker v. Des Moines, 393 U.S. 503 (1969).

RESOURCES

American Civil Liberties Union of Louisiana, 1340 Poydras Street, P.O. Box 56157, New Orleans, LA 70156, phone: 504-522-0617, website: www.laaclu.org. This state branch of the nationwide organization investigates complaints concerning denial of students' civil rights, serves s an advocate for students and their families, publishes a newsletter, provides on-line reports of complaints and legal developments and provides an on-line guide to student rights in Louisiana. The executive director of the ACLU of Louisiana is Marjorie Esman.

Foundation for Individual Rights in Education (FIRE), 170 S. Independence Mall W. Suite 510, Philadelphia, Pa. 19106, phone: 215-717-3473, website: www.thefire.org. This non-profit organization defends students and faculty rights and documents incidents of violations of free speech nationwide. The president of FIRE is Greg Lukianoff.

Journalism Education Association, 103 Kedzie Hall, Kansas State University, Manhattan, KS 66506-1505, phone: 866-532-5532, website: www.jea.org. This non-profit organization sponsors annual national conventions and competitions for high school students and provides resources for teachers. Executive director is Kelly Furnas.

National Scholastic Press Association/Associated Collegiate Press, 221 University Ave. SE, Suite 121, Minneapolis, MN 55414, phone: 612-625-8335, website: www.studentpress.org. This non-profit organization sponsors annual national conventions and competitions for both high school students and college students and provides resources for teachers. Executive director is Diana Mitsu Klos.

Student Press Law Center (SPLC), 1101 Wilson Blvd., Suite 1100, Arlington, Va. 22209-2275, phone: 703-807-1904, website: www.student.org. This non-profit, non-partisan organization serves as an advocate of student free expression rights. It provides legal assistance, classroom resources and even help with term papers and other homework assignments dealing with aspects of the First Amendment. Executive director is Frank LoMonte.

Chapter 7
Courts and Media
By S. L. Alexander, Loyola University, New Orleans

Learning objectives

In this chapter, readers will:
- understand increasing importance of free press/fair trial concerns in the United States
- learn current issues including prejudicial publicity, grand juries, access to proceedings and records, gag orders, anonymous juries, plea bargains, contempt, civil proceedings, courtroom cameras, and virtual courtrooms
- understand relevant cases in Louisiana, in both federal (District, Fifth Circuit) and state (all levels) courts
- learn past and current developments regarding courts and media in the United States and Louisiana today and to predict possible future trends

On July 5, 2011, a jury rendered a verdict in the case of *Florida v. Casey Marie Anthony*. Anthony, twenty-two, had been tried on charges of the first-degree murder of her two-year-old daughter Caylee. Casey and Caylee were living with Casey's parents in Orlando, Florida, when Casey's mother, Cindy Anthony, reported her granddaughter Caylee missing in July 2008. Five months later, searchers found the child's body in a garbage bag in the woods near the Anthony home.

The case attracted sensationalistic media coverage that resulted in some intervention by the court. There were reports of checkbook journalism in which both tabloid and mainstream media outlets paid potential witnesses for access to their planned evidence, thereby tainting their testimony; manipulation of the press by lawyers for both the prosecution and the defense; and a gag order on participants, forbidding them from talking to the press. The possibility of prejudicial publicity was further enhanced by the Internet, for example, due to demand for documents—twenty-five thousand were posted online by the trial's end. In addition, the growth of social media included thousands of bloggers and tweeters weighing in, with some calling Anthony the most hated woman in America.

At the end of the six-week trial, Casey Anthony was found not guilty on any of the child abuse, manslaughter, or murder charges. She was convicted only of four misdemeanor charges of lying to the police. The verdict came after three years of intense publicity during which Anthony's guilt had seemed certain to so many television viewers. Public outrage over the verdict was widespread, with death threats forcing Casey Anthony into hiding.

In 2012, a bizarre $3 billion civil suit was filed against Anthony for allegedly threatening to kill a Pennsylvania woman; the case was quickly thrown out of court. But a serious defamation suit was also filed against Anthony by a woman she had initially claimed kidnapped Caylee, a nanny named Zenaida (Zanny) Gonzalez, who said she had never met Anthony.

As of early 2013, Anthony's appeal of the misdemeanor convictions had led to the striking of two of the four convictions, and Anthony had filed for bankruptcy. Lifetime TV aired a docudrama *Prosecuting Casey Anthony* starring Rob Lowe, and the "Nanny Zanny" defamation case continued. And bloggers, journalists, legal commentators and academics continued to weigh in on the case that *Time* magazine described as the "social media trial of the century."

TRIALS OF THE CENTURY?

In the hundred years before the Anthony case, at least two dozen trials were considered at various times to be the "trial of the century" in the United States. All of them involved widespread coverage by the press and resulted in intervening orders by the court. Factory owner Leo Frank's conviction in 1913 in Georgia for the murder of one of his pencil-factory employees, little Mary Phagan; the Chicago trial of thrill killers Nathan Leopold and Richard Loeb; and the conviction of Ruth Snyder and her lover Judd Gray for the murder of her husband, (with a 1928 *New York Daily News* photograph of Snyder at the moment she was electrocuted, the only execution photograph ever known to be published in the United States), were all considered early candidates for the title.

The first of three major trials competing for that title was the 1935 prosecution of a German immigrant carpenter Bruno Richard Hauptmann for the kidnap and murder of the baby of pioneer aviator Charles Lindbergh, "Lucky Lindy" (*Hauptmann v. N.J.*). Press coverage of the six-week-long trial was the most extensive in history until that time, with seven hundred reporters and photographers along with thousands of spectators crowded around the courthouse in Flemington, New Jersey. The intensity of the coverage of the case against Hauptmann—who was convicted and executed—and particularly the perceived excesses of the still and newsreel photographers, was cited in support of a ban on courtroom cameras at both the state and federal levels. One such ban was imposed by the American Bar Association in 1937 in its *Canons of Professional and Judicial Ethics*. Then after World War II, congress moved in 1946 to keep cameras out of the federal courtrooms if a criminal trial was in progress. The Federal Rules of Criminal Procedure No. 53 prohibited the "taking of photographs in the courtroom during judicial proceedings or the broadcasting of judicial proceedings from the courtroom."

In the 1950s, a "Cold War" developed in the United States against the Soviet Union, and it led to several political trials involving Americans accused of aiding Communists. The federal cases of the "Hollywood 10," Alger Hiss, and that of Julius and Ethel Rosenberg were three such cases. But it actually was another sensational murder trial that deserves to be called the second trial of the twentieth century.

Sam Sheppard was a Cleveland doctor charged in 1954 with murdering his pregnant wife, and from the day he was arrested until he was convicted, the sensationalistic coverage of the case precluded any chance of a fair trial. Newspapers editorialized about Sheppard's guilt, and the judge exercised no control over the press during the trial itself, with reporters sitting near the jurors in the courtroom and then being allowed to sit right outside the jury room where they could hear the deliberations. The U.S. Supreme Court overturned Sheppard's murder conviction on the grounds of prejudicial publicity (*Sheppard v. Maxwell*, 1966).

At retrial in 1966, Sheppard was acquitted, but he lived only a few years after his release from prison. However, his story lives on in nonfiction and dramatized versions in books, TV series, and movies. The most well known was the 1993 feature film starring Harrison Ford as *The Fugitive*.

The 1970s brought one of the longest trials in U. S. history, when a California cult leader named Charles Manson and several followers he called his "family" were convicted in 1971 of the grisly murders of actress Sharon Tate and three others. Also in California, coverage of a criminal case involving kidnapped heiress Patty Hearst included a live national TV broadcast of a shootout in which six people died.

Then "Watergate," the federal case involving misdeeds in regard to the re-election of President Richard Nixon, held the attention of the country for two years and ended in Nixon's resigning in disgrace.

With the advent of Court TV in 1991, the age of televised criminal trials began in earnest, with three criminal cases reaching a new level of media coverage. In Florida, the rape trial of William Kennedy Smith, a nephew of assassinated president John F. Kennedy, was one of the first trials covered gavel-to-gavel, and although Smith was acquitted, his name remained associated with the case.

In California, excerpts from a videotape showing four white members of the Los Angeles Police Department apparently beating Rodney King, a black drunken-driving suspect fleeing the police, was widely broadcast before their trial in 1992. The jury, however, saw the full tape, which included threatening behavior by King. After a month-long trial, the acquittals of all four officers led to three days of rioting, with thousands of injuries and at least fifty people killed in Los Angeles.

Also in California, the 1994 criminal trials of brothers Erik and Lyle Menendez, charged with murdering their parents, were among the first to be broadcast on Court TV and ended in hung juries. Their retrials were not broadcast, and both Erik and Lyle were convicted and received life sentences.

California is the location of the third trial of the century, one that perhaps could have retired the title for the next one hundred years: the 1995 trial of athlete and actor O.J. Simpson, charged with the murders of his ex-wife and her friend.

Nicole Brown Simpson and Ronald Goldman were murdered in June 1994, and the media obsession with the case began when OJ Simpson became a suspect scheduled for arrest. The famous celebrity drove off in a white Ford Bronco, with TV news helicopters following the police chase that was broadcast for hours on live TV. The subsequent nine-month criminal trial dominated the world's press, and an estimated two thousand representatives of the media set up "Camp OJ" outside the courthouse. Millions of viewers were fixated on the gavel-to-gavel courtroom drama on Court TV and other networks.

To the surprise of many commentators, Simpson was acquitted on the criminal charges; however, a year later in civil court, he was found liable for the two deaths and ordered to pay the victims' families $33.5 million, which he reportedly made little attempt to do. More than one hundred books were written about this so-called trial of the century, which generated TV documentaries and docudramas. As of 2013, Simpson remained in prison in Nevada where he was sent after being convicted in 2008 of armed robbery in an unrelated case, with the earliest possible parole date 2017.

Several other cases received widespread media coverage in the new millennium, including the challenge to the U.S. presidential election recount of 2000 that determined that George W. Bush and not Al Gore should be president. Celebrity cases involving famous names such as athlete Kobe Bryant, singer Michael Jackson, business personality Martha Stewart, and actor Robert Blake also received remarkable publicity. The George Zimmerman "Stand Your Ground" proceedings on trial in Florida for the shooting death of Trayvon Martin in 2012-13 followed the Casey Anthony murder trial to be counted among the more recent cases garnering worldwide media attention.

The Trial of the Century: Louisiana

In Louisiana, the trials of prominent politicians, including those charged with corruption, rival each other for pre-eminence in media coverage. Congressman William ("Dollar Bill") Jefferson of New Orleans began serving a prison sentence in May 2012 after a 2009 corruption conviction. Defense attorneys in that case were of the opinion that a postponement was necessary to prevent prejudicial news coverage, such as reports of frozen cash found hidden in the congressman's freezer. The court disagreed.

Back in the day, a Louisiana case that received worldwide press coverage was the 1969 trial against New Orleans businessman Clay Shaw for his alleged involvement in the assassination of President John F. Kennedy in Dallas in 1963. Although the federal government's Warren Commission had concluded that Lee Harvey Oswald had acted alone in shooting the President, Oswald himself was killed shortly after his arrest, leading to numerous conspiracy theories that exist to the present day.

Since Oswald had spent some time in New Orleans, local district attorney Jim Garrison was especially interested in the case. He charged Clay Shaw with having participated in such a conspiracy, which, according to Garrison's theory, involved not only Oswald but also the CIA, the FBI, anti-Castro Cubans, and the Mafia.

Journalists from around the world converged on New Orleans to cover the proceedings against Shaw. After a month-long trial, the jury spent only an hour deliberating before acquitting Shaw, but Garrison continued to insist until his death in 1992 that Shaw (who had died in 1974, a ruined man) had been part of an assassination conspiracy.

Hundreds of books were written about the JFK case, and numerous documentaries and dramatizations popularized conspiracy theories. One of the most well-known was Oliver Stone's 1991 feature film *JFK*. However, most commentators discredited Garrison for his prosecution of Shaw.

Louisiana is famous for flamboyant politicians who attract widespread media attention. The corruption case against four-time Louisiana governor Edwin W. Edwards in 2000 became noteworthy for both its use of new media and measures taken to protect jurors from extrajudicial forms of evidence. Edwards was the chief of seven defendants in a trial involving thirty-three racketeering and extortion charges in connection with riverboat-casino licensing.

The trial, which began in Baton Rouge in January 2000, was the first major Louisiana trial of the twenty-first century, with docket information posted on the court's Web site, extensive use of audio-taped evidence and documentary evidence posted digitally. There were even computer terminals available for everyone in the courtroom, including jurors and members of the press and public. Convicted on most charges, Edwards would serve nearly ten years in prison. After his release, with his new young wife the eight-four-year-old Edwards was scheduled to co-star in a TV reality show *The Governor's Wife*.

The technological advances of the media in covering Edwards's trial—along with extensive use of traditional means of restricting the press, such as closed proceedings, sealed records, and gag orders forbidding participants to comment publicly—dramatized the need for reconsideration of many of the traditional approaches in attempting to balance an accused's Sixth Amendment right to a fair trial with the First Amendment rights of a free press. These sometimes conflicting concerns have been the subject of U.S. Supreme Court consideration over the past eighty years.

FREE PRESS / FAIR TRIAL

The conflict between the rights protected by First Amendment and those of the Sixth Amendment seem to have been inevitable. According to the First Amendment, Congress should make no law abridging freedom of expression including speech and the press. But the Sixth Amendment allows anyone accused of a crime to a speedy and public trial before an impartial judge or jury.

In one brief period during the mid-twentieth century, the U.S. Supreme Court—charged with interpreting government actions in light of the Constitution—overturned a number of criminal convictions on grounds of prejudicial publicity and ordered new trials be held for defendants. In Oklahoma in 1959, local newspapers reported that a defendant charged with dispensing prescription drugs without a license had been convicted of the same crime twice before, evidence that the judge had ordered kept out of the trial (*Marshall v. U.S.*, 1959), and the Court overturned the conviction.

Three cases were important in terms of establishing the effects of pretrial publicity on a fair trial. In southwest Indiana, the murder conviction of Leslie Irvin, described by the press as "Mad Dog Irvin," was overturned after his connection to six murders became the subject of widespread pretrial publicity that included comments from the district attorney and reports of Irvin's confession to police (*Irvin v. Dowd*, 1960). A 1963 Louisiana case featured a filmed confession to a murder that was televised three times before the defendant's trial (*Rideau v. Louisiana*). Finally, a 1965 swindling case in which a pretrial hearing was carried live on radio and TV required a new trial due to the extensive publicity (*Estes v. Texas*).

The most significant of the trial reversals was the case of *Sheppard v. Maxwell*. In

1954, Dr. Sam Sheppard was convicted on charges of murdering his wife. The egregious publicity included live broadcasts of a three-day pretrial inquest and a debate on the case, as well as a prisoner's claim that she had borne Dr. Sheppard's child. The local newspapers competed to determine who had contributed the most to supporting Sheppard's indictment and conviction. Often overlooked in the reversal of this case is the U.S. Supreme Court's determination that the blame for the prejudicial publicity lay primarily with the judge, and not the press. "A responsible press has always been regarded as the handmaiden of effective judicial administration, especially in the criminal field" (*Sheppard v. Maxwell*, p. 350).

Since *Sheppard*, the Court has rejected several attempts to have convictions overturned on the grounds of prejudicial publicity. These failed efforts include the case of "Murph the Surf" Jack Murphy—who was convicted of stealing the Star of India sapphire from a New York museum—but the jurors learned of other crimes including an unrelated murder case. The robbery conviction was sustained—the last of which he unsuccessfully appealed in *Murphy v. Florida* (1975). A high-school math teacher, John Yount, was convicted of murdering one of his students, and the conviction was upheld in 1984 when the Supreme Court ruled there was no "inherent prejudice in the trial setting or actual prejudice from the jury selection process" (*Patton v. Yount*, p. 803).

Dawud Majid Mu' Min, convicted in two separate murder trials, appealed the second conviction on grounds of prejudicial publicity leading to his first conviction. In *Mu' Min v. Virginia* (1991), the U.S. Supreme Court held that in high-profile cases, as long as a court has overseen a careful jury selection, with potential jurors questioned about their ability to put aside whatever publicity they have been exposed to and consider only the courtroom evidence, there is no grounds to overturn a conviction.

In *U.S. v. Skilling* (2010), Enron CEO Jeffrey Skilling was convicted of conspiracy and fraud, but claimed the trial court should have granted his change-of-venue motion due to extensive media coverage in the company's hometown of Houston. The Court held otherwise: "Prominence does not necessarily produce prejudice, and juror impartiality, we have reiterated, does not require ignorance" (*U.S. v. Skilling*, p. 2915). The Court sent back the *Skilling* verdict to the appeals court on other grounds, but the conviction was upheld. Skilling at this writing was serving a twenty-four-year prison sentence.

Several Supreme Court cases have dealt with contempt-of-court citations regarding press coverage of courts. In *Bridges v. California* (1941), a newspaper reported a labor leader's threat to call a strike if a judge's "outrageous" decision regarding a labor action were enforced. The Court held that no one, whether a private citizen or a member of the press, could be held in contempt of court merely for criticizing a judge's actions.

Similar contempt citations were reversed, including one in which a newspaper was found in contempt due to its editorials and a cartoon criticizing the judge's decisions in criminal and gambling cases (*Pennekamp v. Florida*, 1946). The Supreme Court ruled that those articles published by the *Miami Herald* were "legitimate criticism and comment," and posed "no clear and present danger to the administration of justice" (p. 331). Another newspaper was found in contempt for offending the court with an editorial that the judge felt did not correctly and accurately discern the important issues in the case. The contempt citation was reversed by the Supreme Court because journalists should not be held in contempt for failing to cover the important legal points of a trial (*Craig v. Harney*, 1947). Reporters' use of confidential sources also produces contempt citations, which became the subject of a landmark case that led to the creation of "shield laws" extending a privilege of secrecy for certain sources of news.

SHIELDING SOURCES

In 1972, the Supreme Court heard three cases joined together as *Branzburg v. Hayes*, all three involving subpoenaed reporters who refused to obey court orders and reveal the sources of their stories. In the first case, a Kentucky newspaper reporter named

Paul Branzburg was ordered to reveal confidential information about drug activities he witnessed. In Massachusetts, TV reporter Ike Pappas, and in California, *New York Times* reporter Earl Caldwell, were both subpoenaed by grand juries and ordered to reveal information gained from their news coverage of a militant group of activists called the Black Panthers. All three reporters were found in contempt for refusing to testify.

In the consolidated *Branzburg* case, the Court held that the First Amendment did not protect journalists from having to testify before grand juries. But the vote was close, 5-4. The dissent, written by Justice Potter Stewart, included a three-part test which he argued should be applied before punishing journalists: The government should show the journalist had relevant information; the information could not be obtained by other means; and there had to be a compelling need for the information. Although Justice Stewart's dissent did not set any precedent, many states, including Louisiana, subsequently incorporated the "*Branzburg* test" into their state shield laws privileging journalists subpoenaed to testify (Louisiana Shield Law, La Rev. Stat 45:1459). Journalists who violate an agreement with sources not only damage their personal and professional integrity by revealing their names to law enforcement officers, but they can be successfully sued after the fact.

In 1991, the decision in *Cohen v. Cowles Media Co.* dealt with journalists who promised confidentiality to a news source and then violated that trust. Dan Cohen, a public relations practitioner working on a gubernatorial campaign, approached reporters from two Minnesota newspapers and offered them negative information on his candidate's opponent provided they would keep the source of the story secret, which they did. However, when their editors discovered that the information was more in line with a smear campaign than genuine misbehavior on the part of the rival candidate, they decided to publish the source's name. Cohen was subsequently fired from the campaign, and he sued the newspapers.

In an interesting twist, the U.S. Supreme Court held that someone who violates a general law is not exempt just because the violator happens to be a newspaper protected by the First Amendment. Under the principle known as promissory estoppel, the Court said the promise of confidentiality was similar to a contract by which someone offers someone something in exchange for something of value, and it should be treated as such. The case was remanded to the trial court for further action and was subsequently settled in Cohen's favor. Thus, a journalist who refuses to reveal a confidential source may, under *Branzburg*, be found in contempt of court. However, if he does obey the court's order and reveals the identity, under *Cohen v. Cowles Media Co.*, the source may sue him for the equivalent of a breach of contract.

After *Branzburg*, only one other case involving coverage of grand juries reached the U.S. Supreme Court: *Butterworth v. Smith* in 1990. A reporter in Florida who had served as a grand jury witness wanted to write about his own testimony, but he was prohibited by a state law forbidding any participant in a grand jury proceeding from ever revealing anything about the case. A unanimous U.S. Supreme Court struck the Florida law and pointed out that it could be used to silence government criticism, a violation of the First Amendment.

COURT RECORDS

Another area of free press/fair trial concern involves public access to court records and documents. In a Georgia case (*Cox Broadcasting v. Cohn*, 1974), a high-school girl was raped and murdered, and although five of the six defendants pleaded guilty, a sixth defendant refused to do so and went to trial. A TV station covering the trial publicized the name of the victim, which it had obtained from open court records, thus violating a Georgia statute that prohibited publicizing the name of a rape victim.

The Court did not strike the statute but said that the government could not punish someone for publishing accurate information obtained from open court records. More narrow laws that forbid public identification of rape victims remain enforced in Georgia and in several other states.

In a Florida rape case, a weekly newspaper accurately printed a report of the robbery and assault of a woman at a bus stop. The paper had obtained the information from a police report that was supposed to be kept confidential, but the police accidentally released the version of the report that included the victim's name. As in Georgia, Florida had a law forbidding the publication of the name of a rape victim.

In this case (*Florida Star v. BJF*, 1989), the U.S. Supreme Court held that while the law in Florida was valid, a clause that limited punishment to media violators was unconstitutional. Ruling on the narrow grounds unique to the case, the Court held that in this case the newspaper should not be penalized, but in future cases anyone who violated the law by revealing the victim's name, not just members of the media could be punished.

Over a two-year period, three Supreme Court cases involving access to court records were decided in favor of the press. One overturned a state law that prohibited identifying anyone in a juvenile hearing, even a murder defendant (*Oklahoma Publishing v. District Court*, 1977). Another reversal would have punished a newspaper for writing anything about the state judicial review commission (*Landmark Communications v. Virginia*, 1978). And in *Smith v. Daily Mail* (1979), the Court held unconstitutional a West Virginia statute that punished a newspaper for publishing the name of a juvenile defendant accused in a serious shooting incident. Despite the government's argument favoring the need to protect minors from such publicity, the Court refused to affirm the "power of a state to punish the truthful publication of an alleged juvenile delinquent's name lawfully obtained by a newspaper" (*Smith v. Daily Mail*, p. 105-06).

Pretrial Publicity

Even before a criminal case actually comes to trial, there are usually numerous proceedings, such as evidentiary or suppression hearings concerned with whether certain evidence will be allowed. Judges presiding over such high-profile trials are often tempted to issue gag orders, restrictive orders against the press banning the release of certain information that they feel will interfere with a defendant's fair trial rights.

In a Louisiana case (*U.S. v. Dickinson*, 1973) two reporters in Baton Rouge violated a gag order by reporting on the testimony from a judicial hearing involving the state's questionable prosecution of a civil rights leader. The U.S. Fifth Circuit Court of Appeals held that reporters should obey gag orders, even if they appeared to be unconstitutional.

In 1986, a judge punished a reporter for violating his order not to publish information about an organized crime figure, Raymond Patriarca (*In re Providence Journal*). The stories were based on material obtained from FBI files after Patriarca's death. The U.S. First Circuit Court of Appeals overturned the reporter's contempt citation, holding that if the press had made a "good faith effort" to appeal an order before disobeying it, reporters may not be held in contempt for violating it.

However, since the U.S. Supreme Court refused to hear appeals in either the *Dickinson* or *Providence Journal* cases, a contempt charge may be applied differently depending on the jurisdiction where the judge's order was issued: The *Providence* precedent must be followed in the federal First Circuit (which in addition to Rhode Island includes Maine, Massachusetts, New Hampshire, and Puerto Rico), while the *Dickinson* precedent must be followed in the U.S. Fifth Circuit (which in addition to Louisiana covers Mississippi and Texas).

The *Nebraska Press* test

In a landmark gag-order case (*Nebraska Press Association v. Stuart*, 1976), a young man charged with the brutal murders of six members of a neighboring family confessed to the crime, and the judge issued a broad gag order, forbidding the press from reporting on the confession or other details of the case. The journalists appealed the order.

A unanimous U.S. Supreme Court held that the judge should have tried some other means of balancing the defendant's rights with those of the press (such as those described after the *Sheppard* case, above). According to the Court, "Prior restraints on speech and publication are the most serious and the least tolerable infringement on First Amendment rights" (*Nebraska Press Association v. Stuart*, p. 559).

The "*Nebraska Press* test" drawn from this decision suggests that before judges issue gag orders against the press, they should consider three factors: the nature and extent of pretrial coverage, whether other measures could better mitigate prejudicial publicity, and whether the gag order would actually accomplish its goal of lessening the likelihood of interference with the defendant's Sixth Amendment rights.

Since the *Nebraska* case, few judges implement direct gags on the press before or even during a trial, but many indirectly hamper press coverage by ordering lawyers and witnesses (even defendants themselves) not to speak about the case outside the courtroom, a de facto (in effect) gag order because it prevents the press from doing its job.

As far as access to court proceedings, it is in the area of criminal trials that the U.S. Supreme Court has issued the strongest decision upholding access. In *Richmond Newspapers, Inc. v. Virginia* (1980), after a murder case repeatedly ended in mistrials, the judge ordered the courtroom cleared during a retrial, and the press appealed his closure order. The Court issued a landmark decision written by Chief Justice Warren Burger, who although not generally regarded as a friend of the press, held the judge should not have closed the trial without a hearing. He said that the constitutional requirement for public trials was designed to protect defendants facing loss of liberty and even life: "People in an open society do not demand infallibility from their institutions, but it is difficult for them to accept what they are prohibited from observing" (*Richmond Newspapers, Inc. v. Virginia*, p. 572). Burger added, "Open trials assure the public that procedural rights are respected, and that justice is afforded equally. Closed trials breed suspicion of prejudice and arbitrariness, which in turn spawns disrespect for the law" (*Richmond Newspapers, Inc. v. Virginia*, p. 595).

An important stage of a criminal trial is the questioning of potential jurors during *voir dire*, the jury selection. In 1984, in *Press Enterprise v. Riverside Superior Court*, a defendant charged with rape and murder asked that the jury selection be closed to the press and public, and the court agreed to do so. After the defendant was convicted and sentenced to death, the press filed several motions for access to the jury-selection transcripts, which they finally obtained after the Supreme Court held that the party seeking to close the voir dire must show that an open process would prevent a fair trial.

The same newspaper appealed another court ruling in *Press Enterprise v. Riverside Superior Court II* (1986), this time during pretrial hearings. Again the Court held that criminal proceedings should not be closed unless access would prevent a fair trial. This case also has been generally interpreted as applicable whenever there is a question of whether the constitutional presumption of access applies to particular proceedings or records. Called by some commentators the "use and logic test," or the "*Press-Enterprise* test," it calls for consideration of whether the process in question has traditionally been open, and whether access is an essential aspect of the proceeding.

As for pretrial suppression hearings, the Supreme Court ruled in *Waller v. Georgia* (1984) that the right to a public trial includes the right to have such hearings open to the public. The suppression motion concerned evidence obtained through wiretaps that would implicate persons not on trial. The Supreme Court ruled that the right to a public trial also applied to suppression hearings, particularly if it involved wrongly seized evidence.

A more recent U.S. Supreme Court case dealing with access to pretrial hearings is *Presley v. Georgia* (2010). In this case, the judge closed the courtroom during jury selection, and Presley petitioned for his conviction on cocaine-trafficking charges to be overturned due to a violation of his Sixth Amendment right to a public trial. The Court reversed Presley's conviction and said it did not matter whether it was a defendant's Sixth Amendment right or the public's First Amendment right (as in *Press Enterprise I*):

"Trial courts are obligated to take every reasonable measure to accommodate public attendance at criminal trials" (*Presley v. Georgia*, p. 681).

Because lawyers are officers of the court, the U.S. Supreme Court has heard several cases in which additional prohibitions have been placed on lawyers' speech, which affects media coverage of court activities since lawyers are prime sources of information about cases in which they are involved. For example, the Court ruled in *Gentile v. State Bar of Nevada* (1991) that lawyers' speech regarding pending cases might be limited provided such rules are specific. The American Bar Association's canons limit the speech of lawyers and judges in pending cases to descriptions of the general nature of the charges, directory information about defendants (names, addresses, arrest dates), and scheduling details of the phases of a trial.

In *Florida Bar v. Went for It* (1995), after a horrible school bus accident in which parents were immediately contacted by "ambulance-chasing" lawyers, the state bar association passed a rule requiring lawyers to wait at least thirty days before directly soliciting victims to become their clients. The Supreme Court upheld the restrictions, and noted that the Bar has a legitimate interest in protecting the "privacy and tranquility of personal injury victims and their loved ones against invasive, unsolicited contract by lawyers" (at 618). Subsequently several other states, including Louisiana, passed similar restrictions controlling the direct solicitation of clients by lawyers (also called "barratry") in cases of personal injury.

Lawyers may be called upon to participate in political campaigns, particularly in jurisdictions where prosecutors and judges are elected by popular vote rather than appointment. This activity can produce legal restrictions of their freedom of expression. In *Republican Party of Minnesota v. White* (2002), the U.S. Supreme Court held that some restrictions against judges during election campaigns are unconstitutional, such as forbidding them to speak out on controversial issues. This decision emphasized that the Minnesota code of judicial ethics: restricted free speech, which is at the core of First Amendment protection; interfered with a candidate's qualifications for public office; and lacked the narrow tailoring necessary to survive strict scrutiny. However, other restrictions, such as those preventing judicial candidates from making specific campaign promises, were upheld. Legal codes of conduct have also reviewed the impact of courtroom video and photography on a trial's fairness.

CAMERAS IN COURT

As far as the issue of cameras in the courtroom: in the *Estes* case mentioned above, in 1966, the swindling conviction of Billie Sol Estes, an associate of then-president Lyndon Johnson, was overturned due to prejudicial publicity, primarily the use of television. A two-day pretrial hearing had been broadcast live, and excerpts from the trial itself were shown on TV news programs. The court held that television coverage might have affected jurors and witnesses and distracted judges and defendants.

By 1981, many states had developed courtroom camera experiments, and the U.S. Supreme Court decided—despite a defendant's objections in *Chandler v. Florida*—that use of courtroom cameras was not automatically proof of a lack of due process. As of 2013, all fifty states and some federal courts allowed some type of courtroom camera coverage.

FREE PRESS / FAIR TRIAL: LOUISIANA

Two cases that originated in Louisiana had precedential value to the nation. In a 1963 prejudicial publicity case, *Rideau v. Louisiana*, the U.S. Supreme Court heard the appeal of Wilbert Rideau, an African American man in Lake Charles who was charged with a bank robbery and murder. In a pretrial interview broadcast three times during the newscasts of the local TV station in the jurisdiction where the trial was to be held, Rideau confessed to the robbery and the kidnapping of three employees, one of whom was murdered.

The Court held that Rideau did not have a fair trial, and his request for a change of venue should have been granted: "For anyone who has ever watched television, the conclusion cannot be avoided that this spectacle, to the tens of thousand of people who saw it and heard it, in a very real sense *was* Rideau's trial—at which he pleaded guilty to murder." Writing for the majority, Justice Potter Stewart concluded: "Any subsequent proceedings in a community so pervasively exposed to such a spectacle could be but a hollow formality" (*Rideau v. Louisiana*, p. 726).

After a retrial (this trial moved from Calcasieu Parish to Baton Rouge), a second conviction was also overturned because of faulty jury selection. A third conviction in 1970 also included a death sentence, commuted to life when the U.S. Supreme Court in 1973 held that all capital punishment laws were unconstitutional and had to be rewritten. Then decades later, the third conviction was overturned because no African Americans had been on the grand jury that had indicted Rideau.

After a fourth trial in 2004, Rideau was found guilty of manslaughter and sentenced to time served. He wrote a book about his years in Angola prison during which he became a nationally known prison journalist writing about horrendous conditions and was widely known as the "most rehabilitated prisoner in America."

In a second Louisiana case to reach the U.S. Supreme Court (*U.S. v. Dickinson*, 1977), Frank Stewart, a black civil rights worker in the state capital of Baton Rouge was accused of participating in a conspiracy to murder the mayor. State officials were thought to have trumped up the murder charges to punish Stewart because of his civil rights activities. At a hearing in the case, the judge ordered the press not to publish any details of the proceeding, but two reporters including Larry Dickinson of *The* (Baton Rouge) *Advocate* newspaper disobeyed the order.

The Fifth Circuit Court of Appeals held that the order had been unconditional, but held that under normal circumstances journalists must follow orders of the court no matter their apparent unconstitutionality. The U.S. Supreme Court refused to hear that case or a similar one involving the *Providence Journal* in 1986, where the court held that as long as reporters had made a "good faith effort" to follow a seeming unconstitutional order, they could not be punished, which left the issue unsettled outside the jurisdictions of the respective appellate courts. Therefore, reporters in Louisiana (and Mississippi and Texas) must follow the *Dickinson* holding and obey all judges' orders and ask questions later in order to lessen the possibility of charges of contempt.

Courtroom Coverage

The judicial process is adversarial, pitting two sides against each other in accord with the safeguards designated by criminal and civil procedures and the U.S. Constitution. In the federal court system, there are ninety-four trial courts (district courts), at least one in each state, where cases usually begin. There are thirteen intermediate appeal courts (circuit courts), and the U.S. Supreme Court in Washington, D.C.

Each state designs its own court system. In Louisiana, there are more than one hundred trial courts (with cases originating in city, parish, district, and specialized courts); five intermediate appeal courts; and the Louisiana Supreme Court, with seven justices representing districts around the state but chambered in New Orleans. Cases may be civil actions, whereby one party—the plaintiff—sues another, the respondent, or criminal actions—whereby the government prosecutes someone accused of breaking a law.

Most public interest is in criminal cases, which are based on the theory that a defendant is presumed innocent unless the prosecution proves guilt beyond a reasonable doubt. An estimated 95 percent of criminal cases never makes it to trial: about one third are dropped by the prosecution and nearly two thirds are settled before trial in a negotiated settlement, or "plea bargain."

In the small percentage of cases that actually make it to trial, there may be a conflict between a free press and a fair trial. A book-length study found in 2004 that most commentators over-estimate the negative impact of newspaper coverage on the judicial process (Bruschke & Loges). However, balancing these rights has long been the subject of much controversy regarding such issues as prejudicial publicity, access to records and proceedings, and use of cameras in courtrooms.

Prejudicial Publicity

Following the U.S. Supreme Court *Sheppard* decision discussed above, committees of judges and lawyers developed recommended guidelines a judge might follow in conducting a trial in order to mitigate the impact of prejudicial publicity on the defendant's fair trial rights. These included the following:

- continuance—a delay in the case to allow the impact of pretrial publicity to die down
- change of venue—moving the case to another location (as long as it remains in the court's jurisdiction) where the publicity might be less pervasive
- change of venire—similarly, bringing in jurors from another location to lessen the chance of exposure to the intense publicity likely in the locality where a crime occurred
- voir dire—careful questioning of potential jurors during jury selection to determine whether they have followed coverage of the case—and, if so, whether they remain impartial
- admonition—frequent reminders of a judge to jurors to avoid exposure to all media coverage of the case and to avoid discussing the case until they are charged with deliberating at the end of the trial
- sequestration—isolating the jurors from exposure to media coverage by keeping them in a hotel or motel with court oversight of their activities
- severance—in the case of two or more defendants charged in conjunction with a crime, separating their trials to avoid publicity about one defendant from spilling over to another.

A change of venue, for instance, was ordered by the federal court in moving to Denver the trial for those accused of the 1995 Oklahoma City bombing in which 168 people were killed (*U.S. v. McVeigh and Nichols*). The 2003 court proceedings of the Washington, D.C., snipers (*In re Virginia v. Malvo and Muhammed*) was moved on a change of venue from near Washington, D.C., to the tidewater area of Chesapeake, Virginia.

Rather than grant a change of venue, a change of venire was ordered in the Casey Anthony trial for the murder of her daughter, with jurors brought in from Clearwater in Pinellas County to Orlando in Orange County. And as of early 2013, pretrial hearings in the case of George Zimmerman, charged with second-degree murder in the widely publicized "Stand Your Ground" shooting of Trayvon Martin, continued in the Seminole County, Florida, courthouse, the home jurisdiction of those involved in the case.

In Louisiana, change-of-venue motions are seldom granted. The failure to grant Wilbert Rideau's change-of-venue motion for his first trial became one of the grounds for overturning his conviction by the U.S. Supreme Court. Change-of-venue motions were also turned down in the trials of five New Orleans Police Department officers charged with a killing and cover-up as a result of violent incidents on the Danziger Bridge in the aftermath of Hurricane Katrina in 2005.

One Louisiana case in which a change-of-venue motion was granted was the 1998 manslaughter trial of a nanny who had left a three-year-old locked in a van while she played video poker. The trial of Terri Lynn Revere was moved from Bridge City in Jefferson Parish to Lafayette, where she was convicted and sentenced to forty years (*Louisiana v. Revere*, 2008). About a year later, a change of venue was also granted in the case of five Bourbon Street bar bouncers charged with manslaughter. One defendant was acquitted after his trial was moved to Lake Charles, another one after his trial was moved to Baton Rouge, and then charges against the last three defendants were dropped.

Several other Louisiana cases also involved prejudicial publicity and change-of-venue motions including the high-profile case of a police officer charged with murdering three people. Antoinette Frank was an officer with New Orleans Police Department who worked an outside detail as a security guard with fellow NOPD officer Ronald Williams at a Vietnamese restaurant in New Orleans East. On the night of March 4, 1995, Frank and an accomplice returned to the restaurant at closing time and shot Williams and two of the owners' four children while the other two hid in a walk-in cooler. Returning later to the restaurant, Frank said she was responding to the 911 call but the survivors said Frank had committed the crime. She was arrested and charged with three counts of first-degree murder, for which she was convicted and sentenced to death.

One of the grounds for appealing her conviction was Frank's claim that she had not been afforded due process because of prejudicial publicity and the denial of her change-of-venue motion. In 2001, the Louisiana Supreme Court reached a decision on her appeal that included a discussion of change of venue in the state. The court cited the portion of the Louisiana Code of Criminal Procedure (Art 622) dealing with change of venue, and the court's holding in an earlier case which listed factors which should be considered in determining whether to grant such a motion. These factors include the degree of pretrial publicity; the length of time between publicity and trial; and the severity and notoriety of the offenses. The court concluded that in the Frank case, there was no lack of due process due to the denial of her change-of-venue request (*Louisiana v. Frank*, 2001). All appeals by Frank were denied, and she remains on death row at this time.

In 2008, the murder trial of popular New Orleans area broadcast personality Vince Marinello, charged with killing his wife in Metairie, was moved from Jefferson Parish to Lafayette Parish. Defense attorneys cited "highly inflammatory" and "extensive" prejudicial publicity, including widespread coverage of a fourteen-point murder checklist Marinello drew up right after the murder: It listed such items such as "Gun—river on way to Mama" and "Clothes—burn." Marinello was convicted of second-degree murder and sentenced to life in prison, and the verdict was upheld on appeal (*Louisiana v. Marinello*, 2010).

In New Orleans, rapper "C Murder" (Corey) Miller was charged with second-degree murder in the 2002 killing of a teenage fan in a nightclub. A 2003 conviction in the case was overturned due to the prosecutors' withholding of evidence in the case, and in 2006 the state supreme court upheld the order for a new trial. During the six years while Miller was under liberal terms of house arrest awaiting his retrial, his travels to promote his work received extensive publicity and became an issue in the re-election campaign of the presiding trial judge—who was not re-elected.

Miller was not granted his requested change of venue for the retrial, which was finally held in 2009, and he was convicted and sentenced to mandatory life imprisonment. He already pleaded no contest to two counts of attempted second-degree murder stemming from an unrelated, earlier nightclub incident. His murder conviction was upheld in 2011 and left standing in 2013 (*Louisiana v. Miller*).

In an even more recent high-profile case, Telly Terrence Hankton, considered one of the most dangerous violent offenders in New Orleans, was the subject of numerous court cases and extensive local publicity for more than a decade. Finally, in late 2012, federal prosecutors in New Orleans issued a sweeping twenty-two-count racketeering and violent crime indictment against Hankton, two of his cousins, and two others charged with four murders. Eight others were charged with crimes from their activities with the violent drug ring, including Hankton's mother (*U.S. v. Telly Hankton, et al.*).

One of the murder victims mentioned in the new federal indictment had been the brother of a witness who testified against Telly Hankton in his trial for the murder of Darnell Stewart, for which Hankton had been convicted in 2011 and sentenced to life in prison. Earlier in 2011, New Orleans Mayor Mitch Landrieu had called out the "Hankton clan" in a press conference—at which the mayor said he was sending them a message, "We're coming to get you." Police reacted to death threats against the mayor, the district attorney, and others by providing police protection for weeks afterward.

Shortly after the 2012 federal indictment, the court announced that the jury in any forthcoming trials would be kept anonymous. As of 2013, it remained to be seen what additional steps would be taken to balance the fair trial rights of such notorious and feared defendants with the safety of officials, witnesses, and members of the general public who depend on a free press to keep them informed.

GRAND JURIES AND CONTEMPT

A felony involves a crime such as rape or murder, with penalties including prison sentences up to life, as well as capital cases that may lead to execution of the defendant. In most felonies, before a defendant is brought to trial, a prosecutor decides whether enough evidence exists to charge him with a crime. In some states, the prosecutor may do this on his own via an information, but in the majority of felony cases, the state prosecutor presents the evidence to a grand jury to decide (as in the *Branzburg* case also described above).

A grand jury hears only one side of a case—the prosecutor's. A suspect may be told he is the target of an investigation, but he may not bring his lawyer into the grand jury room and may only answer the questions that are asked of him. Since it may well be that the grand jury decides there is not enough evidence to indict a suspect—charge him with the crime—grand jury hearings are closed to the public and records are sealed.

Anyone who violates grand jury secrecy laws is thus subject to charges of contempt. Furthermore, anyone who is subpoenaed, which is officially ordered by the court, to testify before the grand jury, but refuses can be charged with contempt.

In several high-profile cases, journalists found in contempt of court were punished with jail sentences. Vanessa Leggett, an author writing about a Texas murder case in 2001, refused a subpoena to reveal her sources and was jailed for a record 168 days (*Leggett v. U.S.*). Judith Miller, a *New York Times* reporter who refused to reveal her source for a story based on a White House leak, spent eighty-five days in jail before her source allowed her to reveal his name (*In re Grand Jury Subpoena*, 2005).

One Louisiana grand-jury-secrecy case related to the prosecution of Clay Shaw for conspiracy in the assassination of President Kennedy (*Louisiana v. Shaw*, 1969, discussed above). The Orleans Parish District Attorney, Harry Connick Sr., agreed in 1995 during a hearing of the federal government's JFK Assassination Records Review Board in New Orleans to turn over all of the records that had been left in his office from the Clay Shaw prosecution. Connick said he discovered that most of the documents had disappeared prior to his taking over the office in 1974. A former investigator for the D.A.'s office, who said he ignored an order by Connick to destroy all JFK material, turned over the JFK grand jury records to WDSU-TV reporter Richard Angelico, who broadcast stories on the documents, and then gave them to the Review Board. Connick went after Angelico and the investigator, and a judge found them in contempt for violating grand-jury-secrecy laws (Louisiana Code of Criminal Procedure, Article 434) despite the fact that the records in the case were more than thirty years old and Connick had not told the truth about having ordered them destroyed.

Angelico, a highly regarded investigative reporter, had been the subject of contempt citations, including a 1975 case in which the contempt citation had been overturned (*Louisiana v. Angelico*). In the JFK grand jury records case, the Society of Professional Journalists and the Press Club of New Orleans supported Angelico's appeal, and in 1996, the state appeal court reversed Angelico's conviction (*Louisiana in re Grand Jury Transcripts*).

A more recent Louisiana contempt-of-court case involved a journalist who had reported before a murder trial began that the defendant was considering a plea bargain. In 2007, a judge in Orleans Parish criminal court declared a mistrial in the first-degree murder trial after WDSU-TV's Travers Mackel reported that defendant Tyrone Wells was considering a plea in exchange for elimination of the possibility of a death penalty in the first capital case to be heard in New Orleans after Hurricane Katrina (*In re Louisiana v. Wells*).

After two hearings on the matter, the judge dropped the idea of issuing contempt charges against Mackel and reset the murder trial. After a second mistrial, Wells was tried again, convicted of second-degree murder, and in 2010 received the mandatory sentence of life in prison without parole.

Gag Orders

As discussed earlier, ever since the Nebraska case, it has been rare for judges to issue restraining orders ("gag orders") against the press. However, in an effort to provide a defendant with a fair trial, judges do more often extend such orders to trial participants including lawyers, witnesses, and sometimes even the defendant himself.

Several attempts to have orders against the press lifted have been unsuccessful. For instance, the gag was upheld in the civil trial against OJ Simpson, who was acquitted of criminal charges in the murder of his ex-wife and her friend but held liable in a subsequent federal civil trial and ordered to pay the victims' families more than $30 million (*In re Rufo v. Simpson*, 1994). Similarly, a gag order against the media was upheld in the Oklahoma City bombing case (*In re U.S. v. McVeigh and Nichols*, 1997). Gag orders were also issued in numerous cases involving celebrities on trial, such as the federal trial of Martha Stewart (*U.S. v. Martha Stewart*, 2004) and Michael Jackson (*In re California v. Jackson*, 2005). A pretrial gag in the Zimmerman "Stand Your Ground" murder case was struck (*Florida v. Zimmerman*, 2012).

In 2001, a blanket gag order was overturned in *Louisiana v. Lee* on the grounds of its being a prior restraint in violation of the First Amendment. Journalists were less successful in fighting a gag order in the case of Len Davis, a corrupt New Orleans Police Department officer charged with offenses ranging from bribery and drug dealing to ordering the murder of a woman who filed a police brutality complaint against him.

When the *Times-Picayune* filed a petition to overturn the gag order, the court held that the order restrained trial participants, not the press itself, and that alternatives, such as a change of venue or continuances, would not protect the defendant's rights to a fair trial (*In re U.S. v. Len Davis*, 1995). Davis was convicted of numerous charges in 1995, received a federal death sentence in 2006, and as of 2013 remained on death row pending further appeals of his conviction and sentence.

The 2000 trial of (four-time) former Louisiana Gov. Edwin Edwards on federal charges of corruption in connection with the awarding of riverboat casino licenses was replete with restrictive measures, including gags on trial participants and Edwards himself. The gag orders were left standing when the U.S. Fifth Circuit Court of Appeals held it lacked jurisdiction to overturn them (*In Re U.S. v. Edwin Edwards*, 2000).

An attempt to overturn a gag the same year by a co-defendant in another federal case involving Edwards (*U.S. v. Brown*) also failed. Louisiana Insurance Commissioner Jim Brown fought the order against him on constitutional grounds, claiming that it interfered with his Sixth Amendment right to a public trial. He also claimed in his appeal that it was the first time a federal appeals court upheld such a gag order against a defendant who challenged it. Acquitted of all charges, save lying to an FBI agent, Brown served a brief sentence and spent years afterward fighting what he saw as a widespread prosecutorial misconduct, even writing a book about the subject, and taking to broadcast channels and online forums to make his arguments known.

Access To Records

The noticeable gap between the ideal and the reality of judicial access is illustrated by the general failure of courts to provide public access to their records and proceedings. In criminal cases, most records are presumed open, including arrest records and court dockets (schedules of proceedings) even though the Federal Juvenile Decency Act presumes that most juvenile records will be closed unless a child is being prosecuted as an adult.

Some cases in which the press failed to obtain full access to court records included the prosecutions of priests charged with sexual abuse in Los Angeles (*L.A. Times v. Supr Ct*, 2003), the Michael Jackson molestation charges in 2004, and the sexual assault case against NBA's Kobe Bryant (*Colorado v. Bryant*, 2003). In the Bryant case, after a court clerk accidentally released records naming the victim by email, the news media were ordered not to publish the material.

However, the media were more successful in several high-profile cases. The sealed records were opened in the case against the seventeen-year-old D.C. sniper suspect John Lee Malvo (*In re Virginia v. Malvo*, 2003), and in the class-action securities fraud case against Enron (*In Re Enron*, 2003). The press also won its challenge to the closure of pretrial discovery material in the Zimmerman murder case (*Florida v. Zimmerman*, 2012).

The USA Patriot Act of 2001 and the Homeland Security Act of 2002, both passed in response to terrorist attacks on September 11, 2001, made it more difficult to obtain court records regarding security information, although the press had limited success in obtaining release of unclassified documents in *Detroit Free Press v. Ashcroft* (2001), where some records were opened but much information remained sealed.

In its quest to obtain access to evidence such as exhibits and tapes used in trials, the press is often successful, as in the OJ Simpson murder case. After overcoming legal challenges, news media were allowed to obtain copies of tapes of 911 calls Simpson's wife had made during earlier domestic disturbances. In a 2001 case involving the death of well-known race-car driver Dale Earnhardt, the outcome was unfavorable to the news media requests. Not only was the press denied access to the autopsy photos following the racing accident (*Earnhardt v. Volusia County Florida Medical Examiner*), the Florida legislature subsequently passed a law requiring the permanent sealing of some autopsy evidence, such as photographs. Several other states followed suit in exempting them from public records laws, including Louisiana (La R.S. 44:3).

Regarding access to electronic records, the federal government began storing records in electronic databases in 1988, moving them to the Web in 2001. Free access to unsealed records is generally available at computer terminals in the federal courthouse located in the jurisdiction of the case. However, remote online access is more problematic. U.S. Supreme Court and appellate court decisions published in government reports are generally available from the government and various private sources online, but pleadings and trial court records may be available only via a paid subscription to the U.S. court system's PACER (Public Access to Court Electronic Records) service.

In Louisiana, there is a constitutional right to public documents (Art. 12 Sect. 3), and all branches of the government, including the judicial, are included in the Public Records Act (La. R.S. 44). However, in Louisiana, members of the press have often had a difficult time obtaining access to records, particularly in federal court proceedings held in the state. And this is also true in state courts, especially civil courts, despite a successful challenge to sealed documents in an exceptional case involving Leander Perez and other public officials accused of stealing millions of dollars in mineral royalties (*Plaquemines Parish v. Delta Development*, 1985).

For example, the marriage separation proceedings of popular TV newsman Ron Hunter, whose wife killed herself in their New Orleans home in 1990 after the couple had briefly reconciled, had been sealed (*Hunter v. Hunter*, 1988). In the divorce cases of high-profile Popeye's Chicken founder Al Copeland—one of which cases contributed to the criminal convictions of the judge and two Copeland associates—the press successfully fought to obtain access to court records, which in the end were only slightly redacted to exclude the children's home address and the name of their school (*In re Copeland v. Copeland*, 2006, 2007).

The federal courts in Louisiana were often even less welcoming of access. In the riverboat casino case of former governor Edwin Edwards, discussed above (*U.S. v. Edwin Edwards*, 2000), almost all 1500 of the records filed in the case remained sealed until after the trial—including the motion of the Society of Professional Journalists to unseal the records. A separate motion by the *Times-Picayune* newspaper for access to the booking photograph ("mug shot") of Edward De Bartolo, a defendant in the case who entered a guilty plea before the trial began, was also denied (*Times-Picayune v. U.S. Dept. of Justice*, 1999). News media requests for post-verdict access to juror identifying information and questionnaires in the 2001 insurance fraud case of *U.S. v. Jim Brown*, also involving Governor Edwards, were denied by the appeals court that held it was important to maintain juror anonymity in order to prevent "extraneous harassment and intimidation of jurors" (*U.S. v. Jim Brown*, p. 18).

Judges seem to be—understandably, perhaps—reluctant to release records regarding investigations involving other judges. The 2003 corruption investigation involving the case of Ronald Bodenheimer, the state judge accused, among other charges, of fixing the Copeland child custody case; the 2004 perjury and extortion case against state Judge C. Hunter King; and the 2005 case of state Judge Alan Green, accused of conspiracy in a bail bonds case (*U.S. v. Green*) were all subject to sealed-records challenges filed by members of the New Orleans press.

As far as access to electronic records are concerned, there is no uniform access in the state of Louisiana. One reason for this fact is that some courts lack the capacity to provide records online. In the more populous jurisdictions, such as in New Orleans and Baton Rouge, there are electronic records, although as in the federal system, those documents available outside the courthouse are available via a paid subscription.

Civil court records are more problematic, particularly in cases where the permanent sealing of records are made part of a court settlement. Even more difficult can be the challenge of obtaining records regarding legal disputes subject to resolution alternatives such as mediation and arbitration.

Several federal class-action civil cases heard in Louisiana are subject to sealed record closures including a $600 million lawsuit against tobacco companies in 2004 (*Scott v. American Tobacco Co.*) and a 2007 complaint against Shell Oil for tainted gasoline. In the aftermath of Hurricane Katrina, the federal cases involving thirty-four deaths at Memorial Hospital in New Orleans (*In re Investigation*, 2009), as well as the deadly police shootings on the Danziger Bridge, challenged the news media in terms of obtaining access to records.

ACCESS TO PROCEEDING

Among the cases challenging the press beyond gag orders were the ones imposing obstacles to court records and preventive measures to attending proceedings—from pretrial hearings such as jury selection through the trial phase, and afterward. The press in 2000 was successful in obtaining access to the once-closed murder arraignment of Michael Skakel, a nephew of Robert F. Kennedy. Skakel was convicted of murdering his fifteen-year-old Greenwich Connecticut neighbor Martha Moxley when he had been a teenager himself twenty-five years earlier (*Connecticut v. Skakel*, 2000). However, the public was banned from most preliminary hearings when rape charges against famed basketball star Kobe Bryant were heard in Colorado. The stock-fraud pretrial hearings for Martha Stewart were successfully closed as well.

Of particular concern is the use of anonymous jurors, with jury selection closed and juror names and questionnaires sometimes sealed even after the trial has concluded.

The practice was deemed necessary for participants' safety in cases involving gangsters, such as "The Dapper Don" John Gotti, who was acquitted in three cases in the 1980s (although there was speculation afterward of misconduct in the form of jury tampering in those cases). "The Teflon Don" previously escaped conviction, but the racketeering and murder charges in 1998 stuck against Gotti (*U.S. v. Gotti*), and he died in prison in 2002.

More problematic from the viewpoint of the press are cases involving ordinary citizens, such as Scott Peterson, convicted in 2004 of murdering his wife Laci and their unborn child. The court ordered a change of venue in the case, with various alternative cities actually lobbying the court to be selected for the celebrated trial. During deliberations, however, Court TV presented a videotape showing a juror talking to Laci's older brother as they passed by each other in the courthouse, and the juror was replaced. Two other jurors were also replaced, one at his own request after receiving death threats. Peterson was convicted and sentenced to death, and remains on death row while continuing the appeal process, which included charges of prejudicial publicity creating an unfair trial for him (*California v. Peterson*).

In the Casey Anthony trial in 2011, members of the press challenged an order requiring them to sign a confidentiality agreement before the court would disclose to reporters the location where jury selection would take place (*WPTV-TV et al. v. Florida and Casey Anthony*, 2011). The appellate court vacated the portion of the order that implemented the confidentiality agreement but said the court did not have to immediately reveal the location. The names of the jurors in the case were not released until three months after the verdict.

In 2012, in New York, a lawyer convicted on charges relating to his work with immigration applications had his 2011 conviction overturned due to the court's failure to follow the requirements of *U.S. v. Presley* that held the closure of jury selection be allowed only after findings overcome the presumption of openness (*U.S. v. Gupta*, 2012).

One federal case in Louisiana was noted for the judge's issue of a blanket post-trial gag order on jurors. The judge later revised it in order to allow jurors to be interviewed for their "general reactions" without reference to jury deliberations. In New Orleans, federal trial judge Sarah Vance issued the order after a highly publicized trial involving six defendants up on racketeering charges involving the video poker industry. Former Louisiana state senator Larry Bankston, who was convicted of accepting a bribe, and former state senator BB "Sixty" Rayburn, who was acquitted in the case, were among the defendants.

During the trial, the judge refused to release juror names and questionnaires, or even to allow media access to tapes or transcripts of conversations used as evidence in the case. The *New Orleans Times-Picayune* and *The* (Baton Rouge) *Advocate* appealed the orders, but the sealed records were upheld by the appeal court, and the U.S. Supreme Court let the decision stand (*U.S. v. Cleveland*, 1997).

The Governor Edwards riverboat-casino corruption case included an anonymous jury. The issue became of particular concern when the judge dismissed a deliberating juror, known only as "Number 68," reportedly after the judge interviewed all the other jurors and the pastor of Number 68's church, The eleven remaining jurors convicted Edwards and four of his six co-defendants on various charges, with most of the convictions upheld by higher courts (*U.S. v. Edwards*, 2000).

Under Louisiana's constitution (Art. 1 sect. 22), "All courts shall be open." Echoing the Sixth Amendment of the U.S. Constitution, the Louisiana document further states that defendants are entitled to a "speedy, public, and impartial trial" (Art. 2 sect. 16). Most procedures involving juveniles are confidential according to the Louisiana Children's Code (Art. 407, Ar.t 879), but delinquency hearings are an exception.

In one highly publicized case in Jena, Louisiana, six black teenagers were charged in the beating of a white student at Jena High School in 2006, the site of much racial tension. The controversy received widespread publicity, including a song by John Mellencamp. Among the cases tried against the teenagers, nicknamed by the media "The Jena 6," Mychal Bell was first tried as an adult due to his criminal record. His conviction was overturned on the grounds he should have been tried in juvenile court. For the retrial (*Louisiana in re the Interest of Mychal Bell*), the judge closed all proceedings, sealed all records, and imposed a gag order on all participants.

After a consortium of news organizations including the *Chicago Tribune*, the Associated Press, and *The New York Times* filed motions to open proceedings and records, the state appeals court eventually held the proceedings should be opened (*Chicago Tribune v. Mauffray*, 2008). By that time Bell had pleaded guilty, as had the other defendants. As of 2013, the victim had settled with the Jena 6 in a civil suit for monetary damages he had brought against them. Several of the former Jena 6 had subsequently been arrested on various unrelated charges.

In a case involving three juveniles at Lakeshore High School in Mandeville in St. Tammany Parish, police arrested and charged them with planning to shoot a fellow student and teacher on the first day of class in 2011. The *Times-Picayune* filed a motion to grant public access to their hearings and records in this juvenile court case, and eventually were granted access to their hearings. All three boys subsequently pleaded "true" (the juvenile court equivalent of guilty) to various reduced charges of conspiracy to commit violence and were sentenced to serve terms in juvenile institutions.

Cybercourts

Controversies regarding electronic coverage of courtrooms—including still and video photography, radio and television broadcasting, even today's netcasting and use of social media—can be traced to events occuring more than eighty years ago.

As mentioned earlier, the U.S. Supreme Court has heard three cases in which camera usage was an issue: *N.J. v. Hauptmann* (1935) resulted in courtroom camera restrictions that lasted for more than thirty years, and *Estes v. Texas* (1965) reinforced continued restrictions. In 1981, however, in *Chandler v. Florida*, the Court finally held that the issue was a matter for individual states to determine.

The American Bar Association, which sets licensing standards for lawyers in each state, suggests that judges may authorize camera coverage in some cases (see *ABA Standards for Criminal Justice*). However, the government rules governing the federal courts generally presume courtroom cameras will be banned (*Federal Rules of Criminal Procedure #53*).

After conducting a three-year experiment in 1996 the U.S. Judicial Conference, which regulates courtroom standards in the federal courts, voted to allow each of the thirteen appellate circuits to decide whether to permit cameras in federal appeal courts; only the Second Circuit headquartered in New York and the Ninth Circuit in California voted to do so. A handful of judges in the ninety-four federal district courts have allowed some camera coverage of trials on a case-by-case basis.

In 2011, the Judicial Conference began a second three-year experiment with cameras in a limited number of civil district courts, and posted the coverage online (uscourts.gov). In 2014, this pilot program will be evaluated as to the effects the cameras have had on the trials covered.

The U.S. Supreme Court is more readily making available audiotapes of oral arguments. And at various times, Congress has considered "Sunshine in the Courtroom" acts, which would permit coverage of all federal courts at the judge's discretion ("Sunshine in the Courtroom Act," 2012), but so far none have ever made it to the president's desk for his signature.

All 50 states allow some sort of electronic courtroom coverage as of this writing. Courtroom media access ranges from the most permissive (*e.g.*, Florida courtrooms) to the most restrictive (*e.g.*, Indiana and Minnesota). The Radio-Television-Digital News Association Web site (rtdna.org) and that of the National Center for State Courts (ncst.org) track the level of access and legal restrictions.

The Louisiana Supreme Court says judges should prohibit all electronic coverage of trial courtrooms in the state, with a few exceptions for ceremonial or educational purposes. Louisiana judges are allowed to permit camera coverage in state appellate courts, however, provided the media follow specific guidelines spelled out in the Appendix to

Canon 3 (lasc.org). These stipulate that the media must request camera coverage well in advance of the event, and then cooperate with pooled camera coverage: two video cameras, two still cameras, and one audio system for radio are allowed in the courtroom. The video may not be used for commercial purposes or political advertising.

Over the years, various attempts to extend courtroom coverage to trial courts in Louisiana have met with negative results. Most notably, in 1992, the Society of Professional Journalists in Louisiana filed such a motion of access, and after a lengthy study, a Louisiana Supreme Court Task Force recommended implementation of the change. The state's high court, however, rejected the motion by a 6-2 vote in 1996.

In 1999, the National Center for State Courts published a study that predicted that the virtual courtroom, including trials taking place all-electronically, was a future possibility. In Louisiana, the 2000 corruption trial of former Gov. Edwin Edwards was a dramatic demonstration of virtual trial justice. The federal court maintained a Web site with docket information, and during the Edwards trial all participants including the judge, the defendants, lawyers, and jurors donned headsets in order to hear audio recordings and documentary evidence that was posted online and available on various computer terminals in the courtroom.

In 2001, Louisiana banned the use of certain scanners that would allow the user to avoid having to pay the courts for copies of records. The law was struck after a court challenge (*First Commerce Title v. Martin*, 2005), but after the Second Circuit Court of Appeal held that such portable scanners fell outside the prohibition of "placed or installed" copiers the legislature returned to pass an amended ban [La Rev. Stat 44.32(C)(1)(c)] further inconveniencing public access to judicial records.

The state of Florida in 1999 became the first to allow an entire trial to be netcast, and by 2013, various state experiments had started netcasting court proceedings. The Open Court project in Massachusetts, for example, began streaming live in a Quincy courthouse outside Boston, and the Courtroom View Network (CVN) webcasts civil cases from around the country (see http://opencourt.us/ and http://www.courtroom-view.com). A report issued by the office of the New Orleans mayor in October 2012, "A 21st Century Criminal Justice System for the City of New Orleans," indicated the largest city in the state was lagging in its development of virtual courtrooms: "In a world of Microsoft Outlook, the New Orleans criminal justice system is functioning in a bygone era" (The PMV Group, p. 65).

More courts around the country are experimenting with blogging, tweeting, and even texting of court proceedings, although it varies widely from jurisdiction to jurisdiction. However, it cannot be presumed that the same restrictions applying to broadcast coverage will apply to cybercourts given the unsettled state of the law in this area at both national and state levels. The Louisiana rules, for instance, have not been amended since 1993, so the issue has yet to be directly addressed in this state.

Conclusion

As the second decade of the new millennium proceeds, the digital revolution is bringing about dramatic changes in every aspect of the law, including courtroom coverage. The growing field of litigation public relations includes widespread use of Web sites and social media such as Facebook and Twitter by lawyers—and the courts. For example, an estimated 150 million Facebook accounts in the United States alone, have inspired some courts to experiment with serving subpoenas via Facebook. Even the U.S. Supreme Court justices are increasingly going online with personal speeches, television appearances, and their participation on the official Web site (supremecourt.gov).

With these developments, the potential for numerous new conflicts increases. For instance, the growth of "citizen journalists" blogging coverage of courts gives rise to the question: Just who is a journalist? Louisiana's shield law extends a legal privilege for journalists to protect confidential sources and defines a reporter to mean someone "regularly engaged in the business of collecting, writing or editing news for publication through a news media" (Shield law statute, 1964). That definition, however, has not been applied to courtroom coverage in the state.

Web sites created by and for attorneys or their legal firms might include names of potential witnesses that would inhibit such witnesses from testifying. In fact, one independent Web site, <whosarat.com>, founded in 2004 as a free site but currently available only by subscription proved to be problematic. Under the protection of the First Amendment, the Web site published trial-related content, such as the names of informants and protected witnesses,which led the federal courts to more carefully control the details of the plea agreements forged in criminal cases.

Court participants may violate gag orders by using the Internet, and "Google mistrials" may be caused by jurors who violate admonitions not to seek information on cases outside the courtrooms. Judges "friending" courtroom participants on Facebook can cause additional confusion, raising the questions of when a recusal should be required. The greatest problem, perhaps, is the potential for prejudicial publicity due to the ubiquity of social media. The "Twitter effect," including jurors' use of such social media, is met with widely varying responses from the judiciary. One court judge in South Carolina signed an order in 2011 that banned all wireless communication devices in courtroom facilities, while an Iowa district court judge gave a newspaper reporter permission to tweet a trial so long as she sat in the back of the courtroom to avoid creating a distraction (Lozare, 2011)

In the second decade of the new millennium, judges, lawyers, journalists, and legal scholars (many writing at courtsandmedia.org) are studying steps that might be taken to alleviate problems, such as possible bans on cell phones in courthouses and revised jury instructions to include admonitions against any use of the Internet or social media during a trial. The jury instructions for federal criminal cases heard in Louisiana, for instance, were updated more than a decade ago, and do not mention the Internet or social media (La. Pattern Crim. Jury Inst., 2001). In the jury instructions generally applied in state trials in Louisiana, only books are specifically mentioned (18 La. Civil Law Treatise, 2010).

Other suggestions include amending the canons of judicial conduct and the codes of conduct for lawyers to acknowledge the practice of "litigation public relations," and the growth of social media. This might include a voluntary code of conduct for lawyers when they are acting as media legal analysts—even holding lawyers accountable for comments of public relations practitioners hired by lawyers during litigation.

As far as suggestions for journalists: The guidelines for electronic access to courts in each state should be updated and made consistent for coverage of blogging, netcasting, and the use of social media such as Twitter. Enhanced training for journalists covering courts, with an emphasis on journalistic codes of ethics such as those of the Society of Professional Journalists, also should be implemented. Recognizing that these ethical codes apply to those who work for the "legacy media" (primarily newspapers and broadcasters), citizen journalists who are not professionally trained reporters should be encouraged by the courts to follow them. The inherent conflicts in balancing defendants' constitutional guarantees of fair trials with impartial jurors, while accommodating crucial coverage of government by a free press, present new challenges to the goals of a constitutional democracy.

REFERENCES

Alexander, S.L *Courtroom Carnival: Famous New Orleans Trials*, Pelican Publishing, 2011.

_____. *Covering the Courts: A Handbook for Journalists*, Rowman & Littlefield, 2ed, 2003.

_____. *Media and American Courts*, ABC Clio, 2004.

Brown, Jim. *Justice Denied: How the Federal Court System Failed Former Insurance Commissioner Jim Brown*, Lisburn Press, 2004.

Bruschke, Jon, and William Loges. *Free Press v. Fair Trials: Examining Publicity's Role in Trial Outcomes*, Lawrence Erlbaum, 2004.

Coffey, Kendall. *Spinning the Law: Trying Cases in the Court of Public Opinion*, Foreword by Alan Dershowitz, Prometheus, 2010.

David, Richard. *Justices and Journalists: The U.S. Supreme Court and the Media*, Cambridge University Press, 2011.

Rideau, Wilbert. *In the Place of Justice: A Story of Punishment and Deliverance*, Knopf, 2010.

GENERAL CASES CITED

Branzburg v. Hayes, 408 U.S. 665 (1972).

Bridges v. California, 314 U.S. 252 (1941).

Butterworth v. Smith, 494 U.S. 624 (1990).

In re California v. Michael Jackson NBC, Cal. Ct. App. No. B176587, 2005 WL 958201 (Cal Ct App, 4/27/05).

California v. Manson, 61 Cal. App. 3d 102 (1976).

California v. Menendez, 422 F3d 1012 (U.S. Ct. Appl., 9th Cir) (2005), 834 P 2d 786 (1992).

California v. Scott Peterson, Ca. Supreme Court (appeal) San Mateo No. 55500A, filed July 5, 2012 (2004).

California v. Simpson, Ca. Dist. Ct. No. BAO 972111 1995 WL 704581.

Chandler v. Florida, 449 U.S. 560 (1981).

Cohn v. Cowles, 501 U.S. 663 (1991).

Colorado v. Kobe Bryant AP, 94 P 3d 624, 542 U.S. 1301(Colorado, 2004), 125 S Ct 1 (2004).

Connecticut v. Skakel, 549 U.S. 1030, 276 Conn 633 (2006).

Cox Broadcasting v. Cohn, 420 U.S. 469 (1975).

Craig v. Harney, 331 U.S. 367 (1947).

Detroit Free Press v. Ashcroft, 303 F 3d 681 (U.S. 6th Cir. Ct. Appl.) 2002.

In re Enron Securities Legislation (Newby v. Enron), 542 F3d 463 (2008), 302 F3d 295 (2002).

Earnhardt v. Volusia Cty Office of ME, 29 Med. L Rptr. 2173. 2001 WL 992068 (Fla. 7th Cir, 2002), *Campus Communications v. Earnhardt*, 2002 WL 1483806 (Fla. Fifth DCA 2002).

Estes v. Texas, 381 U.S. 532 (1965).

Florida v. Casey Anthony, Fla App Case No 5D11-2357 (2013); 2011 Fla. App. LEXIS 13596, 2011; *WPTV. et al v. Florida and Anthony*, 61 So. 3d 1191 (2011).

Florida v. William Kennedy Smith, Palm Beach County, December 23,1991.

Florida v. George Zimmerman, No 12-CF 1083-A, 40 Med. L Rptr. 2054, July 13, 2012 (records); 40 Med L Rptr 2655, October 29, 2012 (gag).

Florida Bar v. Went For It, 515 U.S. 618 (1995).

Florida Star v. BJF, 491 U.S. 524 (1989).

Gentile v. State Bar of Nevada, 501 U.S. 1030 (1991).

Georgia v. Frank, 237 U.S. 309 (1915).

In re Grand Jury Subpoena [Judith Miller], 397 F3d 964 (D.C. Cir. 2005), *reissued* 438 F.3d 1141 (2006).
Hauptmann v. NJ, 180 A 809 (N.J. Sup. Ct., 1935) *cert. den.* 296 U.S. 649 (1935).
Illinois v. Leopold and Loeb, Chicago, Sept. 10, 1924.
Irvin v. Dowd, 366 US 717 (1961).
("King") In re California v. Powell, 232 Cal. App. 3d 785, 1991.
L.A. Times v. Superior Court, 2003 Cal. App. LEXIS 1853.
Landmark Communications v. Virginia, 435 U.S. 829 (1978).
Leggett v. US, In re Grand Jury Subpoenas, 535 U.S. 1011 (2002).
Marshall v. US, 360 U.S. 310 (1959).
Mu' Min v. Virginia, 501 U.S. 1269 (1991).
Murphy v. Florida, 421 U.S. 794 (1975).
Nebraska Press Association v. Stuart, 427 U.S. 539 (1976).
New York v. Snyder and Gray, 246 N.Y. 491 (N.Y. Sup. Ct.) 1927.
Oklahoma Publishing v. District Court, 430 U.S. 308 (1977).
Patton v. Yount, 467 U.S. 1025 (1984).
Pennekamp v. Florida, 328 U.S. 331 (1946).
Presley v. Georgia, 130 S. Ct. 721 (2010).
Press Enterprise v. Riverside Superior Court I, 464 U.S. 501 (1984).
Press Enterprise v. Riverside Superior Court II, 478 U.S. 1 (1986).
In re Providence Journal, 820 F 2d 1342 (U.S. 1st Cir. Ct. Appl., 1986), *cert. den.,* 485 U.S. 693 (1988).
Republican Party of Minnesota v. White, 536 U.S. 765 (2002).
Richmond News v. Virginia, 488 U.S. 555 (1980).
In re Rufo v. Simpson, No SC 031947 (Cal. Supr. Ct., Aug. 23, 1996).
Sheppard v. Maxwell, Warden, 384 U.S. 333 (1966).
Smith v. Daily Mail, 443 U.S. 97 (1979).
U.S. v. Gotti, 166 F3d 1202 (1998).
U.S. v. Gupta, 699 F3d 682 (2012).
U.S. v. Hearst, 563 F 2d 1331 (U.S. 9th Cir. Ct. Appl., 1977), *cert. den.* 435 U.S. 1000 (1978).
U.S. v. Hiss, 185 F 2d 822 (U.S. 2d Cir. Ct. Appl., 1950); *cert. den.* 340 U.S. 948 (1951).
In re US v. McVeigh and Nichols, 964 F Supp. 313 (1987), 931 F Supp. 753 (1996).
U.S. v. Nixon ("Watergate") 418 U.S. 683 (1974).
U.S. v. Julius and Ethel Rosenberg, 344 U.S. 838 (1952).
US v. Skilling, 130 S. Ct. 2896 (2010); *cert den* 132 S. Ct. 1905 (2012).
US v. Stewart, 317 F Supp. 2d 426 (2004), *ABC v. Martha Stewart,* 360 F 3d 90 (2 Cir. 2004).
[In re Commonwealth of] Virginia v. Malvo [and Muhammad], Criminal No. 102888 (2003).
Waller v. Georgia, 467 U.S. 39 (1984).

LOUISIANA CASES CITED

Chicago Tribune v. Mauffray, 996 So. 2d 1273 (La. Appl., 2008); *Louisiana in the Interest of Mychal Bell,* J-4002 (2007).
In re Copeland v. Copeland, 966 So. 2d 1040 (2007).
First Commerce Title v. Martin, 896 So. 2d 66 (2005), 887 So. 2d 716 (2004).
Marilou Ann Hunter v. Ron Hunter, Petition for Separation 89-162 (1988, New Orleans Parish Civil Dist. C, "Motion to Seal Proceedings" 89-19182 (1989).
Louisiana v. Richard Angelico 378 So. 2d 378 (1975).
Louisiana v. Antoinette Frank, 552 U.S. 1189 (2008), 803 So. 2d 1 (2001).
Louisiana v. Lee, 787 So. 2d 1020 (2001).
Louisiana v. Vincent Marinello, 61 So. 3d 660 (2011); 49 So. 3d 488 (2010).
Louisiana v. Corey Miller, 2013 U.S. Lexis 1095, 89 So. 3d 1191 (2012); 83 So. 3d 178

(2011), 923 So. 2d 625 (2006).
Louisiana v. Terri Revere, 994 So. 2d 14 (2008); 922 So. 2d 529 (2006).
Louisiana v. Clay Shaw, March 1, 1969.
Louisiana in re Grand Jury Transcripts [Angelico], No. 96-K-0916, Sup. Ct. of La. (1996).
In re Louisiana v. Tyrone Wells, No. 441-698 (2007).
In re [Memorial] Investigation, 37 Med. L Rptr. 2130 (La. Sup. Ct.) 2009.
Plaquemines Parish Commission Council v. Delta Development Co., 502 So. 2d 1034 (1987), 472 So 2d 560 (1985).
Wilbert Rideau v. Louisiana, 373 U.S. 723 (1963).
Scott v. American Tobacco, 949 So. 2d 1266 (2004), 36 So. 3d 1046 (2010).
Times-Picayune v. U.S. D.O.J. and U.S. Marshals Service, 37 F Supp. 2d 472 (1999).
U.S. v. Jim Brown, 250 F 3d 907 (Fifth Cir. 2001); 218 F3 415 (2000).
In re US v. Carl Cleveland, 128 F 3d 267 (1997), 1997 U.S. Dist LEXIS 10718.
In re US v. Len Davis, et al, 904 F Supp. 564 (1995), 24 Med. L Rptr. 1083 (1995).
U.S. v. Dickinson, 465 F 2d 496, *cert. den.*, 414 U.S. 979 (1973).
U.S. v. Edwin Edwards, 303 F 3d 606 (2002), *cert. den.* 537 US 1192 (2003); 206 F 3d 461 (2000) (gag).
U.S. v. Alan Green, U.S. v. Bowley, 2005 U.S. Dist. LEXIS 11560 (E.D. La. June 3, 2005).
U.S. v. Telly Hankton, et al, US Dist Ct ED La Superceding Indictment, Criminal Docket No. 12-001, Sect F (10/18/12); *Louisiana v. Telly Hankton, et al*, 58 So.3d 477 (2011).

Legal Citations

Federal Rules of Criminal Procedure, Rule 53 Courtroom Photographing and Broadcasting Prohibited (April 29, 2002).
["Hollywood 10"] Hearings Regarding the Communist Infiltration of the Motion Picture Industry, U.S. 80th Cong. 1st Sess., Oct 1947.
[Louisiana] 18 La. Civil Treatise, Civil Jury Inst., sect. 101 (2nd ed. 2010).
Louisiana Children's Code, Art. 407 Confidentiality of Hearings (1995). Art. 879 Presence at Adjudication Hearing, (2011).
Louisiana Code of Civil Procedure 122 Change of Proper Venue.
Louisiana Code of Criminal Procedure: Article 434 Secrecy of Grand Jury Meetings (1972), 434.1 Exceptions; (2012) Article 622 Grounds for Change of Venue.
Louisiana Constitution Art. 1 Sect. 16 Right to a Fair Trial (1995); Sect. 22 Access to Courts; Art 12 Sect 3 Right to Direct Participation.
Louisiana Public Records Act. (La. R.S. 44:1 *et seq*), inc. 44.32 (C) (1)(c), 2005 (scanner ban).
Louisiana Rev. Statutes Sec. 45:1451-1459 ("Shield Law").
Louisiana Supreme Court Rules (ww.lasc.org/rules/supreme.asp): Louisiana Canon 3 & Appendix: Guidelines for Extended Coverage of Proceedings in Appellate Courtrooms (1985, 1993).
[Louisiana] U.S. Fifth Circuit Court Appeal (www.uscourts.gov.) Fifth Circuit Pattern Jury Instruction Civil Fifth Circuit Pattern Jury Instruction-Criminal 18. La Civ. Treatise 2010.
"Sunshine in the Courtroom Act," H.R. 5163 (112th) 2012.
[Louisiana v. Shaw] President John F. Kennedy Assassination Records Collections Act, 44 USCS Sec 2107 (1992).

Online Material

Administrative Office of the U.S. Courts, *uscourts.gov.*
    Cameras in Courts Digital Video Pilot
    Judicial Conference of the United States
    PACER (Public Access to Court Electronic Records)
American Bar Association: *americanbar.org*

Rules of Professional Conduct of Attorneys: Rule 3.6 Trial Publicity
Standards of Conduct in Criminal Cases, 8-3 (2011 edition)
Louisiana State Bar Association *lsba.org*
Rules of Professional Conduct (with amendments through September 30, 2011)
Shield Law, Louisiana Revised Statutes § 45.1451 (1964). Retrieved June 9, 2013, from http://www.dmlp.org/louisiana-revised-statutes-sec-45-1451-1459
Lozare, N. (2011). More Reporters Tweeting from Courtroom: High-profile Trials can Increase Reporters' Followers by Thousands. *News Media & The Law*, 6. Retrieved June 9, 2013 from http://www.rcfp.org/browse-media-law-resources/news-media-law/news-media-and-law-fall-2011/more-reporters-tweeting-court
National Center for State Courts, *ncsc.org*
2012 CCPIO New Media Survey
Updates to *Managing Notorious Trials*, Timothy Murphy, et al 1998
"Future Trends in State Courts"
inc John Kostouras, "Who Are These Guys? Courts Face a Rapidly Changing News Industry"; David Sluto, "Social Media: A New Way to Communicate That Can No Longer Be Ignored"
Open Court, *opencourt.us*
The PFM Group, *pfm.com*
"A 21st Century Criminal Justice System for the City of New Orleans," October 2, 2012
Radio-TV-Digital News Association, *rtdna.org*
"Cameras in the Court: A State by State Guide"
Reporters Committee for Freedom of the Press, *rcfp.org*
Mary Ellen Roy and Don Zimmerman, "Open Courts Compendium: Louisiana"
"Secret Justice":
Anonymous Jurors, Alternative Dispute Resolution, Access to
Juror Questionnaires, Access to Juvenile Justice, Access to Terrorism
Proceedings, Electronic Access to Court Records, Gag Orders, Grand Juries,
Judicial Speech, Jury Records and Proceedings, Online Access to Plea
Agreements, Secret Dockets, Secret Juries, Star Treatment, Warrants and
Wiretaps
Reynolds Center for Courts and the Media, *courtsandmedia.org*
Reynolds Center for Courts and the Media Law Journal
(Vols 1-3, 2011-2013)
Society of Professional Journalists, *spj.org* SPJ Code of Ethics
U.S. Supreme Court, *supremecourt.gov.*
Who's A Rat, *whosearat.com*

Chapter 8
Access to Public Documents and Meetings
By James Stewart, Nicholls State University

Learning Objectives
In this chapter, readers will:
- be able to identify the First Amendment reasoning of shared information and public governance
- know how press freedoms relate to public access to records and meetings
- understand the arguments for limiting access to certain records and meetings
- be able to define state public-records and open-meetings provisions

In his dissent to the court's ruling in *Branzburg v. Hayes*, U.S. Supreme Court Justice Potter Stewart wrote, "No less important to the news dissemination process is the gathering of information. News must not be unnecessarily cut off at its source, for without freedom to acquire information the right to publish would be impermissibly compromised" (1972, p. 728). The system of self-governance that has evolved in the United States would appear to demand the greatest possible access to information by citizens, particularly to that which relates to the workings of government. News-media responsibilities in facilitating access seem apparent. As Justice William O. Douglas argued in *Branzburg*:

> The press has a preferred position in our constitutional scheme, not to enable it to make money, not to set newsmen apart as a favored class, but to bring fulfillment to the public's right to know. The right to know is crucial to the governing powers of the people (p. 721).

But despite what seems an obvious need for public information about government activities, significant obstacles can work to limit access. Availability can be affected by any number of economic, cultural, and social factors, as the necessity for information must be balanced against legitimate competing interests and historical precedent.

From a legal perspective, attempts to carve out protected rights of access are further complicated by the fact that there is no single body of regulation. In addition to national standards established by the U.S. Constitution and the federal government, there are also fifty state governments, each with its own constitution and policies. While these states and their political subdivisions are not permitted to operate with total autonomy, they retain great latitude in determining their own methods of popular governance.

Separation of powers within the branches of both the national and state governments also complicates the matter. For example, rules for granting access to courts are not the same as those regulations providing access to legislative bodies.

This chapter will examine how Louisiana has attempted to protect the rights of the public, including members of the news media, to acquire information, particularly information related to government action. It will explore the state's open-meetings and public-records laws, as well as its shield laws protecting the confidentiality of news sources.

ACCESS IN GENERAL

The obvious ties between self-governance and free speech and press are so profound that some scholars have argued that the principal, if not the singular, objective of the First Amendment is to protect the exchange of information affecting the political process (Baker, 1989; Bunker, Splichal, Chamberlin, & Perry, 1993; Parks, 1957; Pember & Calvert, 2011; Tedford, 1993). Wallace Parks wrote:

> It is clear that the primary purpose of the freedom-of-speech-and press clause of the First Amendment was to prevent the government from interfering with the communication of facts and views about governmental affairs, in order that all could properly exercise the rights and responsibilities of citizenship in a free society (p. 9).

Alexander Meiklejohn asserts that while private speech is afforded only the limited protections of due process provided by the Fifth Amendment, political speech is shielded by the absolute nature of the First Amendment. Political speech, according to Meiklejohn, is *"beyond the reach of legislation limitation, beyond even the due process of law.* [emphasis added]" (Tedford, p. 377).

Though the merits of these views on the breadth of the First Amendment's application may be debated, it is readily apparent that general acceptance of the perceived political benefits derived from robust communication freedom has been instrumental in the evolution of press-liberties doctrines in this country. Consequently, any government effort to curtail press freedom is suspect. Arguably, governmental restriction of access to its own workings affects press freedoms in an area that will have the most impact on the potential political dividends of these freedoms.

In arguing for "[t]he people's right to know" about government conduct, James Russell Wiggins wrote in 1964 that of the component parts of this right "the first in order of its exercise, and perhaps the first in the order of importance, is the right to get information" (pp. 3-4). Parks asserted:

> Availability is needed in order for the dynamic processes, by which our free democratic society governs itself, to function properly through the franchise, the independent formation of opinion at many levels, the equitable participation in governmental processes of especially interested parties, and the separation-of-powers and checks-and-balances system. (pp. 3-4)

In light of the preceding discussion, it would appear self-evident that there is an incumbent governmental obligation to provide access to its workings. Yet, as Baker wrote, "Almost no access advocate argues that all government information and practice should be public" (1989, p. 238). To make such an argument would be to ignore an array of factors that serve to temper the call for government openness.

To begin, public government itself is of relatively recent origin. Indeed, political philosophers dating back to Plato and Aristotle have long argued against the value of governmental participation by the masses (Ebenstein, 1969). In discussing the writings of Alexis de Tocqueville, William Ebenstein argued that "The first major democracy in the modern world is that of the United States; only after its establishment and success could the issue of democracy be brought down from the clouds of [. . .] hypothetical speculation to the firm ground of positive and empirical observation" (p. 533).

English common law, the basis of much American legal philosophy, placed little emphasis on making government accessible to the people until the late 1800s ("Open meeting statutes," 1962; Pember & Calvert; *Reeves v. Orleans Parish School Board*, 1973; Schewe, 1980; Wiggins; Wright, 1974; Yankwich, 1956). Not content to physically bar members of the press and public from witnessing its deliberations, Parliament for a time placed restrictions on printing information about its proceedings, forcing some members of the press to publish their accounts as thinly disguised works of fiction (Wiggins, 1964; Wright, 1974).

Another factor that should be considered is that despite the volume of rhetoric devoted to the popular aspects of government in the United States, government by pure democracy is the rare exception rather than the rule in America. In describing the form of national government, a model generally adopted on the state and local level, Walter F. Murphy and C. Herman Pritchett wrote:

> The structure that emerged from the Convention at Philadelphia and has evolved since that time is obviously not one of pure democracy in which the people rule directly. Nor is it merely a system of representative democracy in which those elected by popular vote govern. Rather, it is what the framers called "free government," and what most modern writers would label constitutional democracy (1986, pp. 11-12).

It may be argued that practicality might not have been the only advantages the framers saw in representative government. A central thesis of *The Irony of Democracy: An Uncommon Introduction to American Politics* is that the architects of the American political system had every intention of limiting direct public participation in government (Dye, & Zeigler, 1972). Noting that the constitutional convention itself was attended by "the most prestigious, wealthy, educated, and skillful group of 'notables' ever to be assembled in America for a political meeting" and that it was conducted in closed session, the authors contend that the Constitution's drafters felt that the actual administration of government should be left in the hands of the nation's "elites" (p. 34).

Security at the convention was indeed tight. Upon receiving the retrieved copy of proposals that had been misplaced by one of the delegates, George Washington in his capacity as president of the convention admonished the delegates "to be more careful, lest our transactions get into the News Papers and disturb the public response by premature speculation" (Rivers, 1970, p. 9).

To be sure, the architects of the Constitution were expressing democratic principles so extreme that in the eyes of "the aristocratic society of eighteenth-century Europe, the Founding Fathers were dangerous revolutionaries" according to *The Irony of Democracy* (p. 27). However, the founders were not proposing "mass democracy, with direct participation by the people in decision-making. They expected the masses to consent to government by men of principle and property out of recognition for their abilities, talents, education, and stake in the preservation of liberty and order" (p. 39). It was the view of the founders that excessive public involvement in government "could threaten the rights of property, and only a strong central government with limited popular participation could safeguard property from the attacks of the masses" (p. 31).

Irrespective of the motives behind the basic model outlined by the framers and replicated on the state and local levels, it is subject to a basic tension inherent in any system wherein elected representatives must set policy. Roger H. Davidson and Walter J. Oleszek (1994) highlight this philosophic dispute between the "Burkean trustee" and "instructed-delegates [hyphen added]" concepts of representation in their discussion of Congress (p. 135). According to the Burkean model, a representative, once elected, is obligated to look beyond the parochial desires of constituents and take that action he or she perceives is in the best interest of the population as a whole. Those who follow the instructed-delegate approach believe the duty of representatives is to give voice to the wishes of their constituents. Davidson and Oleszek wrote that the distinction is between "lawmakers who follow instructions" and those who "exercise independent judgments" (p. 135).

One implication of the Burkean-trustee model of representation is that there is arguably less need for public access to the actual workings of government. Those who accept the value of the Burkean model, founded on the assumption of the inherent morality of its agents (negating the concern over the potential for corruption stemming from secrecy), would argue that public access may actually be counterproductive. Dye and Zeigler state that this concern may have contributed to the decision to conduct the constitutional convention in closed session. "Apparently the Founding Fathers were aware that elites are most effective in negotiating, compromise, and decision making when operating in secrecy," they wrote (p. 34).

The Senate continued the tradition of secrecy established at the constitutional convention by keeping its sessions closed to the press and public until 1794 (Dye & Zeigler;

"Open meeting statutes"; Rivers; Wiggins). The House, which by design was intended to be more responsive to the general public (Davidson, & Oleszek; Fairfield, 1981), made itself available to public scrutiny from the beginning (Dye & Zeigler; "Open meeting statutes"; Rivers; Wiggins; Wright).

Given this historical precedent of governmental secrecy and the philosophic debate over the basic nature of representative government, it should not be surprising that the courts have been quite circumspect in delineating the boundaries of any right of access under the common law or the Constitution. As Parks wrote (1957):

> So long as the Supreme Court finds that there is some rational basis between the withholding [of information] and the carrying out of legislative or presidential powers, it most probably would be extremely reluctant to review the discretion of the other two branches in determining the scope and importance of the relationship (p. 17).

The reach of access to the other branches might be viewed as a political question beyond the realm of judicial review, according to Parks. There is justification for this conclusion. The American bench has found only a limited right of access to government records (Braverman, & Heppler, 1981; Bunker, et al.) and courts (Bunker, et al.; Pember & Calvert; *Richmond Newspapers, Inc. v. Virginia*, 1980; Tedford) under the common law and/or the Constitution. As Matthew D. Bunker, *et al.* wrote, "The United States Supreme Court has not explicitly found, except in criminal trials, an implied constitutional right of access to government proceedings or records" (p. 546). Indeed, the Supreme Court as recently as Spring 2013 ruled that "the right to access public information is not a 'fundamental' privilege or immunity of citizenship. The Court has repeatedly stated that the Constitution does not guarantee the existence of FOIA [freedom of information] laws" (*McBurney v. Young*, pp. 2-3).

If access must then be provided by statute, a number of factors must be considered in the development of these laws. Parks argued that the justifications for withholding access to information held by the national government include: protecting "personal and property rights"; maintaining "sources of needed information" which might be lost through fear of public disclosure; shielding reputations from "the spreading of false charges"; preventing premature release of information related to investigations of criminal conduct; maintaining an atmosphere in which policy makers can "receive frank and full advice in advance of policy decisions"; preventing "unfavorable economic consequences from the premature release of information or unfair benefits being gained through its acquisition by some in advance of others"; safeguarding security interests; and conducting foreign policy (pp. 5-6). With the possible exception of the foreign diplomacy interests, it is argued in the current analysis that access provisions at any level of government must address these same considerations.

While the rhetoric of full access has its appeal, consideration must be given to these mitigating concerns. As summarized in a 1962 *Harvard Law Review* article on open-meetings law, in the development of access guidelines "a more rational approach would be to seek to devise a legal standard affording the fullest possible degree of openness while recognizing the interests promoted by governmental secrecy" ("Open meeting statutes," p. 1203).

Gaining greater access to government-held information became an increasingly important social issue in the 1950s (Bunker, et al.; "Open meeting statutes"; Parks; Wiggins; Wright). Improving access to the federal government was not the sole objective of the movement. "Local governing bodies, operating under varied local and state laws, still are not generally as accessible to the people as they ought to be in a democracy," Wiggins wrote in 1964 (pp. 16-17). Despairing of the potential for achieving this access through the courts, champions of the cause turned to legislative remedies. In the 1970s there was a renaissance of interest in access issues as indicated by John A. Kidwell's assertion in a

1989 *Wisconsin Law Review* article that a "great majority" of state records statutes were modified, "perhaps in reaction to Watergate and other controversies concerning the concealment of governmental information" (p. 1027). Quite often those representing press interests were the driving force behind the access campaigns (Bunker, et al.; "Open meeting statutes"; Reeves; Wiggins; Wright).

In Louisiana the opportunity to observe the meetings of public bodies and examine documents related to their activities are constitutionally protected by the 1974 revision of the document under Art. 12, §3. This provision states, "No person shall be denied the right to observe the deliberations of public bodies and examine public documents, except in cases established by law."

Meetings

Most federal and state meetings-access statutes were developed in the twentieth Century, many subsequent to World War II. For example, in 1959 only twenty states had open-meetings laws (Van Slyke, & Rushing, 1990; Wright), and by 1974 every state except Mississippi, Rhode Island, New York, and West Virginia had adopted open-meetings statutes (Wright). Access to the meetings of some federal bodies was provided by the government in the Sunshine Act of 1976. Currently all states have some statutory law protecting access to meetings (Pember & Calvert).

The components of effective statutes—those which would attempt to strike the necessary balance between legitimate justifications for confidentiality and the need for public access—were detailed in a seminal 1974 *Mississippi Law Journal* article by William R. Wright II. "Perhaps the most vital provision in an open-meetings law is a statement evidencing a clear, presumptive purpose of the legislature to open the deliberations and actions of government to the people," Wright wrote (p. 1162). Such declarations, he argued, would discourage public officials from attempting to circumvent the law by taking advantage of ambiguities. They also encourage liberal court interpretation in favor of access. The body of the statutes, according to Wright's paradigm, should delineate the law's coverage, define meetings, outline provisions for closed sessions, establish notice procedures, and provide enforcement measures.

LOUISIANA

As noted earlier, personal observation of the meetings of public bodies is a constitutionally protected right in Louisiana. The seeds of Louisiana's current statutory law were planted with passage of Act No. 484 of 1952. However, it may be argued that it was not until the passage of Act No. 665 in 1976 that open-meetings regulation began to take on real meaning (Brown, 1996; Manning, Murchison, Pierce, Songy, & Wear, 1976; Schewe, 1981). That measure, which began as Senate Bill No. 591 authored by then state Sen. James H. "Jim" Brown of Ferriday, made great strides in correcting existing deficiencies in the law, such as restricting topics that would justify an executive session. The current statutes are outlined in *LAS*-Title 42, sections 11 through 28.

The second of these sections (LSA-R.S. 42:12) notes that, as it is vital to the "maintenance of a democratic society that public business be conducted in an open and public manner," open-meetings statutes must "be construed liberally." As it is unreasonable to assume that any set of regulations, no matter how detailed, can anticipate all possible eventualities, this clear statement of legislative intent is critical to the application of the statutes in real-world situations. It requires that under any possible conditions that create gray areas, the Louisiana statutes should be interpreted in favor of providing access.

Likewise, in LSA-R.S. 42:13 the statutes create a broad definition of "public meeting." Under this section, meetings are defined as "the convening of a quorum of a public body to *deliberate or act* [emphasis added] on a matter over which the public body has supervision, control, jurisdiction, or *advisory* [emphasis added] power" (LSA-R.S. 42:13.A.(*1*)). Even if the body is gathering to merely receive information, the statute requires that the meeting adhere to statutory requirements for meetings in general. Public bodies are those "state, parish, [or] municipal" groups with "policy making, *advisory*, [emphasis added] or administrative functions" (LSA-R.S. 42:13.A.(2)). Any entities that report to these bodies are also bound to abide by open-meetings laws. For example, a planning-and-zoning subcommittee formed to simply make a recommendation to a city council would be subject to open-meetings requirements. Exemptions are provided for "chance meetings or social gatherings" at which no official business is discussed (LSA-R.S. 42:13.B).

Not only must the public be admitted to the meetings of public bodies, it must also receive adequate advance notice of such meetings so that those who wish to may attend (LSA-R.S. 42:19).[1] The notice requirement has two components. The first is that public bodies that are legally required to hold regularly scheduled meetings must annually publish the times, dates, and location of these meetings (LSA-R.S. 42:19.A.(1)(a)). For example, if a parish school board is mandated by law to meet on the second and fourth Tuesday of each month, and these meetings take place at 7 p.m. in the board's conference room, the board must post written notice of this schedule at the year's start.

The second is that, except under "extraordinary emergency" circumstances (LSA-R.S. 42:19.A.(1)(b)(iv)), special written notice for all meetings are to be posted at least twenty-four hours in advance of such meetings, even for those meetings whose annual schedule has already been announced (LSA-R.S. 42:19.A.(1)(b)(i)). This notice must include not only scheduling details, but also an agenda (LSA-R.S. 42:19.A.(1)(b)(ii)) and any anticipated executive-session discussions (LSA-R.S. 42:19.A.(1)(b)(iii)). These specific notices of meetings may be posted at the body's "principal office," its meeting location, or in its "official journal" (LSA-R.S. 42:19.A.(2)(a)). The news media may also request special notice of meetings, and in such cases they must be given the same notification as are members of the public body in question (LSA-R.S. 42:19.A.(2)(b)).

The body may address matters not included on the posted agenda; however, doing so requires that a clear explanation of the necessity for adding items should be recorded in the minutes and that there should be a unanimous vote in favor of the addition (LSA-R.S. 42:19.A.(1)(b)(ii)). The body must allow public comment on the motion to add items before a vote is taken. This provision allowing for adding items cannot be used in an attempt to circumvent the law.

Once it has been established that the proceeding in question is subject to open-meetings law, members of the public may not only observe the meeting, they also have the right to record it or broadcast it live, so long as such activities do not disrupt the proceedings (LSA-R.S. 42:23). In addition, LSA-R.S. 42:14 requires that there be time provided for public comment. Furthermore, school boards are specifically required to allow public comment on each agenda item immediately prior to any action (LSA-R.S. 42:15.A). Attempts by a public body to avoid public observation of its actions, such as conducting "secret balloting" (LSA-R.S. 42:14. B), are expressly banned.

The statutes allow for closed meetings under certain conditions (LSA-R.S. 42:16). Justification for executive sessions are outlined under LSA-R.S. 42:17 and include: "Discussion of the character, professional competence, or physical or mental health of a person" (LSA-R.S. 42:17.A.(1)); meetings related to on-going collective bargaining activities (LSA-R.S. 42:17.A.(2)); discussion of security measures (LSA-R.S. 42:17.A.(3)); "Investigative proceedings" (LSA-R.S. 42:17.A.(4)); or "Cases of extraordinary emergency, which shall be limited to natural disaster, threat of epidemic, civil disturbances, suppression of insurrections, the repelling of invasions, or other matters of similar magnitude" (LSA-R.S. 42:17.A.(5)).

Even when there is justification for a public body to consider entering executive session, it must follow detailed procedures for doing so (LSA-R.S. 42:16). The reason for seeking the closed session must be publicly stated, and closure of the meeting requires a two-thirds vote, with the votes of all members on the motion recorded.

No final action can be taken during the closed session, and any attempt to use the session to circumvent the intent of the open-meetings laws is expressly prohibited. In addition, while the body *may be permitted* to enter executive session under the outlined circumstances, the law clearly states that it is *not required* to do so.

In fact, the provision allowing executive-session discussion of a person's "character, professional competence, or physical or mental health" also requires that the subject of such discussion be given twenty-four-hour notice prior of the meeting, barring extenuating circumstance (in such instances the body must still provide what it considers adequate notice for the situation). The subject of the discussion is thus afforded the opportunity and the right to require that this discussion take place in open session (LSA-R.S. 42:17).

The statute also sets limits on executive sessions by the state legislature and its subdivisions (LSA-R.S. 42:18). It establishes conditions allowing for executive session (most similar to those found for public bodies in general) and requires a majority vote before doing so.

Minutes from the meetings of public bodies in general must be made "available within a reasonable time," and must include information such as the votes by individual members of the group (LSA-R.S. 42:20). Minutes' requirements of the legislature and its subdivisions are established by the constitution and chamber guidelines (LSA-R.S. 42:21).

The statutes provide several mechanisms to ensure compliance with their dictates. Anyone may file a complaint with either the local district attorney or state attorney general if he or she believes that the law has been violated (LSA-R.S. 42:25). The office receiving the complaint *must* act on the complaint "unless written reasons are given as to why the suit should not be filed" (LSA-R.S. 42:25.A & B). If either office has reason to believe that the law has been violated, it may file a suit even in the absence of a complaint.

Suits alleging violations are to be heard by the district courts with jurisdiction for the parish where the meeting took place (LSA-R.S. 42:27). They require summary judgments and must be given docket priority, and any appeals resulting from the district court's ruling must be decided "as soon as practicable" (LSA-R.S. 42:27.B). The courts may issue writs of mandamus, provide injunctive relief, or render declaratory judgments (LSA-R.S. 42:26). The court might also award fully successful plaintiffs "reasonable attorney fees and other costs of litigation" (LSA-R.S. 42:26.C). Plaintiffs who are partially successful may receive such awards at the court's discretion. Those who are found to have filed frivolous complaints are subject to paying such fees to the defendant. Those who do not abide by a court's decision can be found in contempt of court (LSA-R.S. 42:26.B).

If a member of a public body is found to have intentionally violated the law, he or she can be held personally responsible for civil penalties up to one hundred dollars per violation (LSA-R.S. 42:24). If a court rules that a public body took action during a meeting that did not comply with open-meetings regulations, that action can be nullified (LSA-R.S. 42:24). In both instances, suits seeking these remedies must be filed within sixty days of the meeting in dispute.

Given that Louisiana's open-meetings laws are primarily found in the statutes, the potential value of examining court decisions in an effort to understand application of the law in a specific instance may be somewhat limited. Statutes can be frequently amended, rendering a particular court ruling no longer applicable. Looking at patterns of interpretation can be instructive, however.

While court decisions in the state have generally promoted access—as might be expected by the requirement that statutes be interpreted liberally—they can be far from consistent. For example, in *Spain v. Louisiana High School Athletic Association* (La. 1981) the state's supreme court took a liberal position in the direction of openness by rejecting the defense argument that the athletic association (LHSAA) should be exempt from the law because it was a private organization.

In reaching the contrary conclusion, the court noted that in effect the association was exercising control over the schools, which are state agencies, by imposing guidelines on their athletic programs. While the court agreed that schools were not required by law to be a member of the organization nor to abide by its rules, it also recognized that it was difficult for high-school athletic programs to survive if they were not association members.

Citing judicial precedent, the court took the position that athletics is an important component of education, which is a state function. In addition, the court found that a great deal of the association's administrative work was conducted by government employees, primarily coaches and principals, and the association was funded by gate receipts, which were held to be state money.

The *Spain* decision can be interpreted as allowing for the application of open-meetings law to any number of agencies operating within the state that are not clearly governmental authorities. In many ways, the National Collegiate Athletic Association is similar in function and organization to the LHSAA. The applicability of access laws to the NCAA was an issue raised by John Tyler (1989).

Tyler was specifically addressing access under records laws. However, there is a great deal of overlap in coverage between meetings and records laws, and arguably inclusion is a significant issue under both. This concern is also of relevance to the status of various academic accrediting organizations, such as the Southern Association of Colleges and Schools and the Accrediting Council on Education in Journalism and Mass Communications.

The openness established by cases such as *Spain* is at times offset by decisions that limit the law's scope. For example, in *Delta Development v. Plaquemines Parish* (1984) the state's Fourth Circuit Court of Appeal ruled that when actions taken in violation of the open-meetings law are voidable, rather than null from inception, it is within the authority of a public body to later ratify such action in a properly conducted meeting. In this case a parish commission council, during a meeting that allegedly violated open-meeting guidelines in several ways, passed a resolution to file a lawsuit to recover mineral rights.

In answer, *Delta*, which held the mineral rights, had filed a lawsuit arguing that the resolution authorizing the suit for reclamation of the rights was invalid because of these alleged violations of open-meetings law. Before the court could rule on the suit seeking nullification, the commission met in a properly conducted meeting and ratified its earlier vote. The circuit court upheld the district-court ruling that the suit for nullification of the resolution was therefore rendered moot. This position suggests that public bodies are free to violate the law, then, if they are caught, they can simply take a *pro forma* vote in a properly conducted meeting in order to avoid nullification of its action.

As recently as 1998 the state's Third Circuit Court of Appeal took that same position (*Marien v. Rapides Parish Police Jury*). It found that the defendant had not given the proper twenty-four-hour notice prior to a meeting. However, because the action it took was later reapproved at a subsequent meeting that did comply with notice requirements, the request for voiding the action under open-meetings statutes had been once again rendered moot. Cases such as these serve as prime examples of the potential weakness in the voidability provisions that Wright warned against. A stronger assurance of compliance with the law would be to require those bodies found in violation of the law to re-initiate the proceedings in question so that the public can observe the entire process.

Technological changes are also raising new concerns in the arena of open-meetings law. The attorney general's office has consistently noted that the law prohibits "walking quorums" (Op.Atty.Gen., No. 12-0177, October 11, 2012, p. 6), a situation where members of a public body cleverly leave a room and other members enter a room to deliberate or discuss an issue so there is never a quorum (a majority of the membership) physically present in the same room as a subterfuge to avoid compliance with open-meetings requirements. Texting, e-mail, instant messaging and other forms of electronic communications and technological advances can create those same dangers as presented by "walking quorums" that might be used by a public body to skirt the intent of open-meetings law and allow a public body to secretly discuss or deliberate on an issue even in the public's presence. For example, members of a public body may text one another during the course of a meeting as a way to avoid vocal discussion of the matter at hand. The attorney general's office has held that the mere use of electronic communication during a meeting is not a de facto violation of open meetings law (Op.Atty.Gen., No. 10-0233, November 8, 2011). The office likened this practice to members of the body passing hand-written notes, which is not prohibited under the law. However, it cautioned that the use of these devices between members of the body in an effort to get out of open discussion might be prohibited. The office noted that:

> La. R.S. 42:14(B) provides that public bodies are prohibited from utilizing any manner of proxy voting procedure, secret balloting, or any other means to circumvent the intent of the Open Meetings Law. Thus, it would not be appropriate for members of a public body to utilize electronic communication to engage in any secret balloting to find out how council members would vote or as a method of circumventing the purposes of the Open Meetings Law. (*Op.Atty.Gen.*, No. 12-0177, October 11, 2012, p. 3)

Such exchanges taking place outside of formal meetings may also constitute a violation of the law. On the other hand, members of the body sending one another electronic messages, even as they relate to issues before the body, is not in and of itself a violation. The key issue is the intended effect. According to the AG's office, if such an exchange "effectively stifles any further discussion of the issue at a public meeting by the public body, this could raise concerns under the Open Meetings Law" (p. 6).

OPEN RECORDS

Wisconsin has provided statutory access to public records since 1849 (Kidwell; Bunker et al.), and currently all states have established records-access provisions (Bunker, et al.; Kidwell; Pember & Calvert; Tyler, 1989; Van Slyke & Rushing). The national government enacted the Freedom of Information Act, which provides access to federal records, in 1966 (Braverman & Heppler; Bunker, et al.; Kidwell; Pember & Calvert), replacing the access provisions of Section 3 of 1966's Federal Administrative Procedures Act (Bunker et al.).

Components of Public Records Laws

Burt A. Braverman and Wesley R. Heppler presented an analysis of public records laws in a 1981 *George Washington Law Review* article similar to the one Wright had authored for open-meetings regulation. They note that a number of states had recognized at least limited "common-law rights of access to public records" long before the development of twentieth-century Sunshine Laws (p. 723).

As a consequence, they suggested that a complete understanding of all the public records provisions, such as the guidelines applicable to court documents, would require the study of multiple sources of law. Among the issues of importance to the development of record statutes which they considered were the definition of public records, exemptions, preconditions for exercising access opportunities, procedures for gaining access, indexing, copying, enforcement, and the relationship between federal and state statutes.

Braverman and Heppler stated public-records laws must establish what agencies, and which of their records, are subject to the law. Often, they wrote, funding is used as a determinant of the law's applicability to agencies. The entity's mission may also be a consideration. Some regulations are applicable to those agencies serving "a governmental or proprietary function for the state" (p. 730), which also may result in the inclusion of private or quasi-public organizations that fulfill some traditional government function. These definitions may also specifically exempt some bodies, such as courts, from a statute's reach.

Braverman and Heppler argue that there are two primary considerations when determining which records should be viewed as public: "(1) the physical form of the information; and (2) the origin, nature, and reason for the agency's creation or acquisition of the records" (p. 732). As most states have implicitly or explicitly established expansive conceptions of what constitutes a record, the latter issue more often creates difficulties.

There are four basic approaches states have taken to establish the public nature of documents, according to Braverman and Heppler. One method states have used has been to define all records held by bound agencies as public. The second state approach has been to restrict applicability to those records related to the discharge of a public duty. The third has been to include within the law's boundaries "only those materials *required to be kept by law* [emphasis in original]" (p. 735). Finally, some state laws permit "public interest" (p. 736) to warrant the exemption of records. Braverman and Heppler argue that this final type of stipulation is so vague that it cannot be categorized among the commonly accepted justifications for exempting specific types of records.

The first approach to defining public documents has the greatest potential application for providing access, though it is often mitigated by exception stipulations. The fourth is the most restrictive. Most states permit the duplication of public records; however, few require the indexing of records as part of the access guidelines.

Enforcement measures should establish a process for challenging a public official's denial of access to, what the requester believes is, a public document and also judicial remedies for inappropriate request rejections. The researchers found that some states hold that intra-agency appeal is the first recourse for those who have been denied access. In these cases, states may mandate the exhaustion of agency appeals before seeking judicial review. Other states permit citizens to apply immediately to the courts when they are denied access to a public document. The laws may also specifically establish court jurisdiction and procedure in application of public-records law. Those laws may also encourage prompt adjudication of civil suits over denial of public access. Some allowed the award of attorney fees or court costs or both to successful plaintiffs in civil suits for access. The recovery of these funds may be dependent upon establishing "bad faith" (p. 756) on the custodian's part in denying the requested record. The plaintiff may also be required to be fully successful in the bid for access before recovery. Some states give courts discretion in these matters; others do not. Some states created civil and criminal penalties for violation of public records law. Generally, statutes require defendants to carry the burden of proof in access suits.

Louisiana

The foundation of Louisiana's law regulating public records was laid in 1940 by Act No. 195 (*LSA-R.S. 44.1 et seq.*), introduced by senators Frank B. Ellis of Covington, W. Davis Cotton of Rayville, and Joe T. Cawthorn of Mansfield as Senate Bill 273 of 1940 (*Acts State of Louisiana 1940*). The legislation's scope was broad. It defined public records as any documents—written or visual, copies or originals—"being in use, or prepared for the use in the conduct" of state business (p. 833). It applied to any entity operating under the auspices of the Louisiana Constitution, including state and local authorities. It also encompassed any financial data associated with "the receipt or payment of any money received or paid by or under" state law (p. 833).

Given the scope of the law, it is to be expected that there would be repeated revisions, and there have been. From its original passage through 1974 alone, the act was amended nineteen times. However, upon adoption of the Louisiana Constitution of 1974, access to public records was lifted from the status of a statutory-granted privilege to a protected right.

Provisions of the state's public-records laws are currently found in Title 44 of the statutes. As with the open-meetings law, the state has set liberal guidelines that, in general, promote access. Unlike the open-meeting statutes, public-records provisions do not include a clear statement of legislative intent in favor of access. However, if the record's custodian denies access to a public document, the custodian bears the burden of providing a justification for this denial (LSA-R.S. 44:31.B.(3) & 44:35.B).

The term "public body" is broadly defined. This definition encompasses both official government entities and their subdivisions—such as city councils and committees answering to them—and any organization created "to perform a governmental or proprietary function" (LSA-R.S. 44:1.A.(1)). Likewise the description of "documents" is expansive. The physical properties of the material are not relevant. The definition includes everything from maps and photographs to electronically stored data (LSA-R.S. 44:1.A.(2)(a)). Nor is the physical location of the material a matter of primary importance. According to the law, "public records" are those "*having been used*, being in use, or *prepared*, possessed, or retained for use in the conduct" [emphasis added] of public policy (LSA-R.S. 44:1.A.(2)(a)).

Access to public records encompasses a wide array of activities. According to the law, "any person of the age of maturity [eighteen] may inspect, copy, or reproduce" these records (LSA-R.S. 44:31.B.(1)). They may also require that the custodian provide a copy of the record (LSA-R.S. 44:31.B.(2) & LSA-R.S. 44:32). In such cases, the custodian may charge "reasonable fees," though they are not required to do so (LSA-R.S. 44:32.C.(1)(a)). Any such fees are to be charged according to a "uniform" schedule established by the appropriate agency (LSA-R.S. 44:32). Free copies or copies at reduced cost may be provided to the indigent or to those who the custodian deems will use the material in the public's interest (LSA-R.S. 44:32C.(2)).

During inspection, those persons accessing the material must receive "all reasonable comfort and facility for the full exercise of" their rights (LSA-R.S. 44:32.A). While the custodian can require documentation establishing appropriate age and that the requester sign a log, no other inquiries may be posed.[2] Supervision of the inspection of documents is limited to those actions necessary to ensure that documents are not damaged or altered. The custodian cannot inspect copies of material created by or provided to those exercising these rights (LSA-R.S. 44:32.A). No fees can be charged for inspections when they take place during normal working hours (LSA-R.S. 44:32.A & C.(3)). Those who wish to examine documents outside of normal working hours can be charged "reasonable" amounts to cover payment for those required to remain during these inspections (LSA-R.S. 44:32.A).

Unless a public document is in active use, it must immediately be made available to the person making the request (LSA-R.S. 44:33.B). In those instances when the material is in active use, the custodian must "promptly" give written notice of a date and time within three working days when the record will be made available. Unless otherwise mandated by state law,[3] all public records must be maintained for at least three years (LSA-R.S.44:36). If the material is for some reason absent, the custodian is required to not only explain in writing "to the best of his knowledge" why the record is absent, but also provide all available information that would allow the requester to access it.

If a custodian deems that material in question is not subject to access under public-records law, within three working days he or she must provide a written explanation—including a reference to the legal justification—as to why the material is being withheld (LSA-R.S. 44:32.D). If the custodian determines that a portion of the material is not subject to public-records law, he or she may remove that material and provide the remaining portion to the requester (LSA-R.S. 44:32.B).

Enforcement mechanisms include both civil and criminal penalties for those who violate the law. Anyone who has received a written denial notice or who has not received such response or access within five working days may file suit in the district court serving the parish in which the request was presented (*LSA-R.S. 44:35.A*). Such petitions can seek "issuance of a writ of mandamus, [and] injunctive or declaratory relief." In these actions, the custodian who has denied access carries the burden of proof (*LSA-R.S. 44:35.B*). The district court must give these cases docket preference (*LSA-R.S. 44:35.C*). The court will issue summary judgments (*LSA-R.S. 44:35.C*). It has the authority to conduct in-camera review of the material (*LSA-R.S. 44:35.B*). Any resulting appeals of the ruling must also be given prompt attention by the appropriate court (*LSA-R.S. 44:35.C*).

Plaintiffs who are fully successful in their action are entitled to recover legal expenses (*LSA-R.S. 44:35.D*). Partially successful plaintiffs can be awarded such fees as the court deems fitting. If the custodian is found to have acted "unreasonably or arbitrarily," the court may also award the plaintiff actual damages (*LSA-R.S. 44:35.E.(1)*). In addition, the court can level civil penalties up to one hundred dollars for each regular workday for which the custodian failed to respond to the request. In these cases the custodian will be held personally responsible for the civil penalties and responsible along with the government agency he or she represents for the plaintiff's legal costs, unless the custodian acted on advice of the agency's attorney (*LSA-R.S. 44:35.E.(2)*). If the custodian uses a personal attorney for defense in the suit (*LSA-R.S. 44:35.E.(2)*), the court may award compensation for these services up to amounts approved by the state's attorney general (*LSA-R.S. 44:35.F*). Failure to comply with court rulings can result in contempt-of-court findings against the custodian (*LSA-R.S. 44:35.B*).

Custodians who prevent access and those who conspire with the custodian to do so can face criminal fines between $100 and $1,000 or jail terms from one to six months for a first conviction (*LSA-R.S. 44:37*). Further convictions can result in fines ranging from $250 to $2,000 and/or jail sentences from two to six months.

Though open-records law does not include the same clear statement of legislative intent toward access (as is found in open-meetings law), in 2001 the Louisiana Supreme Court held that a host of previous court rulings had outlined such a requirement (*Landis v. Moreau*). Quoting from its 1984 decision in *Title Research Corp. v. Rausch*, the majority opinion in *Landis v. Moreau* reaffirmed the court's position that:

> The legislature, by the public records statutes, sought to guarantee, in the most expansive and unrestricted way possible, the right of the public to inspect and reproduce those records which the laws deem to be public. There was no intent on the part of the legislatures to qualify, in anyway, the right of access. [citations omitted]. As with the constitutional provision, the statute should be construed liberally, and any doubt must be resolved in favor of the right of access (p. 4).

As recently as 2003, the state's First Circuit Court of Appeal reached a similar conclusion (*The Times-Picayune Publishing Corporation v. The Board of Supervisors of Louisiana State University*). In that case the First Circuit noted that state Supreme Court decisions had consistently "found that there was no intent on the part of the legislature to qualify, in any way, the right of access." It also reaffirmed that the burden of proof that a record is exempt from disclosure rests with the custodian.

One glaring weakness in the law is the issue of exemptions. In an attempt to simplify determination of information's status under the open-records guidelines, the legislature has decreed, "Any exception, exemption, and limitation to the laws pertaining to public records not provided for in this Chapter or in the Constitution of Louisiana shall have no effect" (*LSA-R.S. 44:4.1*). While this would at first appear to simplify establishing a document's status, just sections *LSA-R.S. 44:4* and *LSA-R.S. 44:4.1* combine to make a list of more than seventy-five items exempt from disclosure. In addition, federal exemptions must also be taken into account. Furthermore, merely listing exceptions does not settle the matter. There remains the issue of interpreting the meaning of the exceptions in application.

This concern is clearly illustrated by one of the most recently contentious regions of exception, those that apply to the governor's office. A clause in *LSA-R.S. 44:5.A* states that all records of the office "relating to the deliberative process of the governor" are not subject to disclosure. Additionally, Section 44:5.B.(2) provides that "a record limited to pre-decisional advice and recommendations to the governor concerning budgeting in the custody of any agency or department headed by an unclassified gubernatorial appointee shall be privileged [exempt from disclosure] for six months from the date such record is prepared."

The legislature added this language to the statutes as part of a 2009 move that was touted as promoting greater openness from the governor's office, which had previously been essentially exempt from open-records law (Blanchard, 2011). However, as Kevin Blanchard argued in a 2011 *Louisiana Law Review* article, the wording is so vague that it "is subject to several interpretations, meaning that the courts will be faced with choices of interpretation that could indeed result in a *less*—not more—transparent government" (p. 706). His concern quickly proved well-founded, as Gov. Bobby Jindal's office denied documents to the media shortly after Blanchard's warning, claiming protection from disclosure under this section of the law (Deslatte, 2012a; Deslatte, 2012b; Maldonaldo, 2012; *The Advocate*, 2012).

As with open-meetings regulations, public-records law can change with each session of the legislature. As a result, statutes carry more weight than case law. That having been stated, study of court decisions can provide insight into the struggles judges face in attempting to achieve a proper balance between the need for access and legitimate limitations. This dilemma was well illustrated by the Fourth Circuit Court of Appeal's ruling in *Times-Picayune Publishing Co. v. Johnson* (1994). In this case the newspaper was attempting to gain access to nominations for scholarships that could be awarded by members of the legislature at the time. Some of these applications were in the possession of Tulane University, a private institution. The court found these nominations prepared by legislators constituted public records accessible under the law. The court held that:

> The contract between the State and Tulane, the manner of its execution, the contractual beneficiaries, and all other related matters concern public business. As such, they are subject to public scrutiny; and we readily conclude that all records related to the contract and the giving of scholarships fall within the broad definition of public records, including the nomination forms herein sought by plaintiffs (p. 1176).

According to the court, the legislators remained custodians of these records, responsible for adhering to the law, even when they had transferred physical possession of the documents to the university. "Custodians of public records [including legislators who are custodians] do not have authority to transfer custody of public records to another so as to insulate those records from public inspection" (p. 1176). By allowing the university to keep the forms, the legislators "tacitly authorized Tulane to respond to requests to make them public in accord with" the law (p. 1176).

This section of the decision appears in keeping with a liberal application of the law, holding that under certain conditions even private entities can become custodians of public records, with attendant responsibilities. Yet, in that same decision the court appeared to apply special exertion in justifying its refusal to take full advantage of enforcement mechanisms. It ruled that although the plaintiff was entitled access to the documents, it found no justification for issuing the requested writs of mandamus (which had been among the forms of relief sought by the plaintiff), as there was no evidence that the custodians would not abide by the declaratory judgment defining the records as public. Because the petition for writs was denied, the court argued that the plaintiff had only been partially successful in its suit. It therefore overturned the district court's award of attorney fees.

An emerging area of contention is the status of e-mail under the law. As noted earlier, the statutes broadly define public records to encompass a wide range of material regardless of their physical properties or location (*LSA-R.S. 44:1.A.(2)(a)*). However, it is the "public" nature of e-mails produced or received by government officials that has created some difficulty. Louisiana has decided that "e-mails of a purely personal nature received or transmitted by a public employee which have no relation to any function of a public office" (*Op.Atty.Gen.*, No. 10-0272, April 13, 2012, p. 2). The attorney general's office has held, "A record's mere existence in a public office does not automatically make such document a 'public record.' It is the opinion of this office that the definition of 'public records' requires a content-driven analysis for a connection between the record and the conduct of public business or the functioning of a public body" (p. 2).

A district court in *Suire v. Murphy* (2011) agreed with the position of the attorney general's office. It found that the conflict over the status of personal e-mails is one between privacy rights protected by the state's constitution and public-records law. It ruled that even though government employees have only a limited expectation of privacy for messages they send using work computers, "a document's content must have a connection to a government function" to be considered a public record (p. 7).

While these interpretations do provide some protection from disclosure for e-mails, they also reinforce the idea that the law requires access to documents regardless of their physical properties. The fact that a document is electronic does not exempt it from disclosure.

SHIELD LAWS

Government policy may have an impact on a journalist's ability to gather information even when the information is not necessarily in the government's possession. Arguably there are times when the only way that a journalist can gain access to information is to promise the source that his or her identity will be kept secret. Journalists may refer to these informants as "unnamed sources," "informed sources," "Deep Throat," or similar designations. Obviously there are many reasons why a source may wish to avoid being identified. However, there are also many instances in which government officials and the public may want to know the names of such sources. These situations lend themselves to a clash concerning the public good derived from disclosure, the journalist's responsibility to inform the audience, and a professional ethic that demands honoring a commitment. In these battles the journalist has limited protection under the First Amendment. As has already been discussed, there is little historical or judicial precedent for a "right" to gather information in general, much less one that would set journalists apart as a protected class.

Generally, there are three ways by which the government may use the force of law to extract information from an individual: compelled testimony, search warrant, and subpoena of data. As they relate to journalists, the objectives of these inquiries might be anything from attempting to uncover the name of a confidential source to gathering unpublished potential evidence related to a criminal investigation, such as photographs of a crime scene.

Given the clear need for courts and legislative bodies to have access to as much information as possible so that they can reach the optimal decisions, protections from forced disclosure of information are the rare exception. And, these protected areas are not absolute. For example, in general there exists a right of patient-doctor confidentiality. However, under certain circumstances, not only is a doctor *allowed* to report what he or she has learned from a patient, the doctor is *required* to do so, such as when a patient describes a concrete plan to commit suicide. From a constitutional perspective, the seminal ruling is the U.S. Supreme Court's 1972 holding in *Branzburg v. Hayes*. In that ruling the court consolidated two judgments arising from Kentucky (both involving Paul Branzburg, a reporter for the *Louisville Courier-Journal*), one from Massachusetts (*re Pappas*), and one from California (*United States v. Caldwell*) to explore the question of whether a journalist can be forced to reveal the identity of a confidential source to a grand jury. In each case the journalists had been called to testify before grand juries and had refused to do so, citing, among other claims, an implied right under the First Amendment to gather information through the use of confidential sources.

The U. S. Supreme Court, in a 5-4 decision with one justice filing a concurring opinion, held that there were no First Amendment considerations that would necessarily preclude a court from compelling journalists to reveal the identity of confidential sources before a grand jury. Noting that as early as 1958 the federal bench had rejected the argument that journalists were exempt under the First Amendment from revealing confidential information in response to a subpoena, Justice Byron White, writing for the Court argued:

> Citizens generally are not constitutionally immune from grand jury subpoenas; and neither the First Amendment nor any other constitutional provision protects the average citizen from disclosing to a grand jury information that he has received in confidence (p. 682).

Justices Warren Burger, Harry Blackmun, and William Rehnquist endorsed the finding. Justice Lewis Powell supported the ruling, but filed a concurring opinion.

Although the majority refused to exempt journalists from grand jury testimony under the First Amendment, even it suggested in that opinion that certain access rights did exist under its umbrella. Justice White wrote:

> We do not question the significance of free speech, press or assembly to the country's welfare. Nor is it suggested that news gathering does not qualify for First Amendment protection; *without some protection for seeking out the news* [emphasis added], freedom of the press could be eviscerated (p. 681).

The court ruled that the rights of journalists to gather news are generally no greater than the rights of the public at large to acquire information. In few instances are citizens protected from grand jury testimony. Those in the majority were loath to add another protected group. For the courts to operate efficiently and fairly, they must have access to as many sources as possible; thus the judicial branch ruled in favor of its own access to information, to the detriment of journalists' access.

The final decision was a near thing. The final vote was 5-4 with a concurring opinion. In that concurring opinion, Justice Powell wrote that he had sided with the majority only because of the narrow nature of the holding. In his view, even the majority had accepted in general terms a public right to gather information, but it was simply not automatically exempting testimony before grand juries by journalists. Apparently in support of the perceived public good occasionally served by the use of confidential sources, the majority opinion had suggested alternative means for government establishing a privilege it could not find under the First Amendment, including statutory exemption. For its part, the dissent presented persuasive arguments for expanding First Amendment rights to gather information to include exemptions for journalists from such testimony. Justice Potter Stewart, joined by justices William Brennan and Thurgood Marshall, wrote:

> A corollary of the right to publish must be the right to gather news. The full flow of information to the public protected by the free-press guarantee would be severely curtailed if no protection whatever were afforded to the process by which news is assembled and disseminated (p. 727).

Stewart outlined the conditions that should be met before journalists could be compelled to reveal their sources. These include situations in which the government could show an "overwhelming and compelling interest in the information" (p. 743) and that the information could not be gathered by other means. Justice William Douglas, in his dissent, wrote, "A reporter is no better than his source of information. Unless he has a privilege to withhold the identity of his source, he will be the victim of governmental intrigue or aggression" (p. 722).

The practical impact of this decision is mixed. Lower courts, perhaps influenced by the judicial uncertainty suggested by the split vote, have generally read the case to give it its narrowest possible scope. States have stepped into the void. Forty have established journalist-privilege statutes, also known as shield laws (Pember & Calvert).

The Supreme Court addressed the use of search warrants and subpoenas *duces tecum* to acquire information from journalists in its 1978 *Zurcher v. Stanford Daily* ruling. In 1971 demonstrators had barricaded themselves in Stanford University Hospital. After a standoff of more than twenty-four hours, officers from the police and sheriff's departments forced their way into the hospital. As they did so, demonstrators fled through a doorway at the opposite end of the corridor. Fleeing demonstrators ran into the nine law officers posted outside of the door. During the ensuing melee, all nine officers were injured, including one who received a broken shoulder. The *Stanford Daily* published an article with accompanying photographs about the incident. In an effort to identify those involved in the demonstration, the district attorney secured a warrant to search the news offices for "negatives, film, and pictures showing the events" (p. 551).

Staff members filed a civil suit seeking declarative and injunctive relief under the First, Fourth, and Fourteenth amendments to the U.S. Constitution. They argued that newsroom searches are potentially disruptive, and confidential material lying outside the scope of the warrant would also be made available to searchers. Their position was that a subpoena duces tecum, which requires the recipient to provide indicated documents rather than allowing police officials to search for them, would have been a more appropriate way to gain access to information in the possession of journalists.

The U.S. Supreme Court ruled 5-3 that there was no special exception to search warrants issued against journalists to be found under the First Amendment. In the majority opinion, Justice White noted that warrants are not directed at people, but at searching places and seizing things. They do not even require that a person be named. According to the majority, precedent established that justification for warrants is, in fact, higher for those suspected of having committed criminal acts than for other parties. Justices in the majority rejected the notion of a *per-se* requirement that subpoenas be used in place of search warrants just because journalists were involved. They pointed out that warrants could be issued only upon establishment before a magistrate that there was good cause to justify the warrant. As a result there existed ample protection from harassing or unduly disruptive searches. They held that "prior cases do no more than insist that the courts apply the warrant requirements with particular exactitude when First Amendment interests would be endangered by the search" (p. 565). These requirements "should afford sufficient protection against the harms that are assuredly threatened by warrants for searching newspaper offices" (p. 565). The federal government would later limit warrant-based searches of newsrooms with the Privacy Protection Act of 1980 (Pember & Calvert).

In summary, with *Branzburg* and *Zurcher* the court rejected the notion that journalists under the First Amendment are granted special exemptions from compelled testimony or searches of their offices. Both decisions were narrow victories for the majority. In both, the dissent offered persuasive arguments for contrary findings, and even the majority opinions acknowledged that special consideration should be given journalists in these matters. The majority opinions also offered alternative resolutions to the dilemma, strongly hinting that other branches of government might step in to fill the void left by constitutional protections for confidential information.

Louisiana and compelled disclosure by journalists

There may be a common perception that Louisiana is not among the most progressive of states in the protection of civil liberties. Given the state's history in such areas as segregation, some justification exists for that perception. However, it is argued here that Louisiana has in fact been proactive in this area of law. The state statutorily created a shield law for reporters in 1964 (*LSA-R.S. 45:1451-1454 et. seq.*), eight years before the U.S. Supreme Court's *Branzburg* holding. Special statutory protections from warrant-based searches were created in 1981 (*LSA-R.S. 15:42*), and the legislature enacted provisions for issuing subpoenas in 1986 (*LSA-R.S. 45:1455-1459 et. seq.*). These laws followed the Supreme Court's ruling in *Zurcher* by three and eight years, respectively.

Under *LSA-R.S. 45:1451 et. seq.* Louisiana's statutes provide journalists a special, conditional privilege from compulsory disclosure of unidentified sources. It first defines those covered by the law. According to *LSA-R.S. 45:1451*:

> "Reporter" shall mean any person regularly engaged in the business of collecting, writing or editing news for publication through a news media [sic]. The term *reporter* shall include all persons who were previously connected with any news media as aforesaid as to the information obtained while so connected.
> "News Media" shall include:
> (a) Any newspaper or other periodical issued at regular intervals and having a paid general circulation;
> (b) Press associations;
> (c) Wire service;
> (d) Radio;
> (e) Television; and
> (f) Persons or corporations engaged in the making of newsreels or other motion picture news for public showing.

For those covered by the provisions, the law states:

> Except as hereinafter provided, no reporter shall be compelled to disclose in any administrative, judicial or legislative proceedings or anywhere else the identity of any informant or any source of information obtained by him from another person while acting as a reporter. (*LSA-R.S. 45:1452*)

The protection can be revoked. As noted in *LSA-R.S. 45:1453*, a district court can issue an order to remove the privilege in response to a request by a party or parties seeking the information. Those seeking revocation of the privilege must demonstrate "why the disclosure is essential to the protection of the public interest." If, after a hearing, the order to revoke is granted, the media have a right to appeal. The privilege remains in effect until appeals are exhausted.

This area of law is narrower in scope than open-meetings or public-records law, and there has been little change in the statutes since their adoption. Likewise there have been correspondingly few reported court interpretations of the laws. The shield law has been the most adjudicated of the three statutory measures to protect information possessed by journalists. There have been four published and one unpublished appellate-court rulings related to the law. The two significant aspects of the law examined by the courts concern the definition of reporter and the nature of the information journalists may withhold.

Louisiana appellate courts have twice examined the law's definition of reporter. As the Fifth Circuit Court of Appeal noted in the unpublished case of *State v. Fontanille* (1994), the central issue in defining a reporter under the law is determining whether the legislature intended the detailed list of those protected by the law to be exclusive or inclusive. In *Becnel v. Lucia* that same court twelve years earlier had ruled that an owner-publisher of a weekly newspaper was a reporter for the purposes of the law. In that case the publisher had refused to reveal the identity of an author of a published letter to the editor to a district court. The appellate court pointed out that the statute afforded protection to "*any* person *engaged* in the *business* [emphasis in the original] of collecting, writing or editing news for publication through a news media [sic]" (p. 1175). This, in the eyes of the court, encompassed both editors and owners.

In *Fontanille* the court was asked to determine if the statute protected the writer of a true-crime book. The three-judge panel appeared to stop short of ruling that the statute's protection extended that far. Passing on the question of whether the list was meant to be exclusive or inclusive, it held that "book authors do not fit comfortably under these statutes" (p. 2). However, it did rule that the writer, Joseph Bosco, could find protection elsewhere if the statute was not applicable. Quoting from the *Branzburg* decision and referring to the Louisiana constitution, the court found that Bosco was protected from forced disclosure of his source's identity.

In a concurring opinion, Judge Grisbaum argued that the statute did in fact protect Bosco. Grisbaum pointed out that the statute holds that news media "shall include" the listed outlets. He contended that the list was "not intended as a restrictive parameter but indicates what news media must encompass as a bare minimum" (p. 4). He compared the language used in this section of the statutes with that which defines reporter. There the legislature had used the phrase "shall mean" as part of the definition. It was his position that "shall mean" indicated a legislative intent to outline "the entire parameters of what constitutes a reporter" (p. 4). He noted that LSA-R.S. 45:1459(A) defined news as "any written, oral, pictorial, photographic, electronic, or other information or communication, whether or not recorded, concerning local, national, or worldwide events or other matters of public concern or public interest or affecting the public welfare" (p. 4). This definition, he held, would include books.

The state's high court has ruled that once it has been determined that the subject is protected by the law, all information related to the identity of the source is protected as well. In *Re Burns* the state's supreme court held that a trial court had ruled incorrectly that the law was inapplicable when a reporter was asked if his source was an employee of a particular government office. The trial court had ruled that asking this question did not constitute asking for the identity of the source. When Michael Burns, a reporter for a local paper, continued to invoke the privilege after the judge's ruling, he was ordered jailed. The appellate court concurred with the lower court's rulings. The Louisiana Supreme Court reversed.

In a *per curium* opinion, the court found that identifying a source included not merely releasing the name, but also any information which might tend to identify the source. The court decided, "Otherwise, through a series of indirect questions, the identity of the informant could be obtained without the need to ask for the informant's name directly, resulting in subversion of the reporter's privilege" (p. 659).

Ten years earlier, a circuit court had found that the shield law extends even to information that was never published. In *Dumez v. Houma Municipal Fire and Police Civil Service Board* (1981), the First Circuit ruled that a reporter was not required to reveal the source of "off the record" comments. Police officer Keith Dumez was appealing his dismissal from the force. The department's civil service board held a hearing on the matter and upheld the dismissal. Dumez took the matter to district court and deposed Thomas Abrams, a local reporter. Dumez was attempting to establish that he had not been given a fair hearing by the board. Abrams told the court that he had spoken with several members of the board before the hearing who gave him their personal opinions regarding the likely outcome. These opinions had not been published. Dumez sought the names as part of his appeal. The district court ruled that Abrams could not claim privilege, given that the information did not relate to revealing the source of the comments, but to the comments themselves. The circuit court ruled that the district court's position was "an erroneous finding of fact" (p. 1208). The circuit court found that the line of questioning directed at Abrams would have forced him to reveal the identity of his source. This would have violated the protections afforded by the shield law.

The courts have consistently noted that the journalists' privilege is not absolute. The statute, for example, does not protect information, only its source. As one judge noted in *Dumez*, "while some states have statutorily extended the newsman's privilege to information received . . . our statute grants the privilege only as to the identity of the informant and to the source of the information, and not to the information itself" (p. 1208). The Louisiana Supreme Court echoed this position in *Re Grand Jury Proceedings* (*Ridenhour*, 1988).

Information has some protection in Louisiana, however. The state's supreme court has read *Branzburg* as providing a First Amendment protection. In *Re Grand Jury Proceedings*, the Louisiana court noted that in the wake of *Branzburg*, the "vast majority of the courts" had been persuaded by the dissent and had created a qualified privilege, except in cases in which the reporter witnessed a crime or had physical evidence of a crime (p. 375). To justify revocation of the privilege, the trial judge must determine that the subpoena was issued in good faith and not as "a mere fishing expedition" or as harassment. The party seeking revocation of the protection must show a legitimate public interest served by the disclosure of information, which outweighs the potential "chilling effect" on news-gathering of such disclosure (p. 376). The standard of proof is raised when the journalistic efforts involve investigation of governmental activity. Noting the important role of the media as a governmental watchdog, the state supreme court held that "additional weight should be given to the reporter's interest when the information concerns his investigation of or criticism of the government" (p. 376). In a concurring opinion, one judge wrote that he read the state's constitution to afford journalists the level of protection described by the dissent in *Branzburg*.

Louisiana law also provides protections for instances in which the purpose of the subpoena is to compel journalists to produce documents rather than provide testimony. Subpoenas can be issued against journalists or news media only upon a showing by parties seeking such information that the information sought is "highly material and relevant," critical to resolving a matter before the court and, perhaps most importantly, "Is not obtainable from any other source" (LSA-R.S. 45:1459.B.(1)(c)). This provision is applicable in any arena, judicial or legislative, in which the governing authority has subpoena and contempt powers. The limitation on subpoenas issued to journalists extends this privilege beyond the definition of news media and reporter found at *LSA-R.S. 45:1451*. It also encompasses the "custodian of records, or other representative of any news media operation" (LSA-R.S. 45:1459.B.(1)). It protects both published and unpublished information.

The privilege dictates that the journalist be given ten days to respond to the subpoena (LSA-R.S. 45:1456.A) and provides for contradictory hearings. It allows the journalist to estimate the costs of complying with the order, and requires the requesting party to deposit these funds with the governing authority (LSA-R.S. 45:1456). It stipulates that courts are to consider such estimates reasonable unless the requesting party calls for a hearing and can prove otherwise. More than once the statutes note that if the news organization is successful in seeking protections afforded by the law, it can recover court costs and attorney fees associated with defending its position. In those instances in which the governing authority determines that the requesting party has established grounds for revoking the privilege, the journalist or organization has a right to appeal, and the protections remain in place until appeals have been exhausted and the governing authority's ruling has been affirmed (LSA-R.S. 45:1459).

Research for this chapter uncovered no instances in which an appellate court published a ruling regarding these provisions. However, one instance of a law-enforcement agency's seizing material from a news organization received considerable coverage in the popular press, including a front-page story in the *Wall Street Journal* (Wartzman, 1995). The legal battle concerned a security-camera videotape of a fight on a school bus. Following settlement of criminal charges resulting from the fight, a local television news organization used the state's public records law to obtain a copy of the tape from the sheriff's office (DeSantis, 1996a; DeSantis, 1996b; DeSantis, 1996c; DeSantis, 1996d; DeSantis, 1996e; DeSantis, 1996f). The district attorney's office brought new charges in relation to the fight and seized the copy under a court order before it could be aired. The news organization filed suit to regain possession of its copy. The district attorney argued that the original tape was exempt from disclosure, as it was once again related to pending criminal litigation. Ultimately, the new charges were ruled to constitute double jeopardy, halting the prosecution.

The tape was returned to the news organization, which asked for a court ruling on the tape's status before it would be aired (DeSantis, 1996c; DeSantis, 1996e; DeSantis, 1996f). The district attorney's office countered by seeking a court order to have the tapes destroyed (DeSantis, 1996d; DeSantis, 1996f). The court ruled that the original tape should be sealed and all copies destroyed, save for the one possessed by the news organization (DeSantis, 1996f). The court declined to rule on the question of the station's right to broadcast the tape. The district attorney, who maintained that the tape should not have been released initially, refused to state that no action would result should the tape be aired. No discussion was given to the question of whether the tape had been properly confiscated initially. The station eventually showed the tape and there were no consequences (Folse, 2013).

The state legislature has prohibited the use of search warrants against journalists or the organizations they work for "unless there is probable cause, established by affidavit, to believe that such person or an employee thereof has committed a criminal offense and that the search or seizure is directed toward that offense" (*LSA-R.S. 15:42*). For the purposes of this statute, news media have been defined as "newspapers or other periodicals issued at regular intervals, press associations, wire services, radio, and television." No published appellate court decisions addressing the matter were discovered during research for this chapter.

Conclusion

It has long been argued that the rights of free speech and press imply a right to gather information, particularly that which relates to government action. While that position has strong appeal, it flies in the face of federal precedent. It has largely fallen to the states through their constitutions, court rulings, statutes, or some combination thereof, to carve out this right. Louisiana, seldom a pioneer in the area of protecting civil liberties, has been one of the nation's leaders in doing so. This progressiveness may be the result of the state's civil law tradition, discussed elsewhere in this volume.

Whatever the motivation, the state, through various mechanisms, has established strong protections for access to government meetings and public records, as well as affording journalists the privilege of using confidential sources. To be sure, there are gaps. The nullification provisions of public-meetings regulations could be strengthened. The list of exempted public records is extensive. The shield law's definition of "journalists" is vague.

While each of these deficiencies can be addressed by the legislature, it is unreasonable to expect that perfection is achievable. The impact of court interpretation will therefore continue to be extremely significant. Ultimately, legislative and judicial action will be heavily influenced by continuing public support for the position that there is a right to know, which is of paramount importance to the nation's political and cultural systems.

Special thanks to Ryan Brown of Roedel, Parsons, Koch, Blache, Balhoff & McCollister Civil Litigation for his assistance.

FOOTNOTES

1 The legislature has its own notice requirements under the state's constitution and procedural rules of each chamber (LSA-R.S. 42:19.B)
2 Provisions of this law do not apply to those who are in custody for a felony conviction (LSA-R.S. 44:31.1), and custodians are permitted to inquire if the requester falls within this category.
3 For example, mortgage and similar records must be permanently archived (LSA-R.S. 44:36.A).

REFERENCES

Acts State of Louisiana 1940, No. 195.
Acts State of Louisiana 1952, No. 484.
Acts State of Louisiana 1976, No. 665.
Baker, C. E. (1989). *Human liberty and freedom of speech.* New York: Oxford University Press.
Becnel v. Lucia, 420 So. 2d 1173 (La. App. 5th Cir., 1982).
Blanchard, K.M. (2011). From sunshine to moonshine: How the Louisiana Legislature hid the governor's records in the name of transparency. *Louisiana Law Review, 71,* 703-747.
Branzburg v. Hayes, 408 U.S. 665 (1972).
Braverman, B. A., & Heppler, W. R. (1981). A practical review of state open records laws. *George Washington Law Review, 49,* 720-760.
Brown, J. H. (1996, March 27). Letter to author. Copy held by author.
Bunker, M. D., Splichal, S. L., Chamberlin, B. F., & Perry, L. M. (1993). Access to government-held information in the computer age: Applying legal doctrine to emerging technology. *Florida State University Law Review, 20,* 543-598.
Davidson, R. H., & Oleszek, W. J. (1994). Congress and its members (4th ed.). Washington, D. C.: CQ Press.
Delta Development Co. v. Plaquemines Parish Commission Council, 451 So. 2d 134 (La.App. 4 Cir. 1984).
DeSantis, J. (1995, December 24). Random checks find jail booking practices lacking. *The Courier,* pp. 1A, 9A.
_____. (1995, December 24). What happens when a book is not a book? *The Courier,* pp. 1A, 9A.
_____. (1996a, March 26). Greenburg plans to return tape. *The Courier,* pp. 1A, 9A.
_____. (1996b, March 26). Supreme Court blocks Mart prosecution. *The Courier,* pp. 1A, 9A.
_____. (1996c, March 27). HTV officials await judge's ruling on tape. *The Courier,* pp. 1A, 11A.
_____. (1996d, March 29). District attorney wants videotape of fight destroyed. *The Courier,* pp. 1A, 11A.
_____. (1996e, March 29). HTV awaits judge's ruling on videotape of fight. *The Courier,* pp. 1A, 11A.
_____. (1996f, April 23). Judge orders tape copies destroyed. *The Courier,* pp. 1A, 9A.
Deslatte, M. (Aug. 9, 2012). Voucher documents being kept secret. *The Advocate,* p. 2A.
_____. (July 18, 2012). Jindal budget office refuses to provide tax credit records. *The Advocate,* p. 10A.
Dumez v. Houma Municipal Fire & Police Civil Service Board, 408 So. 2d 403 (La.App. 1 Cir. 1981).
Dye, T. R., & Zeigler, L. H. (1972). *The irony of democracy: An uncommon introduction to American politics* (2nd ed.). Belmont, CA: Duxbury Press.
Ebenstein, W. (1969). *Great political thinkers: Plato to the present* (4th ed.). New York: Holt,

Rhinehart, & Wilson.

Edwards, V. E., Jr. (1970). *Journalism in a free society*. USA: Wm.C. Brown.

Faifield, R. P. (ed.). (1981). *The Federalist Papers: A collection of essays written in support of the Constitution of the United States* (2nd ed.). Baltimore, MD: Johns Hopkins University Press.

Folse, M. (2013, May 10). Telephone interview.

Force, R., & Griffith, L. (1982). The Louisiana Administrative Procedure Act.

Kidwell, J. A. (1989). Open records laws and copyright. *Wisconsin Law Review*, 1021-1031.

La.Const. Art 12, § 3.

Landis v. Moreau, Lexis 621 (La. 2001).

LAS-R.S. 15:42.

LAS-R.S. 42:11-28.

LAS-R.S. 45:1451-1454.

LAS-R.S. 45:1455-1459.

LAS-R.S. Title 44.

Louisiana Press Association. (May, 2013). Inquiry: Whether all emails of a public employee or official constitute a public record?

Maldonaldo, C. (Oct. 10, 2012). The Jindal administration and "deliberative process": Charles Maldonaldo on the governor's favorite excuse for ignoring public document requests. *Gambit*. http://www.bestofneworleans.com/gambit/the-jindal-administration-and-deliberative-process/Content?oid=2093004.

Manning, K., Murchison, M. S., Pierce, J. F., Songy, R. C., & Wear, J. C. (1976). The work of the Louisiana Legislature for the 1976 regular session. *Louisiana Law Review*, 37, 89-202.

Marien v. Rapides Parish Police Jury, La.App. 3rd Cir., Lexis 1601 (1998).

McBurney v. Young, 569 U.S. _____. Slip opinion (http://www.supremecourt.gov/opinions/12pdf/12-17_d1o2.pdf) (2013).

Murphy, W. F., & Pritchett, C. H. (1986). *Courts, judges, & politics: An introduction to the political process* (4th ed.). New York: McGraw-Hill.

Op.Atty.Gen., No. 10-0233, November 8, 2011.

Op.Atty.Gen., No. 10-0272, April 13, 2012.

Op.Atty.Gen., No. 12-0177, October 11, 2012.

Open meeting statutes: The press fights for the "right to know." (1962). *Harvard Law Review*, 75, 1199-1221.

Parks, W. (1957). The open government principle: Applying the right to know under the Constitution. *George Washington Law Review*, 26, 1-22.

Pember, D.R., & Calvert, C. (2011). *Mass Media Law* (17th Ed.). McGraw Hill: New York.

Re Burns, 484 So. 2d 658 (La. 1986).

Re Grand Jury Proceedings (Ridenhour), 520 So. 2d 372 (La. 1988).

Reeves v. Orleans Parish School Board, 281 So. 2d 719 (La. 1973).

Richmond Newspapers, Inc. v. Virginia, 100 S.Ct. 2814 (1980).

Rivers, W. (1970). *The adversaries: Politics and the press*. Boston: Beacon Press.

Schewe, B. V. (1980). Entering the door opened: An evolution of rights of public access to governmental deliberations in Louisiana and a plea for realistic remedies. *Louisiana Law Review*, 41, 192-219.

Schewe, B. V. (1981). Tilting against windmills: A solitary rejoinder. *Louisiana Law Review*, 41, 1279-1294.

Seghers v. Community Advancement, Inc., 357 So. 2d 626 (La.App. 1 Cir. 1978).

Spain v. Louisiana High School Athletic Association, 393 So. 2d 226 (La.App. 1 Cir. 1980).

State v. Fontanille, La.App 5th Cir., Lexis 191 (1994).

Suire v. Murphy, No. C594000, (19th Judicial Dist. Court Parish of Baton Rouge, LA, 2011)

Tedford, T. L. (1993). *Freedom of speech in the United States* (2nd ed.). New York: McGraw-Hill, Inc.

The Advocate. (July 22, 2012). Jindal blocks state records, p. 6B.
The Times-Picayune Publishing Corporation v. The Board of Supervisors of Louisiana State University, La.App. 1st Cir., Lexis 1351 (2003).
Times-Picayune Publishing Co. v. Johnson, 645 So. 2d 1174 (La.App. 4 Cir. 1994).
Tyler, J. (1989). State open records laws and the NCAA: Does the NCAA qualify as a 'governmental body' and, if so, may its members invoke the privilege of self critical-analysis. *Journal of College and University Law, 15,* 349-368.
Van Slyke, L., & Rushing, T. (1990). Sunshine in Mississippi: The Open Meetings Act. *Mississippi Law Journal, 60,* 283-309.
Wartzman, R. (1995, October 11). Should graphic video of a violent incident be shown to public? *The Wall Street Journal,* pp. 1A, 8A.
Wiggins, J. R. (1964). *Freedom or Secrecy* (rev. ed.). New York: Oxford University Press.
Wright, W. R. II (1974). Open meetings laws: An analysis and a proposal. *Mississippi Law Journal, 45,* 1151-1190.
Zurcher v. Stanford Daily, 436 U.S. 547 (1978).

Chapter 9
Obscenity
By William R. Davie, University of Louisiana at Lafayette

Learning Objectives
In this chapter, readers will:
- identify the history of obscenity laws
- discover how Louisiana's obscenity laws evolved over time
- contrast federal and state opinions in obscenity cases
- describe the concept of variable obscenity
- understand how child pornography is set apart from obscenity offenses
- distinguish the laws against obscenity by channel of communication
- examine the void by vagueness rationale used to challenge obscenity laws
- consider the efforts to regulate obscenity on the Internet

Obscenity is one of those terms that cause both controversy and confusion. It takes on one meaning in conversation and casts a different meaning in the courtroom, although it is certainly no easier to define in law than in conversation. Obscenity is often defined by the layperson as either sexually offensive language or simply objectionable behavior, but in the legal sense it is used to forbid sexual activity or hardcore pornography. Recognizing the subjective nature of this term, one Supreme Court justice famously concurred, "I know it when I see it" (*Jacobellis v. Ohio*, 1964). He was judging the French film, *Les Amants* (*The Lovers*), and declared, "I shall not today attempt further to define the kinds of material I understand to be embraced within that short hand description (hardcore pornography); and perhaps I could never succeed in intelligibly doing so. But I know it when I see it, and the motion picture involved in this case is not that" (Justice Potter Stewart in *Jacobellis v. Ohio*, 1964, p. 197).

The task of "trying to define what may be indefinable," as Justice Stewart put it, has confounded lawmakers and jurists for years, including the ones judging books such as *God's Little Acre* (see *Attorney General v. The Book Named "God's Little Acre,"* 1950), and *Memoirs of Hecate County* (see *Doubleday & Co. v. New York*, 1948). Both works were considered obscene in some states but not in others. Observers have attributed this phenomenon to the conflicted thinking of "promiscuous puritans" (Odysseus, 2013), but the problem of determining when the natural interest in sex becomes an unnatural, harmful offense poses a significant legal challenge even today.

Given that crimes such as robbery, assault, and murder vary slightly by definition, it is remarkable how widely obscenity varies from place to place and time to time. Today's notion of obscenity, for instance, requires an average person reflecting on contemporary, community standards drawn by the collective wisdom of the jury or the considered opinion of the judge. This all requires an understanding of how Louisiana has prosecuted obscenity over time. Strictures defining obscenity can be traced to jurists' shaping the law in the nineteenth century.

HISTORY OF OBSCENITY

American courts inherited from the British common law a concept of obscenity that deemed printed material to be criminal when it threatens the public's decency and morality. To enlighten the reasoning behind such prosecutions one British scholar, Sir Francis Ludlow Holt, described obscenity as a libel against morality and the law of nature that tends to "poison the springs and principles of manners, and disturb the peace and economy of the realm" (Holt, 1818, p. 82). The royal monarchy during Queen Victoria's reign defended British morality against pornography's threats to decency and civil manners. Joining Holt in his opposition to "filthy prints" was the son of an Anglican minister, Sir John Campbell, who advanced the British church's aim to rid pornography from the country. The Obscene Publications Act of 1857 did little to identify obscenity precisely, but it did hand over to the crown the legal power to seize suspect materials and bring unwilling authors and printers to trial for distributing it. One case in particular established the key elements for prosecuting obscenity.

In *Regina v. Hicklin* (1868), the court's interpretation of the Obscene Publications Act gave rise to the Hicklin Rule. Chief Justice Sir Alexander Cockburn presided over the appeal of Henry Scott, a leader of the Protestant Electoral Union imprisoned for circulating an anti-Catholic pamphlet titled, "The Confessional Unmasked" (1867). Its vivid passages contained Catholic women's confessions to their priests and held forth "impure and filthy acts, words, and ideas" (*Regina v. Hicklin*, 1868). The court found that those salacious sentences had the tendency "to deprave and corrupt those whose minds are open to such influences." Those words were sufficient to seal Scott's fate for printing such an obscenity. There was no need to consider the pamphlet as a whole; Justice Cockburn affirmed the crime was committed even though half of Scott's pamphlet had nothing to do with sex.

The Hicklin Rule actually divided obscenity into parts by dealing first with the identification of provocative passages, and then by showing how their impact would influence susceptible readers that might be depraved by its influence. Susceptible minds were generally viewed at the time as including children, women, or weak-minded adult men. If any passage of an explicit print would likely produce lascivious feelings among such members of the population, then it all was to be banned as obscene. Since any sexual material could accidentally make its way eventually into the hands of a child, woman, or adult male, this essentially meant that all sexual material met the definition of obscenity under the Hicklin rule. Even before the Hicklin Rule was imported into U.S. jurisprudence in the Supreme Court case of *Rosen v. United States* (1896), U. S. customs agents were working dockside to stop cargo boxes with erotic works aboard.

Pre- and Post-Civil War Pornography

In the United States, a federal law act was signed to keep pornography from offloading European ships, especially those cargo vessels arriving from France. The Tariff Act of 1842 banned the "importation of all indecent and obscene prints, paintings, lithographs, engravings and transparencies," and it gave the federal government the authority to dispose of obscene cargo from any foreign port (Dennis, 2007, pp. 43-95). In the mid-nineteenth century, sexually explicit artwork was seized at port if sexual intent was detected, while other legal guardians stood vigilant watch over carriers by land.

In 1873, a veteran union officer and postal clerk from Connecticut, Anthony Comstock, founded and led the New York Society for the Suppression of Vice. His followers devoted to anti-pornography crusades chose a book-burning scene as their emblazoned emblem of righteousness. Comstock personally boasted of setting ablaze tons of sordid books and photos. He was incensed by the use of postal mails to distribute artwork that unveiled too much feminine flesh, and sought vigilance from public officials; he asked New York district attorneys to redouble prosecutions of this sordid content.

In the corridors of congress, Comstock is credited with an 1873 act titled the "Suppression of Trade in, and Circulation of Obscene Literature and Articles of Immoral Use," also known as the Comstock Act. It not only authorized the U.S. Postal service to confiscate mail that contained obscene pictures or publications, but also any contraceptive devices or sex toys (The Comstock Act 17 Stat. 598). His crusade against "obscene, lewd, or lascivious" works, including the plays of George Bernard Shaw earned a label for his lobbying efforts: "Comstockery." Combined with the Hicklin Rule, the Comstock Act characterized the Victorian-era zeal against erotica.

Hicklin's Retreat

The foundation supporting the Hicklin Rule as a legal tool eroded early in the twentieth century. An erotic novel prosecuted in 1913—the story of young New York woman Hagar Revelly's sexual misadventures—prompted Judge Learned Hand to question whether mid-Victorian morals should take precedent over "truth and beauty . . . too precious to society at large to be mutilated in the interests of those most likely to pervert them to base uses" (*United States v. Kennerly*, 1913). Judge Hand doubted that Americans were simply "content to reduce our treatment of sex to the standard of a child's library" (p. 121). When Theophile Gautier saw his writings put on trial in 1923, the judge was asked whether he should ban the *Mademoiselle de Maupin*. Instead he saw in its passages "purity and beauty" along with ones "undoubtedly vulgar and indecent" (*Halsey v. New York Society for the Suppression of Vice*, 1922). Still the court in *Halsey* refused to magnify the troubling references of sex scattered through pages of Gautier's book and protected the whole work's survival.

Literary Test Case

James Joyce's *Ulysses* attracted little attention from federal customs agents until Random House strategically promoted the book's sexual content so that it actually would be seized for the purposes of a test case. Random House sought a court ruling in order to secure future imports of the book. In the trial court's opinion, *Ulysses* did contain multiple passages that could be described as "coarse, blasphemous, and obscene, [but] it does not in our opinion, tend to promote lust" (*United States v. One Book Entitled Ulysses by James Joyce*, 1934). Judge Woolsey's ruling, and the appeal in his favor, exonerated *Ulysses*, a stream-of-consciousness look at a single day in Dublin, largely on its literary merits. The impact of this decision began to sway courts away from gauging works on the basis of their sensational but isolated passages that inflame unsophisticated readers.

Roth-Memoirs Test

Following Justice William Brennan's lead, the U.S. Supreme Court in 1957 adopted a new perspective on obscenity. It joined two cases from lower appellate benches: the conviction of Samuel Roth for marketing erotic materials such as *American Aphrodite*, and the conviction of David Alberts of Los Angeles, for operating a mail-order business. In combining the cases, the Court fashioned a three-prong test for differentiating obscenity from acceptable content. Justice Brennan held that an average person—not a person of a heightened sexual appetite or an individual with sensitive aversions—but someone who would be considered normal, would be provoked by the content. Then, in order to determine if the material is obscene, contemporary community standards would be used to test if the content's dominant theme taken as a whole would appeal to prurient (sexual) interest and would be patently offensive. Finally, the court would need to be convinced that the material was "utterly without redeeming social importance" and thus undeserving of constitutional protection (*Roth v. United States*, 1957).

The majority upheld the convictions of Roth and Alberts, but the First Amendment issues underscored the dissents. The anti-social behavior in Roth's case involved only "morbid and shameful" lusts, according to dissenting Justice Douglas, and "arousing of sexual thoughts and desires happens every day in normal life in dozens of ways" (*Roth v. United States*, 1957, p. 509). How could punishment be "inflicted for provoking, in (normal, average adults), undesirable sexual thoughts, feelings, or desire—not overt dangerous or anti-social conduct, either actual or probable" (*United States v. Roth*, 1956, p. 802).

On the same day Nico Jacobellis, a cinema theater manager in Cleveland Heights, Ohio, won his Supreme Court appeal and was allowed to show the aforementioned French film about an extramarital affair, the Court considered a second case of obscenity against *Tropic of Cancer*, a novel that had received conflicting judgments in state trials.

Depending on the jury, Henry Miller's fictionalized account of sexual encounters in which he had participated, or had heard about, in Paris, was either a damnable obscenity or acceptable literature. As far as the appellate court in Florida was concerned, "the filth which is packed into the work and in its narration of a procession of sexual episodes" requires no elaboration (*Grove Press, Inc. v. State Ex Rel. Gerstein*, 1963, p. 537), and so Miller's work failed the test in that state. The Supreme Court reversed this decision against *Tropic of Cancer*, based on the *Jacobellis* reasoning (*Grove Press, Inc. v. Gerstein*, 1964). That is, neither work—the French film or the novel, when taken as a whole—would be judged as obscene using the Roth test.

Sexual Orientation and Nude Portrayal

While the Roth test determined that the law must consider whether the work as a whole appealed to prurient interests before defining it as obscene, another question was raised regarding homosexual literature. In *Manual Enterprises, Inc. v. Day* (1962), the U.S. Post Office seized a large order of mail-order magazines appealing to gay men with photos of nude males. The postmaster of Alexandria, Virginia, seized six parcels of the magazines that he declared to be obscene and refused to deliver them. The postmaster's opinion was challenged before the U.S. Supreme Court. The evidence that photos of nude male models were patently offensive, and an affront to contemporary, community standards was insufficient (*Manual Enterprises, Inc. v. Day*, 1962). Writing for the majority, Justice John Harlan found that it was not acceptable to condemn magazines like *Grecian Guild Pictorial* and *Trim* merely because they appealed to homosexual men. Male nudes "cannot fairly be any more objectionable then many portrayals of the female nude that society tolerates," ruled the Court (p. 490). Four years earlier, the Supreme Court (*ONE, Inc. v. Otto K. Olesen, Postmaster of Los Angeles*) issued a single sentence ruling from the bench (*per curiam*) that reversed an obscenity conviction against *ONE: The Homosexual Magazine*, but the Court did not elaborate on its decision except to cite *Roth* (1957).

Redeeming Value

In 1966, the Supreme Court took another turn at defining obscenity by combining three standards into a test for the lower courts to apply. *Memoirs of a Woman of Pleasure* was an early British novel imagining the escapades of Fanny Hill, a young orphan woman's journey into the eighteenth-century world of prostitution that devoted page after page to vivid descriptions of orgies, sexual intercourse, flagellation, and other erotic episodes. Writing from prison and publishing the book in two installments, John Cleland was rewarded with the judicial threat of more jail time. He instead chose to renounce the novel, while Fanny Hill's adventures continued to garner attention long after Cleland and the British courts had disposed of it.

Legal authorities in Massachusetts first prosecuted Fanny Hill's exploits in 1821, and banned the book in Boston. One hundred forty-five years later Cleland's *Memoirs of a Woman of Pleasure* was reprinted by Putnam Books (1963), and again was declared obscene. In the midst of the American sexual revolution, the U.S. Supreme Court issued a landmark reversal in what became known as the *Memoirs* case, adding one more standard to the obscenity test (*Memoirs v. Massachusetts*, 1966). Yes, it was written to inflame immoral lusts of a prurient nature, and yes it was patently offensive by contemporary, community standards, but was it "utterly without redeeming social value" as Roth required? No, the Court held, because *Memoirs of a Woman of Pleasure* "displays a skill in characterization and a gift for comedy," and because it also "contains a moral, namely that sex with love is superior to sex in a brothel" (*Memoirs v. Massachusetts*, 1966, p. 419). The Roth test then became the Roth-Memoirs test based on Justice Brennan's opinion that the social value of this book "plays a part in the history of the development of the English novel" (p.419).

PANDERING PORN

Beyond the new standard of the Roth-Memoirs test came another offense, the activity of advertising or marketing pornography that is defined as pandering. Ralph Ginzburg's promotions emphasizing the erotic nature of his mail-order trade earned him a conviction for pandering to prurient interests. Ginzburg was a well-known journalist who had on his résumé stints with the *Washington Times Herald*, NBC, *Reader's Digest*, and *Esquire* Magazine. He turned to publishing erotica and began promoting books and magazines devoted to the sexual revolution: *The Housewife's Handbook on Selective Promiscuity*, a "magbook," *Eros*, and a newsletter, *Liaison*—for which he gained mailing privileges from double entendre addresses (e.g., Blue Ball, Pa., and Middlesex, N.J.). In a 5-4 ruling, the Supreme Court affirmed that advertising porn would be a crime if "the purveyor's sole emphasis is on the sexually provocative aspects of his publications" (*Ginzburg v. United States*, 1966). Justice Black reasoned in his dissent that the ruling ill served justice because neither Ginzburg nor anyone else would have known the reading material involved was obscene (*Ginzburg v. United States*, 1966). Ginzburg spent eight months in prison, but contended that his crime was without definition or a victim.

Sex and Violence

When the Court was called upon to judge depictions of sadomasochism in 1966, new legal parameters were set to judge perverse sexual content. Manhattan bookseller Edward Mishkin's conviction was affirmed for selling fifty books, mostly paperback, that dealt with the fetish of bondage, punishment, and sexual abuse (*Mishkin v. New York*, 1966). In his appeal, the defense reasoned that this genre of pornography could not possibly meet the "average person" test because no average person would find such depictions alluring. As a result the Roth-Memoirs standard would not apply. Justice Brennan, writing for the Supreme Court at this point, adjusted the obscenity standard by noting that brutal depictions of sex are utterly without redeeming social value, patently offensive, and of sufficient prurient interest to be condemned as obscene. As a result the prurient appeal requirement was adjusted to specify "a clearly defined deviant sexual group, rather than the public at large" (p. 508).

Variable Obscenity

The earliest laws against obscenity made reference to the necessity of protecting youth from the harmful social effects of consuming sexual content prematurely. Outlawing the marketing of erotic materials to minors produced a legal principle known as "variable obscenity," which gauges the harm of the explicit material as it varies according to the intended audience's level of maturity. It was first accepted as a standard in 1968 when the U.S. Supreme Court affirmed a New York statute preventing the sale of nude magazines to consumers seventeen years old or younger. A sixteen-year-old purchased two magazines depicting female nudity from a store in Long Island, operated by Sam Ginsberg, who was convicted of selling an erotic magazine to minors (*Ginsberg v. New York*, 1968). The revealing photos were not put to the test of obscenity because the state of New York considered its province to include limiting the access of minors to sexually graphic material by using a proof of age requirement. Under the doctrine of *variable obscenity*, the sale of erotic materials—even those that are not necessarily obscene—is a crime when directed at minors.

LOUISIANA'S OBSCENITY LAWS

Variable obscenity is up to the states to enforce, and Louisiana recognized this standard as a valid limitation of the First Amendment. *The Louisiana Law Review* warned its readers that "serious dangers lurk in the dissemination of obscene and pornographic materials throughout the United States" (*Graphia*, 1963, p. 604). This warning was prompted by a statistical rise in sex crimes among juveniles attributed to the spread of communism and the "attempted demoralization of youth through the dissemination of such materials" (as cited in the Joint Committee on Continuing Legal Education of ALI and ABA, *The Problems of Drafting an Obscenity Statute*, No. 9, 67, 68, 1961). Financial profit rather than political conspiracy might better explain the motive of pornography today, but regardless of the motive, defining its elements has proved to be difficult. Louisiana judges began trying to define immoral and indecent acts over a century ago and prosecuted a range of offenses.

In 1913, Joe Comeaux was indicted in Vermilion Parish for a crime that was described as an "indecent assault" (*State v. Comeaux*, 1913). The state supreme court refused to affirm his conviction because the legislature had failed to specify in concrete terms what exactly would constitute an indecent assault. After critiquing the law's vagueness, the court declared it invalid. Such crimes are statutory, and cannot be prosecuted unless clearly "defined and denounced by statute" (p. 620).

In 1947, the Louisiana Supreme Court acknowledged its confusion over another law proscribing "disorderly" and "immoral" acts that were not enforceable terms with sufficient definition. F. L. Truby and his wife Amelia operated a café on Second Street in Alexandria, Louisiana, and were put on trial for "Keeping a Disorderly Place," which in Article 104 of the state's criminal code was defined as the "intentional maintaining of a place to be used habitually for any illegal or immoral purpose" (*State v. Truby*, 1948). Did such words necessarily mean a "meeting place for prostitutes and men desirous of their company," as the state alleged? Rather than leave the interpretation open to diverse judges and juries (p. 765), the court refused to uphold the law against "Keeping a Disorderly Place" because citizens need to know precisely where such lines are drawn.

Louisiana's justices evaluated another vague section of the criminal code after two men were convicted of contributing to the delinquency of a juvenile (*State v. Vallery*, 1948). Jimmy and Gordon Vallery of Rapides Parish appealed their convictions for enticing a "child under the age of seventeen to . . . perform an immoral act" (p. 330). The court simply could not discern what immoral act was specified in this law, and refused to guess because that presumption would usurp legislative power. Consequently, the convictions of both men were set aside and the law was invalidated.

In 1948, the state supreme court wondered aloud in its ruling if Samuel Wooderson's sexual advances were what the state's obscenity statute meant by "performing an act of lewdness in a public place" (*State v. Wooderson*, 1948, p. 369). Wooderson had propositioned a woman on the front porch of a New Orleans home, and while his invitation was unwelcome the court could not say exactly whether his overture was an act of lewdness fit for punishment. Wooderson was exonerated because of the law's vagueness.

Overbroad and Vague

One New Orleans resident, who had been convicted of showing an obscene cinematic work, won his appeal based on lack of clarity in the law. Film owner Ted Kraft was fined $301 for displaying an "indecent print, picture, written composition, model or instrument" (*State v. Kraft*, 1948). Kraft held in his possession a black-and-white film titled *Mom and Dad* depicting graphic sexual acts between an unmarried man and woman in a bedroom. Kraft's lawyer challenged his conviction because censoring any "indecent print, picture" was "too broad and indefinite to inform anyone as to when or whether his conduct would constitute a violation of the statute" (p. 816). The Louisiana Supreme Court agreed that the term *indecent* did not adequately inform Kraft of the type of films it would be a crime to show, which was essential to the guarantee that "in all criminal prosecutions the accused shall be informed of the nature and cause of the accusation against him" (p. 816). Kraft's case and the ones preceding it prompted the legislature in Baton Rouge to review this part of the state criminal code.

In 1950, lawmakers revised the obscenity statute, adding only one word, "*sexually* indecent print" (La. Acts 1950, No. 314, Section 1). The state supreme court gave its approval to this revision in *State v. Roth* (1954) when it held that "sexually indecent" was certain enough to satisfy the constitutional requirement. Even though the legislature redrafted Louisiana's obscenity statute and issued a new criminal code (La. R.S. 14:106A(2), every few years another legal challenge would arise. From 1950 to 1973, Louisiana enforced its criminal statute against "the intent to primarily appeal to the prurient interest of the average person, or of any lewd, lascivious, filthy, or sexually indecent written composition" in the form of books, magazines, newspapers, films, or records, including "auditory visual or sensory representations of such sexually indecent character" (La. R.S.14:106A 9(2), 1950) as amended, La. Acts 1958, No. 388, Sec. 1, La. Acts 1960, No. 199). Still the void for vagueness argument would not go away.

In 1954, the state supreme court affirmed the New Orleans case against Roth (*State v. Roth*, p. 393) because the addition of *sexually* before *indecent* sufficed to clarify the nature of the crime, making it neither too broad nor vague. Roth's attorney then tried to convince the court that the state failed in proving all the material was conclusively "obscene, lewd, lascivious or filthy," but the court ruled that proving any one of those offenses sufficed. After the *Roth* decision, another obscenity appeal came forward challenging the one-word edit to the crime of indecency.

New Orleans merchant James Esposito was convicted for possession and sale of "sexually indecent" prints (*State v. Esposito*, 1954). Citing its precedent in *Roth*, the Louisiana Supreme Court turned back Esposito's appeal by noting how "*sexually indecent* has an accepted meaning, not susceptible to misunderstanding" (p. 28).

Maurice Roufa of New Orleans was arrested for displaying sexually indecent prints but his appeal challenged the law for lacking a *scienter* provision. The requirement of *scienter* means that a defendant must be shown not only committing illegal acts, but also realizing at the time that it was wrong to do those acts. If a defendant lacks "*scienter*," a personal knowledge of the criminal nature of the alleged crime, an appeals court may consider that ignorance to be legal grounds for acquittal. Roufa's appeal failed to persuade the court, even though that use of the terms "intent" and "intentional" were not comparable. "It leaps to the mind that knowledge is necessary to intention and that one cannot have intention without knowledge" (*State v. Roufa*, p. 747). The court's decision also dismissed Roufa's vagueness argument because "perfect precision in language" is not required, only that the law use "constitutional and valid" terms (p. 747).

Erotic Dancing

In the "Cat Girl" case of 1960, the obscenity statute targeted the erotic moves of Ms. Lilly Christine of 318 Dauphine Street in New Orleans, who was convicted of "lewd and indecent dancing" (*State v. Christine*, 1960, p. 403). Law enforcement officials relied on La. R.S. 14:106(3) that forbade "grossly scandalous" movements that would tend to "debauch the morals and manners" of observers. The state supreme court reversed the trial judge's decision favoring Ms. Christine, even though the trial judge had found the law's wording "too broad and indefinite" to inform her of the nature of her crime (*State v. Christine*, 1960, p. 403). The supreme court opined that the words *indecency* and *lewdness* somehow would forewarn the Cat Girl and artists like her what dance moves and dress actually were proscribed by law. As for "grossly scandalous," the court simply ruled that the community's feelings were "grossly shocked and offended" (p. 407). Ms. Christine's case was remanded for trial.

A New Iberia storekeeper in 1966 tried to convince the Louisiana Supreme Court of three reversible errors committed at his trial on obscenity (*State v. Henry*, 1967, p. 891). Percy Henry sold magazines with nude pictures in New Iberia, and was convicted following warnings from police about local residents' complaints. First, he claimed that he had no guilty knowledge at the time of his arrest, and second he challenged the prosecution's case for not listing all the titles of the confiscated magazines. Finally, he objected to the lack of a national community standard to clearly define obscenity. The state court saw no need for a written inventory of confiscated publications, nor did it judge the lack of a "national yardstick" on community standards to be a reversible error. As for *scienter*, Henry's conversation with police describing the magazines before his arrest (pp. 891, 896) convinced the justices his claim was false. Henry's day in court was not done, though. Following a 1967 landmark decision, the U.S. Supreme Court gave his and another Louisiana case further consideration.

Ramifications of Redrup

In *Redrup v. New York* (1967), the U.S. Supreme Court joined three obscenity cases involving pulp fiction works and magazines in Arkansas, Kentucky and New York City. Defendant Robert Redrup was a Times Square newsstand merchant who sold William Hamling's *Lust Pool* and *Shame Agent* to police officers. With financial support from the author Hamling, Redrup appealed the obscenity decision against him and won. In a per curiam decision, the Court applied the Roth-Memoirs test and found the erotic publications did have some redeeming social value. This decision meant that centerfold magazines and paperback narratives with some erotic descriptions were constitutionally protected. After the *Redrup* ruling, *Henry v. Louisiana* (1968) was reversed along with *Conner v. City of Hammond* (1967). The *Redrup* precedent reversed both Conner's conviction in the 21st Judicial District Court for Tangipahoa Parish and Henry's conviction in Iberia Parish.

Three years later, a New York publisher and a Louisiana merchant were in court for obscenity based on two different laws. August M. Ledesma of Delta Book Distributors was convicted under both the state law forbidding lewd and lascivious literature, and an ordinance in St. Bernard Parish. The poorly worded parish ordinance was declared invalid by a federal judge, and a three-judge federal panel found the seizure of Ledesma's newsstand periodicals to be unlawful. The panel also issued a suppression order effectively preventing the state's prosecution of the "illegally seized" evidence (*Delta Book Distributors, Inc. v. Cronvich*, 1969). A federal panel intervened and declared the suppression order invalid because the defense could make such a constitutional claim at the proper time during the trial. The state law against obscenity, however, remained intact and produced further charges against New Orleans cinema theaters.

Prior Adversary Hearing

The Louisiana law on obscenity prior to the filing of charges calls for an adversary hearing to be held in order to determine if the seized materials actually may be considered obscene. In 1972, the state supreme court considered whether the failure to hold such a preliminary hearing represented a reversible error in *State v. Eros Cinema, Inc.* After reading affidavits that detailed the filmed activities in *Studs Galore*, *Four Women in Trouble*, and other likeminded motion pictures, the high court concluded that such a hearing was unnecessary based on the police report.

A plainclothes officer took notes at Le Banque Cinema, Cinema One, and Cinema Two in New Orleans, and filed affidavits that were "fully descriptive, reciting in detail the various sexual activities performed" (*State v. Eros Cinema, Inc.*, 1972). Each affidavit was brought before a criminal district court judge, who authorized the seizure of the reels of film and the arrests of those responsible for showing the "lewd, lascivious, filthy and sexually indecent motion picture film" (La. R.S. 14:106(A)(2)). Eros Cinema claimed that its rights were violated because the law called for a prior adversary hearing in order to determine if the communication was potentially obscene. The state supreme court ruled that the affidavits accompanied by the search warrants and the judge's orders were sufficient, and added it "would be ridiculous" to require more.

THE MILLER STANDARD EMERGES

Courts in Louisiana used elements of the obscenity statute in light of the Supreme Court standard set in *Roth v. United States* (1957), which meant that isolated passages of eroticism were not to be judged without examining the works in their entirety (p. 489). Another U.S. Supreme Court decision, *Kingsley International Pictures v. Regents* (1959), which justified the novel *Lady Chatterly's Lover*, was applied to give some First Amendment protection for controversial ideas including those supporting adulterous relationships. Still, problems persisted.

The Roth-Memoirs test required a showing of patently offensive content appealing to an average person's prurient interest based on contemporary, community standards, and that the material was "utterly without socially redeeming value." But what if a court could not determine exactly what constituted utterly worthless material? The Supreme Court chose to deal with that issue in *Miller v. California* (1973). The medium of direct mail promoting sexually oriented literature produced this federal decision that changed the way obscenity law would be enforced in Louisiana.

The genesis of the *Miller* case was an upset mother and her son who encountered hardcore pornography sent via U.S. postal mail. The unidentified restaurant owner in Newport Beach, California opened an envelope containing pictorial advertisements of four book titles including *An Illustrated History of Pornography* and *Sex Orgies Illustrated*, and a motion picture titled *Marital Intercourse*, all advertised in bulk mail by pornographer Marvin Miller. California law prohibited the distribution by mail of knowingly obscene materials, and so Miller was convicted of a misdemeanor at trial, but appealed to the U.S. Supreme Court, believing that his brochures had some redeeming social value. The Court found that the burden of finding something to be "utterly without redeeming social value" impossible to meet under the criminal standards of proof, and dropped the short-lived Memoirs test in favor of something more specific (*Miller v. California*, 1973).

Chief Justice Warren Burger wrote the majority opinion revising the third prong that defines the offense of obscenity. States were within their constitutional rights to punish content that was "prurient, patently offensive depiction or description of sexual conduct" absent "serious literary, artistic, political or scientific value to merit First Amendment protection" (pp. 23-24). Because the allegedly obscene content must be lacking only *serious* specific values, it relieved prosecutors of having to prove a complete lack of redeeming value. Affirming all three questions meant a pornographer could be punished for obscenity crimes without offending constitutional rights. For Miller, the decision meant that his mail-order advertisements might fit the description, and if so, then no protection would be granted because that "demeans the grand conception of the First Amendment and its high purposes in the historic struggle for freedom" (*Miller v. California*, 1973). The Court thus remanded the case back to the lower court so that it could apply the new definition of obscenity based on Miller's bulk mail items.

Privacy and Pornography

The same year *Miller* was decided, the Supreme Court took up an adult movie theater case seeking to allow adults a right to private viewing of erotic cinema fare. This defense relied on the earlier decision in *Stanley v. Georgia* (1969), wherein the high court ruled that Robert Eli Stanley's private collection of film reels was of no legal interest to state law enforcement in Georgia. The Stanley case involved the discovery of pornographic films that police seized in the midst of their search for illegal gambling evidence. Stanley was prosecuted for possession of obscene films, although the reels were neither covered nor anticipated by the search warrant concerning gaming activities. The Court ruled that Stanley's right to privacy within his own home allowed him to possess sexual material for his own private noncommercial use, even if the material would otherwise meet the definition of obscenity.

A majority of the justices in *Paris Adult Theatre I v. Slaton* (1973) refused to accept the comparison to *Stanley* and said that the public exhibition of movies is not comparable to the privacy the law affords to one's home. The Court held in its 5-4 ruling that the state's interest in decency outweighed any interest in privacy in the cinema theater case. Two films, *Magic Mirror* and *It All Comes Out in the End*, were showing at the Paris Adult Theatre I of Atlanta were judged to be "hard core pornography" that Georgia had a right to prohibit. The ruling was justified by social interests against obscenity, including the protection of a community's quality of life for families, social decency, public safety, and the "social interest in order and morality" (p. 61).

Aftermath of *Miller* in Louisiana

The impact of the decisions of *Stanley* and *Paris Adult Theater I* in light of the new *Miller* standard meant that the Louisiana legislature needed to go back again and revise the state obscenity statute. In applying the *Miller* standard, two cases had been reversed by the Louisiana Supreme Court. First came the appeal of Richard Lee McNutt, who was charged with the sale of obscene magazines. He had been found guilty of obscenity under the *Roth* test, fined $500 and sentenced to serve six months in jail, but the Louisiana Supreme Court reversed that action citing the *Miller* decision (*State v. McNutt*, 1973). The court also reversed the decision reached against the Shreveport News Agency, Inc., charged with selling sexually indecent magazines. In *State v. Shreveport News Agency* (1973), the high court found the obscenity law "totally lacking in specificity which would comply with the requirements of *Miller v. California*." (p. 469). The court added that because the statute was "over-broad, too general, and without the required specificity to withstand the constitutional attack under the United States Constitution" (p. 470), the legislature would need to do something about it. The majority opinion held that the most sensible approach would be for lawmakers to repair the state obscenity statute in Baton Rouge: "We have left the specific definition and regulation of obscenity to the legislature" (p. 471).

As noted, the short-term consequences of *Miller v. California* (1973) were supreme court reversals in *State v. McNutt* (1973) and *State v. Shreveport News Agency, Inc.* (1973), but during its 1974 regular session the state legislature chose to rewrite the law in six different bills. These acts dealt with a range of sexual matters from movie ratings to the prohibition of "lewd or immoral acts" where alcoholic beverages are sold (Acts 279 and 496). The most important act redefined obscenity at great length and in much detail.

1974 Obscenity Acts

At first glance the 1974 legislative act on obscenity (La. R.S. 14:106) appears to be a collection of redundancies complicated by digressions into indecent exposure and lewd performances. Its first subsection targets public exposure, followed in the second subsection by a law against public performances of a sexual nature for commercial gain. Act 274 mirrored the three-part test in *Miller v. California* (1973), but it also added a list of activities classified as patently offensive beyond the "ultimate sex acts, masturbation, excretory functions, and lewd exhibition of the genitals" recommended by *Miller*. There is reference to the "lewd exhibition, actual, simulated or animated," of sexual and excretory organs (genitals, breast nipples, vulva, anus, pubic hair, etc.) and depictions of fondling or caressing those areas of the anatomy were outlawed.

A writer for the *Louisiana Law Review* questioned how the new rule would fare in light of *Jenkins v. Georgia* (1974). In that case, a Hollywood film, *Carnal Knowledge*, was excused for its depictions of extramarital sex, because "nudity alone is not enough to make material legally obscene under the Miller standards" (p. 161). Would the qualifying term "lewd" in Louisiana's 1974 Obscenity Act sufficiently differentiate pictures of breastfeeding from sexually oriented pictures of breasts? Louisiana's statutory expansion of *Miller* also made it a crime to display sadomasochistic conduct, whippings, beatings, torture, and mutilation of the human body (R.S. 14:106(A)(6)). This description perhaps could be legally challenged because such acts were of violence rather than sex. The Supreme Court held that sadomasochistic pornography could be deemed criminal in *Mishkin v. New York* (1966). The provision against sadomasochistic violence, along with other provisions, became part of Louisiana obscenity law:

> R.S. 14 §106. Obscenity A. The crime of obscenity is the intentional:
> (1) Exposure of the genitals, pubic hair, anus, vulva, or female breast nipples in any public place or place open to the public view, or in any prison or jail, with the intent of arousing sexual desire or which appeals to prurient interest or is patently offensive.
> (2)(a) Participation or engagement in, or management, operation, production, presentation, performance, promotion, exhibition, advertisement, sponsorship, electronic communication, or display of, hard core sexual conduct when the trier of fact determines that the average person applying contemporary community standards would find that the conduct, taken as a whole, appeals to the prurient interest; and the hard core sexual conduct, as specifically defined herein, is presented in a patently offensive way; and the conduct taken as a whole lacks serious literary, artistic, political, or scientific value.
> (b) Hard core sexual conduct is the public portrayal, for its own sake, and for ensuing commercial gain of:
> (i) Ultimate sexual acts, normal or perverted, actual, simulated, or animated, whether between human beings, animals, or an animal and a human being; or
> (ii) Masturbation, excretory functions or lewd exhibition, actual, simulated, or animated, of the genitals, pubic hair, anus, vulva, or female breast nipples; or
> (iii) Sadomasochistic abuse, meaning actual, simulated or animated, flagellation, or torture by or upon a person who is nude or clad in undergarments or in a costume that reveals the pubic hair, anus, vulva, genitals, or female breast nipples, or in the condition of being fettered, bound, or otherwise physically restrained, on the part of one so clothed; or
> (iv) Actual, simulated, or animated touching, caressing, or fondling of, or other similar physical contact with a pubic area, anus, female breast nipple, covered or exposed, whether alone or between humans, animals, or a human and an animal, of the same or opposite sex, in an act of apparent sexual stimulation or gratification; or
> (v) Actual, simulated, or animated stimulation of a human genital organ by any device whether or not the device is designed, manufactured, or marketed for such purpose.
> (3)(a) Sale, allocation, consignment, distribution, dissemination, advertisement, exhibition, electronic communication, or display of obscene material, or the preparation, manufacture, publication, electronic communication, or printing of obscene material for sale, allocation, consignment, distribution, advertisement, exhibition, electronic communication, or display.
> (b) Obscene material is any tangible work or thing which the trier of fact determines that the average person applying contemporary community standards would find, taken as a whole, appeals to the prurient interest, and which depicts or describes in a patently offensive way, hard core sexual conduct specifically defined in Paragraph (2) of this Subsection, and the work or thing taken as a whole lacks serious literary, artistic, political, or scientific value.
> (4) Requiring as a condition to a sale, allocation, consignment, or delivery for resale of any paper, magazine, book, periodical, or publication to a purchaser or consignee that such purchaser or consignee also receive or accept any obscene material, as defined in Paragraph (3) of this Subsection, for resale, distribution, display, advertisement, electronic communication, or exhibition purposes; or, denying or threatening to deny a franchise to, or imposing a penalty, on or against, a person by reason of his refusal to accept, or his return of, such obscene material.

Louisiana Supreme Court Affirmation

The Louisiana Supreme Court defended the 1974 legislature's work and its complicated overhaul of the obscenity statute in *State v. Amato* (1977). Frank Amato was arrested in New Orleans for "exhibiting five pornographic magazines for commercial gain" (p. 678). At trial, the district judge quashed the obscenity charges pending against him because he found the phrases, "contemporary community standards" and "patently offensive" to be unconstitutionally vague. The state supreme court noted that those were the precise terms used in *Miller v. California* (1973), and must be regarded as the law in the state. Amato's attorney noted how Louisiana leaped beyond *Miller's* "few plain examples" and even proscribed lewd depictions of the "female breast nipple." The court disagreed with that argument, contending that the plain examples of obscenity cited in Miller were not intended to be an exhaustive list. The high court also dismissed Amato's argument against the "hypothetical statewide community" because the judge or jury's assessment would serve that purpose (p. 702).

Justice Dixon issued a dissenting opinion in *Amato* that made two substantive points. He felt it was constitutionally impermissible to put citizens in the position of having to imagine what sort of sexual material would offend community standards as patently offensive in terms of an average person's prurient interest, while at the same time having to guess at the undefined standards of serious literary, artistic, political, and scientific value that would pardon sexual material from prosecution.

Retail Employees

The state supreme court took another critical look at the law in cases involving store and cinema employees who legitimately claim to hold no interest in the sale of sexual merchandise other than simply to earn their wages as employees. The court joined the appeals of Stephen W. Johnson, convicted for showing two pornographic films, and Kenneth V. Hensley, convicted for displaying five sexually oriented magazines. A district court sided with both Johnson and Hensley based on the law's ambiguous wording regarding when a bookstore or theatre employee might be arrested for presenting hardcore sexual movies or magazines for sale. Because Johnson and Hensley had no financial interest or managerial authority over the content, the court granted "immunity from conviction to all theater and bookstore employees having no managerial duties and financial interest, other than wages, in the dissemination of obscene materials" (*State v. Johnson*, 1977, p. 709). The court also noted a drafting error in the new law that refers to *obscure* rather than *obscene* materials, but considered that flaw to be immaterial.

Constitutional Flaws

Lawyers make a living finding reversible errors, to gain their clients freedom from adverse judgments. In *State v. Luck* (1977), Tommy's News and Gilmore's Newsstand were held in violation of the obscenity statute for their sale of sexually oriented magazines, but their lawyers challenged a provision in the act that exempted "schools, churches, museums, medical clinics, hospitals, public libraries, and governmental agencies," from prosecution. The court agreed that exemption is constitutionally suspect under the equal protection clause of the U.S. Constitution. Luck and Gilmore also challenged the state provision for a pre-arrest obscenity hearing, but such a preliminary examination was deemed necessary, to avoid any prior restraint on protected forms of expression (*State v. Luck*, 1977). The main point of the *Luck* case was that it required the prosecution to prove pornographic material is obscene *beyond a reasonable doubt*.

Ultimate Sex Acts

The following year Louisiana justices wrestled with what exactly are "ultimate sex acts" in *State v. Gambino* (1978). Warren Gambino faced charges of obscenity at his convenience store near a Catholic school in New Orleans, where he prominently displayed sexually flavored magazines "in such a manner that school children could see and buy them" (p. 1109). He was convicted on obscenity charges, fined, and sentenced to serve six months in jail. Gambino's lawyer appealed his conviction because he was denied a preliminary hearing, and "no person shall be arrested or charged with an obscenity violation involving any material (except for hard-core pornography explicitly showing ultimate sex acts)" without such a hearing (see La. R.S. 14:106 (F), 1974). The magazine for sale, *National Screw*, contained a lesbian pictorial that Gambino argued was free of hard-core sexual content because "none of the photographs depict penetration, which . . . is essential to the ultimate sex act" (p. 1110). The court defined *ultimate sex acts* as "coitus, anal and oral intercourse" (p. 777), and by oral intercourse it held that lesbian acts fit the description. "Thus in our independent review we agree with the jury, which is the repository of community standards in this case, that the photographs in question depict the 'ultimate sex acts' contemplated" (p. 1111).

Gambino's case also took up the question of whether material extraneous to an offensive sexual display would be safeguarded from obscenity charges due to its serious artistic and literary value. The high court concluded that "it is the offensive depiction of sexual conduct itself which must have 'serious literary, artistic, political or scientific value' to merit First Amendment protection," (pp. 1111-12) ignoring the requirement that a work suspected of obscenity must be regarded in its entirety and not just in its parts.

The Louisiana Supreme Court decided to correct this error in *State v. Walden Book Co.* (1980). This case pitted the government's prosecution of *Penthouse* magazine in Alexandria against the magazine publisher, Walden Book Company. After law enforcement authorities served notice that an adversary hearing would be held to determine if *Penthouse* was classified as obscene or not, five retail businesses in Rapides Parish removed this magazine from their shelves and chose not to participate in the trial.

Walden Book Co. took up the defense of *Penthouse* on its own, lost and appealed to the state supreme court, which creatively chose to review the contents of the magazine qualitatively and quantitatively. The justices inspected every page of one edition in order to see whether it had "serious value" or not. After examining 228 pages (excluding advertisements), the Louisiana Supreme Court held that 67 pages of *Penthouse* contained some serious literary, artistic, political or scientific value including articles about films, fashion, consumer cameras, and assorted news items. On the other hand, 161 pages of Penthouse "depicts hard core sexual conduct which appeals to the prurient interest and is patently offensive under our statute but it cannot be obscene unless taken as a whole it lacks serious value beyond a reasonable doubt" (p. 346). The high court evaluated the whole work, and in a footnote reversed its Gambino position (*State v. Walden Book Company*, 1980, p. 346).

Six-Member Juries

One of Louisiana's extraordinary statutory provisions is its reliance upon six-member juries used to determine guilt or innocence in criminal cases for non-petty offenses. That fact along with the non-unanimous verdicts afforded to small juries was addressed by Daniel W. Burch of New Orleans, who appealed his obscenity conviction for operating peep shows in the backroom of the Mid-Town News store (*State v. Wrestle, Inc.*, 1978). Burch first appealed his conviction by claiming that the obscenity statute was "vague, arbitrary, and overbroad," particularly in its use of terms such as "contemporary community standards," "prurient interest," and "patently offensive" (p. 834). The state supreme court rejected this challenge, along with his claim of ignorance about the peep shows' content, because a witness testified seeing Burch building the coin-operated booths.

What became a matter of interest to both the state supreme court and the U.S. Supreme Court was Burch's argument that a six-person jury reaching a 5-1 verdict should not be allowed to render conviction, given that ordinarily one dissenting vote would be a hung jury. The state supreme court countered that a 5–1 decision amounted to eighty-three percent concurrence, and that should be acceptable because a verdict by nine of twelve jurors (representing seventy-five percent concurrence) was affirmed by the U.S. Supreme Court in an earlier case. On appeal, the U.S. Supreme Court disagreed. In Burch's situation, Louisiana was not to allow a conviction by five of six jurors for non-petty offenses because to do so "violates the right of an accused to trial by jury guaranteed by the Sixth and Fourteenth Amendments" (*Burch v. Louisiana*, 1979, p. 130). Non-unanimity is permissible when twelve jurors are used, but when only six jurors are used unanimity is required.

Video Porn

Whenever a new channel of communication is invented, it seems only a matter of time before that medium becomes a platform for pornography. Following the success of videocassette recorders in the 1980s, the Peacock Inn of New Orleans began offering its motel guests "adult" movies by video cassette for guests who had an extra three dollars to spend for this form of entertainment. The motel's namesake, Raymond Peacock, and his colleague Barbara Dearman were convicted under the obscenity statute. They chose to appeal on the grounds that viewing videocassettes in the privacy of one's motel room did not constitute a "public portrayal," but to no avail. "Whether or not the room in the Peacock Inn is public or private is irrelevant to this case," ruled the state supreme court (*State v. Peacock*, 1984, p. 1044). Presumably such a ruling would discourage a defendant from continuing to rent video porn, but the Peacock Inn's management was back in court on obscenity charges the next year (*State v. Price*, 1985). The court in this appeal was asked to decide how many counts of obscenity should be assessed per video rental. One count per arrest was the answer (also see *State v. Hungerford*, 1973). The ratio changed, though, when courts dealt with the crime of child pornography.

A Different Attack on Porn

During the so-called "golden age of cinema pornography" when movies such as *Deep Throat* and *Behind the Green Door* were celebrated by the mainstream media and following the *Miller* ruling in 1973, feminists became alarmed by how many women were subjected to gang rape, bestiality, and worse for the benefit of porn merchants. Legal scholar and feminist Catherine MacKinnon took up the case of Linda Boreman, also known as Linda Lovelace, the star of *Deep Throat*. Boreman had been violently coerced by her husband to participate in that movie that netted hundreds of millions of dollars. MacKinnon, as her attorney became convinced that pornography was not so much a moral question as it was a "form of forced sex, a practice of sexual politics, and institution of gender inequality" (MacKinnon, 1989, p. 197). She abandoned the criminal approach to obscenity and chose instead to seek civil justice as a means to fight it.

MacKinnon drafted an anti-pornography civil rights ordinance that was adopted by the city of Indianapolis in 1985. It defined "pornography" as the "graphic sexually explicit subordination of women, whether in pictures or in words. . . . presented as sexual objects for domination, conquest, violation, exploitation, possession, or use, or through posture or positions of servility or submission" (Indianapolis Code, Sec. 16-3(q)).

Even though this measure also applied to men, children, and transsexuals, an appellate court ruled that it had failed to meet the standards of the *Miller* test for obscenity, and restricted ideas that are protected under the First Amendment (*American Booksellers v. Hudnut*, 1985). More recently, a majority of Americans—sixty-six percent according to the Gallup poll's 2013 data—believe that pornography is morally wrong, and want something done about its many permutations.

CHILD PORNOGRAPHY

The Louisiana law against child pornography (La. R.S. 14:81.1) was enacted in 1977 following congressional hearings in Washington, D.C., because "the commercial exploitation of child pornography had exploded and a national movement directed at curbing that market had emerged" (*State v. Fussell*, 2008, p. 1235). The Louisiana legislature moved to prevent children in the state from being victimized by passing a tough law against the following activities:

- The photographing, videotaping, filming, or otherwise reproducing visually of any sexual performance involving a child under the age of seventeen.
- The solicitation, promotion, or coercion of any child under the age of seventeen for the purpose of photographing, videotaping, filming, or otherwise reproducing visually any sexual performance involving a child under the age of seventeen.
- The intentional possession, sale, distribution, or possession with intent to sell or distribute of (sic) any photographs, films, videotapes, or other visual reproductions of any sexual performance involving a child under the age of seventeen.
- The consent of a parent, legal guardian, or custodian of a child under the age of seventeen for the purpose of photographing, videotaping, filming, or otherwise reproducing visually any sexual performance involving the child.

The state supreme court commented on the intent of this law in 2008: "Simply stated, preventing any child from being sexually victimized is the end to be achieved, and punishing both producers and consumers of child pornography equally is the legislature's chosen means by which to achieve this end" (*State v. Fusssell*, 2008, p. 1235). The *Miller* standard for obscenity does not apply in child pornography cases because the harm inflicted to children is too severe to allow such deliberations over its value.

In *New York v. Ferber* (1982), the U.S. Supreme Court found that child pornography is, in some ways, worse than direct acts of sexual abuse due to the repeated circulation of the visual depictions of the child abuse long after the act had occurred. Manhattan bookstore owners Paul Ferber and Tim Quinn were arrested for selling films of adolescent boys masturbating. The Court concluded that child pornography is too great a threat to society so that no judge or jury should consider community standards or the serious social value that Miller would have dictated in obscenity trials. The physical and psychological harms inflicted by sexually exploiting children, and the lasting record of their visual depictions scarring victims long after the acts were sufficient reasons for the government to exercise full censorship in dealing with such materials.

While the *Ferber* case dealt with the act of merchandising child pornography at the federal level, the U.S. Supreme Court later upheld a ban on simple possession. In Ohio, Clyde Osborne received mail order pictures of fourteen-year-old boys in sexually explicit poses that caught the attention of the postal inspector, who notified local police. Officers searched Osborne's home, seized the pictures, and charged him under an Ohio law that proscribed individuals from possessing nude pictures, not of their own children, but others without any consent from the parents. In light of the *Ferber* decision, the Ohio law charged as criminal the mere possession of child pornography and the Court affirmed Osborne's conviction (*Osborne v. Ohio*, 1990). The Court differentiated the *Ferber* ruling from *Stanley v. Georgia*, by holding that although possession of obscene material that portrays adults is protected by the privacy of the home, child pornography will receive no such protection, as the state's interest in protecting children outweighs any privacy interests of the person viewing such material at home. Thus, *child pornography* is without any constitutional protection whatsoever, which is reflected in Louisiana criminal law.

Following the *Ferber* decision, the Louisiana state legislature promptly amended La. R.S. 14:81.1, separating it from the state obscenity statute and seeing to it that the law outlawed not just *acts of sexual conduct* with children, but targeted all "obscene, lewd, or lascivious exhibition of the genitals or pubic area" (see H.B. 720, 1981 Regular Session, as enacted in Acts 1981, No. 502, Sec. 1). Committee minutes showed that the legislature sought "to tighten a loophole in the law which allowed juveniles to be photographed in an obscene manner as long as no sexual conduct is included" (as cited in *State v. Fussell*, 2008, p. 1236).

The appeal of Leon Fussell came before the Louisiana Supreme Court in 2008, which asked how many individual offenses are committed by each owned picture of child pornography, which in Fussell's case would mean sixteen convictions for possession. The state supreme court ruled that "an individual offense is committed each time one visually reproduces any sexual performance involving a child, [or] possesses any single visual reproduction of a child's sexual performance" (p. 1238). Unlike obscenity law, each item of child pornography is thus viewed as a separate offense with criminal penalties to match.

Sexting Laws

American youth generally embrace innovation and experimentation, especially in media, and mobile media today is one popular way for youth to convey their feelings. So what happens when the teenage discovery of sexuality comes in contact with the tools of digital media and images of young people in daring, sexual poses are circulated via instant text, photo, and video messaging? The National Campaign to Prevent Teen and Unplanned Pregnancy estimated in 2008 that one out of five young people between thirteen and twenty-six years of age has shared nude or semi-nude pictures of themselves, and an even greater percentage has sent sexually explicit messages by mobile phone (The National Campaign to Prevent Teen and Unplanned Pregnancy, 2008). Pew Center data show that fifteen percent of American teens have received sexually suggestive, nude, or nearly nude images from someone they know and also received them from third parties (as cited by Potter, 2011, p. 3). More common are the "selfies" (self-taken photos) involving teenagers, some of whom share partially nude photos. This practice raised the question among lawmakers of how such an activity should be judged: as freedom of expression, child pornography, or as a special "sexting" offense?

Louisiana was one of the first states to take action against the practice of *sexting* when the state legislature voted in 2010 to charge juveniles under the age of seventeen with the crime of having in their possession nude photos of friends transmitted by mobile phones or computers. The "sexting" law that Governor Jindal signed into effect made it a crime for anyone under the age of seventeen to knowingly possess or transmit an indecent visual depiction. "Indecent visual depiction" is defined as "sexually explicit conduct," which is further defined in graphic detail as "masturbation or lewd exhibition of the genitals, public hair, anus, vulva, or female breast nipples of a person under the age of seventeen years" (La. R.S. 14:81.1.1 A(2) B(1)(2)). The problem with Louisiana's anti-sexting law (R.S. 14:81.1.1A(1)) is that a young teen could go to jail for just receiving a nude image of another teenager even though he or she had never asked for such a picture. Some critics also asked that the crime of sexting be removed from the classification of child pornography and placed instead under the state's children's code.

In *Family Law Quarterly*, Andrea Potter (2011) argued that Louisiana's sexting law could possibly mean jail time and fines for teens, and would label as sex offenders those who have no history of delinquent behavior. The offense must be "committed by a child of ten years of age or older which if committed by an adult is designated an offense under the statute or ordinances of this state" to receive delinquent punishment (as cited in Potter, 2011, p. 9). Because there is no corresponding adult crime, delinquent treatment is denied. Louisiana has a state policy that recognizes "a child has the right to non-criminal rehabilitative treatment" (La. Const., Article V. sec. 19), but punishment for sexting is a fine for first offenders of between $100-$250 with the possibility of up to ten days in jail (La. R.S. 14:81.1.1.C (1)). Louisiana law makes the record of this crime difficult to expunge since it requires at least two years causing more harm to the juvenile offender in the meantime.

The American Civil Liberties Union in 2009 filed a lawsuit in Pennsylvania against a district attorney, who threatened to proceed with the prosecution of several teenage girls on child pornography charges if they did not enter a counseling program. The girls shared by mobile phone their personal semi-nude photos in bras and bath towels. High School officials in Tunkhannock, Pennsylvania, confiscated the pictures from student cell phones and fourteen girls entered a counseling program rather than face child pornography charges while three others refused. District Attorney George Skumanick threatened the teen holdouts but was enjoined from proceeding against the girls by the Third Circuit Court of Appeals because his counseling program violated their constitutional rights of freedom of expression. No decision though was reached in terms of the pornographic nature of the photographs (*Miller et al. v. Skumanick*, 2009). Writing for the American Bar Association, Hannah Geyer (2009) recommended a "Romeo and Juliet" exception for juveniles who "sext" each other in order to avoid the prospect of criminal prosecution, especially for child pornography.

Victim's Privacy

What happens to the privacy rights of victims of sexual depictions when photos are seized in evidence for the prosecution of criminal acts of obscenity, child pornography, and sexting? The state legislature adopted a law (La. Rev. Stat. Ann. §14:1845) designed to protect the privacy of a victim when evidence pertaining to child pornography, video voyeurism, or obscenity comes to court. The law allows for a hearing to determine if the court should issue an order to protect the victim's privacy by limiting access to child pornography evidence, video voyeurism recordings, or other obscenity items obtained in the alleged commission of a crime. However, in deciding what privacy protections to implement, the statute advises courts to balance the public's right to know and freedom of expression with the right to privacy and right to a fair and impartial trial, among other interests (La. Rev. Stat. Ann. §14:1845 (F)(2) (a-f)).

Congressional Acts

For more than three decades, Congress has worked to ban Internet pornography of children at the national level. In three laws passed during the 1980s and 1990s, Congress defined both criminal acts and civil causes of action for children to recover damages for personal injuries sustained in child pornography. The Child Protection and Obscenity Enforcement Act of 1988 made it a crime to use a computer to transport, distribute, or receive child pornography. In 1990, it became a federal crime to possess visual depictions of minors engaged in sexually explicit behavior. And in 1996, a law was passed to ban the use of minors in sexually explicit roles directed at computer-generated images of children in nude portrayals. The Child Pornography Prevention Act (CPPA) was the subject of a Supreme Court case pitting the U.S. Attorney General against the Free Speech Coalition and the American Civil Liberties Union.

Child Pornography Prevention Act

Child pornography was given special unprotected status outside the law of obscenity, but if no children are involved in the sexually explicit content as in animated pornography, what happens then? A challenge to CPPA was issued by a trade group for California's "adult entertainment industry" that included artists specializing in nudes and a photographer devoted to erotic subject matter. This 1996 law's prohibition against "any visual depiction, including any photograph, film, video, picture, or computer-generated image" was challenged along with its pandering language that banned "any sexually explicit image that was advertised, promoted, presented, described, or distributed" as child pornography (*Ashcroft v. Free Speech Coalition*, 2002).

Because child pornography fell outside the reach of the *Miller* test, the CPPA conceivably could be used to ban images of pre-adult teenagers engaged in sexual activity without weighing any sort of literary or artistic merits. At one extreme, it could prohibit the digital transmission of *Romeo and Juliet* because nowhere did the law require evaluating a work in its entirety; a "single explicit scene" could produce criminal consequences. Theoretically, it also would outlaw sexual content where adult actors are advertised as younger than eighteen years of age, even if they were not.

The *Ashcroft* decision meant that the government would first have to show how CPPA would protect real children from exploitation, and not just hypothetical beliefs about how sexually explicit content provokes perverse behavior. The dissenting opinions in Ashcroft pointed out that the harms of incitement found in such child porn—real or virtual—could be used to encourage child molesters to assault children.

Communications Decency Act

The Communications Decency Act (CDA) added another safeguard against child pornography designed to punish anyone who used the Internet to reach a minor with content featuring "sexual or excretory activities or organs" that would be deemed "patently offensive as measured by contemporary community standards." The act also barred transmitting "obscene or indecent" material to minors. Such terms approximated FCC regulations used to bar radio and television stations from broadcasting indecent content. The bill was signed in February 1996, and within months of its passage a panel of federal judges in Philadelphia called it to a halt, striking down the terms that were designed to shield minors from pornography (Title 47:5, II, I Sec. 230).

Insofar as the law's indecency provisions were concerned, the CDA's demise was sealed in *Reno v. American Civil Liberties Union* (1997). In that case, the government tried to defend it by comparing the Internet's sexual content to court rulings dealing with the sale of erotic magazines to minors (*Ginsberg v. New York*, 1968), profane monologues on daytime radio (*F.C.C. v. Pacifica Foundation*, 1978), and rezoning of adult cinema theaters (*Renton v. Playtime Theaters*, 1986). The Court held that the CDA was overly vague and too blunt an instrument to achieve the goal of denying minors access to "potentially harmful speech" because it would suppress a wide swath of online communication that adults would be entitled to share as free expression. Two justices who basically agreed with the majority suggested technology should allow for some sort of online zoning to protect children from obscene content.

Child Online Protection Act

In 1998, Congress tried again to protect minors by passing the Child Online Protection Act (COPA), which would block online sites from giving children access to sexually explicit materials. The punishment for conviction would be up to six months in prison and a $50,000 fine, but this law was never enforced. A federal judge in 2007 declared COPA failed to meet strict scrutiny because less restrictive means were available for handling the danger of online pornography reaching minors. Installing software filters, for example, would block the content at the receiver's end. COPA's critics noted that the law was well behind the Internet's developments. No provisions were drafted to cover e-mail attachments, streaming video images, or social networking sites, and the law failed to specify how the U.S. government could police foreign sources transmitting explicit sexual content to children. COPA failed in both its technical and legal aspects.

Children's Internet Protection Act

A parent in Livermore, California, was distressed in 1998 to discover that her child had used the Internet at a local library to download sexually explicit content. She filed a lawsuit to force the library to install gate-keeping software and prevent access to minors

(*Kathleen R. v. City of Livermore*, 1998). Her lawsuit failed; however, it did reach the attention of Congress, where members championed the mother's case for web filtering. Sen. John McCain (R-Ariz.) drafted a bill to protect children from accessing explicit content online by curtailing federal funds for libraries that did not prevent the access of explicit images that might be "harmful to minors" through filtering technology.

Once it became law, the American Library Association challenged the Children's Internet Protection Act (CIPA) because it felt libraries must stand free as public forums. A federal panel declared it unconstitutional, but the Court upheld CIPA on appeal. In *United States v. America Library Association* (2003), the Supreme Court ruled 6-3 that the law should be reinstated because libraries still had the freedom to offer unfiltered online access by simply refusing to accept federal monies. The court rejected the public forum analysis because a library is not bound to "create a public forum for Web publishers ... any more than it collects books in order to provide a public forum for the authors of the books to speak" (*United States v. America Library Association*, 2003).

PROTECT Act

Congress continued in 2003 to pursue its goal of protecting children from sexual exploitation by passing the "Prosecutorial Remedies and Other Tools to end the Exploitation of Children Today" (PROTECT Act–Public Law 108-21, S. 151, 2003). This law reworded the ban on computer-generated child pornography by prohibiting a "computer-generated image that is, or appears virtually indistinguishable from that of a minor engaging in sexually explicit conduct" (amend. 1466, 18 U.S.C. sec. 2256(8)(B)). It also brought the Miller test to bear in terms of examining sexually explicit depictions of minors, if found to be outside the bounds of actual child pornography. The new law was challenged in *United States v. Williams* (2008), but the majority opinion of the Supreme Court found the PROTECT law was not unconstitutionally overbroad and upheld it.

CONCLUSION

Louisiana's obscenity laws developed from the common law traditions of Britain. The offense is based on sexually provocative literature that poses such a threat to morality it is deemed worthy of punishment. An English magistrate's ruling in 1868 known as the Hicklin Rule defined material that has a tendency to "deprave and corrupt those whose minds are open to such influences," and American courts came to judge as criminal those creative works that were in whole or in part a sexual enticement to the most susceptible people.

The U.S. Supreme Court dealt with the crime of obscenity and adopted the Hicklin rule in 1896, but later completely redefined the offense in the landmark case of *Miller v. California* in 1973. This decision modified the test crafted by the Court in *Roth* and *Memoirs*, which required that suspect material appealing to an average person's prurient interest must be judged as patently offensive by contemporary community standards. *Miller* further clarified that obscene material need not be utterly lacking in socially redeeming value, but need only lack serious literary, artistic, political, and scientific value.

Miller v. California (1973) had an immediate impact on Louisiana jurisprudence. It caused the reversal of two court decisions and prompted the state legislature to re-draft a complicated statute on obscenity that deals with public exposure, nude dancing, and other forms of sexual portrayals that go beyond the so-called plain examples recommended in the *Miller* decision. Louisiana also takes into consideration the standards of variable obscenity, which makes it a crime to sell non-obscene pornography to some teenagers. Under the principle of variable obscenity, the state punishes the sale or distribution to minors—young people under the age of seventeen—pornography without declaring it as obscene under the *Miller* test. Louisiana's law against sexting covers not only sexually offensive transmissions by mobile media, but offers penalties for sending or receiving such images.

Child pornography is considered to be of such significant harm to minors that Congress and the courts have criminalized its possession and sale without requiring that it be judged by the standards under *Miller*. Neither its degree of offensiveness to an average person, nor the contemporary standards of that community, nor any social value the material might have, are in any way legally relevant—child pornography is absolutely prohibited. Louisiana's law against child pornography punishes offenders for each item in their possession.

Congress has passed multiple laws to restrict access to Internet pornography. Most of these laws have been struck as unconstitutional given their infringement of the free expression of adults who wish to exchange communication of a sexual nature online. In 2003, the Supreme Court upheld the Children's Internet Protection Act that requires public libraries to block access to online pornography that would be harmful viewing for children or offensive to other patrons. The Court held that a public forum analysis did not apply in this instance, and libraries that do not want to install software filters to block sexual content on the Internet can simply refuse federal funds in order to overcome any intereference such filters would otherwise impose on free expression.

Louisiana has drafted several laws designed to prevent obscenity in various forms of expression. Over the years, the statutes have been challenged repeatedly on the void for vagueness and overbroad doctrines. This fact has led observers to conclude that obscenity is ultimately a problematic concept under the First Amendment, given its reliance on imprecise, subjective, and generalized reactions to sexual portrayals.

REFERENCES

Dennis, D. I. (2007). Obscenity Law and its Consequences in Mid-Nineteenth Century America. *Columbia Journal of Gender and Law* 16:1, 43-95.

Geyer, H. (2009, June). Sexting—The ineffectiveness of child pornography laws. Juvenile-Justice (e-newsletter), 3. Retrieved from http://www.abanet.org/crimjust/juvjust/newsletterjune09/june09/sexting.htm

Graphia, A.J. (1963, April). Criminal Law - The Louisiana Obscenity Statute And Freedom of Speech. *Louisiana Law Review* 23:3, 604-609.

Holt, F. L. (1816). "Of Libels against Morality and the Law of Nature," in *The Law of Libel* (London: J. Butterworth & Son)

MacKinnon, C. (1989). *Toward a Feminist Theory of the State*. Cambridge: Harvard University Press.

Newport, F. & Himelfarb, I. (2013, May 20). In U.S., Record-High Say Gay, Lesbian Relations Morally OK. Retrieved from www.gallup.com/poll/162689/record-high-say-gay-lesbian-relations-morally.aspx

Potter, A. E. (2011). Sexting and Louisiana's punishment for the children the law intends to protect from prosecution under child pornography statutes. *Family Law Quarterly* 45, 419-442.

Richards, D.A.J. (1974, Nov.). Free speech and obscenity law: Toward a moral theory of the First Amendment. *University of Pennsylvania Law Review* 123:1, 45-91.

_____ .2009 "Sexting" legislation. National Conference of State Legislatures.com (2009). Amend. 1466A, 18 U.S.C. sec. 2256(8)(B)

The Communications Decency Act, Title 47:5, II, I Sec. 230.

The Comstock Act, 17 Stat. 598.

The Joint Committee on Continuing Legal Education of ALI and ABA. (1961). The problems of drafting an obscenity statute, 9, 67-68.

The national campaign to prevent teen and unplanned pregnancy, sex and tech. (2008). Results from a Survey of Teens and Young Adults, 11.

Louisiana State Senate Committee on Judiciary, Minutes of Meeting, July 7, 1981, p. 1

La. Acts 1974, Nos. 274, 275, 277, 279, and 496.

La. Acts 1950, No. 314, Sec. 1.

La. Acts 1958, No. 388, Sec. 1.

La. Acts 1960, No. 199.

La. Acts 1981, No. 502, Sec. 1.

La. Child Code Ann. Art. 804(2) (2010).

La. Const., Art. V, sec. 19.

La. R.S. 13:4711-4717.

La. R.S. 14:81.1.

La. R.S. 14:106.

La. R.S. 14:1845(F)(2)(a-f)

Louisiana Legislature. (1981) H.B. 720, Regular Session.

Louisiana State Senate Committee on Judiciary. (1981, July 7). Minutes of meeting, p. 1

Obscene Publications Act of 1857 (20 & 21 Vict. c.83).

Odysseus. (2013, March 20). The Party of Promiscuous Puritans. The Cassandra Times. Retrieved at http://www.cassandratimes.com/?p=1147

PROTECT Act, Pub. Law 108-21, 117 Stat. 650, S. 151, enacted April 20, 2003

CASES CITED

American Booksellers v. Hudnut, 771 F.2d 323 (7th Cir. 1985).
Ashcroft v. Free Speech Coalition, 535 U.S. 234 (2002).
Attorney General v. The Book Named "God's Little Acre," 326 Mass. 281 (1950).
Burch v. Louisiana, 441 U.S. 130 (1979).

Conner v. City of Hammond, 389 U.S. 48 (1967).
Delta Book Distributors, Inc. v. Cronvich, 304 F. Supp. 662 (1969).
Doubleday & Co. v. New York, 335 U.S. 848 (1948).
F.C.C. v. Pacifica Foundation, 438 U.S. 726 (1978).
Ginsberg v. New York, 390 U.S. 629, 8 S.Ct. 1274 (1968).
Ginzburg v. United States, 383 U.S. 463, 86 S.Ct. 942 (1966).
Grove Press, Inc. v. State Ex Rel. Gerstein, 156 So. 2d 537 (1963).
Grove Press, Inc. v. Gerstein, 378 U.S. 577 (1964).
Gulf State Theatres of La, Inc. v. Richardson, 287 So. 2d 480 (1973).
Halsey v. New York Society for the Suppression of Vice, 234 N.Y. 1, 136 N.E. 219 (1922).
Henry v. Louisiana, 392 U.S. 655 (1968).
Jacobellis v. Ohio, 378 U.S. 184 (1964).
Jenkins v. Georgia, 418 U.S. 153 (1974).
Kathleen R. v. City of Livermore, Appeal to the Court of Appeal to the State of California, First Appellate District, Div. 4, Appeal No. A086349 (1998).
Kingsley International Pictures v. Regents, 360 U.S. 684 (1959).
Manual Enterprises v. Day, 370 U.S. 478, 82 S. Ct. 1432 (1962).
Memoirs v. Massachusetts, 383 U.S. 413 (1966).
Miller v. California, 413 U.S. 15 (1973).
Miller, et al. v. Skumanick, 605 F. Supp. 2d 634 (M.D. Pa. 2009).
Mishkin v. New York, 382 U.S. 502, 88 S.Ct. 958 (1966).
New York v. Ferber, 458 U.S. 747 (1982).
ONE, Inc. v. Otto K. Olesen, Postmaster of Los Angeles, 355 U.S. 371 (1958).
Osborne v. Ohio, 495 U.S. 103 (1990).
Paris Adult Theatre I v. Slaton, 413 U.S. 49 (1973).
Redrup v. New York, 386 U.S. 767 (1967).
Regina v. Hicklin, L.R.2 Q.B. 360 (1868).
Reno v. American Civil Liberties Union, 524 U.S. 844 (1997).
Renton v. Playtime Theaters, 475 U.S. 41 (1986).
Rosen v. United States, 161 U.S. 29 (1896).
Roth v. United States, 354 U.S. 476, 77 S.Ct. 1304 (1957).
Stanley v. Georgia, 394 U.S. 557 (1969).
State v. Amato, 343 So. 2d 698 (1977).
State v. Christine, 118 So. 2d 403 (1960).
State v. Comeaux, 131 La. 930 (1913).
State v. Eros Cinema, Inc., 264 So. 2d 715 (1972).
State v. Esposito, 75 So. 2d 27 (1954).
State v. Fussell, 974 So. 2d 1223 (2008).
State v. Gambino, 362 So. 2d 1107 (1978).
State v. Gay Times, Inc., 274 So. 2d 162 (1973).
State v. Henry, 198 So. 2d 889 (1967).
State v. Hungerford, 278 So. 2d 33 (1973).
State v. Johnson, 343 So. 2d 705 (1977).
State v. Kraft, 37 So. 2d 815 (1948).
State v. Luck, 353 So. 2d 225 (1977).
State v. McNutt, 287 So. 2d 478 (1973).
State v. Price, 475 So. 2d 6 (1985).
State v. Roth, 74 So. 2d 302 (1954).
State v. Roufa, 129 So. 2d 743 (1961).
State v. Shreveport News Agency, 287 So. 2d 464 (1973).
State v. Truby, 211 La. 178, 29 So. 2d (1948).
State v. Vallery, 212 La. 1095, 34 So. 2d 329 (1948).
State v. Walden Book Company, 386 So. 2d 342 (1980).
State v. Wooderson, 213 La. 40, 34 So. 2d 369 (*1948*).

United States v. America Library Association, 539 U.S. 134 (2003).
United States v. Kennerly, 209 Fed. 119, S.D. New York (1913).
United States v. One Book Called Ulysses, 5 F. Supp. 182 (S.D.N.Y. 1933).
United States v. One Book Entitled Ulysses by James Joyce, 72 F2d. 705, (2nd Cir. 1934).
United States v. Roth, 237 F.2d 796 (2nd Cir. 1956).
United States v. Williams, 553 U.S. 285 (2008).

Chapter 10
Intellectual Property
By Steven J. Dick, University of Louisiana at Lafayette

Learning Objectives
In this chapter, readers will:
• understand the basics of copyright and trademark law
• know how to establish a copyright
• discern various types of works
• recognize the rights that are protected by copyright
• identify what constitutes infringement
• find out how copyright holders license a work
• consider how Creative Commons offers an alternative to copyright
• differentiate trademark from copyright protection
• know what is necessary to establish a trademark

Media industries sell stories, ideas, and information. Once created, others can easily appropriate the property. Intellectual property (IP) law defines the ownership rights for content produced through the creative labors of the mind, and in the digital age a good deal of money is spent, lost, and invested in "IP" by media organizations around the world. At the state level, the Louisiana Office of Entertainment Industry Development (Loren C. Scott & Associates, 2013) in 2012 reported nearly $800 million in terms of media productions including $11 million in the creation of infrastructure for state-based productions. Protecting media products is essential to this continuing investment and that requires some legal oversight. The state of Louisiana defines IP as an "incorporeal" (Incorporeal movables, LA Civ Code 473), which means that IP is regarded the same as stocks, bonds, and other financial instruments minus a tangible nature for the purposes of financial liabilities and control. IP law protects the creator by insuring a chance of profitability. There are generally three areas of IP protected by law—patents, trademarks, and copyright.

THREE AREAS OF INTELLECTUAL PROPERTY

Patentable inventions are beyond the focus of this chapter because they generally are not media products, but they are a form of IP. From the patent pools of early radio to the politicized maneuvering of digital television standards, patent disputes have shaped the media marketplace by defining the nature of home media inventions and their costs. Similar to copyright in this respect, patents protect the IP of inventions, processes, and useful adaptations of existing ideas. The intention of patent protection is to promote the creative process by allowing the inventor a limited period of exclusivity for profit making based on a registered patent for the original design and execution.

Trademarks

While copyright and patents protect creative ownership rights, another set of IP rights affect market behavior. Laws that regulate branding through trademarks and service marks primarily exist to keep competitors from acting unfairly concerning product identification. Establishing a product identity (or brand) can be a complicated and expensive process that may involve icons, names, and slogans such as "ONE LOVE," the motto used by Raising Cane's Chicken Fingers, or the iconic trademark of the black-and-gold fleur-de-lis used by the New Orleans Saints. Properly maintained, a product or organization's trademark establishes a corporation's image (or brand) in the marketplace. The intention of this marketed identification is to afford consumers a symbolic association between the product and its provider so that they can make a reasonable choice based on their preference for what the service mark or trademark represents. Trademark law is covered more completely at the end of this chapter.

Copyright

Copyright protects original works of authorship such as literary, musical, pictorial, or graphic expressions including some forms of computer software (Copyright Act, 17 U.S.C. § 102 (1976)). The work must be original to the copyright holder and have a certain minimum amount of authorship that can be attributed to them. Names, titles, and short phrases do not qualify for copyright protection but may qualify for trademark protection. The goal is to protect the actual expression of the idea; the mere idea itself lacks protection of copyright. For example, HBO's *True Blood* copyright protects literary and cinematic elements associated with that television series—the script, music, and videos—but it does not protect any story idea about vampires living in a small town. Otherwise, the *Twilight* movie franchise using this narrative approach would have to answer to possible claims of infringement.

Once copyrighted, the 1976 Act grants at least five specific rights to the holder including the most important one—the right to *reproduce* (or control reproduction) the work. Second, the right allows the user to *prepare derivative* works, such as translations, or transpositions of the work into a different medium, and it also protects serializing the work as well. Third, the right grants control over the *distribution* of copies and makes the work available for sale by the owner. Fourth and fifth, public *performance* and *display* rights allow the copyright holder to control the venue, including the time of presentation and to what public it is shown beyond the circle of family and friends. Broadcasting involves rights to a public performance of copyrighted works, but stations must have a license to allow such use.

The IP chart below compares the various rights. Readers will note most of the legal authority resides with the federal government, but a state such as Louisiana can exercise its interest in trademark protection through the secretary of state's office and provides some protection to copyrighted works. It also is important to understand that different titles of law protect IP, including copyright, trademarks, and the patents. The duration period for the different areas of IP—copyright, trademark, and patents—also varies according to the terms of different statutes.

Intellectual property law enforcement

	Copyright	Trademark	Patent
Protects	Original expression of an idea	Promotion material or corporate image that identifies an entity	Useful invention or method
Protection Starts	When fixed in tangible form	Use in commerce or registration of intent to use	On registration
US Statute	17 U.S.C.	15 U.S.C § 1123 35 U.S.C § 2	35 U.S.C.
LA Statute	14 LA R.S. § 73.2	51 LA R.S. § 211- 300	
US Agency	Copyright Office, Library of Congress	United States Patent and Trademark Office	United States Patent and Trademark Office

LA Agency		Louisiana Secretary of State	
Current Length of Protection	Author's life plus 70 years. Others: 95 years from first publication or 120 years from creation (whichever ends first)	As long as used in commerce. Federal registration lasts 10 years, but is renewable	Utility and plant: 20 years Design patents: 14 years

LEGISLATIVE HISTORY

In 1556, the charter of the Stationers' Company in Great Britain created the process to regulate printing, and stamp out the Protestant Reformation. Queen Mary was intent on helping the Catholic clergy put an end to the distribution of Protestant literature. The British Stationers' Company was empowered with royal backing to approve books and presses, plus search out illegal prints, and destroy non-approved books and presses. Following her reign, Queen Mary's successors turned the tables on the Catholic Church and used this tool of censorship to advance the Anglican cause. By 1710, protests over the despotism of the Stationers' Company prompted Queen Anne to adopt the world's first copyright law with parliamentary approval. The Act prescribed a copyright term of fourteen years with the opportunity to renew it once amounting to twenty-eight years of exclusive control before the copyright expired and the work entered the public domain. This copyright bill remained in effect in Britain until 1842 when the duration of copyright protection was extended to forty-two years.

IP legislation became part of the foundation of the newly formed legal system of the United States. Even before ratification of the Constitution, twelve of the original 13 colonies approved copyright protection while the federal government operated under the Articles of Confederation (Patterson, 1993). In 1787, the U.S. Constitution prominently featured in the first article IP's foundation in law:

> The Congress shall have Power . . . To promote the Progress of Science and useful Arts, by securing for limited times to Authors and Inventors the exclusive Right to their respective Writings and Discoveries.
> –*United States Constitution, Article I, Section 8*

The "exclusive right" feature of IP rights eventually would come into conflict with the rights of free expression protected by the First Amendment of the Bill of Rights, and later guaranteed by the Louisiana Constitution in Article 1, Sec. 7. On one side, copyright law creates a predictable media marketplace by defining rules and responsibilities. Creators gain the *right* to control the use of the content and the revenue it generates. On the other side, copyright law denies to others the right to express the same ideas in the same fashion, giving to certain authors the exclusive use of this IP. This exclusivity is understandable given that copyright law was, at its origin, a government sanctioned monopoly (Patterson, 1993).

Although the constitutional provision set down the basic principles of IP, the necessary regulations were implemented at several levels. The U.S. Congress acted swiftly to create the statutory protection necessary for its enforcement. The first Copyright Act of 1790 granted authors the basic protection of printed works for fourteen years and this right was renewable for an additional fourteen years. Congress approved revisions to the original copyright law in 1831, 1870, 1909, and 1976, by either creating new forms of protected expression, such as musical compositions, or extending the term of ownership. Not long after the revision of 1831, the U.S. Supreme Court affirmed copyright policy. In 1834, *Wheaton v. Peters* (1834) confirmed that copyright was not a perpetual right, which was set at twenty-eight years plus a fourteen-year extension.

In addition to the U.S. Constitution, copyright protection was upheld by the authority of legislation and the courts. Regulatory agencies are also charged with the day-to-day interpretation and enforcement of copyright law. As opposed to the "laws" created by the Constitution and the Congress, these agencies create "regulation," but the term *regulation* reflects the guidance or control aspect of duties charged to government agencies overseeing IP rights briefly described below.

Copyright Office in the Library of Congress. Established in 1870, this office houses the Register of Copyrights. The Copyright Office examines applications, and records the registration of original and renewal claims. The Copyright Office administers compulsory and statutory licensing discussed below for public performances, transmission, and Internet connection.

Copyright Royalty Board. This board maintains a record of service providers for infringement cases, as well as the tools to find the owner of registered material. It is a part of the Library of Congress, and was created by the Copyright Royalty and Distribution Reform Act of 2004 (Proceedings by Copyright Royalty Judges, 17 U.S.C. § 8, 10: 801-805).

United States Patent and Trademark Office. This agency is part of the U.S. Department of Commerce. As its name implies, it grants to applicants patents and registers trademarks. It also maintains a searchable registry and advises the president and the Congress about the status of patent and trademark policy both in the United States and in global tribunals.

World Intellectual Property Organization (WIPO). The WIPO is the United Nations agency dedicated to the protection of IP through international trade. The WIPO was created in 1970, following the recommendations of the 1967 WIPO Convention. It replaced the *United International Bureaux for the Protection of International Policy*. The *United International Bureaux* created in 1893 was in response to the 1883 Paris Convention for the Protection of Industrial Property and the 1886 Berne convention for the Protection of Literary and Artistic Works (World Intellectual Property Organization, 2013). Together, the Paris and Berne Conventions established the rules for copyright protections between countries. The Paris Convention helped holders gain copyright protection in countries outside their own. The Berne Convention was the first multinational treaty protecting copyright for economic interests.

Enforcement Bureaus. While most IP enforcement actions come from owners, enforcement agencies work to control the more organized efforts. The Federal Bureau of Investigation, White Collar Crime Division and U.S. Customs and Border Protection work to discourage criminal copyright and trademark violations that include commercial operations and Internet distribution, specifically covering those items with a value of more than $1,000 over 180 days (Criminal Infringement, 17 U.S.C. § 5:506). In addition, the Office of the Intellectual Property Enforcement Coordinator, part of the White House Office of Management and Budget, works with federal and international agencies to protect U.S. IP at home and abroad.

Private and Non-Governmental Organizations. There are private organizations integral to the protection of IP, especially copyright. Some of which operate through contractual arrangements with owners to collect payment. For example, the American Society of Composers, Authors, and Publishers (ASCAP) and Broadcast Music Incorporated (BMI) work with artists and broadcasters in order to manage licensing fees. The trade group Recording Industry Association of America (RIAA) is well known for actively pursuing copyright litigation against people and software systems that promote file sharing among consumers sharing music and movies on the Internet. Other groups such as the Harry Fox Agency and Copyright Clearance Center (CCC) identify content owners and negotiate the fair payment for specific uses of the recordings.

Trade groups such as the National Association of Broadcasters (NAB), National Cable & Telecommunications Association (NCTA), Consumer Electronics Association (CEA) and Motion Picture Association of America (MPAA) have helped shape policy for their industries. At the same time, groups such as American Library Association,

Creative Commons and Electronic Frontier Foundation (EFF) aim from a consumer perspective to expand the rights of users. While the agencies and groups identified above are not an all-inclusive list of arbiters, they do represent major overseers of IP rights. Consider a scenario addressing some basic questions that arise in the legal process of copyright management.

ESTABLISHING OWNERSHIP

Scenario: Two photographers with similar cameras independently walk up to Jackson Square in New Orleans. They produce nearly identical pictures. Who owns the copyright on the image? Both? Neither? Is it the first one to take it, or any one of the many photographers who had taken that picture before then?

The answer is that both photographers, along with many others, own the copyright to the Jackson Square pictures. Copyright protects the unique expression of an idea, but uniqueness is defined as "independently created." The fact that the two photographers did not have a particularly novel idea is not as important as the fact that they did their own work. As a professional matter, publishers may demand something more imaginative, but that does not deny the photographer a right to claim personal ownership of the fixed expression of this visual idea.

It may seem strange that the law protects intangible IP when it is fixed (recorded) "in tangible form," but that it is really not the idea; rather it is the tangible expression of the idea that specifies exactly what is protected in law. The tangible expression can be through the means of videotape, a script, a musical score, a recording, a painting, a book, or even a choreography notation. As of 1980, tangible forms would include electronic, or machine-readable records, software, and digital files, which are protected under federal law (Regarding Computer Programs, 17 U.S.C. §101 and §117 (1980)).

Once the work is fixed in its tangible form, two additional steps are needed to strengthen the protection, which are copyright *notice* and *registration*. Neither one is required, but both are useful in order to strengthen a claim of ownership by indicating the intent to protect the content, and by establishing the date of creation and location.

The city of Chicago discovered the trouble that occurs when these steps are ignored. Prior to 1976, a copyright notice was required for protection. In 1967, an untitled model of a proposed grand sculpture by Pablo Picasso in Chicago's Daley Plaza was unveiled without any such notice. After his monumental sculpture was completed, Chicagoans discovered something about it: The city could not enforce its copyright ownership. Under the laws of the time, the lack of copyright notice on the model placed it in the public domain. The full size sculpture was considered a derivative or the original model. Since the model was in the public domain, the derivative monumental sculpture also entered the public domain (*The Letter Edged in Black Press, Inc. v. Public Building Commission of Chicago*, 1970). The 1976 revision to the Copyright Act removed the requirement of notice to afford some protections under law.

The Berne Convention Act adopted by the U.S. Congress in 1988 brought federal law into compliance with the Berne Convention—an international agreement from 1886 achieved in Berne, Switzerland. Works published after March 1, 1989 no longer required a visible copyright. As a result, three rules were authorized to guide copyright holders based on their publication date. Prior to January 1, 1978, a visible copyright notice is required, but after that time from January 1, 1978, to March 1, 1989, certain exceptions are allowed mainly for accidental omissions of the visible notice. The contemporary rule assumes someone owns title to the creative work, and that they do not have to sacrifice their copyright for lack of notice (Sheldon Mak Rose and Anderson, 2013). Unpublished works do not require a copyright notice.

Despite changes in the law, copyright notice is a good idea. The notice informs the public of an author's intent to protect copyright, identifies the author or owner, and the year of its creation. Works without notice are open to an "innocent infringement" defense, where the violator reasonably can claim they did not know the work was protected, which would mean a possible reduction in damages, or no compensation at all would be awarded if a dispute arose.

The visually perceptible notice contains three parts. First, the indication of copyright can be "Copyright," "Copr" or the © character. Second, the year of the current work's first publication—even if it a derivative, or compilation of previous works. Third, the name, or generally recognized abbreviation of the copyright owner's name or organization (e.g., ABC or NFL). The complete copyright notice would look something like, "©2014 Steven J. Dick," or "Copyright 2013 ABC Television." The notice should be clearly visible to the observer and normally at or near the title. Works published primarily in electronic form may place the notice with the credits at the end of the work in digital form, or at the end of printouts (US Copyright Office, 2013).

Copyright owners may strengthen their protection by registering the work with the U.S. Copyright office. However, registration is not required, unless the copyright holder is planning legal action against an infringer. Registration with the copyright office also may require the owner to deposit two of the copies with the Library of Congress. Notice with the U.S. Copyright Office creates a public record of the original work and provides a certificate of registration, and includes other advantages if registered in the first five years.

Derivative Works

Creating a bestselling book may be profitable, but the movie version, a new edition, a translation, or even a spinoff can produce substantial additional profits. All of these are derivative works. The derivative work may claim a new copyright, but only for additional material. For example, the 1946 novel by Robert Penn Warren, *All the Kings Men*, gave the copyright holder benefits of the book until 2059 (author's death in 1989 plus seventy years). Yet a 2005 audio version of the same name carries a copyright title that will not expire until 2100. From 2059 to 2100, the text of the book will be in the public domain, but the audio performance will be covered by copyright for an additional forty-one years assuming no future changes in the law.

The television producer must worry about accidentally creating a derivative work. Works of art, even published books that are visible in the background of TV scenes can leave a video producer open to a copyright complaint (Lyras, 1992). Second, digital editing capacity makes it easier to borrow sounds or pictures from copyrighted sources. The process called *sampling* lifts a phrase or sound from one song in order to make it a part of a new recording. Negotiating a copyright clearance for such a sample can be difficult and prohibitively expensive. There is no standard formula to calculate the terms of such an agreement. In addition, secondary users may want to negotiate for two copyright clearances—one from the writer of the song and one from the performer of the sampled version.

Compilations

A compilation is simply a collection of previous works, as in a body of known information. As such, the compilation copyright protects the work of creating/organizing the original material. Unlike a derivative work, which is considered a new product with its own copyright, the compilation copyright does not create a new copyright for that previous material—nor is it intended to protect the purely mechanical arrangement of information, such as the white pages of the telephone directory. The compilation copyright covers anthologies, some magazines, or other collections.

Collective work

A similar concept is known as the *collective work*, where each separate contribution is new and added by a different creator. Individual contributions would then earn separate copyrights while the compilation, as a whole would be copyrighted for the original work held by the organizing owner. The owner of the collective work license then would only have the right to publish the individual contributions under detailed conditions. Consider this book, individual chapters were written by separate authors and the editors unified and arranged the content. Similarly, newspapers can enforce a collective work copyright on the newspaper as a whole, while individual stories carry their own copyright as well.

Works for Hire

Much of the media depend on "works for hire." A work for hire is a copyrightable product that is created as part of one's employment. In such cases, the employer becomes the owner of copyright. This type of relationship between creator and owner falls into two broad categories—works prepared within the scope of employment (e.g., full time reporter) or those commissioned and ordered for a specific project (e.g., music for a motion picture). In *Community for Creative Non-Violence v. Reed* (1989) the Supreme Court outlined specific limitations based on the nature of the employee and contractor relationship. The Court set out specific rules to ensure that the relationship for creating a work for hire was an intentional one, and that it would prevent creators from losing copyright by mistaken oversight. An employer must exercise control over the employee's work, workplace, and payments. The employee must be hired to do the type of work covered by the copyright, and ideally, the business would support that particular kind of work. Suppose a barista sketched an image of a coffee cup in her spare time, would she lose claim to copyright of her artwork? It depends on whether this was something she was expected to do as part of her job, and if the work was done during work hours and with employer resources.

An independent contractor relationship is legally defined by certain terms, and generally is limited to nine specific commissions: 1) collective works; 2) audiovisual works; 3) translations; 4) supplementary content to another work (e.g., illustrations, forward); 5) compilations; 6) instructional texts; 7) tests; 8) test answers, 9) atlases. New media content are likely to challenge these categories given the growing use of crowd-sourced materials where multiple authors submit an original work in digital format for use by others.

Length of Protection

The duration of copyright protection is dependent upon when it was created, or first published, and who actually holds the copyright. Most works published after January 1, 1978 would be protected for the author's life, plus an additional seventy years. Anonymous authors, pseudonym authors, or works for hire would be protected for ninety-five years from the date of first publication, or 120 years from the content's creation, whichever ends first.

For works published prior to 1978, the rules regarding control become more complicated. The Copyright Act of 1909 established a duration of twenty-eight years of ownership with an optional license renewal for a second twenty-eight-year term combined for a total possible holding of fifty-six years. The Copyright Act of 1976 automated the renewal to forty-seven years, or a total of seventy-five years for two terms (depending on the year of the original copyright). The 1998 Copyright Term Extension Act, named after U.S. Rep. Sonny Bono who was responding to the interests of Hollywood owners, added another twenty years, for ninety-five years in all (U.S. Copyright Office, 2013). Before the passage of the 1976 Act, Congress passed nine interim extensions for copyrights that began with one starting in 1918. The effects of these term extensions were to allow the earlier works to grandfather the prior holdings into the extended protection. One exception was granted to works that began their first term between 1950 and 1963, and that still required renewal after twenty-eight years for continued protection.

First Sale Doctrine

The first sale doctrine (Limitations on exclusive rights, 17 U.S.C. § 109) limits the control of a copyrighted work to the first time a copy of the original work is sold. In effect, once a book, CD, or DVD is sold to a consumer, the copyright owner no longer has the right to control later resale or loan of that work. This doctrine not only protects libraries, but marketing of used media and rentals as well.

As new media promote more creative works for online distribution, there is the question of copyright enforcement through digital rights management, which is where the *first sale doctrine* comes into play. It is unclear if digital copies enjoy the same rights under the first sale doctrine as analog versions (Asay, 2013), and the American Library Association (2013) suggests two other issues. First, digital rights management threatens the legitimate secondary transfer of IP. Second, there is the growing trend to rent/license content (for a limited time), so that most consumers never actually own a copy.

Infringement

Anyone who violates the exclusive rights of the copyright holder commits infringement. The owner may go to court and seek a civil action, asking for relief within three years for civil infringement and five years for criminal infringement (Limitations on Actions, 17 U.S.C. § 507). Relief may come in the form of an injunction to halt the infringing use while the court decides the case. The next step in a successful claim would be to impound the infringing material, and safeguard those items used to create infringing copies (e.g., molds, masters, film negatives), and finally the destruction of the infringing content is required (Copyright Infringement and Remedies, 17 U.S.C. § 501-513).

In addition to the destruction of copies, a copyright holder can demand actual damages, in terms of lost revenue, and the infringer's profits or statutory damages. Recovering statutory damages relies on two steps in the process. First, the court must find that the infringement was intentional. Second, the judge must arrive at a just settlement. For non-intentional uses, statutory damages range from $750 to $30,000 per work that was infringed. If the copyright owner can show intentional infringement, statutory damages may increase to $150,000 per work. Criminal infringement occurs when the reproduction of more than one copyrighted work occurs in a 180-day period, which has a total retail value of more than $1,000. The remedies are the same for civil infringement, along with the addition of a $2,500 fine for someone who intentionally removes, alters, or places a false copyright notice on someone else's work. In addition, the defeated party in a copyright trial may have to pay the cost of the court and attorney's fees (Copyright Infringement and Remedies, 17 U.S.C. § 501-513).

FAIR USE

Copyright was not intended to limit public criticism or to impede education through its restriction on uses. There is also the reasonable expectation that a person who has a legal copy can actually view it. Fair use is the section of the copyright law that defines the acceptable uses of a copyrighted work (Limitations on Exclusive Rights: Fair Use, 17 U.S.C. § 107). Unfortunately, fair use is not a bright line test but one determined by applying the criteria of four factors regarding the use of copyrighted material:

> (1) **Purpose** and character of the use, including whether such use is of a commercial nature or for nonprofit educational purposes;
> (2) **Nature** of the copyrighted work. Does the work lend itself to commentary or is it purely factual material?
> (3) **Amount** and substantiality of the portion used in relation to the copyrighted work as a whole; and
> (4) **Effect** of the use upon the potential market for or value of the copyrighted work.

The Copyright Act (17 USC 112) also created a specific statutory license that, although it is not fair use, does provide the right to the public performance of a copyrighted work and allow the recording of a copy to facilitate broadcasting. This provision means a broadcaster can place a copy of a copyrighted song on a server for later transmission, or hold one in its archives without violating the terms of its license.

Plagiarism

Plagiarism extends the concept of copyright infringement to an ethical duty for creators. The term essentially defines the unethical representation of another person's work as one's own. An individual can infringe on a copyright without representing it as their personal work, such as selling pirated music, but plagiarism defines a misrepresentation made of another author's work without attribution to it creating a false impression that it belongs to the secondary user. Plagiarism protects moral rights rather than legal rights of ownership, and though not necessarily illegal, it can easily violate contractual relationships. In absence of agreements, organizational policies usually guide any determination of plagiarism. As in copyright violations, there are two broad areas of concern—the *value* and the *amount* of the misrepresented material.

Value. In almost all copyrighted material, there are some truly unique ideas, sounds, or images. It does not take much for secondary authors to violate the creator's rights; key concepts and novel interpretations should be properly attributed. Facts that are not generally available, or known, must be referenced. In academic or journalistic writing, the advantage of source citations is found in the validity and credibility given to a work by connecting it to existing experts and their authority.

Amount. A large volume extracted from a single source can easily raise suspicion of plagiarism even when partially cited. In 2003, Pulitzer Prize winning journalist, Rick Bragg covered the Southeast for *The New York Times*, while based in New Orleans. The national newspaper, still smarting from the sting of a national scandal involving admitted plagiarist Jayson Blair, suspended Bragg for two weeks when it came to light that a mostly unpaid reporter was sent to Apalachicola, Florida, in order to gather facts for a story about oystermen that appeared under Bragg's byline without acknowledgement of his help. Bragg admitted he had done little first hand reporting for the piece, and only flew into town to write and file the story under his name. His account of the reporting raised questions about whether another interviewer and fact collector should be given some byline credit for the article. Bragg was suspended for two weeks, but then he resigned his position in protest.

LICENSING RIGHTS

Most of the time, a copyrighted product comes with restrictions. The process of carefully defining what a customer can do with copyrighted material is called "licensing." The limits placed on buyers insure the copyright owners' ability to maximize their revenue. It may sound sort of greedy but it is a necessary and practical reality of the media marketplace. There are a limited number of distribution opportunities for most media authors and composers. Most creators often expect only a single run of their work. Once an audience member has paid ten dollars to see a movie, the willingness to pay again is substantially reduced. The cost of the license is based on the original value of the material, and the potential for a secondary market. The ten dollar price of a DVD is based on the assumption that it will be used for home entertainment and nothing more. In order to have the right to exhibit the film publicly, it would reasonably cost more.

Licensing is the right, granted by the copyright holder, that is necessary for the buyer (licensee) to be entitled to broadcast, recreate, or perform a recorded copy of the copyrighted work. Types of licensing contracts can include: 1) A flat fee for a defined period of usage, or 2) Royalty payments determined by the number of copies of the work sold based on the total revenues acquired. Most music licensing agreements include some form of compensation for the copyright owner—when and if the work becomes part of another creative production (i.e. movie, play, television show) according to the profits gained from the new product.[1]

Producers of video content may wish to include copyrighted works within a larger production, and so legally binding agreements are necessary to protect the original producer. Two specific licenses are common. The *synchronization* license allows the use of musical works as background in a motion picture, television program, video, DVD, or other video production. The *master use* license allows use of the musical work as a soundtrack, bumper, lead-in, or background to a motion picture. In addition, a license might be limited by the duration of use, number of times performed/displayed, size of venue, and exclusivity.

Syndication, a common method for licensing rights, involves selling the product across several media outlets. Rather than charging the same cost for all outlets, the cost is calculated based on potential audience. A group of media outlets with each one licensed to present syndicated content to their audiences within a defined geographic area. Popular television programs, radio shows, and newspaper features including editorial columns and cartoons, are syndicated today for distribution throughout parts or all of the United States. Suppose an outlet in Baton Rouge would be asked to pay more for the same syndicated content than it would have to pay in Alexandria, Louisiana. As cable television and the Internet expand the boundaries of the media marketplace, so too are syndication deals adjusted. Cable television brings stations into markets outside the normal coverage area, and while this expansion not only increases the station's reach it also distributes syndicated content beyond the originating station's regional boundaries.

Compulsory licenses

Certain media outlets, including broadcast stations, produce a compilation of so many copyrighted products and programs that it becomes nearly impossible for a reasonable market to do business without a standardization of payment. For some purposes, the U.S. Congress has enacted specific laws to create a standardized price for copyright payments. These are called compulsory licenses or sometimes, statutory licenses. In most cases, media companies record their use of the content and make a standard payment to an arbitration panel. The arbitrator assigns a payment to each copyright holder.

After years of battles between cable/satellite companies and traditional broadcast companies, a state of relative calm has been achieved through the use of a compulsory license scheme that allows cable and satellite television systems to rebroadcast terrestrial television (Limitations on Exclusive Rights, 17 U.S.C. § 111 and 119). This license allows cable and satellite operators to retransmit TV station programming into their local markets without negotiating for individual programs. There is no set rate for these "retransmission consent" agreements so broadcast stations (or groups) are pitted against cable/satellite operators for carriage fees. Problems arise when negotiations reach a stalemate and channel blackouts become the result.

Radio stations, both online and traditional broadcasters, play so many songs on a daily basis that negotiating with each copyright owner would become a practical impossibility. So three types of distributors and two methods of licensing are used in order to make it manageable. Distributors include traditional broadcasters, Internet broadcasters, and online jukeboxes. Traditional broadcasters include radio, television stations, and Internet networks, but the interactivity of online audio streams allows for even more options. First, there are web radio stations that may be Internet streams of traditional stations, or they may be Internet-only stations. Internet jukeboxes allow the user to select songs or create a custom audio stream by selecting and rejecting content and include popular services such as Pandora and Spotify.

Blanket licenses are private agreements between the distributor and the copyright owner; usually offered in bulk on behalf of several copyright owners. Traditional radio and television stations and some Internet broadcasters prefer these private agreements made through companies such as ASCAP or BMI. However, a number of Internet broadcasters, and most Internet jukeboxes, prefer compulsory licenses from the Copyright Royalty Board (CRB). In January 2006, the Library of Congress established the CRB—three judges who oversee the copyright law's compulsory license by setting rates and distributing payment to the copyright owners. The process has been complicated by litigation and changing legislation but benefits both sides in the process. The music industry gains an automated payment system and users gain the interactivity of radio services that react to their music tastes (jukeboxes).

Internet

IP on digital platforms like the Internet poses a challenge in terms of detecting stolen property and guarding against future abuses. Consider the petty theft that occurs when a person shoplifts a candy bar from a grocery store. The store owner is no longer in possession of that item and therefore cannot profit from it. When a person takes an MP3 song without payment, the owner still has the song and can continue to sell it. The music industry admonishes consumers that they are purchasing digital music for personal use only, but it would be laughable for a candy store owner to restrict when and how someone uses the candy purchased, or with whom they share it. The candy thief takes only one item, while anyone with a digital pirated copy can continue to distribute the recording with equal quality as the original version.

Nowadays popular activities like fan fiction, memes, and AV sampling can violate IP. Some of the harshest and possibly justified criticisms of IP policy emanate from the struggle to balance the competing rights. For example, the length of copyright protection should be expansive enough to encourage and reward authorship, yet brief enough to fulfill the "for limited times" clause of Article 1, Sec. 8, which would grant public access after an interval of time. Over the years, legislators and courts have tried to strike a balance between these interests. Thus, an ongoing battle exists between technologies, licensing, and public mores to determine the shape of the future market for IP on the Internet.

Creative Commons

There is recognition that some copyright holders profit greatly from someone else's work, but the increasing trend toward sampling sounds of favorite music, fan fiction, group stories, and free software has created a general desire to establish a legal space for non-profit or low profit content.

In response to a number of factors such as lengthening copyright terms, the social nature of media production, more information sources, and digital technologies, one group has taken action to lighten the burden of copyright laws. The Creative Commons movement was an attempt to formalize this space for the free exchange of ideas and information. Content producers were encouraged to distribute their products with a mark that would define allowable low cost uses. Broad parameters were recommended, including adaptation with or without attribution, allowing adaptation for free distribution, and even offering works for commercial adaptation. Producers were encouraged to place this notice on their work or web pages: "This work is licensed under a Creative Commons Attribution 4.0 International License" (Creative Commons). Enforceability of the Creative Commons license is yet to be legally tested, but the innovation of such licenses is becoming more popular since it affords innovative space for IP development.

BRANDING AND TRADEMARK

Identifying marks have been used over the millennia to distinguish the creative works of artisans and artists. Egyptian stonecutters, European potters, and printers have "signed" their products one way or another. These symbols and logos were especially important to the trade guilds of medieval England. The stronger the reputation the guild enjoyed, the better it was for the prosperity of the host towns and villages (McKenna, 2007). The concept of branding actually came from the cattle owners of the old American West, who with hot irons burned into the hide of their livestock an identifying symbol of possession. As the cattle grazed and traveled together, it became necessary to observe by brand which rancher owned which cattle. Today trademark law achieve the same goal, which is to make it clear for all to see which product comes from which supplier. The purpose of this section is to discuss how IP law protects the intangible assets of advertising through government oversight.

The reasoning behind trademark law is to provide consumers with information and protect the substantial investment made in the creation and promotion of brand names or trademarks. In one early case, *Coats v. Holbrook* (1845) the court's ruling supported legal protection from an illegitimate diversion of trade (McKenna, 2007). Congress passed two trademark acts in 1870 and 1876, but the controlling legislation today is the Lanham Act of 1946 (Rules and Practice in Trademark Cases, 37 C.F.R. § 2). Congress introduced minor changes in 1988 in order to protect trademarks not yet offered in commerce, and then again in 1995 and 2006 in order to guard against trademark dilution.

In today's interconnected world, the brand image may be the only thing that connects the consumer with the customer. For example, we can accept the Café Du Monde of New Orleans might be just as successful operating under a different name given its investment in advertising, customer service, and product quality. However, the Café Du Monde name itself is valuable due to its long-term investment in New Orleans, and it would be unfair for a rival business to disrupt its position by profiting from the confusion of brand identification.

Still, there are reasonable limits that do not affect the investment. Should the Café Du Monde be allowed to restrict the literal English translation of its name—"Coffee of the World"? Would protecting its brand integrity mean that *Le Café du Monde* in Quebec should change its name to avoid confusion? In some ways, it may depend on a business decision and a willingness to invest in the protection. While Café du Monde did not seek to protect its name against the Quebec company, Dominique Ansel, the creator of the *cronut* (promoted as a combination of a croissant and a donut), has aggressively protected his trademark (Collen, 2014) including one derivation in Louisiana. A Shreveport restaurant, Sevendipity Café, received a cease-and-desist letter for its use of the name "creaux-nuts," which Ansel felt was too similar to go unchallenged (Associated Press, 2014).

Trademark Law

In just about any market, businesses operate with similar names or brand logos (e.g., Agave and Blue Agave restaurants). If these businesses choose to ignore the potential confusion created by a similar service or trademark, they can weaken their own identity. What if a similar logo indicates a business with a bad reputation and that impacts the original trademark holder, or suppose a third business chooses a similar sounding name (e.g., Wild Agave) that could convince the public it is a spinoff of the original? A protected service or trademark must be specific and unique to the trademark company.

Once established, it comes under the legal protection of federal law and that protection lasts for as long as the registered mark is used. There are four categories related to the legal concept of trademark. Strictly speaking, "trademarks" are names for tangible products only. Abita Beer has a *trademark* on its brand name while the telecommunications firm, *CenturyLink*, has a *service mark*. In the United States, there is virtually no difference in the protection provided, and trademark has become a generic term.

A third category covers the product brands managed by groups. These items include the *certification mark*, the *collective mark*, or the *collective membership mark*, and typically are owned by a group for the benefit of its members (Bitlaw, 2013). The certification mark

> **The intellectual property of fried chicken: One Love?**
>
> Raising Cane's Chicken Fingers is a fast-food restaurant headquartered in Baton Rouge, La. The popular chicken eatery has grown to operate dozens of restaurants in seven states following its debut in 2001 near the LSU campus. Raising Cane's discovered in 2013 that not everyone is a fan of its brand, or more exactly the terms used to describe its passion for fried chicken. For years, Raising Cane's labeled its passion for cooking fried chicken with the motto, ONE LOVE. But the chicken franchise discovered that its registered motto was the subject of a trademark lawsuit from the estate of famed Jamaican reggae singer, Bob Marley.
>
> In representing the deceased singer's widow and children, the Marley estate sought to trademark the phrase, but Raising Cane's legally registered ONE LOVE eight years earlier. The trademark infringement suit was filed after the U.S. Patent and Trademark Office denied the estate's application, and Marley's legal counsel felt it necessary to sue the Louisiana restaurant chain in order to reclaim use of the phrase. The suit claimed that ONE LOVE was associated with a popular Bob Marley song of the same name, and charged Raising Cane's Chicken Fingers with "willful and deliberate" trademark infringement in creating a false association with the singer's recording, and intentionally interfering with the Marley estate's business relations.
>
> It seems unlikely that Raising Cane's Chicken Fingers expected the Marley estate to register those two words and enter into the restaurant business, but in trademark property law one key question concerns the likelihood of confusion in the consumer's mind regarding any slogan or symbols used by competing entities. In order to prevail in such a lawsuit, the plaintiff's attorneys would have to successfully show that consumers would confuse the fast-food restaurant's use of ONE LOVE with the reggae singer's song from 1977 with the same name. From the singer's perspective, it is valuable to show all potential infringers that it protects its trademark. Did the chicken restaurant define ONE LOVE well enough to be separate in the consumers' minds? In the end, the Bob Marley estate settled out of court with Cane's and did not disclose the settlement details.

does not protect a specific product, but the endorsement of a product (International Trademark Association, 2013), such as, the Louisiana Department of Agriculture and Forestry's Certified Louisiana, Certified Cajun, and Certified Creole marks (Louisiana Department of Agriculture and Forestry, 2013). A collective mark is similar to a trademark, or service mark, except that its owner generally does not sell anything while the membership collectively uses it in commerce. For example, the Louisiana Association for Justice does not provide legal services, but its members may promote their services under the collective mark of its banner. The collective membership mark can create controversy though once others latch onto it. In 2011, the Zulu Social Aid and Pleasure Club sought to bar the Mardi Gras Beads Factory in Bridge City from selling items using the Krewe's collective mark (Associated Press, 2013).

The fourth category is classified as *trade names*. The trade name is the official corporate name—anything other than the real name of the person. Registration of a trade name generally includes where and how you are going to use it. For example, the common corporate name "Cajun" is not helpful because there are more than 250 variations on that name in Louisiana. However, K-Jon Sewer and Septic Service in Lake Charles, Louisiana is far more specific. Registering the trade name establishes a record of the brand and corporation (Beesley, 2013). Many states record, and some even require, official corporate names as a matter of law. Louisiana requires government registration when trade names are used in communication and commerce.

Within the media, a corporate name is common and when media consolidate, one company may continue operating under the new name. In Shreveport Louisiana, KDKS joined The Radio Group, which became a part of Access 1 Communications (The Radio Group, 2013). The trade name may have evolved from KDKS, The Radio Group, to Access 1 Communications. At the same time, the service mark for KDKS was maintained; except for the lesser protection given to trade names, the concepts are substantially similar.

A corporation may have any of the above identifying marks and products to promote with it. Ampex, for example, provides AMPEX videotape and AMPEX Duplication Services. It may also contract with private companies for AMPEX certified repairs. The protection is similar across these brands in the United States but may appear to be quite different when protected in other countries.

The diversity of brands and their protected marks discourage infringement of the company's name. In 2009, a version of Popeye entered the public domain and others like it eventually will reach that destination. In 2023, for example, the first of the popular Disney characters will lose copyright protection. There is a wrinkle though, while copyright ownership lasts for a fixed period, trademark law sustains a brand image so long as it is used in commerce.

The question to consider then is: "What can be done to protect an image that is both part of the public domain and also in use as a corporate trademark?" Will the less familiar version of Mickey Mouse—Steamboat Willie—allow for more lucrative images to follow it into the public domain, such as Disney's popular array of princesses?

Registration

Registration is not required for protection but remains the best proof in legal disputes. The bad news is that trademark registration can be difficult to obtain, and it is an expensive, complicated, and time-consuming process. In the end, the applicant may not obtain the trademark desired. Beyond the local market it is risky to leave a prominent brand unregistered. The Louisiana Secretary of State's office registers businesses, and its trademark registration records the historic use of the trademark, but this office does not guarantee the exclusivity that is needed for legal protection. The registration may not be entirely effective but then it does not cost much either. In mid-2013, Louisiana's registration fee was only seventy-five dollars per mark, plus the cost of new or changed business registration. While legal assistance is not required, the help of a qualified attorney is recommended by major agencies regularly involved with securing or maintaining service marks and trademarks.

The secretary of state's database in Louisiana will check for the same, or similar names. Images are more challenging to find due to the difficulty of automatically differentiating images. Lutzker (2003, p. 100) noted how "trademark searching is like digging a hole looking for something that may not exist." Due diligence is difficult to achieve especially when similar icons and words are overlooked in the search process, which can cause problems later. An honest attempt to search for conflicting brands may show good faith, which will mitigate damages later, especially in cases of unintended infringement.

Applicants should perform their own search to identify anyone else using their desired logo or brand image. An overlooked contender to a trademark or service marks can set the process in reverse. Federal protection is obtained through the U.S. Patents and Trademarks Office, and registration with that office gives pretenders a notice that the trademark is off limits. It increases penalties, affords some international and Internet protection. Organizations and businesses also may register an "intent to use" form for a trademark up to three years in advance. Federal registration also can be expensive. The base fee was $375 at this writing (United States Patent and Trademark Office, 2013), and additional fees due to errors, or multiple filings in the process, will add up in terms of time and expense. The process easily can take more than a year and cost thousands of dollars. Despite the involved costs and risks, registration affords dividends once a brand mark establishes prestige in a particular market.

International protection is beyond the space available here necessary to detail each country's legal system, particularly since not all countries recognize international protection, and fewer enforce it. It is a step though that should not be taken lightly or without assistance since it could mean an additional three years in the process. In domestic or global quarters, registration of a trademark is a good investment, given what it offers for the design, advertising, and promotion of the brand. As the company grows in reputation and goodwill, the value of the brand will outweigh the costs of registration.

Strength

Some brands are easier to defend than others. The relative potential of a brand to be associated only with a corporation is referred to as the *strength* of the brand. For example, Kodak was long considered to be a strong trademark because it had no meaning outside of the product. Center City Television, on the other hand, is simply descriptive. Customers may know the *company*, but the *mark* would be harder to defend. The new company, Center City Radio, may successfully argue that it does not infringe on the earlier trademark. One way to think of trademarks is by considering their distinctive quality on a continuum from strongest to weakest:

Fanciful names are those terms of marketing devoid of meaning outside of the company. In Louisiana that would bring to mind, "Tabasco," the famous hot sauce that is both trademarked and patented. Even though the etymology of the word *tabasco* has Hispanic and Native American origins describing the nature of soil, it is better known as the brand of hot sauce manufactured by the McIlhenny family of New Iberia, Louisiana and placed on restaurant tabletops around the world. The principal advantage of fanciful trademarks is they have little or no meaning beyond the product itself, which gives them a stronger position in the marketplace.

Arbitrary names have meaning but that meaning is usually not associated with the product itself, such as *Zatarain's* food and spice company of New Orleans. It is a family name, but one that is more associated with food than its founder. Emile A. Zatarain registered his trademark in 1889 in order to sell his brand of root beer in Gretna, Louisiana, and today the *Zatarain's* brand is famous for pre-packaged Cajun and Creole seasonings and other food products.

Suggestive names have meaning somewhat associated with the product such as *Maison Blanche*, which refers in French to the "white house" chain of department stores that grew out of the first white house located on Canal Street in New Orleans.

Descriptive names simply state what the product offers in simple terms, such as, *Community Coffee* or *Capital City Press*, both of which are firms based in Baton Rouge.

Generic words, such as Channel Six Television, cannot be trademarked and are considered weak product brands. Even a weak trademark can be defended though; it is just harder to do. The company must show that it has invested in the brand name and it has acquired secondary meaning in the public's mind. If a TV station is using "Storm Team" to describe its weathercast for example, it would be a fairly weak trademark given its almost generic popularity. Stations must show that their audience understands that the "Storm Team" refers to the weather programming on Channel Six, rather than say the "Weather Friends" on a rival channel.

Television stations are in a unique position. Their call letters can become a descriptive brand, such as WXXX-TV 12, which would be unique to the nation. Normally the call letters summon that channel to the public's mind without confusion. However, a problem could arise supposing a new station adopts call letters or a name similar to a station already broadcasting in the market, such as KISS-FM. The FCC stopped negotiating such disputes in the 1980s, which now are simply a trademark matter.

> ### Case in point: Who Dat?
>
> For the football fans of New Orleans, the phrase "Who Dat?" is a shorthand version of the chant, "Who dat say dey gonna beat dem Saints?" and a common cheer heard among team fans on certain Sundays in the Superdome. It also is a familiar sight to see the phrase on T-shirts around town. In 2010, the National Football League (NFL) sent letters to several T-shirt outlets demanding that they stop the unlicensed distribution of shirts with the phrase, "Who Dat". The NFL claimed it owned the trademark of the name through the New Orleans Saints. Sports marketing is one of the few areas where trademark images create substantial revenue for a professional sports franchise, a university, and other teams. Thus, the battle over the phrase was waged more than just to protecting corporate symbolism, and the controversy clearly created outrage when the governor and other legislators began issuing public comments against the NFL. The question turned on the rights of the powerful NFL ownership versus small shopkeepers in New Orleans. Key issues were public domain ownership and competing company ownership.
>
> The phrase "Who Dat?" is nonstandard English, but it does have a long history in Louisiana, and especially in New Orleans sports. There is documented evidence of its use dating back a full century. The historic use of the phrase led several merchandisers to claim that "Who Dat?" was not owned by anyone and that the NFL should recognize its rightful place in the public domain. The alternative argument was that business corporations often use phrases that are in common use but register them for marketing purposes. It is the association with the business that makes them defensible as a trademark, and does not impose any ban on their common use. Neither the New Orleans Saints nor the National Football League represent unique terms, but both are trademarks. In all practicality, the T-shirts being sold would be of far less value without their association with the NFL's Saints.
>
> On the other hand, even if the phrase is associated with the Saints, who rightfully should own the phrase (if anyone)? Did the NFL, or the Saints, invest sufficiently in the phrase to justify the exclusive profits? It could be argued that the T-hirt shop identified the importance of the phrase and risked their effort and money to create the T-shirt market. While "Who Dat" is far less valuable without its association with the Saints, the NFL had not solely made the investment to market it successfully. Yet this case did not go to trial, and a court will probably never make a final determination on the competing claims. As often happens, the trademark dispute was settled out of court, and the NFL's registration of the phrase remained intact.

Slogans and More

Disputes also can arise over similar slogans and jingles. Slogans are too short for effective copyright protection but are subject to trademark protection. The University of Louisiana at Lafayette registered "Geaux Cajuns!" as a trademark in order to associate the slogan with its university athletic sports programs and souvenirs. With slogans, applicants must understand why the trademarks are protected in the first place. Trademark law does not give ownership rights, only the exclusive-use rights. There is no problem with the fact that multiple Eyewitness News programs use that brand in this country, but there is a problem if two or more stations compete using that name in one market since it would tend to confuse the audience.

Market

Active brand protection is a necessity if any infringement becomes a fact of the marketplace. If an introduced product brand resembles an existing company's images or name, the owner is legally required to respond or risk losing their interest in the property. Disney is often put in the uncomfortable position of asking schools and pre-schools to remove unlicensed images, but the issue is not just corporate profits from use of the images, it is also the fact that poorly drawn infringing images distort or dilute the brand. Protection requires an awareness of the brand's image and impression in the market that goes beyond competitor's marketing.

Registration of a trademark is dependent on how a company defines its market. The investment would be lost if the trademark was not used in the registered area. Not only would it be a waste of money and time to register it, the protection provided by the registration would diminish the meaning for the brand actively used in commerce. If infringement occurs without complaint or challenge from the owner, it is lawfully considered to be abandonment, which is defined by the Lanham Act as the non-use of a trademark for three consecutive years (International Trademark Association, 2013).

Trademark protection can be difficult to maintain given such vagaries. A timid approach is ill advised, and yet it also would be unwise to exaggerate minor similarities in court. Trademarks are tools that are used and reused, but valuable ones must be vigorously defended. In the fast-paced world of competitive industry, market leaders are diligent in creating a trademark protection plan that would encompass at least four objectives: 1) market awareness; 2) business awareness; 3) audience awareness; 4) documented history; and 5) consistency.

1. Market Awareness. If a media outlet hopes to defend its service or trademarks, it must do so by not stepping on the rights of others. A good trademark policy begins by understanding the market. How do the customers differentiate products? How diverse are their products? What marks are being used and recalled? Because media markets differ, the audience in one market may see things quite differently from those in other communities.

2. Business Awareness. Media companies tend to be full of creative people who create valuable products all the time. Smart competitors evaluate their media workers and content for exploitation. Are rivals stealing ideas from in-house authors and artists or vice versa? Media professionals must pay close attention to stringers, contractors, and part-timers. Have they taken something that does not belong to them? Do they own their creations? Successful firms identify media products for exploitation and evaluate how to protect them. In order to make the policy clear and avoid misunderstanding, they circulate internal memos and press releases to clarify it.

3. Audience Awareness. A trademark's value also hinges on the audience's awareness and understanding. Can the company show it has achieved that valuable "secondary meaning" of brand identification? Where, when, and how strong is this impression? This information not only helps in product recognition, but also supports the owner's ability to defend the trademark as necessary.

4. Documented History. As in other forms of IP, creation details define the limits of protection. When was the brand created, by whom, and when it was first shown to the public are important elements under the law. Continuous records use and consistent image can be essential to its protection. In 2013, a federal judge in Louisiana ruled against the New Orleans based firm *Action Ink* that sued Anheuser-Busch for its use of the phrase "Ultimate Fan." *Action Ink* claimed to have coined and used the phrase since 1983, but the judge ruled that the company had abandoned its use of the phrase and lost trademark protection (Brown, 2013).

5. Consistency. The ideal trademark is immediately recognized and associated with the corporation or product. A trademark is strongest when the keepers are absolutely fanatical about expressing it exactly the same way on every occasion. It is easiest to make this association if there is rigorous consistency in the presentation of the brand. While it is always tempting and sometimes necessary to update corporate images, great care is necessary. Radical alterations or too many changes reduce the advertising power of the brand image, and may require new legal protection.

THE INTERNET

As the Internet expands its global reach to various corporate markets, it also increases the need to protect the brand online. Establishing a brand on the Internet expands the target market from a regional to international sphere. Companies hoping to build a campaign have to protect their investment. Otherwise, they open themselves up to challenges beyond their customary geographic market. For example, Blue Sky Foods of Franklinton, Louisiana, may eventually want to discuss a trademark agreement with Blue Sky Vineyard of Illinois to avoid any confusion.

The most common cause of an Internet trademark dispute is based on the universal resource locator or URL—commonly known as the web address. There have been a number of disputes involving the use of a trademark name in a URL, and one major threat was posed by "cybersquatting"—trafficking in web addresses for desirable trademark names to profit through intentional misspellings of web addresses resembling familiar products and services.

In 1999, the Uniform Domain Name Dispute Resolution Policy (UDRP) was introduced in order to manage such disputes. This policy was used to settle domain name disputes covering more than 31,000 URLs. The United States represented forty-two percent of the claims (World Intellectual Property Organization, 2010). In addition, the U.S. Congress passed the Anticybersquatting Consumer Protection Act (False designations of origin, false descriptions, 15 U.S.C. § 1125(d)). The law directed the Secretary of Commerce to recommend to Congress the appropriate guidelines for resolving such disputes. By pointing in part to the UDRP, the Secretary of Commerce urged no action (United States Patent and Trademark Office, 2013).

The Internet Corporation for Assigned Names and Numbers (ICANN) established a procedure for actions complaint filed for the following reasons:

- One domain name is identical, or confusingly similar, to a registered trademark or service mark in which the complainant has rights.
- One domain name owner has no rights, or legitimate interests in the domain name, and because the domain name has been registered, the filing was made in bad faith.

Once these circumstances are verified by ICANN, the URL registry will be transferred to the complainant but no financial penalties or fines are levied against the cybersquatter under this act. However, the Anticybersquatting Consumer Protection Act did create a means for a trademark owner to recover the use of the URL and possible damages from the cybersquatter in federal court. In order to achieve that end, the trademark holder must show the following in evidence:

- The domain name registrant acted in bad-faith with intent to profit from the trademark.
- The trademark was distinctive at the time the domain name was first registered.
- The domain name registered is identical to, or confusingly similar, to the trademark, and
- It qualifies for protection under federal trademark laws—that is, the trademark is distinctive and its owner was the first to use the trademark in commerce.

The last requirement poses the biggest obstacle to the media industry. If a cybersquatter learns of a program or production that has yet to be released, it can register the trademark name before it is used in public.

Fair and Unfair

Aggressive corporate marketing produces innovative efforts to expand trademark protection beyond simply controlling infringing competitors. New means of protection have achieved limited success and include the following noteworthy activities:

- Apple computer designs attempted to control its "look and feel" (Jack Russo, 1993).
- Harley Davidson attempted to trademark the sound of its engine (O'Dell, 2000).
- T-Mobile attempted to trademark magenta (Techdirt5, 2008).

Other means to aggressively manage a branded look are generally for more advanced companies and include two main protections-trade dress and trademark dilution. Trade dress attempts to establish protection for the overall look of a product. It essentially protects the presentation and design of a brand, such as the famous Tabasco bottle's barrel shape topped by a long thin neck and cap. Trade dress can protect the unique exterior and interior design of a store or restaurant such as the wooden porch of Cracker Barrel Old Country Store and Restaurant or the familiar golden arches of McDonald's. In such cases, the customer instantly recognizes the product from its trade dress without having to read the name of the store. Trade dress protection requires that the design element not be functional but aesthetic (Borghese Legal, LTD, 2011). For example, the overall shape of the Tabasco bottle can be protected by trade dress but the regulating lip at the top of the bottle is functional and not protected by trade dress.

One of the strongest measures to prevent competitors from infringing on a trademark emanates from the Federal Trademark Dilution Act of 1995 and 2006. Dilution takes two forms in trademark law. First, there is the "blurring" of a trademark name that causes the quality of the brand product to become unclear in the mind of the consumer. Imagine if a power company called *Entergy* suddenly becomes aware of a new firm titled *Entergy Fitness*. There is little reason to believe that customers might be confused into thinking that there is a partnership between the two companies, and yet the use of the name in terms of fitness would tend to blur the association between the name Entergy and its electricity service.

The second form of dilution is called tarnishment, which occurs when a second company uses the brand name in such a way that its association with the trademark becomes an embarrassment. Suppose that another group calling itself Entergy Nights uses this name to promote an adult nightclub featuring erotic dancers. Local residents are not likely to confuse the club with the electric service company but the association might prove objectionable to the power utility. Nonetheless, Entergy, the electric service company, would have to establish that its trademark deserves the same order of protection that more famous brands such as Starbucks and Disney require in law. The test for defending such a brand under law is based on these criteria:

- The duration and extent of use of the mark
- The duration and extent of advertising for the mark
- The geographic area in which the mark has been used
- The degree of distinctiveness of the mark (either through the nature of the mark itself, or through acquired distinctiveness)
- The degree of recognition of the mark
- The method by which the product was distributed and marketed (the "channels of trade")
- The use of the mark by third parties
- Whether the mark was federally registered (False designations of origin, false descriptions, 15 U.S.C. § 1125(d))

The three areas of *nominative use*, *fair use*, and *parody* are widely recognized exceptions in trademark protection law (Trademark Education & Information, 2013). Nominative use protects nonfiction authors, including journalists, in their ability to comment on the products, or services, offered under a trademark within the limits of libel law. Thus, competitors, reviewers, and even angry consumers are allowed to use brand names in order to provide fair and honest comment. In order to qualify as a nominative use, three conditions must be met (*New Kids on the Block v. News America Publishing, Inc.*, 1999):

- The owner's product and service cannot be easily identifiable without the use of the trademark.
- The author uses as little of the trademark as possible to identify the trademark owner's products or services.
- The author does nothing that suggests to the reader, sponsorship or endorsement of the nominative use by the trademark owner.

Fair use for trademarks normally refers to the passing use of trademarks such as the incidental or original use of a trademarked word. For instance, it is fair to write about apples when not referring to Apple Computer (Trademark Education & Information, 2013). It will be more difficult to determine the protection for books, such as *Because of Winn-Dixie* (using the trademark Winn Dixie) in the era of trademark dilution suits. The most important element remains that the person using the protected name NOT appear to be associated with the company, speaking for the company, or in business with the company.

Transformative Value

One area where the First Amendment protects use of trademarks or service marks comes in the form of parody or satire, especially if it involves political speech. Gov. Bobby Jindal of Louisiana joined forces with several other Republican governors in refusing to accept the federal expansion of Medicaid found in President Obama's affordable health care act. In response, the liberal political action group, MoveOn.Org, leased billboards in several states including Louisiana, posted YouTube videos, and took out TV spots criticizing the partisan refusal to accept this form of health care on behalf of poor residents. Drawing on the state's tourism campaign featuring a plate of crawfish and the capitalized red spelling of the state's names with exclamation marks, the MoveOn.Org billboard read: "LOU!SIANA Pick your passion! But hope you don't love your health. Gov. Jindal's denying Medicaid to 242,000 people." The question of Service Mark infringement was raised when Louisiana elected leaders decided to file suit.

Lieutenant Governor Jay Dardenne filed against MoveOn.Org for service mark infringement claiming the licensed and proprietary interests of the state Department of Culture, Recreation and Trade were at stake, but the liberal group whose billboard campaign was only contested in Louisiana felt the transformative value of political parody and satire took precedence over this IP issue cited. That constitutional viewpoint was affirmed by U.S. District Court Judge Shelly Dick (no relation to the chapter author), who sided with MoveOn.org in affirmation of the organization's rights to freedom of expression in political discourse. "The State has failed to demonstrate a compelling reason to curtail MoveOn.org's political speech in favor of protecting of the State's service mark," Dick held in her ruling. She added that Louisiana's tourism campaign would not suffer "irreparable injury" if the billboard remained on the highway (McGaughy, NOLA.com). Third-party use of a service mark or trademark is lawful for the transformative purposes of commenting through parody, satire, or just simple statement.

CONCLUSIONS

IP law defines the rules by which media professionals treat each other in terms of inventions, product brands, and their original creativity. In some ways it defines the rules of the media marketplace. The two major areas covered in this chapter—copyright and trademark—represent the types of IP most used by the media. Anyone studying this area should be able to identify what is protected, when that protection starts, how to secure protection, and how to profit from their newly created products. In the realm of original creative content such as a song or photograph, it is important to understand that copyright occurs at the moment the author or artist fixes their work in a tangible medium, but for the purposes of commercial protection and to guard against infringing uses, it is best to register the work with the U.S. Copyright Office that is easily online at www.copyright.gov. The law has amended several times over the years to protect various types of works from music to plays, from maps to poetry. Expressions that cannot be protected by copyright are generally ones that are simply factual and functional like a weight chart, a business form, or a telephone book.

Media practitioners need to be able to identify what constitutes infringement, a broad legal term that encompasses uses without permission, pay, or in the case of plagiarism, clear attribution. Plagiarism can be either an ethical and/or legal issue depending on the nature of the content and possible fair use, which is determined by assessing the secondary use's purpose, nature, amount, and effect on the market for the original work.

It is not difficult for copyright holders to license a work for others in either music industries or media entertainment, but in the digital age, alternatives have been recommended through the use of Creative Commons for those who prefer not to register with a federal agency. In the business world, service marks and trademarks may seem like copyright, but actually are protected more for reasons of product identification than to reward creativity and the progress of the useful arts. In all three areas of IP, there is an ongoing legal struggle between the forces of free expression and access in opposition to proprietary uses by copyright holders and trademark owners, which is why the rule of law is so important.

REFERENCES

American Library Association. (2013, July 1). *Digital Rights Management (DRM) & Libraries*. Retrieved from American Library Association: http://www.ala.org/advocacy/copyright/digitalrights

Asay, C. D. (2013, May 7). *Kirtsaeng and the First-Sale Doctrine's Digital Problem*. Retrieved from Stanford Law Review Online: http://www.stanfordlawreview.org/sites/default/files/online/articles/Kirtsaeng.pdf

Associated Press. (2014, July 14). *Cronut Creator goes after mom-and-pop creaux-nut bakery*. Retrieved from New York Post: http://nypost.com/2014/07/14/cronut-creator-goes-after-mom-and-pop-creaux-nut-bakery/

Associated Press. (2013, August 1). *Zulu Mardi Gras knew files suit accusing company of trademark violations*. Retrieved from The Times Picayune: http://www.nola.com/mardigras/index.ssf/2011/02/zulu_mardi_gras_krewe_files_su.html

Beesley, C. (2013, January 9). *The Difference Between a Trade Name and a Trademark – and Why You Can't Overlook Either*. Retrieved from U.S. Small Business Administration: http://www.sba.gov/community/blogs/community-blogs/business-law-advisor/difference-between-trade-name-and-trademark-%E2%80%93-a

Bitlaw. (2013, August 1). *TMEP 1302 Collective Marks Generally*. Retrieved from Welcome to Bitlaw: http://www.bitlaw.com/source/tmep/1302.html

Bitlaw. (2013, February 10). *Trademark Dilution*. Retrieved from Welcome to Bitlaw: http://www.bitlaw.com/trademark/dilution.html

Borghese Legal, LTD. (2011). *What is trade dress and how id trade dress protected?* Retrieved from Borghese Legal, LTD: http://borgheselegal.com/news/40-trademark/79-what-is-trade-dress-and-how-is-trade-dress-protected

Brown, L. (2013, July 18). *A-B wins trademark fight over 'Ultimate Fan" use*. Retrieved from St. Louis Post-Dispatch: http://www.stltoday.com/business/local/a-b-wins-trademark-fight-over-ultimate-fan-use/article_61422f6f-7f98-541a-ad9f-2b1a62dd6d98.html

Coats v. Holbrook, 7 N.Y. Ch. Ann. 713, (1845)

Collen, J. (2014, April 8). *Will Trademark Testing Heat Up Over Half-Baked Claims To 'Cronut'?* Retrieved from Forbes.com: http://www.forbes.com/sites/jesscollen/2014/04/08/cronut-wars/

Community for Creative Non-Violence ET AL. v. Reid, 88-293 (Supreme Court of the United States March 29, 1989).

Copyright Act, 17 U.S.C. § 102 (1976). (n.d.).

Copyright Infringement and Remedies, 17 U.S.C. § 501-513. (n.d.).

Creative Commons. (n.d.). *Creative Commons – Attribution*. Retrieved July 30, 2014, from Creative Commons: http://creativecommons.org/licenses/by/4.0/

Criminal Infringement, 17 U.S.C. § 5:506. (n.d.).

False designations of origin, false descriptions, 15 U.S.C. § 1125(d). (n.d.).

Incorporeal movables, LA Civ Code 473. (n.d.).

International Trademark Association. (2013, March 24). *Loss of Trademark Rights*. Retrieved from International Trademark Association: http://www.inta.org/TrademarkBasics/FactSheets/Pages/LossofTrademarkRightsFactSheet.aspx

International Trademark Association. (2013, August 1). *Certification Marks*. Retrieved from International Trademark Association: http://www.inta.org/TrademarkBasics/FactSheets/Pages/CertificationMarks.aspx

Jack Russo, J. N. (1993). *Lawyers of the Internet Economy*. Retrieved July 20, 2014, from Computer Law: http://www.computerlaw.com/CM/Articles/Look-Feel-in-Computer-Software.asp

Limitations on Actions, 17 U.S.C. § 507. (n.d.).

Limitations on exclusive rights, 17 U.S.C. § 109. (n.d.).

Limitations on Exclusive Rights, 17 U.S.C. § 111 and 119. (n.d.).

Limitations on Exclusive Rights: Fair Use, 17 U.S.C. § 107. (n.d.).

Loren C. Scott & Associates. (2013). *The Economic Impact of Louisiana's Entertainment Tax Credit Programs*. Baton Rouge, LA: Office of Entertainment and Industry Development, Louisiana Department of Economic Development.

Louisiana Department of Agriculture and Forestry. (2013, August 2). *Certified Logos*. Retrieved from Louisiana Department of Agriculture and Forestry: http://www.ldaf.state.la.us/portal/Offices/MarketingAgriculturalEconomicDevelopment/CertifiedLogos/tabid/322/Default.aspx

LSU Eunice. (2013, June 2). *The LSU Eunice Logo*. Retrieved from Public Affairs - Graphics: http://www.lsue.edu/site113.php

Lutzker, A. P. (2003). *Content Rights for Creative Professionals: Copyrights and trademarks in a digital age*. Burlington, MA: Focal Press.

Lyras, A. (1992). *Incidental Artwork in Television Scene Backgrounds: Fair use or Copyright*. Retrieved from *Fordham Intellectual Property, Media, and Entertainment Law Journal*: Volume 2, Issue 2: http://ir.lawnet.fordham.edu/cgi/viewcontent.cgi?article=1021&context=iplj

McKenna, M. P. (2007). *The Normative Foundation of Trademark Law*. Retrieved from International Trademark Association: http://www.inta.org/Academics/Documents/finalndlawreview.pdf

New Kids on the Block v. News America Publishing, Inc., 971 F.2d 302 (9th Cir 1999).

O'Dell, J. (2000, June 21). *Harley-Davidson Quits Trying to Hog Sound*. Retrieved August 1, 2014, from Los Angeles Times: http://articles.latimes.com/2000/jun/21/business/fi-43145

Patterson, L. R. (1993). Copyright And `The Exclusive Right' Of Authors." *Journal of Intellectual Property*, 1 (1), 1-48.

Proceedings by Copyright Royalty Judges, 17 U.S.C. § 8, 10: 801-805. (n.d.).

Regarding Computer Programs, 17 U.S.C. §101 and §117 (1980). (n.d.).

Rules and Practice in Trademark Cases, 37 C.F.R. § 2. (n.d.).

Sheldon Mak Rose and Anderson. (2013, June 20). *Coping with the Berne Convention*. Retrieved from Sheldon Mak & Anderson Intellectual Property Law: http://www.usip.com/pdf/Article_Patents/BerneConvention.pdf

Techdirt5. (2008, March 31). *Engadget Mobile Threatened For Using t-Mobile's Trademarked Magenta*. Retrieved from Techdirt: http://www.techdirt.com/articles/20080331/134624706.shtml

The Letter Edged in Black Press, Inc. v. Public Building Commission of Chicago, 353 (US District Court for the Northern District of Illinois, Eastern Division December 22, 1970).

The Radio Group. (2013, June 20). *The Radio Group*. Retrieved from http://www.radiogroupshreveport.com/

Trademark Education & Information. (2013, June 1). *What is Trademark Fair Use?* . Retrieved from Trademarks 101: http://www.trademark-education.com/fairuse.html

United States Patent and Trademark Office. (2013, April 12). *Report to Congress: The Anticybequatting Consumer Protection Act of 1999*. Retrieved from USPTO.gov: http://www.uspto.gov/web/offices/dcom/olia/tmcybpiracy/repcongress.pdf

United States Patent and Trademark Office. (2013, March 19). *USPTO Fee Information*. Retrieved from USPTO.gov: http://www.uspto.gov/web/offices/ac/qs/ope/fee031913.htm#tm

US Copyright Office. (2013, May 21). *Copyright Nocies*. Retrieved from United State Copyright Office: http://www.copyright.gov/circs/circ03.pdf

US Copyright Office. (2013, May 10). *Duration of Copyright*. Retrieved from United States Copyright Office: http://www.copyright.gov/circs/circ15a.pdf

Wheaton v. Peters, 33 U.S. 591 (1834).

World Intellectual Property Organization. (2010, March 23). *Brands Tackle Cybersquatters in 2009, UDRP becomes Eco-Friendly*. Retrieved from WIPO.int: http://www.wipo.int/pressroom/en/articles/2010/article_0007.html

World Intellectual Property Organization. (2013, June 23). *WIPO - A Users Guide*. Retrieved from WIPO: http://www.wipo.int/freepublications/en/general/1040/wipo_pub_1040.html

Chapter 11
Commerical Law Restrictions on Expression
By Rick J. Norman, McNeese State University

Learning Objectives
In this chapter, readers will:
- distinguish commercial speech from non-commercial speech
- recognize the limits of controlling speech through contracts
- identify a "contract of silence"
- contrast the principles the protecting free speech rights of private-sector employees from those protecting the free speech rights of government employees
- understand the conflict between free speech rights and the right to equality in the workplace
- recognize the limits of controlling speech through commercial laws and regulations
- become familiar with the conflict between intellectual property rights and free speech rights

Since ancient times, the free flow of information between individuals has been recognized as having a high social value. Now, the free flow of information between businesses and individuals has a huge monetary value. The question for contemporary society is whether it will consider the exchange of information between businesses and individuals as valuable and as worthy of protection as the exchange of information between individuals.

Twenty-five hundred years ago, the Chinese philosopher Confucius recognized that the accuracy and free flow of information was critical to the maintenance of a just society:

> Now, if names of things are not defined, words will not correspond to facts. When words do not correspond to facts, it is impossible to perfect anything. Where it is impossible to perfect anything, the arts and institutions of civilization cannot flourish, law and justice do not attain their ends; and when law and justice do not attain their ends, the people will be at a loss to know what to do. (Confucius, *The Analects,* 1938, xiii, 3)

Twenty-three centuries after Confucius, the framers of the U.S. Constitution sought to protect the free flow of information with the First Amendment, which has been called "the Constitution's most majestic guaranty" (Tribe, 1978, p. 576). And as noted in previous chapters, the free speech guarantees of the Louisiana Constitution (Article 1, Sec. 7) are at least as extensive as those of the federal First Amendment. It is doubtful, however, that Confucius or the founding fathers, men from Agrarian economies, could have anticipated how commerce would come to dominate modern society. Nothing in late eighteenth century America gave the framers of the First Amendment a reason to predict the power and influence of today's global businesses.

CONTROL OF COMMERCE THROUGH THE CONTROL OF SPEECH

As commerce has permeated every aspect of modern society, the lines of demarcation between commercial and non-commercial speech are somewhat blurred. The town square has, to a large extent, become as commercialized as a shopping mall, raising certain First Amendment questions. Are restrictions on free speech, which would be unlawful in the town square, acceptable in the shopping mall as simply the mall owner's right to control his commercial property? In this age of ever-expanding information in the form of digital data, speech is information and information is speech. Efficient commerce requires the free flow of information or "free speech." A business whose information flows more freely has an advantage over a competitor whose information is restricted. At the same time, though, a business with a monopoly on the use of information may want to restrict or even prevent the flow of that information. To the extent the First Amendment can be used to promote or restrict the free flow of information, there is a temptation for business to manipulate it to gain a competitive advantage.

The modern trend has been towards the concentration of economic power. In 1967 Professor Lawrence Blades wrote, "It is a widely accepted proposition that large corporations now pose a threat to individual freedom comparable to that which would be posed if governmental power were unchecked" (Blades, 1967). As will be shown below, with the concentration of power in the hands of business has come the tendency of business to use the First Amendment as both a sword and a shield.

CONTROL OF SPEECH THROUGH COMMERCIAL LAWS

Speech may be regulated by the government where: (1) the regulation is content-neutral (i.e. does not specify what can and cannot be said), (2) it furthers a significant governmental interest, and (3) other opportunities exist for exercising First Amendment rights (*U.S. v. Grace*, 1983). Regulations infringing on the content of protected speech are presumed unconstitutional (*U.S. v. Eichman*, 1990).

The Supreme Court and legal scholars initially considered the flow of information related to business (i.e. commercial speech) less worthy of protection and so subject to more regulation than other forms of expression. As Professor Baker stated: "the profit-motivated speech of the marketplace of commodities . . . does not seem to deserve the same status as the speech of the marketplace of the mind . . . [and] justifies excluding this commercial speech from constitutional protection" (1989, p. 198). However, gradually the courts have afforded commercial speech more and more protection. But the initial question is always: "What is commercial speech?"

Commercial speech is not always easy to identify. It is generally held to refer to expressions that propose a commercial transaction (*Virginia State Board of Pharmacy v. Virginia Citizens Consumer Council*, 1976), that is likely to influence consumers in their commercial decisions (*Kasky v. Nike, Inc.*, 2002), or that is related solely to the economic interests of the speaker and the audience (*Central Hudson Gas & Electric Corporation v. Public Service Commission of New York*, 1980; *Gregory v. Louisiana Board of Chiropractic Examiners*, 1992). For example, protected commercial speech is not limited to spoken words but includes billboards, video, audio, and other forms of expression (*Metromedia, Inc. v. City of San Diego*, 1981). However, even the Supreme Court has acknowledged that the definition of commercial speech is confusing and often vague (*Greater New Orleans Broadcasting v. U.S.*, 1999). The Supreme Court has noted that commercial speech is often, increasingly, "inextricably intertwined" with noncommercial speech (*Riley v. National Federation of the Blind of North Carolina, Inc.*, 1988).

Once identified, however, not all of commercial speech can be protected. The government has a legitimate interest in regulating speech for lawful goods and services, but it also penalizes commercial speech that is false, deceptive, or misleading (*Greater New Orleans Broadcasting v. U.S.*, 1999). Freedom of speech cannot be denied on the pretext of government regulation. Commercial speech is protected from unwarranted governmental regulation where it is neither misleading nor in furtherance of unlawful activity.

The government is not allowed to regulate commercial speech unless the governmental interest is substantial, the regulation restricting speech directly advances the governmental interest, and the regulation is not more extensive than is necessary to serve that governmental interest. There must be a "reasonable fit" between the government's reason to regulate speech and the method of regulation chosen. The method need not be the least restrictive method, but it must be narrowly tailored to achieve the desired objective (*State University of New York v. Fox*, 1989; *Florida Bar v. Went For It, Inc.*, 1995). For example, in one outdoor advertising case (*Longview Outdoor Advertising Co., LLC v. City of Winter Garden, Fla.*, 2006), it was determined by the court that the city's interest in safety and aesthetics was sufficient to uphold a city ordinance that allowed businesses to put up signs, and yet limited those signs to the location of their business but not elsewhere.

Freedom of speech may be subordinated to the police power of the government in furtherance of a substantial public interest. In the *City of Ladue v. Gilleo* (1994), the Supreme Court was forced to balance two competing interests. The first was the authority of the state to regulate speech in furtherance of an aesthetic purpose. The second concern was the right of a citizen to express her political beliefs while on her private property. In that case, Margaret Gilleo displayed a sign on her lawn that read: "Say No to War in the Persian Gulf, Call Congress Now." The town of Ladue had an ordinance prohibiting lawn signs but allowing the town council to make exceptions where the public interest would be best served. The Supreme Court ruled that the ordinance violated Ms. Gilleo's right to free speech. The First Amendment requires that the government's restriction on speech actually be necessary to achieve its interest and that there be a direct causal link between the restriction and the injury to be prevented.

From No Protection to Full Protection

Each year, billions of dollars are spent by businesses on advertising. Advertising promises to further commerce by stimulating demand from consumers. And what better way for a business to stimulate demand and, thereby, commerce, than through freedom of speech? The First Amendment, originally intended for the protection of speech in the town square, now is used to protect speech directed principally at increasing sales and promoting a brand image. However, advertising and other profit-motivated, commercial speech were not constitutionally protected until fairly recently. Three quarters of a century ago, commercial speech was afforded no protection. Slowly, as its monetary value has increased, commercial speech has been given more and more protection.

In 1942, the Supreme Court unanimously ruled that commercial speech was not protected at all by the First Amendment. In what has come to be known as the *Submarine* case, a Florida businessman, F.J. Chrestensen, moored a submarine in New York City's East River and distributed handbills advertising tours of his boat. When New York City Police Commissioner Valentine stopped him from distributing his handbills because of a city ordinance prohibiting such advertisements, he cleverly printed the handbills with a political protest on one side and the advertisement for his submarine on the other. The Supreme Court upheld the ordinance and dismissed his First Amendment claims stating "We are . . . clear that the Constitution imposes no . . . restraint on government as respects purely commercial advertising" (*Valentine v. Chrestensen*, 1942, p. 54).

Since the *Submarine* case, the Supreme Court has used the First Amendment both to expand the free speech rights of business and to slowly restrict government regulation of business. The Supreme Court's first recognition of commercial free speech rights, although minimal, began in the 1970s with the *Bigelow* case (*Bigelow v. Virginia*, 1975). In *Bigelow*, the Court invalidated a Virginia statute prohibiting the advertisement of abortion services. The Court balanced the importance of commercial expression against Virginia's interest in protecting the public, and held in favor of the newspaper editor's decision to advertise for the Women's Pavilion of New York, an abortion referral service.

One year later, in the *Virginia Pharmacy* case, the Court overturned a Virginia law that prohibited pharmacists from advertising drug prices. The Court held that the statute violated the rights of consumers to the free flow of information from those selling important products. The Court reasoned that the pricing of prescription medications was vital to the quality of life of those dependent on them. The Court determined that a business may be a "speaker" with free speech rights and that even "purely economic" speech, such as advertising, enjoys some First Amendment protection. Justice

Rehnquist's dissent, however, scolded the majority for "elevat[ing] commercial intercourse between a seller hawking his wares and a buyer seeking to strike a bargain to the same plane as has been previously reserved for the free marketplace of ideas . . ." (*Virginia State Board of Pharmacy v. Virginia Citizens Consumer Council, Inc.* 1976, p. 781).

In the *Central Hudson Gas* (*Central Hudson Gas & Electric Corp. v. Public Service Commission of New York*, 1980) case, an electric company challenged a government regulation that banned promotional advertising by utilities because, arguably, such advertising encouraged consumers to use more energy. The Supreme Court said that, when determining the outcome of a commercial free speech challenge, a four-step analysis was required. The court must determine: (1) whether the advertising deals with lawful activity and is not misleading; (2) whether the government's interest in regulating the speech is substantial; (3) whether the regulation directly advances that government interest; and (4) whether the regulation is narrowly drawn so as not to be overly intrusive. The Court noted that the government had a substantial interest in lowering energy use and that the regulation banning advertising by utilities directly advanced that governmental interest. Even though the Court determined that the government satisfied the first three standards of the four-step test for validity, it held that the regulation was too broad because banning advertising that was unrelated to conservation violated the utility company's right to commercial expression.

A purely pro-business approach to the First Amendment would make three assumptions in arguing that commercial speech is entitled to full protection. First, it would suppose that all speech enjoys full First Amendment protection. Second, it would assume that all information disseminated by a business is "speech" for purposes of the First Amendment. Third, it would claim that the identity of the "speaker" is irrelevant in determining whether protection is afforded by the First Amendment. If one accepts all three assumptions, commercial speech by a business would enjoy the full protection of the Constitution. However, such is not the case and, by the end of the 1970s, the Supreme Court declared truthful, non-misleading speech about commercial matters protected but in a "subordinate position in a scale of First Amendment values" (*Ohralik v. Ohio State Bar Association*, 1978). In a 1993 decision overturning a state law prohibiting Certified Public Accountants from soliciting business in Florida, the Supreme Court stated:

> The commercial marketplace, like other spheres of our social and cultural life, provides a forum where ideas and information flourish. Some of the ideas and information are vital, some of slight worth. But the general rule is that the speaker and the audience, not the government, assess the value of the information presented. Thus, even a communication that does no more than propose a commercial transaction is entitled to the coverage of the First Amendment. (*Edenfield v. Fane*, 1993; *Virginia State Board of Pharmacy v. Virginia Citizens Consumer Council, Inc.*, 1976)

Any authority—be it government or professional organization—seeking to restrict commercial speech has the burden of justifying the restriction (*Thompson v. Western States Medical Center*, 2002) under the application of the *Central Hudson* test. In the *Lorillard Tobacco* case (*Lorillard Tobacco Co. v. Reilly*, 2001), the U.S. Supreme Court was called upon to determine whether a Massachusetts regulation prohibiting outdoor advertising of tobacco products within 1,000 feet of schools violated the tobacco corporation's free speech rights. The Court held that this advertising was for a legal activity (i.e. the sale of tobacco products), the government had a substantial interest in curbing youth smoking, and banning advertising within 1,000 feet of schools advanced that governmental interest. However, the Court determined that the prescribed distance went too far to satisfy the "narrowly-tailored" requirement of the *Central Hudson* four-part test. The Court ruled that the regulation of free speech cannot "unduly impinge" on the ability of a business to propose a commercial activity, nor impinge upon the rights of a consumer to obtain information regarding a proposed commercial activity.

The trend of the Supreme Court has steadily been to put commercial speech on closer footing with non-commercial speech. The shift by the Supreme Court from no First Amendment protection for commercial speech to what is known as intermediate scrutiny can place commercial business and advertising interests on a collision course with the government's efforts to protect consumers, employees, and other individuals.

CONTROL OF SPEECH BY CONTROL OF ADVERTISING

Keep in mind that it is only truthful advertising related to lawful activities that is protected by the First Amendment, but any law or regulation that restricts truthful advertising is subject to judicial scrutiny to determine the rule's validity. Deceptive advertising is not protected by the First Amendment and, in fact, the government may prohibit it entirely (*In re. RMJ*, 1982). Advertising that is potentially misleading may be regulated but that regulation must be reasonably related to the government's interest in preventing the deception of consumers (*Zaunderer v. Office of Disciplinary Counsel of Supreme Court of Ohio*, 1985).

Any governing body seeking to uphold a restriction on commercial speech must justify the restriction (*Bolger v. Youngs Drug Products Corp.*, 1983). The burden is a substantial one, and may not be satisfied by mere speculation or conjecture (*Edenfield v. Fane*, 1993). Again, the regulation restricting advertising is appropriate if the regulation directly advances a substantial government interest and is not more extensive than is necessary to serve that interest (*Central Hudson Gas & Electric Corp. v. Public Service Commission of New York*, 1980). In the *Bad Frog Brewery* (*Bad Frog Brewery, Inc. v. New York State Liquor Authority*, 1998) case, an appellate court ruled that the Liquor Authority could not prohibit a beer label displaying a frog giving an insulting hand gesture. Because the labels were not

Attorney Advertising

If there is any question that commercial speech has a different level of protection in terms of the First Amendment, look no further than rules governing the use of advertising publicity for lawyers. The practice of directly soliciting clients, known as barratry, has long been considered illegal, but that tactic is not quite the same as publicizing a lawyer's practice through the media. In terms of lawyer advertising the picture becomes murkier and the style of marketing varies from state to state. In New York, for example, lawyers had taken to using special effects in their TV spots with explosions and jingles accompanying enlarged visuals of them towering over tall buildings and promising results that would impress. In 2008, the Louisiana Supreme Court adopted new rules regulating attorney advertising, but those regulations were challenged in court by the consumer advocacy group, Public Citizen. The Federal Fifth Circuit Court of Appeals ruled in the lawyers' favor and held that the limits on publicity lawyers were allowed to use in the state to promote their practice infringed on First Amendment rights. Specifically, the complaining lawyers did not want to be told they had to keep silent about their legal record of success, nor did they want to be forced to announce disclaimers in commercial messages similar to those non-prescription medicine companies have to use at the close of television spots to warn customers of potential side effects. The lawsuit filed in Louisiana on behalf of the advertising attorneys was not deemed a total victory for their commercial speech, however, since the state's lawyers were still prevented from using mottos or nicknames indicating their success in litigation. They also were prohibited from using scenes of courtroom judges and juries, and from using commercial messages that promised results for their clients. In addition to banning any misleading, false or deceptive messages in legal advertising the rules also restricted advertising promotions on attorney's Web sites.

misleading or related to an illegal activity and the regulation did not directly advance the government's interest in protecting children from vulgar advertising, the label was deemed commercial speech protected by the First Amendment.

Commercial speech also may be curtailed in the regulation of professions (*The Florida Bar v. Catarcio*, 1998). In *Gregory v. The Louisiana Board of Chiropractic Examiners* (1992), the Louisiana Supreme Court struck down a statute that prevented chiropractors from soliciting potential patients who were known to have been involved in motor vehicle accidents. The Court ruled that, although the state is not required to use the least restrictive means of regulating commercial speech, it is required to choose a reasonable means of regulation that is in proportion to the interests which are served. Similarly in *Public Citizen, Inc. v. Louisiana Attorney General Disciplinary Board* (2011), the U.S. Fifth Circuit Court of Appeals ruled that the Louisiana Rules of Professional Conduct governing attorney advertisement were overly restrictive.

The Federal Trade Commission regulates misleading advertising on a federal level (15 U.S.C.A. Sec. 53), and the Louisiana Office of Attorney General, Consumer Protection Section, regulates misleading advertising on a state level (La. R.S. 51:1404). The Federal Securities and Exchange Commission regulates misleading speech with respect to the sale of corporate stock and other securities (15 U.S.C.A. Secs. 78d, 78j). The state Office of Financial Institutions, Securities Division, regulates misleading speech with respect to state corporate and securities matters (La. R.S. 51:710, 712). Of course, their regulations are subject to First Amendment protections.

Laws to Restrict Speech to Protect Business from Criticism

Commercial laws are sometimes used to stem public criticism of a business. For example, agricultural disparagement laws (La. R.S. 3:4501-3:4504), criticized as "veggie libel" laws, were originally enacted to protect producers of farm products from potentially huge losses that could result from false claims that might cause perishable produce to be kept off the market and thus not sold before spoiling. One of those agricultural disparagement laws was used against a celebrity trying to alert the public to potential health hazards.

In 1998, television talk show host Oprah Winfrey was sued by a group of cattle lot operators in Texas under the Texas Food Disparagement Law after Oprah made disparaging comments on her television show about beef. Unlike in a defamation suit, where the plaintiff must prove that the defendant deliberately and knowingly spread false information, under the Texas Food Disparagement Law the food lot merely had to prove that Oprah's statements were not based on reasonable and reliable scientific inquiry, facts, or data (*Texas Beef Group v. Winfrey*, 2000). In other words, the food lot only had to prove that Oprah did not do her homework, not that Oprah intentionally lied. Even though Oprah eventually won the case, she no longer speaks publicly on the issue (Rampton & Stauber, 1997, p. 192).

Laws that Restrict Competitive Speech to Protect Business

A number of commercial laws are used to protect businesses by restricting the free speech of competitors or potential competitors. For example, the Louisiana Unfair Trade Practices Act (La. R.S. 51:1401 to 51:1422) (LUTPA) generally prohibits unfair competition. The definition of "unfair" under the LUTPA is very nebulous. A practice is considered "unfair" under the LUTPA when it offends established public policy or when the practice is unethical, oppressive, unscrupulous, or substantially injurious to a business competitor (*Family Resource Group, Inc. v. Louisiana Parent Magazine*, 2001). For example, solicitation of business customers by an employee for personal interest rather than on behalf of the employer is a violation of the LUTPA if the solicitation occurs while the employee is still employed (*Dufau v. Creole Engineering, Inc.*, 1985; *United Group of National Paper Distributors, Inc. v. Vinson*, 1996; but see *SDT Industries, Inc. v. Leeper*, 2001; *Innovative Manpower Solutions, LLC v. Ironman Staffing*, 2013).

Compelling Commercial Expression and Reception

Sometimes the government may run afoul of the First Amendment by attempting to compel speech rather than to silence it. The Supreme Court has held that there may be a difference between compelled speech and compelled silence but, in the context of First Amendment protection, the difference is without constitutional significance because "... the First Amendment guarantees 'freedom of speech,' a term necessarily comprising the decision of both what to say and what *not* to say" (*Riley v. National Federation of the Blind of North Carolina, Inc.* 1988, pp. 796-797).

Until recently, it was generally understood that the government, acting in the interest of the public, had the authority to force businesses to convey non-ideological, government-mandated messages, so long as it was apparent that it was the government speaking, not the business. Examples of this compelled speech include the familiar warnings on cigarette packages. But the First Amendment also has been used to limit such government regulations. For example, in 2001 the federal National Labor Relations Board (NLRB) released a new rule requiring businesses to display a poster that notified employees of their union rights under the federal NLRA. Business groups argued that the rule forced them to speak against their will in violation of their rights under the First Amendment. Within a year of the NLRB rule, a federal appellate court struck down the rule on First Amendment grounds (*National Ass'n of Mfrs. v. N.L.R.B.*, 2013).

What surprised legal scholars was that, less than ten years before, one of the judges on the three judge appellate panel had affirmed the legality of an executive order of President George W. Bush requiring federal contractors to put up anti-union posters in the workplace. The same judge ruled that the First Amendment prohibited the government from requiring a business to post a pro-union poster but the same First Amendment allowed the government to require the business to post an anti-union poster (*UAW Labor Employment and Training Corp. v. Chao*, 2003). Critics argued that free speech protection should not depend on the content of the message.

The First Amendment sometimes pits rights of speakers against the privacy rights of unwilling viewers or listeners. For example, the government may act to prohibit intrusion into the privacy of the home. There is no constitutional right to force speech into the ear of an unwilling listener (*Frisby v. Schultz*, 1988). Nothing in the Constitution requires a person to listen to or view even the best ideas. For that reason, a statute that requires a business to remove unwilling recipients from its mailing list does not violate the First Amendment (*Rowan v. U.S. Post Office Dept.*, 1970). Such restrictions, however, are valid only when the speaker intrudes on the privacy rights of the targeted audience (*Erznoznil v. City of Jacksonville*, 1975).

Protecting the Commercial Speaker

A person who does business as a sole proprietor and persons who combine to do business as a partnership are personally liable for the debts and liabilities of their respective businesses. The owners of sole proprietorships and partnerships put all of their personal property and all of their business property at risk. This potential liability acts as a disincentive to business owners to take even modest commercial risks. One wrong move or a little bad luck and an owner doing business as a sole proprietor or in a partnership could lose everything. In order to give business owners an incentive to take more risks, Louisiana and other states allow them to do business in the form of a limited liability entity such as a corporation or a limited liability company. The advantage of doing business through a limited liability entity is that, if something goes wrong, a creditor of the business can take what the business owns, but it cannot take what the business owner owns personally. As a result, most business in the United States is done through an entity with limited liability protection.

Such limited liability entities (e.g. corporations and limited liability companies) are deemed "persons" for some purposes but not all. For example, a corporation is entitled to file a lawsuit but is not entitled to vote. A corporation is not a "citizen," however, so the question naturally arises whether a corporation's speech is protected by the First Amendment. In the United States, corporations and other legal entities have been elevated gradually in terms of constitutional protection. In the famous *Citizens United* case (*Citizens United v. Federal Election Commission*, 2010), the Supreme Court held that any law constraining corporate political expenditures is a violation of corporate rights of free speech. The Court also held that a corporation is a person for purposes of free speech. This holding was reached despite Justice John Marshall's pronouncement in 1819 that "a corporation is an artificial being, invisible, intangible, and existing only in contemplation of law" (*Trustees of Dartmouth College v. Woodward*, 1819). In bitter dissenting opinions in *Citizens United*, Justices Stevens and Breyer concluded that the Court was perverting the First Amendment by giving corporate speakers the same rights as citizens and by providing commercial speech with the same protection as political speech.

CONTROL OF SPEECH THROUGH THE "EMPLOYMENT AT WILL" DOCTRINE

The "state action" doctrine provides that constitutional guarantees of individual rights only protect individuals from governmental interference (Tribe, 1988). Because the First Amendment only proscribes government restrictions on free speech, its constitutional guarantee is inapplicable to private-sector employees (*Tiernan v. Charleston Area Med. Ctr., Inc.*, 1998). As a result, private-sector employees do not have First Amendment free speech rights concerning most of what they say at or about their job.

With rare exceptions, free speech in the workplace is a matter of employer prerogative. Employers typically regulate speech with the actual or implied threat of dismissal. The right of an employer to fire its employees at any time for no reason has a tendency to limit free expression in the workplace.

Most of the debate over restricting speech in the workplace pits the employee's free speech desires against the employer's near absolute right to fire the employee under Louisiana's employment-at-will doctrine. The "at-will" employment doctrine has its basis in the Louisiana Civil Code (La. Civil Code art. 2747), which provides that employment not guaranteed for a specific period of time may be terminated by either the employee or the employer at any time, so long as the reason for termination is not unlawful. Reasons for termination of or by an at-will employee need not be accurate, fair, or reasonable (*Mix v. University of New Orleans*, 1992).

Most other states protect an employee from being discharged for reasons that violate or offend public policy (see e.g., *Petermann v. International Brotherhood of Teamsters, Chauffeurs, Warehousemen, and Helpers of America, Local 396*, 1959). Louisiana, however, does not recognize this "public policy" exception to the doctrine of at-will employment (*Guillory v. St. Landry Parish Police Jury*, 1986). Even though the Louisiana free speech protections in Article I Section 7 of the Louisiana Constitution are broader than those of the federal First Amendment, Louisiana courts have not seized upon this protection to fashion a public policy exception to the rule of at-will employment. As a result, with only a few exceptions, private-sector employees may be fired for exercising their free speech rights.

Speech Involving Concerted Activity of Employees Protected

Even though private-sector employees have limited freedom of expression, there are a few rights protected by federal labor law. Employees have a protected right to talk to each other about their working conditions, and such employee speech is protected by the National Labor Relations Act (NLRA) when it involves concerted activities for the employee's mutual benefit (29 U.S.C.A. art. 157; *N.L.R.B. v. Magnavox Co. of Tennessee*, 1974). "Concerted activities" must be in contemplation of further group action by the employees. Consequently, employer rules prohibiting employees from discussing their working conditions or their compensation violate the NLRA (*Cintas Corp. v. NLRB*, 2007).

The NLRA has been interpreted, for example, to proscribe employer rules: (1) prohibiting employees from making disparaging remarks against their employer's business or its management (*Dish Network Corporation and Communication Workers of America, Local 6171 and Eric Sutton*, 2013), (2) prohibiting employees from contacting the media (*DirectTV U.S. DirectTV Holdings, LLC and International Association of Machinists and Aerospace Workers, District Lodge 947, AFL-CIO*, 2013), and (3) prohibiting employees from disseminating personal or financial information (*MCPC, Inc. and Jason Galanter*, 2014). In all of these cases, it was determined that the employers' rules could discourage employees from discussing their working conditions.

The NLRA also protects employees against retaliation for their concerted activities and restricts employer speech that threatens reprisal against employees involved in concerted activities (*N.L.R.B. v. Gissel Packing Co.*, 1969). In one case, it was held that an employer violated the NLRA by firing employees for posting messages on Facebook about their working conditions (*Design Technology Group, LLC d/b/a Bettie Page Clothing and DTG California Management, LLC d/b/a Bettie Page Clothing, a Single Employer and Vanessa Morris*, 2013).

Free Speech Rights of Government Employees

Since the Supreme Court's 1968 decision in *Pickering v. Board of Education* (1968), the First Amendment has been interpreted to give government employees free speech protection. In *Pickering*, a public school teacher was fired after the local newspaper published his letter criticizing the Board of Education's allocation of funds to athletics rather than to improve classrooms and educational facilities. The Supreme Court balanced the teacher's interest in free speech and the school's interest in running an efficient school system and found that the former outweighed the latter (see *Duke v. North Texas State University*, 1972).

As noted in *Pickering*, a government employee's speech enjoys First Amendment protection when: (1) the speech involves a matter of public concern, and (2) the employee's free speech interests outweigh the government employer's interests as an employer. The employee's right to speak must be balanced against the government employer's interest in promoting the efficient fulfillment of its responsibilities (*Bolton v. City of Dallas*, 2006; *Communications Workers of America v. Ector County Hospital District*, 2006).

Even government employers may regulate workplace speech when it involves personal matters rather than matters of public concern (*Connick v. Myers*, 1983). A government employer may impose certain restrictions on the speech of its employees which would be unconstitutional if the government attempted to apply those restrictions to the general public (see e.g., *Faculty Rights Coalition v. Shahrokhi*, 2006). Government employees have less First Amendment protections when speaking about matters arising within the scope of their employment. For example, a government employee's complaints about his working conditions, if not voiced to co-employees, are not protected because they are not a matter of public concern (*Adamson-James v. Florida*, 2013).

A government employee, however, may not engage in speech that disrupts the efficient delivery of public services by the employer unless an overwhelming public interest is at stake that does not involve the personal interest of the employee. In one case, a government employee's statement that he hoped President Reagan would be assassinated was held to be accorded constitutional protection because it addressed a matter of public concern and it did not interfere with the business of the government employer (*Rankin v. McPherson*, 1987). Again, the free speech of public employees is protected so long as it does not adversely impact the business of government.

Prohibited Retaliation for Engaging in Free Speech

Whistleblower laws prohibit employers from taking adverse employment action against an employee because the employee discloses information that he believes evidences a violation of law by his employer. An employer may not retaliate against an employee who is acting in good faith by reporting the suspected violation of law (R.S. 23:967(a); *Matthews v. Military Dept. ex rel. State* (2007). The protections of the Whistleblower statutes are available to both public and private employees (*Puig v. Greater New Orleans Expressway Commission*, 2000).

The federal Whistleblower Protection Act (5 U.S.C.A. Art. 2302 (b) (8)) prohibits federal agencies from taking adverse employment action because an employee disclosed information that he believed evidenced either a violation of law by the federal government or gross mismanagement of federal funds (see e.g., *Crawford v. U.S. Dept. of Homeland Security*, 2007). Other federal statutes similarly protect whistleblowing employees from retaliation (see e.g., Consumer Product Safety Improvement Act of 2008, 15 U.S.C.A. Sec. 2087). For example, federal securities laws (15 U.S.C.A. Arts. 78a to 78pp.) and commodities laws (7 U.S.C.A. secs. 1 to 27f) provide "bounties" to whistleblowers who report illegal trading (15 U.S.C.A. secs. 78a to 78pp). Financial services employees are protected from retaliation when they disclose or object to fraudulent or unlawful conduct related to offering or providing financial products or services to consumers (12 U.S.C.A. sec. 5567). Federal criminal law also prohibits retaliation against individuals who report the commission of any federal offense to law enforcement (18 U.S.C.A. sec. 1513 (e)).

Generally, to be successful in a whistleblower claim, an employee must prove: (1) the employer violated the law through a workplace act or practice, (2) he informed the employer of its violation, (3) he refused to participate in the unlawful act or practice, (4) he threatened to disclose the unlawful act or practice, (5) he was fired as a result of that refusal to participate or threat to disclose, and (6) the employer actually committed a violation of law (*Corley v. Louisiana ex re. Division of Administration, Office of Risk Management*, 2011).

Other laws similarly protect employee free speech rights. An employer may not retaliate against an employee for reporting the sexual abuse of a minor child by a fellow employee (R.S. 23:968(A); for reporting environmental violations (La. R.S. 30:27); voicing concern about safety (La. R.S. 30:2027) or for refusing to work because of safety concerns (*Odyssey Capital Group, L.P. III*, 2002). Employers are also prohibited from restricting the political speech of their employees. Louisiana law prohibits employers from discriminating against employees based on their political beliefs, from attempting to control the vote of their employees, and from preventing their employees from participating in politics (La. R.S. 23:961, 962).

Restricting Speech to Advance Privacy

In the context of free speech, the right to privacy can be seen as the right not to furnish information about one's self to another. Both the federal and Louisiana constitutions recognize this right to privacy (La. Const. Art. 1I, Sec. 5). Laws protecting privacy limit the flow of private information by imposing liability on persons who invade the zone of privacy of another either by (1) compelling that person to disclose personal and private information, or (2) by disclosing private information about that person. Both disclosure of private information about someone and obtaining private information about someone without his or her permission may result in liability for invasion of privacy (*Time, Inc. v. Hill*, 1967).

An employer may not intrude upon an employee's zone of privacy (*Love v. Southern Bell Telephone & Telegraph Co.*, 1972; *Phillips v. Smalley Maintenance Services, Inc.*, 1983; *East Bank Consolidated Special Service Fire Protection Dist. v. Crossen*, 2004, writ denied, 2005), or publicly disclose private facts about an employee (*Lambert v. Dow Chemical Company*,

1968; *Karraker v. Rent-A-Center, Inc.*, 2005). An employer that does so may be liable to its employee for invasion of privacy (see Louisiana Database Security Breach Notification Law, n.d.; *Landrun v. Board of Commissioners of the Orleans Levee Dist.*, 1996; *Fox v. City of Alexandria*, 2007; see *National Aeronautics and Space Administration v. Nelson*, 2011). Even the disclosure of truthful facts may be actionable if the facts concern the private affairs of an employee or other private individuals (*Stewart v. Courtyard Management Corp.*, 2005).

The reasonableness of an employer's conduct is determined by balancing the employer's interest in pursuing its invasive conduct with the employees' interest in protecting their privacy (*Jaubert v. Crowley Post-Signal, Inc.*, 1979; *Carr v. City of New Orleans*, 1993). An employer's liability for invasion of privacy may be based, for example, on (1) unreasonable public disclosure of private facts about an employee (see e.g., *Landrum v. Board of Commissioners of the Orleans Levee Dist.*, 1996; (2) intrusion into its employee's private life; *Phillips v. Smalley Maintenance Services, Inc.*, 1983; (3) portraying an employee in a false light in the public eye (see e.g., *Watkins v. General Refractories Co.*, 1992); or (4) misappropriation of an employee's likeness (see e.g., *Moore v. Big Picture Co.*, 1987).

Suppose you are an employee who believes that your privacy has been invaded by your employer. Your legal complaint would involve either claims of unreasonable intrusion into your zone of privacy or unreasonable disclosure of your private affairs. To prevail, you must generally show both that you had a reasonable expectation of privacy and there was a highly offensive intrusion or disclosure by your employer. The court then must decide whether you had an actual or subjective expectation of privacy and whether society is prepared to recognize your expectation as reasonable (*East Bank Consolidated Special Service Fire Protection Dist. v. Crossen*, 2004, writ denied, 2005). Again, courts balance the employee's expectation of privacy against his employer's interest in efficient business operations (see *U.S. v. Ziegler*, 2007).

Federal and state laws prohibit wiretapping and secret recording of employees where the employee has a reasonable expectation of privacy (Electronic Communications Privacy Act of 1986; R.S. 15:1303). Those laws do not prohibit obvious video surveillance so long as there is no audio recording and the employee has no reasonable expectation of privacy (see *Singletary v. Fridley*, 2000). An employer may monitor or tape an employee's conversation if one party to the conversation consents and the taping is not done for the purpose of committing a crime or injury, or if it is done by using a telephone extension and the conversation is in the "ordinary course of business" (18 U.S.C.A. Art. 2510 (5)(a)(i)).

Compelled Speech in the Workplace

The free speech rights of government employees include the right to refrain from speaking (*Langford v. Lane*, 1991). A private sector employee may refuse to answer the employer's questions on any basis, including on the basis of the First Amendment right of free speech or the Fifth Amendment right against self-incrimination. However, a private-sector employee who is fired for invoking such constitutional rights has no cause of action against the employer because of the at-will employment doctrine (*Winn v. New Orleans City*, 2013).

The Federal Employee Polygraph Protection Act (1988) makes it unlawful for most employers to either (1) require or request a prospective employee to take a polygraph (i.e. lie detector) test or (2) use the result of a polygraph test to make an employment decision (29 U.S.C.A. sec. 2002; *Worden v. SunTrust Banks, Inc.*, 2008). Testing employees is generally unlawful except in connection with an ongoing investigation of a workplace incident that resulted in loss or injury or when the employer has a reasonable suspicion that the employee was involved in the incident (e.g., embezzlement) (29 U.S.C.A. sec. 2007(d); *Cummings v. Washington Mut.*, 2011).

Restricting Free Speech in Furtherance of Equality

Louisiana and federal employment laws protect employees from discrimination and retaliation based on certain protected characteristics of employees such as their race, religion, disability, or gender. These various statutes protecting individuals from discrimination, retaliation, and harassment pose an inherent conflict in the workplace, however, between the right to free speech and the guarantee of equality. Traditionally, courts have enforced laws that infringe on free speech when the enforcement is necessary to correct unlawful conduct. Statutes, such as those prohibiting employment discrimination, provide courts with justification for limiting free speech when that speech contravenes the purpose of those statutes. Consequently, an employee's right to a harassment free workplace may trump the free speech rights of the employer and its other employees. Like speech constituting a crime which is not protected by the First Amendment (e.g. threats of terrorism or other violence, blackmail), neither is speech in furtherance of employment discrimination.

Anti-discrimination laws necessarily restrict speech. For example, in order to combat discrimination, the government may prohibit job advertisements that indicate a preference for employees who are not in a protected class (e.g., "only whites need apply") (*Passaic Daily News v. Blair*, 1973). Job advertisements are unlawful if they indicate a preference for a particular gender or age range unless those characteristics are bona fide qualifications for the job (42 U.S.C.A. sec. 2000e-3(b)).

In the case of *Dixon v. Coburg Dairy, Inc.* (2004), a white employee was terminated for refusing to remove two confederate flag stickers from his toolbox after an African American coworker complained. The trial court refused to give the white employee First Amendment protection and allowed his discharge to stand. On appeal, the appellate court first noted that Congress has not created a federal remedy for the private workforce whose employers restrict their freedom of speech. Nevertheless, in ruling for the African American employee, the court concluded that the First Amendment must be applied flexibly when it conflicts with other civil rights. Otherwise, the First Amendment would be a mockery (*Joseph v. U.S. Civil Service Commission*, 1977).

The conflict between free speech rights and the right to equality in the workplace might be best demonstrated in the context of religious discrimination. Both Title VII of the Civil Rights Act of 1964 (42 U.S.C.A., Secs. 2000e to 2000e-17) and the Louisiana Employment Discrimination Law (La. R.S. 23:301-369) protect an employee from discrimination based on that employee's religion. The term religion is not limited to "traditional organized religion but includes all aspects of religious observances and practices as well as beliefs" (42 U.S.C.A. sec. 2000e-(j); *Noyes v. Kelly Services*, 2007). An employer that voices or allows its other employees to voice a derogatory opinion about an employee's religion may be liable for religious discrimination if it can be shown that the employee suffered adverse employment action because of his religious beliefs.

In *E.E.O.C. v. Sunbelt Rentals, Inc.* (2008), Ingram, a veteran of the United States Army, proved that he suffered harassment in the workplace because he was a Muslim. The Court stated in its opinion that the speech of Ingram's co-employees resulted in liability to Ingram for religious discrimination as the following excerpt clearly indicates.

> Ingram was also the object of anti-Muslim crudities that associated Ingram, and the Muslim faith, with violence and terrorism. For instance, one time Gray was carrying a metal detector and, as Ingram walked by, he raised the metal detector to Ingram's head garment. Presumably because the detector did not go off, Gray called Ingram a 'fake ass Muslim want-to-be turbine wearing ass.' On another occasion, Gray, while holding a stapler in his hand, told Ingram that 'if anyone upsets you pretend this stapler is a model airplane [and] just toss it in the air, just repeatedly catch it, just don't say anything.' For Ingram, the implication was clear: Gray was trying '[t]o connect me and my religion as terrorists [and] the ones who . . . took the planes that smashed into the buildings September 11th (*E.E.O.C. v. Sunbelt Rentals, Inc.* 2008, p. 317).

Just as the free speech rights of the employer and co-employees are restricted when balanced against the rights of the religious employee, the free speech rights of the religious employee may also be restricted in the workplace. That is, your religious beliefs are protected against discrimination if your personal expression of those beliefs at work outweighs the interests of your employer and fellow employees (29 C.F.R. Sec. 10605.1, 1996). Consequently, employers may restrict their employees from proselytizing or preaching to their coworkers in the workplace. However, an employer is not required to insulate its employees from the religious expression of another employee merely because that religious expression is annoying (*Powell v. Yellow Book USA, Inc.*, 2006). Creative expression through your manner of dress also may be restricted by your employer. For example, an employer may adopt dress code policies to promote a particular company image (see *Cloutier v. Costco Wholesale Corp.*, 2004).

CONTROL OF SPEECH THROUGH CONTRACT

The First Amendment protects the right to speak and the right not to speak (*U.S. v. Phillip Morris USA, Inc.*, 2009). As for the First Amendment, there is no difference between compelled speech and compelled silence because "freedom of speech" includes the decisions of what to say and what not to say (*Riley v. National Federation of the Blind of North Carolina, Inc.*, 1988). If a person has the right not to speak, may he go one step further and legally bind himself not to speak?

The law generally allows you to voluntarily restrict your own free speech rights. "Freedom of contract" signifies that people have the right to construct their own bargains (La. Civil Code art. 1971; *Louisiana Smokes Products, Inc. v. Savoie's Sausage and Food Products, Inc.*, 1997). People may agree to contract for any object that is lawful, possible, and determinable (La. Civil Code art. 1971). All things that are not forbidden by law may legally become the subject of, or the motive for, contracts (*Hayes v. Muller*, 1963; *Lewis v. Liberty Industrial Life Ins. Co.*, 1936). As the U.S. Supreme Court has said regarding contracts in the context of free speech, "The parties themselves . . . determine the scope of their legal obligations, and any restrictions that may be placed on the publication of truthful information are self-imposed" (*Cohen v. Cowles Media Co.*, 1991). Once a lawful contract is entered into, it becomes the law between the parties (La. Civil Code art. 1983).

Contracts of Silence

A contract of silence is an agreement whereby you agree not to disclose certain information. In *Cohen v. Cowles Media Co.* (1991), the Supreme Court held that contracts not to speak are enforceable and do not implicate the First Amendment. People often use contracts of silence to protect their personal privacy. For example, contracts between banks and their customers commonly include an agreement by the bank to keep the customers' account information private. Another reason to seek a promise of silence is to protect a commercial secret or other information that a business feels is important to protect. For commercial advantage, businesses commonly require legally enforceable confidentiality and non-disclosure agreements wherein you agree that you will not disclose commercial information.

There are often good reasons for enforcing contracts of silence. A business may spend millions of dollars developing information that gives it a competitive advantage that it would not enjoy if that information became available to its competitors. Such information is commonly referred to as a "trade secret." Requiring its employees to sign a contract of silence may give the trade secret owner the protection it needs to preserve its competitive advantage.

Contracts of silence are considered so important to society that the law imposes them in certain circumstances. For example, a part of any contract between a lawyer and a client is that the lawyer may not disclose information supplied by the client in confidence (State Bar Articles of Incorporation, Art. 16; Rules of Professional Conduct, Rule 1.6; La. R.S.37:222; La. Code of Evidence art. 501). Similarly, a covenant by an employee not to disclose the employer's commercial secrets is an implied term of every employment relationship (*NCH Corp. v. Broyles*, 1985) even in the absence of a specific contract not to disclose them. Every employee has a legal duty not to communicate information given by the employer in confidence or to use the information to the competitive disadvantage of the employer, unless the information is a matter of general knowledge (*SDT Industries, Inc. v. Leeper*, 2001).

In Louisiana, all agreements that restrict competition are usually null and void. However, it is also true that you may agree by contract that after your period of employment ends with a particular business you will refrain from soliciting any former customers provided that the contract of silence is applied in strict accordance with Louisiana law (La. R.S. 23:921). That law requires that the area of the restriction be clearly defined and that the restriction not last more than two years.

Sometimes it becomes important for an individual or an organization, in fact any professional relation, to forge an agreement so that you will not say bad things about them. You, in fact, can legally bind yourself, through a non-disparagement agreement, to speak no ill about another party. And if you do start talking critically about that person or party, you will have breached the agreement, which will entitle them to seek damages and perhaps even an injunction against you (see *JetPay Merchant Services, LLC v. Tepoorten*, 2009). For example, the National Football League players are commonly required to sign a contract containing a restricted speech clause that allows the team to take away a player's signing bonus if the player publicly criticizes the team, and such contracts have been affirmed by the courts in at least two instances (Groeschen, 2001; Fielder, 2002).

There are situations, however, when it would be inappropriate to enforce a contract of silence, such as when the object of the contract is to conceal criminal conduct, suppress information regarding public safety, or otherwise conceal important information about public officials.

Courts often are unable to agree on whether persons should be allowed to contract away their free speech rights, especially when stopping information from becoming public might adversely affect others. In a series of related cases involving dangerous truck fires, one court stopped a General Motor's employee from testifying as an expert witness about the danger of fires resulting from collisions involving GM pickup trucks (*Smith v. Superior Court*, 1996). The employee had left his employment with GM on bad terms but had agreed with GM in a contract of silence not to testify about his research into truck fires. Although one court entered a permanent injunction preventing the employee from testifying, the courts in other states allowed him to testify, with one court characterizing the contract of silence between GM and its former employee as an agreement to suppress evidence (*Smith v. Superior Court*, 1996).

Settlement agreements ending disputes between private parties are also contracts that are enforced according to the principles of contract law (*Soileau v. Smith True Value and Rental*, 2013). Settlement agreements typically prevent the parties from disclosing whether anything was paid to settle their dispute. Most of the time, private parties are free to agree to keep the terms of their settlement confidential (*Society of Professional Journalists, Headliners Chapter v. Briggs*, 1988). However, critics question whether the free flow of information advanced through public court proceedings can be "privatized" through a contract between the litigants. Critics claim that private, confidential settlement agreements ending public court proceedings keep crucial information from the public, particularly about defective or dangerous products (see Luban, 1995; Marcus, 1991; Nader & Smith, 1996; Bechamps, 1990).

In the case of *Bowman v. Parma Board of Education* (1988), a teacher signed a confidential settlement agreement with the school district terminating the investigation of the teacher's alleged inappropriate sexual conduct with female students. Despite the confidentiality provision in the settlement agreement, when a neighboring school district called for a job reference on the teacher, a school board member disclosed that the teacher was being terminated for "child molesting." The teacher sued the school board for violating the confidentiality agreement but the court held that the agreement was void because it violated public policy. The court said that a ruling for the teacher upholding the contract of silence "would be to expose our most vulnerable citizens to a completely unacceptable risk of physical, mental, and emotional harm" (p. 667). The public policy of protecting children outweighed the rights of the parties to enforce the contract of silence.

The Louisiana Civil Code provides that a contract is rendered null and void if it violates a rule of public order, such as when the object of the contract is illicit or immoral (La. Civil Code art. 2030). Persons simply may not enter into a binding contract where the object of the contract is contrary to public policy (*Buck's Run Enterprises, Inc. v. Mapp Const., Inc.*, 2001). The Supreme Court has stated that "[A] promise is unenforceable if interest in its enforcement is outweighed in the circumstances by a public policy harmed by enforcement of the agreement" (*Town of Newton v. Rumery*, 1987). For example, a contract whereby one party agrees to warn the other party about a police investigation into the latter's unlawful activities violates a rule of public order and is absolutely null and unenforceable (*Jones v. Chevalier*, 1991). This is because public policy encourages reporting of crimes and discourages suppressing information about criminal conduct (*Branzburg v. Hayes*, 1972). By the same reasoning, a contract whereby the alleged victim of a crime receives compensation from the perpetrator in exchange for a promise not to report the crime is also illegal. The United States Supreme Court has said, "[I]t is obvious that agreements to conceal information relevant to the commission of a crime have very little to recommend them from a standpoint of public policy."

If, therefore, contracts of silence can be declared unenforceable when they are contrary to public policy, the question then becomes: What is "public policy?" Sometimes, laws that have been enacted provide a clear indication of public policy. But, sometimes public policy is not readily apparent. As Professor Corbin has quipped about public policy in his treatise on contracts, "The loudest and most confident assertions as to what makes for the general welfare and happiness of mankind are made by the demagogue and ignoramus" (Corbin, 1950). Consequently, if a contract of silence violates an ascertainable public policy, it is unenforceable. Otherwise, a contract of silence becomes the law between the parties.

Government Action in Enforcing Contracts of Silence

Any contract is only as good as the court system that must enforce it. If one party breaches a contract, the other party may sue in a court of law to enforce the contract and to recover damages (La. Civil Code art. 1986). Consequently, a contract has the potential to move any dispute between the parties out of the court of public opinion and into a court of law.

Even though a contract of silence certainly restricts free speech rights, albeit voluntarily, the First Amendment is usually not implicated because only private parties are involved in the contracting process. The Constitution does not protect you from allowing others to interfere with your free speech rights; it simply protects you from governmental interference with your freedom of expression (*Columbia Broadcasting System, Inc. v. Democratic Nat. Committee*, 1973).

Yet as stated above, a contract is only enforceable by a court. A court is part of the judicial branch of the government. Consequently, the judicial enforcement of a contract of silence may constitute government action sufficient to implicate the First Amendment. In *New York Times Co. v. Sullivan*, the Supreme Court held that, if a court applied a state law in a manner that restricted free speech, the court's action implicated the First Amendment. The Court explained, "the test is not the form in which state power has been applied but, whatever the form, whether such power has in fact been exercised"

(*New York Times Co. v. Sullivan*, 1964).

The argument against the court's enforcement of a contract being considered the requisite government action necessary to trigger First Amendment protection is that a court asked to enforce a contract of silence does not, technically, stop anyone from speaking. Rather, the court merely stops the would-be speaker from breaking the voluntary promise not to speak. The court is simply enforcing an obligation that the would-be speaker assumed himself through the contract of silence. In *Cohen v. Cowles Media Co.*, the Supreme Court suggested that no constitutional violation occurs when the "law simply requires those making promises to keep them" (1991).

Contractual Waiver of Free Speech Rights

The Supreme Court has suggested that First Amendment rights might be waived in a contract. In *Snepp v. U.S.* (1980), the Supreme Court upheld a contract between the federal Central Intelligence Agency ("CIA") and a CIA agent whereby the agent agreed to submit any books he might write to the CIA for review before publishing. Because the agent had voluntarily agreed that his free speech would be limited by the requirement that he submit his book to the government for review, he could not later complain that the government was restricting his free speech. However, in *Curtis Publishing Co. v. Butts* (1967), the Supreme Court refused to enforce an alleged waiver of free speech rights that would have prevented the person who gave the waiver from interjecting a First Amendment defense to a defamation claim against him. The Supreme Court ruled that the waiver was not exact enough to be enforceable, and suggested that a waiver of free speech rights should be given more scrutiny by the Court than other waivers. The Supreme Court held that "[w]here the ultimate effect of sustaining a claim of waiver might be an imposition on [First Amendment rights], we are unwilling to find waiver in circumstances which fall short of being clear and compelling" (p. 145).

Finally, there is a natural conflict between the desire to keep information private and the First Amendment's aversion to restricting the communication of information. Contracts of silence undoubtedly aid commerce when used to protect commercial information from misappropriation. However, contracts of silence do not aid legitimate commerce when used to suppress speech that would otherwise benefit the public. For the reasons stated above, courts should not simply ignore the free speech implications of a contract of silence, as the trial court did initially in *Cohen v. Cowles Media Co.*, when it declared that: "[t]his is not a case about free speech, rather it is one about contracts" (14 MediaL.Rep. (BNA) 1460, 1987). A case to enforce a contract of silence may involve both contractual freedom and freedom of speech.

CONTROL OF SPEECH THROUGH CONTROL OF PROPERTY RIGHTS

Legal scholar Thomas Emerson concluded that speech "in connection with commercial transactions generally relates to a separate sector of social activity involving the system of property rights rather than free expression (Emerson 1966, p. 105). In other words, commerce involves owning things and ownership gives the owner an expectation of control extending even to the right to control expression. A property right is a right to exclude others from using that property (*Kaiser Aetna v. U.S.*, 1979). An intellectual property right is the right to exclude others from communicating certain information or, in other words, the right to stop others from speaking about it.

Under the federal Copyright Act, one author may prevent another from plagiarizing from his book. However, the copyright law does not prevent the second author from using facts or ideas from the first book, only from copying the way the first author expressed those facts and ideas. The second author "possesses an unfettered right to use any factual information revealed in [the first book]," but he may not copy the creative expression of the first author (*Harper and Row Publishers, Inc. v. Nation Enterprises*, 1985). Even though it restricts expression, the Copyright Act does not violate the First Amendment because the Copyright Act restricts copyrightable expression rather than the free flow of un-copyrightable facts and ideas (*Harper*, 1985).

Similarly, federal and state trademark laws restrict the use of trademarks that cover a product but do not restrict the commercial speech that communicates facts or opinions about the product, even if the speech uses the product's name. In the *Gay Olympics* (*San Francisco Arts & Athletics, Inc. v. U.S. Olympic Committee*, 1987) case, the Supreme Court upheld the right of the U.S. Olympic Committee to prohibit the sponsors of the gay Olympics from using the word "Olympic" for advertising and promotional purposes. The Court said that by prohibiting the use of the word "Olympic" for particular purposes, neither the Congress nor the U.S. Olympic Committee prohibited the persons trying to stage the gay Olympics from conveying the "Olympic message." In other words, the term "Olympic" was the property of the Olympic Committee which could control its use. However, the Olympic ideal could not be controlled.

In *Zacchini v. Scripps-Howard Broadcasting Co.* (1977), a television station was prevented from rebroadcasting Hugo Zacchini's human cannonball act. The Court stressed that it was not restricting the station from describing or commenting on Zacchini's act. Although this right of publicity generally prevents the use of someone's name, image, and other attributes of identity "in commerce" or "for trade purposes" (see e.g., Restatement Third of Unfair Competition Art. 46), the use of a person's name or likeness in news reporting or in works of fiction or nonfiction is not prohibited because of free speech concerns (see e.g., *Eastwood v. Superior Court*, 1983; *Hicks v. Casablanca Records*, 1978).

A "trade secret" is information that has independent economic value because it is not generally known or regularly ascertainable and because efforts have been taken to maintain the information's secrecy (*United Group of National Paper Distributors, Inc. v. Vinson*, 1996). Examples of trade secrets would be customer lists, price lists, and marketing plans. Unlike with a copyright or patent, the fact that information is a trade secret does not give its owner an exclusive right to use the information. Anyone who acquires the information lawfully may use it. Consequently, the owner of a trade secret must protect it from public disclosure. This is often done through non-disclosure agreements.

The Louisiana Uniform Trade Secret Act (La. R.S. 51:1431 to 51: 1439) (LUTSA) prohibits the misappropriation of trade secrets by improper means. The purpose of the LUTSA is to deter injury to business competitors by preventing one business from profiting from a secret developed by another business (*Stork-Werkspoor Diesel V.V. v. Koek*, 1988).

Restricting Free Speech Using Commercial Laws Protecting Property Rights

The ability of the government to restrict free speech in traditional public forums is limited (*Kohn v. Southwest Regional Council of Carpenters*, 2003). Traditional public forums are places historically devoted to assembly and debate such as streets and parks. Only reasonable, content-neutral restrictions on speech as to time, place, or manner are permissible in traditional public forums (*Snyder v. Phelps*, 2011). Private property owners may restrict, generally, First Amendment privileges on their property. (*People v. Bush*, 1976). The Supreme Court has held that a shopping center is not a public forum so as to require that the owner allow distribution of handbills and circulars (*Lloyd Corp. v. Tanner*, 1972).

CONTROL OF SPEECH THROUGH COURT PROCEEDINGS

Businesses sometimes find it commercially expedient to use the court system to limit commercial speech. Occasionally in litigation, a judge determines that privacy concerns or commercial interests outweigh the right of the public to monitor judicial proceedings. In such rare cases, a court will issue a gag order or order a court record sealed from the public. Louisiana law, however, prohibits sealing court records where environmental claims are involved (La. Code of Civil Procedure art. 1426(C), (D), and (E)).

Use of Tort Suits

Louisiana courts generally interpret the state and federal constitutions as granting the same free speech rights (*Delcarpio v. St. Tammany Parish School Board*, 1994), even though the free speech clause of the Louisiana Constitution, Article 11, Section 7, contains a concept alien to the First Amendment. It reads: "Every person may speak, write, and publish his sentiments on any subject, but is responsible for abuse of that freedom."

An abuse of a right that is otherwise lawful may be enjoined or may give rise to damages (*Hero Lands Co., Inc. v. Texaco, Inc.*, 1975). Louisiana has long recognized that this constitutional right of expression can be abused when it injures another person but brings no benefit to the person exercising the right. This concept of the abuse of free speech rights is a basis for a number of "speaking" torts by which liability is imposed on the speaker, such as defamation, negligent misinformation, invasion of privacy, and intentional infliction of emotional distress (*White v. Monsanto*, 1993). However, exposure to this potential civil liability has a tendency to discourage free speech. Consequently, the state's enforcement of an action for liability based on a "speaking" tort implicates the First Amendment (*New York Times Co. v. Sullivan*, 1964; *Economy Carpets Manufacturers and Distributors, Inc. v. Better Business Bureau of Baton Rouge Area, Inc.*, 1976), because requiring someone to pay damages for their statements obviously restricts their freedom of speech.

Defamation suits, or the threat thereof, are sometimes used to restrict expression. Defamation of character (i.e., making false statements about another person) is generally an exception to speech protected by the First Amendment. Defamation, as noted in an earlier chapter, is both a crime under Louisiana law (La. R.S. 14:47) and grounds for civil liability (La. R.S. 13:3602). For example, an employer that discloses false information about an employee may be liable to the employee for defamation (*Stewart v. Courtyard Management Corp.*, 2005). However, statements made during private, intra-company investigations conducted in good faith are not defamatory but enjoy a qualified privilege (*Ruffin v. Wal-Mart Stores, Inc.*, 2002; *Lewis v. Meredith Corp.*, 2008).

Louisiana commercial laws often protect speakers from liability when free speech is deemed important enough to commerce. In Louisiana, advertisers have a qualified privilege to protect them from criminal charges of defamation where they make assertions about the products they advertise and have a "reasonable belief" that those assertions are true (La. R.S. 14:49(2)(b)).

Civil liability has been imposed on the basis of negligent misinformation and negligent misrepresentation, which may also limit free expression. For such claims to arise, the person who provided the incorrect information must have had a legal duty to supply correct information, the breach of which duty caused damage to the recipient (*Kadlec Medical Center v. Lakeview Anesthesia Associates*, 2008). Liability has also been imposed on the basis of negligent misrepresentation when the recipient of the information relied on the information to his detriment (see *Kent v. Cobb*, 2002).

Speech may reach a level of causing the hearer to suffer emotional distress and subject the speaker to tort liability. An employer may be liable for conducting a workplace investigation in such a harsh and insensitive manner as to subject it to damages for intentional infliction of emotional distress on its employee. However, liability does not extend to mere insults, indignities, annoyances, or other trivialities. Employees must be hardened to occasional inconsiderate and unkind acts and to insults, indignities, and annoyances that are not extreme or outrageous (*King v. Phelps Dunbar, L.L.P.*, 1999). The Supreme Court has determined that a court imposing liability on the speaker for the tort of intentional infliction of emotional distress may also implicate the First Amendment (*Hustler Magazine, Inc. v. Falwell*, 1988).

The potential for "speaking" tort liability has discouraged free speech to such an extent regarding some commercial matters, that the Louisiana legislature has granted immunity to some speakers to encourage the free flow of information. For example, job references, particularly those supplied by former employers, provide a wealth of information to an employer evaluating a prospective employee. Many employers are reluctant to provide information about former employees because the risk of being sued for defamation greatly exceeds any benefit the former employer might obtain from providing a helpful job reference to another, perhaps competing, employer. As a result, the potential liability for supplying job references hampers the exchange of valuable information and negatively impacts all employees, good and bad. To encourage employers to provide job references, Louisiana has enacted a statute that grants civil immunity to employers who provide references, and to the employers who rely on those references. However, if a job reference is provided, it must be accurate and be provided in good faith or else "speaking" tort liability may result (see La. R.S. 23:291; *Kadlec Medical Center v. Lakeview Anesthesia Associates*, 2008).

Potential liability for these "speaking" torts necessarily hampers free speech. As noted above, a court's enforcement of a contract of silence has First Amendment implications. Similarly, a state's enforcement through its courts of tort law claims can also trigger First Amendment protections (see e.g., *Hustler Magazine, Inc. v. Falwell*, 1988; *Time, Inc. v. Hill*, 1967).

CONCLUSIONS

As detailed in this chapter, commercial laws are often at odds with free expression. When it is advantageous to business to expand its influence or avoid government regulation it will often invoke the First Amendment protections recently accorded commercial speech. On the other hand, when it is advantageous for business to restrict free expression in an effort to maximize profits, business is often quick to decry the speech of others as a violation of its property rights and so not entitled to First Amendment protection.

Since the *Submarine* case in 1942, commercial speech has been afforded more and more protection. Businesses are now recognized as persons under the law and afforded, essentially, the same free speech rights as citizens. Although the wise Confucius and our forefathers could not have foreseen the trend to consider commercial speech as worthy of the same protection as political speech, Justice Rehnquist realized the threat such equivalency posed to our society and warned in 1980, in his dissenting opinion: "In a democracy, the economic is subordinate to the political, a lesson that our ancestors learned long ago, and that our descendents will undoubtedly have to relearn many years hence" (*Central Hudson Gas & Elec. Corp. v. Public Service Commission of New York*, 1980). So long as commercial and political power is concentrated in business, ordinary citizens will have to remain vigilant to insure that the First Amendment does not become for business both an irresistible sword and an impregnable shield and become for the common man a mere memory.

REFERENCES

44 Liquormart, Inc. v. Rhode Island, 517 U.S. 484, 116 S.Ct. 1495, 134 L.Ed.2d 711 (1996).
Accardo v. Louisiana Health Services & Indemnity Co., 943 So. 2d 381 (La.App.1st Cir. 2006).
Adamson-James v. Florida, 6:11-cv-00628 (M.D. Fla.2013).
Age Discrimination in Employment Act, Pub. L. No. 90-202, 29 U.S.C. secs. 621-634 (2011).
Americans with Disabilities Act of 1990, 42 U.S.C.S. secs. 12100-12213 (2009).
Bad Frog Brewery, Inc. v. New York State Liquor Authority, 134 F.3d 87 (2nd Cir.1998).
Bain v. Georgia Gulf Corp., 462 Fed. Appx. 431 (5th Cir. 2012).
Baker, C. E. (1989). *Human liberty and freedom of speech.* New York: Oxford University Press.
Barrie v. V.P. Exterminators, Inc., 625 So. 2d 1007 (La. 1993).
Beard v. Seacoast Electronics, Inc., 951 So. 2d 1168 (La. App. 4th Cir. 2007).
Bechamps, A. (1990). *Note, sealed out-of-court settlements: Does the public have a right to know?* 66 Notre Dame L. Rev. 117.
Benoit v. Roche, 657 So. 2d 574 (La. Ct. App. 3d Cir. 1995).
Berry v. Department of Social Services, 447 F.3d 642 (9th Cir. 2006).
Bhandari v. First National Bank of Commerce, 829 F.2d 1343 (5th Cir. 1987).
Bigelow v. Virginia, 421 U.S. 809, 95 S.Ct. 2222, 44 L.Ed. 600 (1975).
Blades, L. E. (1967). *Employment at will versus individual freedom: On limited the abusive exercise of employer power.* 67 Colum.L.Rev. 1404.
Bolger v. Youngs Drug Products Corp., 463 U.S. 60, 103 S.Ct. 2875, 77 L.Ed.2d 469 (1983).
Bolton v. City of Dallas, Tex., 472 F.3d 261 (5th Cir.2006).
Bowman v. Parma Board of Education, 542 N.E.2d 663 (Ohio App. 1988).
Branzburg v. Hayes, 408 U.S. 665, 92 S.Ct. 2646, 33 L.Ed.2d 626 (1972).
Brown v. Polk County, 37 F.3d 404 (8th Cir. 1994).
Brown v. Polk County, Iowa, 61 F.3d 650 (8th Cir. 1995).
Briggs v. American Air Filter Company, Inc., 630 F.2d 414 (5th Cir.1980).
Buck's Run Enterprises, Inc. v. Mapp Construction, Inc., 808 So. 2d 428 (2001).
Carr v. City of New Orleans, 622 So. 2d 819 (La. App. 4th Cir. 1993).
Central Hudson Gas & Electric Corp. v. Public Service Commission of New York, 447 U.S. 557, 100 S.Ct. 2347, 65 L.Ed.2d 341 (1980).
Chalmers v. Tulan Company of Richmond, 101 F.3d 1012 (1st Cir. 2004).
Chelette v. State Farm Mutual Auto Insurance Co., 2006 WL 2513918 (W. D. La. 2006).
Child Evangelism Fellowship of Maryland, Inc. v. Montgomery County Public Schools, 457 F.3d 376 (4th Cir. 2006).
Cintas Corp. v. N.L.R.B., 482 F.3d 463 (D.C. Cir. 2007).
Citizens United v. Federal Election Commission, 558 U.S. 310, 130 S.Ct. 876, 175 L.Ed.2d 753 (2010).
Civil action for deprivation of rights, 42 U.S.C. sec. 1983.
City of Ladre v. Gilleo, 512 U.S. 43, 114 S.Ct. 2038, 129 L.Ed.2d 36 (1994).
City of San Diego, Cal. v. Roe, 125 S.Ct. 521, 160 L.Ed.2d 410 (2004).
Cloutier v. Costco Wholesale Corp., 390 F.3d 126 (1st Cir. 2004).
Cohen v. Cowles Media Co.,14 MediaL.Rep. (BNA) 1460 (D. Minn. 1987).
Cohen v. Cowles Media Co., 501 U.S. 663, 111 S.Ct. 2513, 115 L.Ed.2d 586 (1991).
Columbia Broadcasting System, Inc. v. Democratic National Committee, 412 U.S. 94, 93 S.Ct. 2080, 36 L.Ed.2d 772 (1973).
Communication Workers of America v. Ector County Hospital District, 467 F.3d 426 (5th Cir. 2006).
Confucius, & Waley, A. (1938). *The analects of Confucius.* New York: Random House.
Connick v. Myers, 461 U.S. 138, 103 C.T. 1684, 75 L.Ed.2d 708 (1983).
Consumer Product Safety Improvement Act of 2008, Pub. L. No. 110-314 (2008).

Corley v. Louisiana ex rel. Div. of Admin., Office of Risk Management, 816 F.Supp.2d 297 (M.D. La. 2011).
Crawford v. U.S. Dept. of Homeland Security, 345 Fed.Appx. 369 (5th Cir. 2007).
Cummings v. Washington Mutual, 650 F.3d 1386 (11th Cir. 2011).
Curtis Publishing Co. v. Butts, 388 U.S. 130, 87 S.Ct. 1975, 18 L.Ed.2d 1094 (1967).
Delcarpio v. St. Tammany Parish School Board, 865 F.Supp. 350 (E.D.La. 1994).
DeSalvo v. State, 624 So. 2d 897 (La. 1993).
Design Technology Group, LLC d/b/a Bettie Page Clothing and DTG California Management, LLC d/b/a Bettie Page Clothing, a Single Employer and Vanessa Morris, 359 NLRB No. 96 (2013).
Desilets v. Wal-Mart Stores, Inc., 171 F.ed 711 (1st Cir. 1999).
Deus v. Allstate Insurance Co., 15 F.3d 506 (5th Cir. 1994).
Diaz v. Superior Energy Services LLC, 341 Fed.Appx. 26 (5th Cir. 2009).
DirectTV U.S. DirectTV Holdings, LLC and International Association of Machinists and Aerospace Workers, District Lodge 947, AFL-CIO, 359 NLRB No. 54 (2013).
Dish Network Corporation and Communication Workers of America, Local 6171 and Eric Sutter, 359 NLRB No. 108 (2013).
Dixon v. Coburg Dairy, Inc., 369 F.3d 811 (4th Cir. 2004).
Dorris v. Absher, 179 F.3d 420 (6th Cir. 1999).
Double Eagle Hotel & Casino v. N.L.R.B., 414 F.3d 1249 (10th Cir. 2005).
Dufau v. Creole Engineering, Inc., 465 So. 2d 752 (La.App. 5th Cir. 1985).
Duke v. North Texas University, 469 F.2d 829 (5th Cir. 1972).
East Bank Consolidated Special Service Fire Protection Dist. v. Cossen, 892 So. 2d 666 (La. Ct. App. 5th Cir., 2004), writ denied, 897 So. 2d 608 (La. 2005).
Eastwood v. Superior Court, 149 Cal.App.3d. 409, 198 Cal.Rptr. 342 (Cal.App.2Dist., 1983).
Economy Carpets Manufacturers and Distributors, Inc. v. Better Business Bureau of Baton Rouge Area, Inc., 330 So. 2d 301 (La. 1976).
Edenfield v. Fane, 507 U.S. 761, 113 S.Ct. 1792 (U.S. Fla. 1993).
E.E.O.C. v. Sunbelt Rentals, Inc., 521 F.3d 811 (4th Cir. 2004).
Electronic Communications Privacy Act of 1986, Pub. L. 99-508, 18 U.S.C. 2510 (1986).
Emerson, T. I. (1966). *Toward a general theory of the First Amendment.* New York: Random House.
Employee Polygraph Protection Act, Pub. L. No. 100-347, 29 U.S.C. secs. 2001-2009 (1988).
Employee Protection, 15 U.S.C. sec. 2622.
Engineered Mechanical Services, Inc. v. Langlois, 464 So. 2d 329 (La.App. 1st Cir. 1984).
Equal Pay Act of 1963, Pub. L. No. 88-38, 29 U.S.C. 206 (1963).
Equal Rights Under The Law, 42 U.S.C. sec. 1981.
Erznoznil v. City of Jacksonville, 422 U.S. 2005, 95 S.Ct. 2268, 45 L.Ed.2d 125 (1975).
Faculty Rights Coalition v. Shahrokhi, 204 Fed.Appx. 416 (5th Cir. 2006).
False advertisements; injunctions and restraining orders, 15 U.S.C. sec. 53.
Family Resource Group, Inc. v. Louisiana Parent Magazine, 818 So. 2d 28 (La.App. 1st Cir. 2001).
Fauntelroy v. Rainbow Marketers, 888 So. 2d 1045 (La.Ct.App. 3rd Cir. 2004).
F.C.C. v. Pacifica Foundation, 438 U.S. 726, 98 S.Ct. 3026, 57 L.Ed.2d 1073 (1978).
Federal Executive Order 11141, 3 C.F.R., p. 179 (1964).
Federal Executive Order 11246, 3 C.F.R., p. 339 (1965).
Fielder, T. E. (2002, Spring/Summer). *Keep your mouth shut and listen: The NFL's player right to free expression,* 10 U. Miami Bus. L. Rev. 547.
The Florida Bar v. Catarcio, 709 So. 2d 96 (Fla. 1998).
Florida Bar v. Went For It, Inc., 515 U.S. 618, 115 S.Ct. 2371, 132 L.Ed.2d 541 (1995).
Fox v. City of Alexandria, 971 So. 2d 468 (La. App. 3rd Cir. 2007).
Frisby v. Schultz, 487 U.S. 474, 108 S.Ct. 2495, 101 L.Ed.2d 420 (1988).

Goulas v. LaGreca, 2013 WL 1947476 (E.D. La. 2013).
Greater New Orleans Broadcasting Association, Inc. v. U.S., 527 U.S. 173, 119 S.Ct. 1923, 144 L.Ed.2d 161 (1999).
Gregory v. Louisiana Board of Chiropractic Examiners, 608 So. 2d 987 (La. 1992).
Groeschen, T. (2001, Jan. 23). Bengal's loyalty clause is upheld: Will be included in "most" contracts. *The Cincinnati Enquirer*. Retrieved from: http://bengals.enquirer.com/2001/01/23/ben_bengals_loyalty.html
Guillory v. St. Landry Parish Police Jury, 802 F.2d 822 (5th Cir. 1986).
Hale v. Touro Infirmary, 886 S.2d 1210 (La.Ct.App. 4th Cir. 2004).
Harper and Row Publishers, Inc. v. Nation Enterprises, 471 U.S. 539, 105 S.Ct. 2218, 85 L.Ed.2d 588 (1985).
Hayes v. Muller, 245 La. 356, 158 So. 2d 191 (La. 1963).
Hero Lands Co. v. Texaco, Inc., 310 So. 2d 93 (La. 1975).
Hicks v. Casablanca Records, 464 F.Supp. 426 (S.D. N.Y. 1978).
Hustler Magazine, Inc. v. Falwell, 485 U.S. 46, 108 S.Ct. 876, 99 L.Ed.2d 41 (1988).
In re. R.M.J., 455 U.S. 191, 102 S.Ct. 929, 71 L.Ed.2d 64 (1982).
Immigration Control and Reform Act, Pub. L. No. 99-603, 8 U.S.C. 1324(a) and (b) (1986).
Innovative Manpower Solutions, LLC v. Ironman Staffing, LLC, 2013 WL 883698 (W.D. La. 2013).
Jackson v. Village of Bellwood, 1992 WL 9203 (N.D. Ill. 1992).
James v. Newspaper Agency Corporation, 591 F.2d 579 (10th Cir. 1979).
Jaubert v. Crowley Post-Signal, Inc., 375 So. 2d 1386 (La. 1979).
Jespersen v. Harrah's Operating Co., 444 F.3d 1104 (9th Cir. 2006).
JetPay Merchant Services, LLC v. Tepoorten, 2009 WL 3047730 (N.D. Tex. 2009).
Jones v. Chevalier, 579 So. 2d 1217 (La. App. 3 Cir. 1991).
K-Mart Corp. Store No. 7441 v. Trotti, 677 S.W.2d 632 (Tex. App. Houston 1st Dist. 1984).
Kadlec Medical Center v. Lakeview Anesthesia Associates, 527 F.3d 412 (5th Cir. 2008).
Kaiser Aetna v. U.S., 444 U.S. 164, 100 S.Ct. 383, 62 L.Ed.2d 332 (1979).
Kammler v. Rent-A-Center, Inc., 411 F.3d 831 (7th Cir. 2005).
Kasky v. Nike, Inc., 27 Cal.4th 939, 45 P.3d 243 (2001).
Kent v. Cobb, 811 So. 2d 1206 (La. App. 2nd Cir. 2002).
King v. Phelps Dunbar, L.L.P., 743 So. 2d 181 (La. 1999).
Kitsap County v. Mattress Outlet, 153 Wash.2d 506, 104 P.3d 1280 (2005).
Knight v. Connecticut Department of Public Health, 275 F.3d 156 (2nd Cir. 2001).
Kohn v. Southwest Regional Council of Carpenters, 289 F. Supp. 2d 1155 (C.D. Cal. 2003).
La. Civ. Code art. 1971.
La. Civ. Code art. 1983.
La. Civ. Code art. 1986.
La. Civ. Code art. 2030.
La. Civ. Code art. 2747.
La. Code Civ. Proc. art. 1426 (C), (D), and (E).
La. Code Civ. Proc. art. 5251(12).
La. Code Ev. art. 501.
La. Const., art. I, secs. 3 and 12.
La. Const., art. X.
La. R.S. 13:3602.
La. R.S. 14:47.
La. R.S. 14:49(2)(b).
La. R.S. 23:291.
La. R.S. 23:631.
La. R.S. 23:921.
La. R.S. 23:961.
La. R.S. 23:966.

La. R.S. 23:967.
La. R.S. 23:967(a).
La. R.S. 23:968(f).
La. R.S. 23:1361.
La. R.S. 30:27.
La. R.S. 30:2027.
La. R.S. 37:222.
La. R.S. 51:710.
La. R.S. 51:1404.
La. R.S. 4501-4504.
Lambert v. Dow Chemical Company, 215 So. 2d 673 (La. App.1st Cir. 1968).
Landrum v. Board of Commissioners of the Orleans Levee District, 685 So. 2d 382 (La. Ct. App. 4th Cir. 1996).
Lansford v. Lane, 921 F.2d 677 (6th Cir. 1991).
Lee v. Pennington, 2002-0381, 830 So. 2d 1037 (2002).
Lewis v. Liberty Industrial Life Insurance Co., 185 La. 589, 170 So. 4 (La. 1936).
Lewis v. Meredith Corp., 293 Ga. App. 747, 667 S.E.2d 716 (2008).
Lloyd Corp. v. Tanner, 407 U.S. 551, 92 S. Ct. 2219, 33 L.Ed.2d 131 (1972).
Longview Outdoor Advertising Co., LLC v. City of Winter Garden, Fla., 426 F. Supp.2d 1269 (M.D. Fla. 2006).
Lorillard Tobacco Co. v. Reilly, 533 U.S. 525, 121 S.Ct. 2404, 150 L.Ed.2d 532 (2001).
Louisiana Employment Discrimination Law, La. R.S. 301-369.
Louisiana National Guard and Reserve Law, La. R.S. 29:38-38.3.
Louisiana Smoked Products, Inc. v. Savoie's Sausage and Food Products, Inc., 96-1716, 696 So. 2d 1373 (1997).
Louisiana State Bar Articles of Incorporation, Art. 16.
Louisiana Unfair Trade Practices Act, La. R.S. 51:1401-1422.
Louisiana Uniform Trade Secret Act, La. R.S. 51: 1431-1439 (1997).
Louisiana White Cane Law, La. R.S. 46:1951-1959.
Lowe v. Southern Bell Telephone & Telegraph Co., 263 So. 2d 460 (La. App. 1st Cir. 1972).
Luban, D. (1995). *Settlements and the erosion of the public realm*, 83 Geo.L.J. 2619.
Mabry v. Andrus, 34 So.3d 1075 (La. Ct. App. 2nd Cir. 2010).
Manipulative and deceptive devices, 15 U.S.C. sec. 78j.
Marcus, R. L. (1991). *The discovery conifidentiality controversy*. 1991 U.Ill.L.Rev. 457.
Mashburn v. Collin, 359 So. 2d 879 (La. 1977).
Matthews v. Military Dept. ex rel. State, 970 So. 2d 1089 (La. App. 1st Cir. 2007).
MCPC, Inc. and Jason Galanter, 360 NLRB No. 39 (2014).
McCann v. Iroquois Memorial Corp., 622 F.3d 745 (7th Cir. 2010).
McLachlan v. New York Life Insurance Co., 488 F.3d 624 (5th Cir. 2007).
Media General Operations, Inc., 341 NLRB No. 18 (2004).
Merrell Dow Pharmaceuticals, Inc. v. Thompson, 478 U.S. 504, 106 S.Ct. 3229, 92 L.Ed.2d 650   (1986).
Metromedia, Inc. v. City of San Diego, 453 U.S. 490, 101 S.Ct. 2882, 69 L.Ed.2d 800 (1981).
Military Service Relief Act, La. R.S. 29:401 to 29:426.
Miller v. California, 413 U.S. 15, 93 S.Ct. 2607, 37 L.Ed.2d 419 (1973).
Miller v. Motorola, Inc., 202 Ill.App.3d 976, 148 Ill.Dec. 303, 560 N.E.2d 900 (1st Dist. 1990).
Minimum wage, 29 U.S.C. sec. 206.
Mix v. University of New Orleans, 609 So. 2d 958 (La. App. 4th Cir. 1992).
Moore v. Big Picture Co., 828 F.2d 270 (5th Cir. 1987).
Moranski v. General Motors Corp., 433 F.3d 537 (7th Cir. 2005).
Myers v. BP America, Inc., 2010 WL 3878920 (W.D. La. 2010).
Nader, R. & Smith, W. J. (1996). *No contest: Corporate lawyers and the perversion of justice*

in America. New York: Random House.
National Aeronautics and Space Administration v. Nelson, 131 S.Ct. 746, 178 L.Ed.2d 667 (2011).
National Association of Manufacturers v. N.L.R.B., 717 F.3d 947 (C.A. D.C, 2013).
NCH Corp. v. Broyles, 749 F.2d 247 (5th Cir. 1985).
New York Times Co. v. Sullivan, 376 U.S. 254, 84 S.Ct. 710, 11 L.Ed.2d 686 (1964).
N.L.R.B. v. Gissell Packing Co., 395 U.S. 575, 89 S.Ct. 1918, 23 L.Ed.2d 547 (1969).
N.L.R.B. v. Gissell Packing Co., 218 F.3d 531 (6th Cir. 2000).
Noyes v. Kelly Services, 488 F.3d 1163 (9th Cir. 2007).
Odyssey Capital Group, L.P. III, 2002 WL 1881220 (N.L.R.B. 2002).
Ohralik v. Ohio State Bar Association, 436 U.S. 447, 98 S.Ct. 1912, 56 L.Ed.2d 444 (1978).
Passaic Daily News v. Blair, 63 N.J. 474, 308 A.2d 649 (N.J.1973).
People v. Bush, 39 N.Y.2d 529, 349 N.E.2d 832 (N.Y.1976).
Petermann v. International Brotherhood of Teamsters, Chauffeurs, Warehousemen, and Helpers of America, Local 396, 174 Cal. App.2d 184, 344 P.2d 25 (Cal. App. 2nd Dist. 1984).
Phillips v. Smalley Maintenance Services, Inc., 711 F.2d 1524 (11th Cir. 1983).
Pickering v. Board of Education of Township High School District 205, Will County, 391 U.S. 563, 88 S.Ct. 1731, 20 L.Ed.2d 811 (1968).
Polkey v. Trustees Corp., 404 F.3d 1264 (11th Cir. 2005).
Powers v. Vista Chemical Co., 109 F.3d 1089 (5th Cir. 1997).
Powell v. Yellow Book USA, Inc., 445 F.3d 1094 (8th Cir. 2006).
Pregnancy Discrimination Act of 1978, Pub. L. 95-555, 42 U.S.C. sec. 2000e (1978).
Prohibitions on lie detector use, 29 U.S.C. sec. 2002.
Protection against discriminatory treatment, 11 U.S.C. sec. 525(b).
Protection of jurors' employment, 28 U.S.C. sec. 1975.
Public Citizen, Inc. v. Louisiana Attorney General Disciplinary Board, 632 F.2d 212 (5th Cir. 2011).
Puig v. Greater New Orleans Expressway Commission, 712 So. 2d 842 (La.App. 5th Cir. 2000).
Ramptor, S. & Stauber, J. (1997). *Mad cow USA: Could the nightmare happen here?* Monroe, Maine: Common Courage Press.
Rankin v. McPherson, 483 U.S. 378, 107 S.Ct. 2891, 97 L.Ed.2d 315 (1987).
Rehabilitation Act of 1973, 29 U.S.C.S. secs. 701 to 796 (2009).
Reingold v. Swiftships, Inc., 126 F.3d 645 (5th Cir. 1997).
Religious Freedom Restoration Act, Pub. L. No. 103-141, 42 U.S.C. Secs. 2000bb to 2000bb4 (1993).
Restatement (Third) Of Unfair Competition, Sec. 46.
Retaliating against a witness, victim, or informant, 18 U.S.C. sec. 1513(e).
Riley v. National Federation of the Blind of North Carolina, Inc., 487 U.S. 781, 108 S.Ct. 2667, 101 L.Ed.2d 669 (1988).
Rocket Learning, Inc. v. Rivera-Sanchez, 715 F.3d 1 (1st Cir. 2013).
Rowan v. U.S. Post Office Dept., 397 U.S. 728, 90 S.Ct. 1484, 25 L.Ed.2d 736 (1970).
Ruffin v. Wal-Mart Stores, Inc., 818 So. 2d 965 (La. Ct. App. 1st Cir. 2002).
San Francisco Arts & Athletics, Inc. v. U.S. Olympic Committee, 583 U.S. 522, 107 S.Ct. 2971, 97 L.Ed.2d 427 (1987).
Schenck v. U.S., 249 U.S. 47, 39 S.Ct. 247, 63 L.Ed. 470 (1919).
SDT Industries, Inc. v. Leeper, 793 So. 2d 327 (La. App. 2nd Cir. 2001).
Securities and Exchange Commission, 15 U.S.C. sec. 78d.
Singletary v. Fridley, 762 So. 2d 692 (La.App. 1st Cir. 2000).
Smith v. Superior Court, 41 Cal.App.4th 1014, 49 Cal.Rptr.2d 20 (Cal. App. 5th Dist. 1996).
Snepp v. U.S., 444 U.S. 507, 100 S.Ct. 763, 62 L.Ed.2d 704 (1980).
Snyder v. Phelps, 131 S.Ct. 1207, 179 L.Ed.2d 172 (2011).
Society of Professional Journalists, Headliners Chapter v. Briggs, 687 F.Supp. 1521 (D.

Utah 1988).
Soileau v. Smith True Value and Rental, 2012-1711, 2013 WL 3305265 (La. 2013).
Stark-Werkspoor Diesel V.V. v. Koek, 534 So. 2d 983 (La. App. 5th Cir. 1988).
Stein v. Marriott Ownership Resorts, Inc., 944 P.2d 374 (Utah. Ct. App. 1997).
Stewart v. Courtyard Management Corp., 2005 WL 3114914 (5th Cir. 2005).
Stewart v. Pantry, Inc., 715 F.Supp. 1361 (W.D. Ky. 1988).
Texas Beef Group v. Winfrey, 201 F.3d 680 (5th Cir. 2000).
Thompson v. Western States Medical Center, 535 U.S. 357, 122 S.Ct. 1497, 152 L.Ed.2d 563 (2002).
Tiena v. Charleston Area Medical Center, Inc., 203 W.Va. 135, 506 S.E.2d 578 (W.Va. 1998).
Time, Inc. v. Hill, 385 U.S. 374, 87 S.Ct. 534, 17 L.Ed.2d 456 (1967).
Title VII of the Civil Rights Act of 1964, Pub. L. 88-352, 42 U.S.C. sec. 2000e-2 (1964).
Town of Newton v. Rumery, 480 U.S. 386, 107 S.Ct. 1187, 94 L.Ed.2d 405 (1987).
Tribe, L. (1978). *American Constitutional Law* (1st Ed.). New York: Foundation Press.
Tribe, L. (1988). *American Constitutional Law* (2nd Ed.). New York: Foundation Press.
Trustees of Dartmouth College v. Woodward, 17 U.S. 518, 1819 WL 2201, 4 L.Ed. 629 (1819).
Uniformed Services Employment and Reemployment Rights Act, Pub. L. No. 103-353, 38 U.S.C. secs. 4301-4335 (1994).
United Group of National Paper Distributors, Inc. v. Vinson, 666 So. 2d 1338 (La. App. 2nd Cir. 1996).
Unlawful access to stored communications, 18 U.S.C. 2701(c).
U.S. Const. amend. I.
U.S. Const. amend. VI
U.S. Const. amend. XIV.
U.S. Const., art. VI, sec. 3.
U.S. v. Alvarez, 132 S.Ct. 2537, 183 L.Ed.2d 574 (2012).
U.S. v. Eichmann, 496 U.S. 310, 110 S.Ct. 2404, 110 L.Ed.2d 287 (1990).
U.S. v. Grace, 461 U.S. 171, 103 S.Ct. 1702, 75 L.Ed.2d 736 (1983).
U.S. v. Hunter, 459 F.2d 205 (4th Cir. 1972).
U.S. v. Phillip Morris USA Inc., 566 F.3d 1095 (C.A. D.C. 2009).
U.S. v. Torres, 751 F.2d 875 (7th Cir. 1984).
U.S. v. U.S. Dist. Court for Eastern District of Michigan, Southern Division, 407 U.S. 297, 92 S.Ct. 2125, 32 L.Ed.2d 752 (1972).
Valentine v. Chrestensen, 316 U.S. 52, 62 S.Ct. 920, 86 L.Ed. 1262 (1942).
Virginia State Board of Pharmacy v. Virginia Citizens Consumer Council, Inc., 425 U.S. 748, 96 S.Ct. 1817, 48 L.Ed.2d 346 (1978).
Warden v. SunTrust Banks, Inc., 549 F.3d 334 (4th Cir. 2008).
Watkins v. General Refractories Co., 805 F.Supp. 911 (D.Utah 1992).
White v. Monsanto, 585 So. 2d 1205 (La. 1991).
Winn v. New Orleans City, 919 F.Supp.2d 743 (E.D. La. 2013).
Young v. Southwestern Savings & Loan Association, 509 F.2d 140 (5th Cir. 1975).
Zacchini v. Scripps-Howard Broadcasting Co., 433 U.S. 562, 97 S.Ct. 2849, 53 L.Ed.2d 965 (1977).
Zauderer v. Office of Disciplinary Counsel of Supreme Court of Ohio, 471 U.S. 626, 105 S.Ct. 2265, 85 L.Ed.2d 652 (1985).

Chapter 12
Digital Media
By Ashley Packard, University of Houston - Clear Lake

Learning Objectives
In this chapter, readers will:
- describe the circumstances in which employer retaliation for online speech may be prohibited
- describe the circumstances in which school retaliation for online student speech may be prohibited
- articulate the categories of speech that do not receive First Amendment protection online
- explain how protection for Internet libel varies depending on whether the speaker is addressing a matter of public interest or a private concern
- describe libel tourism and how the SPEECH Act is used to discourage it
- explain the ways that Internet service providers are shielded from liability for libel or copyright infringement resulting from material their users post
- explain when it is illegal in Louisiana to impersonate someone online
- describe ways that the government and commercial interests monitor online communications
- explain how protections for children and adults differ with respect to the collection of personal information online
- explain how copyright law's derivative right applies to digital works
- describe the actions that transform the use of a trademark in a domain name into cybersquatting

Protections and limitations for speech online are similar to those in the offline world because courts and legislatures have worked diligently to adapt laws related to freedom of expression, libel, privacy, and intellectual property to the digital environment. But there are still important differences. First, law cannot move as quickly as technology, so courts consistently face legal questions that emerge from the new and sometimes unexpected things technology enables people to do. Second, the simplicity of the technology allows almost anyone to publish. People do so in haste, without an editor to review their work, and often with no legal training to understand the risks involved. Third, the geographic reach of online speech is virtually limitless. Conflicts that were once localized more frequently cross state and even international borders.

FREEDOM OF EXPRESSION

The Internet has been a boon to expression, opening up an enormous marketplace of ideas. Online forums, social networks, blogs, and review sites have become the twenty-first-century equivalent of the public square. The Supreme Court has given Internet sites full First Amendment protection (*Reno v. ACLU*, 1997). But it is important to remember that the First Amendment only protects against government censorship. Private online services and social networks are not bound to honor their users' freedom of expression and may suppress content they do not like or disable a user's account for violating their terms of service. In *Estavillo v. Sony Computer Entertainment* (2009), for example, the Northern District of California held that a user banned from a video game network with virtual spaces had no First Amendment claim against Sony because the company was providing a commercial product, not performing municipal functions in a virtual world.

As a private provider of digital services, there was no sufficient nexus to the government to justify the application of First Amendment protection. Nevertheless, sites like Twitter and Reddit have cultivated a sense of community by encouraging freedom of expression, and their policies provide users with a great deal of latitude.

The sense of freedom that people feel when they are online—particularly when they are writing from the privacy of home—can overcome reservations they might have about sharing opinions and information under other circumstances. Bigoted or indiscreet speech posted online can result in retaliation offline. Cold Stone Creamery, for example, fired an employee who posted on her Facebook page after President Obama was re-elected, "another 4 years of the (n - - - - -). Maybe he will get assassinated this term . . ! !" (as cited in Associated Press, 2012). The *Los Angeles Times* suspended one of its pressmen for blogging about the newspaper's production problems. In his last post the pressman wrote, "So much for first amendment rights" (Padgett, 2010). It is a common misconception that the First Amendment applies in the workplace or to employers generally. U.S. law presumes employers have the right to hire and fire at will, unless the company has otherwise specified it will only terminate employees for just cause (Muhl, 2001).

In most states, including Louisiana, employment may be terminated for any reason—including an employee's actions away from work—as long as the termination is not discriminatory.

An exception may apply to employers' freedom to retaliate for online speech if the employee was engaged in a discussion of work conditions with coworkers. The National Labor Relations Board states that workers have a right to discuss labor conditions without fear of retribution and has ordered some employers to reinstate employees fired for criticizing their companies online (*Hispanics United of Buffalo*, 2012; *New York Party Shuttle*, 2013). The key to NLRB relief is concerted activity "for mutual aid or protection" (29 U.S.C. Sec. 157, 2012). For example, the NLRB ordered Bettie Page Clothing to reinstate three employees who were terminated following a Facebook exchange in which they complained about the company's lack of action in addressing their concerns about their direct supervisor, whom they felt was abusive (*Design Technology Group, LLC d/b/a Bettie Page Clothing*, 2013). However, the NLRB will not step in to reverse the termination of employees on lone rants or who have simply exercised poor judgment. It rendered no aid to a reporter fired by the *Arizona Daily Star* for a Twitter post on a slow news day that said "What?!?!?! No overnight homicide . . . You're slacking, Tucson," followed by, "You stay homicidal, Tucson" (Greenhouse, 2013).

Although the First Amendment protects against government censorship, public employers can punish their employees for speech that interferes with the government office's ability to "efficiently provide services" by undermining the integrity of the office or staff morale, particularly when the expression has no bearing on the public interest (*Connick v. Myers*, 1983). In *Connick v. Myers* (1983), the Supreme Court held that Orleans Parish District Attorney Harry Connick did not violate the First Amendment rights of an assistant district attorney in his office by firing her after she circulated a petition through their office questioning his management, because her speech was primarily concerned with internal affairs and could have interfered with close working relationships.

However, when a government employee is speaking as a citizen on a matter "of public concern," courts must balance the employee's First Amendment rights against the employer's interest in promoting the efficiency of public services (*Pickering v. Board of Education*, 1968). The Ninth Circuit struck that balance in a school district's favor when it supported the administration's right to transfer an instructional coach who posted personal and critical comments about her employers and fellow teachers on her blog (*Richardson v. Beckon*, 2009). The court acknowledged that the employee's speech touched on a matter of public concern, but concluded that the school's legitimate administrative interests outweighed the employee's First Amendment rights (*Richardson v. Beckon*, 2009). By publicly criticizing her colleagues, she lost their trust, inhibiting her ability to continue to coach them.

The balance tipped in the other direction in a case involving a Virginia sheriff who refused to renew the contracts of two employees who had "liked" or commented on his opponent's Facebook page during an election campaign. In *Bland v. Roberts* (2013), the U.S. Court of Appeals for the Fourth Circuit held that the employees were speaking as private citizens on matters of public concern and that their interests in expressing support for the opposing candidate "outweighed the Sheriff's interest in providing effective and efficient services to the public." The appellate court also settled the question of whether the act of pressing the "like" button constituted speech that merits constitutional protection. It held that an action generating a statement that one likes something "is itself a substantive statement"(*Bland v. Roberts*, 2013).

Employers are generally prohibited from retaliating against employees for their political positions (*Branti v. Finkel*, 1980). The Supreme Court has held that employees may not be hired, promoted, transferred, or fired based on their political affiliations, unless "party affiliation is an appropriate requirement for the effective performance of the public office involved" (*Branti v. Finkel*, 1980; *Rutan v. Republican Party*, 1990). The Court acknowledged that political affiliation may be relevant in policy-making positions because there is a legitimate government interest in ensuring political loyalty (*Elrod v. Burns*, 1976). It was significant to the Fourth Circuit that the plaintiffs in *Bland v. Roberts* (2013) were not engaged in policy making.

Government supervisors may not suppress employee speech that has no bearing on job performance (*United States v. National Treasury Employees Union*, 1995). Private contractors operating under government contracts receive similar protections (*Board of County Commissioners, Wabaunsee County v. Umbehr*, 1996).

Public schools have also wrestled with the level of control they may exert over students' online speech. The controlling case for student speech is *Tinker v. Des Moines Independent School District* (1969). Students who were dismissed from school for wearing black armbands to protest the Vietnam War challenged the action as a violation of their First Amendment rights and won. The Supreme Court held that while the free speech rights of students are not coextensive with those of adults, student speech should not be restricted unless it disrupts class work, creates substantial disorder, or interferes with the rights of others. This precedent is now applied in an online environment. Courts have vindicated the rights of students who have used online media to criticize school officials when their speech, although lewd or misleading, was not substantially disruptive on campus (*Beussink v. Woodland R-IV School District*, 1998; *J. S. v. Blue Mountain School District*, 2011; *Layshock v. Hermitage School District*, 2011). However, courts have sided with schools when student speech impaired school function. For example, in *Doninger v. Niehoff* (2008), the Second Circuit upheld a school's punishment of a student who complained about the postponement of a school concert on her blog and then invited readers to respond by contacting school officials. The court concluded that the student should have foreseen that her actions off campus would lead to disruption on campus when her readers complied (*Doninger v. Niehoff*, 2008). In *J.S. v. Bethlehem Area School District* (2002) a student posted a picture of his teacher's severed head, dripping with blood, paired with a request for funds to pay for a hit man. The teacher was so upset that she took medical leave for the rest of the year, clearly bringing about a disruption on campus. Pennsylvania's Supreme Court upheld the student's permanent expulsion.

The issue of punishing speech posted off campus is more complicated when the speech is not particularly directed at the school, but violates campus policies. For example, the Fourth Circuit considered a case in which a West Virginia high school student created a MySpace page called "Students Against Sluts Herpes" to bully another student (*Kowalski v. Berkeley County Schools*, 2011). The court concluded that the school's suspension of the poster did not violate her First Amendment rights. Although the speech on the social networking site was not directed at the school, school officials could reasonably foresee that the student's page, which invited other students to join in the bullying, would lead to more serious harassment and disruption on campus, particularly given students' access to computers, smart phones, and other electronic devices at school.

The Supreme Court has offered lower courts no guidance on how to apply its decisions related to expression among secondary school students to university student speech. The Ninth Circuit upheld a lower court's decision to dismiss a First Amendment complaint that a university student filed against administrators at Southern Oregon University after they disciplined him for repeatedly attacking other students on the discussion board of an online class. The court concluded that the administrators were immune from the suit because the question of university students' speech rights was still unclear. The Minnesota Supreme Court upheld the University of Minnesota's right to discipline a student in its mortuary science program for posting pictures of her cadaver on Facebook, along with "satirical commentary and violent fantasy" (*Tatro v. University of Minnesota*, 2012). But it based its decision on narrowly tailored rules regarding her violation of "established professional conduct standards" rather than any disruption her speech caused on campus.

Certain categories of speech also stand outside First Amendment protection. One is the communication of a true threat (*Virginia v. Black*, 2003). It is a federal crime to communicate a threat that crosses state lines (18 U.S.C. Sec. 875(c), 2012). The Fifth Circuit interprets a threat to be unprotected if "in its context [it] would have a reasonable tendency to create apprehension that its originator will act according to its tenor" (*United States v. Morales*, 2001). However, it also follows the Supreme Court's admonition that threats "must be distinguished from what is constitutionally protected speech" (*Watts v. United States*, 1969). In *U.S. v. O'Dwyer* (2011), the Fifth Circuit upheld a lower court's dismissal of charges against a man accused of emailing a threat to a bankruptcy court employee in the Eastern District of Louisiana. Ashton O'Dwyer, a former New Orleans attorney in bankruptcy proceedings, wanted to obtain leave from the judge to use part of his Social Security check to pay for his anti-depressant medication. O'Dwyer wrote, "Maybe my creditors would benefit from my suicide, but suppose I become `homicidal'? . . . a number of scoundrels might be at risk if I DO become homicidal. Please ask His Honor to consider allowing me to refill my prescription. . . . (*U.S. v. O'Dwyer*, 2011). The appellate court, treated O'Dwyer's references to becoming homicidal as hyperbole, observing that he never identified anyone he wanted to harm. In contrast, a defendant's act of posting a video on YouTube, promising to kill the judge overseeing his child custody dispute if the judge made the wrong decision, followed by his act of publishing links to the video on Facebook to attract attention to it, was considered a true threat in *United States v. Jeffries* (2011).

In a threats case, a court must determine not only whether a reasonable person would interpret the statement in question as a threat, but also whether the speaker intended the statement to be a threat (*Virginia v. Black*, 2003). When Barack Obama was running for president, Walter Bagdasarian published two statements on a Yahoo! financial message board that led to his conviction for violating a federal statute that criminalizes threats to harm or kill a major candidate for president. The first post, "Obama: fk the niggar, he will have a 50 cal in the head soon," was followed by a second calling for someone to "shoot the nig" (*United States v. Bagdasarian*, 2011). Secret Service agents, alerted to the posts by a member of the online board, discovered a .50 caliber rifle in his home and emails of a similar vein (*United States v. Bagdasarian*, 2011). The Ninth Circuit found the speech deplorable but protected. One statement was a prediction Obama would be shot; the other called on others to do it. The court said neither amounted to an actual threat on Bagdasarian's part.

Exhorting others to commit acts of violence is more appropriately classified as incitement, another category of speech denied First Amendment protection. But the standard of proof the government must meet to establish incitement results in few successful prosecutions and none so far in the digital realm. The government must demonstrate not only that the defendant intended to arouse others to violence, but also that imminent harm was likely to occur.

Cyberstalking and cyber harassment are both prohibited by federal law and in many states, such as Louisiana (La. R.S. Sec. 14:40.3). Cyberstalking applies to anyone who "uses . . . any interactive computer service, or any facility of interstate or foreign commerce to engage in a course of conduct that causes substantial emotional distress to that person or places that person in reasonable fear of death, or serious bodily injury. . . ." (18 U.S.C. Sec. 2261A, 2012). For example, a Montana man was convicted of cyberstalking after sending his ex-girlfriend twenty-two threatening emails and fifty threatening text messages. One warned that he would enjoy slitting her throat and watching her gasp for air (*United States v. Grob*, 2009).

Cyber harassment applies to the "use, in interstate or foreign communications, of a telecommunications device, whether or not conversation or communication ensues, to annoy, abuse, threaten, or harass someone anonymously (47 U.S.C. Sec. 223(a)(1)(C), 2012). The statute was applied to a Seattle man who disseminated false information about his victim to her coworkers and posted sexual invitations in her name in chat rooms" (Ho 2004, p. B1).

Obscenity is another category of speech that receives no First Amendment protection. It is illegal to produce obscene material intended for sale, or to transport obscene materials (including via a computer service) for the purpose of sale or distribution (18 U.S.C. Secs. 1461, 1462, & 1465, 2012). Likewise, the act of making, distributing, or soliciting child pornography, by any means, including a computer, is a felony (18 U.S.C. Sec. 1466A, 2012). Indecency, on the other hand, is protected speech, and the Supreme Court has held restrictions on Internet indecency to be unconstitutional (*Reno v. ACLU*, 1997).

Federal and state legislatures have engaged in numerous efforts to protect minors from exposure to sexual content on the Internet (*Reno v. ACLU*, 1997; *ACLU v. Ashcroft*, 2003). Legislatures in Louisiana, Nebraska, and Indiana have passed laws banning registered sex offenders from using social networking sites, to reduce their potential online interaction with minors. All have been held to be unconstitutionally overbroad, although Louisiana has since passed a narrower version (*Doe v. Jindal*, 2012; *Doe v. State of Nebraska*, 2012; *Doe v. Prosecutor*, 2013). Louisiana's first attempt left the definition of a social networking site open so that it potentially encompassed any interactive site (*Doe v. Jindal*, 2012). The revised statute defines a networking site as "facilitating social interaction with other users of the Web site" with the capability to allow its users "to create web pages or profiles about themselves that are available to the general public or to any other users." The statute applies to anyone convicted of indecent behavior with juveniles, pornography involving juveniles, computer-aided solicitation of a minor, or video voyeurism; or who was convicted of a sex offense in which the victim was a minor (La. R.S. 14:91.5, 2013). Registered sex offenders convicted of lesser crimes may still use social networking sites, but may not want to because Louisiana law requires them to indicate their sex offender status in their profile pages, along with the crime of which they were convicted, the jurisdiction for the conviction, a description of their physical characteristics, and their residential address (La. R.S. 15:542.1 (D)(1), 2013).

DEFAMATION

Defamation—the communication of a false statement that exposes a person to hatred, contempt or ridicule, or that injures a person or business' reputation—is one of the fastest-growing areas of digital law (La. R.S. 14:47, 2013). According to the Media Law Resource Center, bloggers have faced more than $47 million in defamation judgments (*Media Law Resource Center*, n.d.; Springer, 2011).

Defamation has two categories: A defamatory statement communicated verbally to a limited group is classified as slander; one published or broadcast is categorized as libel. In the digital realm, where all statements are published, the terms defamation and libel may be used interchangeably.

How a court treats a libel case largely depends on its assessment of whether the speech addresses a matter of public interest. In the United States, defendants speaking on matters of public interest receive more protection than defendants speaking about private concerns. Plaintiffs suing for libel are required to prove the falsity of the defendant's statements and a minimum of negligence on the defendant's part (*Gertz v. Robert Welch, Inc.*, 1974). If the plaintiff is a public figure or official, he or she is required to prove a higher standard of fault called *actual malice*, which demands evidence that the defendant published a statement with knowledge of its falsity or with reckless disregard of the truth (*New York Times v. Sullivan*, 1964).

In *Baxter v. Scott* (2003), a Louisiana appellate court dismissed a libel case filed by Richard Baxter, the former Vice President for University Advancement and External Affairs at the University of Louisiana-Monroe, against an economics professor who started the anonymous Web site "Truth at ULM" to comment on the university's administration. The court concluded that Baxter had little chance of winning because he was a public figure suing over statements about issues of public concern. As such he would be required to prove that the defendant acted with actual malice toward him. The court noted that while the defendant had posted comments that were untrue, he had also presented evidence of his reasonable belief that they were true at the time. Other comments that were just mean-spirited, such as the defendant's reference to the plaintiff as the "Vice President of Excremental Affairs," were nothing more than rhetorical hyperbole, protected because no one would believe them to be fact.

This case was the first in which a Louisiana court applied the state's statute barring "strategic lawsuits against public participation" (La. Code of Civ. Proc. art 971). SLAPP suits, as they are known, stifle criticism on issues of public concern while presenting no legitimate potential for success at trial. Defendants challenging the merits of a libel claim under the SLAPP statute are required to establish that their speech concerned a public issue. Once they do, the burden shifts to the plaintiff to demonstrate that his or her claim has sufficient merit to move forward to trial. If the plaintiff cannot show the potential for success, the court will dismiss the suit before it wastes more time and resources.

In contrast, when no issue of public concern is apparent and the libel appears to emanate from a private grievance, courts have shown a willingness to issue astounding damage awards. A Texas jury awarded Orix, a servicer of mortgage-backed securities trusts, a $12.5 million judgment against a Houston family that attacked the lender on the web after it foreclosed on property they owned in Louisiana (*Orix Capital v. Super Future Equities*, 2009). The defendants in *Orix Capital v. Super Future Equities* (2009) set up a cleverly named gripe site, called Predorix.com, that falsely claimed the plaintiff was guilty of tax fraud and facing a federal investigation for racketeering.

Because the court concluded that Orix was a private figure, the company was only required to prove negligence on the defendants' part. The Fifth Circuit decides whether companies are public or private by using a nonexclusive, three-factor test that considers:

> the corporation's notoriety among average individuals within the relevant geographical area; the nature of the corporation's business (whether it makes or markets consumer goods); and the frequency and intensity of media scrutiny. (*Snead v. Redland Aggregates Ltd.*, 1993)

Orix is a successful company within its industry, but it does not market a consumer product or advertise, so the court classified it as private.

Second—and more significantly—despite the site's focus on mortgaged-backed securities in the midst of the financial system's meltdown, the court concluded that the contested speech did not involve a matter of public concern, but rather "unsolicited comments on a private lawsuit" (*Super Future Equities v. Wells Fargo*, 2008). While *New York Times v. Sullivan* (1964) enhanced protection for defendants in libel cases, states are not obligated to apply it in cases involving both private figure plaintiffs and private speech. In such cases, both Louisiana and Texas revert to traditional common law rules requiring defendants to bear the burden of proving the truth of their assertions.

Before their case went to trial, the defendants in Orix attempted to argue the libel claim was unwarranted because their speech was protected opinion, satire, or parody. However, the court documents, deposition videos, and news articles they had posted in support of their accusations undermined their argument (*Super Future Equities v. Wells Fargo*, 2008). A disclaimer on the Web site labeling the information as opinion did not help either (*Super Future Equities v. Wells Fargo*, 2008). As the Supreme Court has pointed out, attaching a provable assertion to the phrase "in my opinion" does not transform it into an opinion (*Milkovich v. Lorain Journal Co.*, 1990). A real opinion cannot be proved true or false (*Milkovich v. Lorain Journal Co.*, 1990).

Until *Orix*, the highest online libel award was an $11.3 million judgment issued in *Scheff v. Bock* (2006) against a Louisiana resident who posted statements on Internet bulletin boards accusing the plaintiff of being a "crook," a "con artist," and a "fraud." The defendant, Carey Bock, contacted Sue Scheff, the operator of an online referral service for parents of troubled teenagers seeking help to extricate her sons from a boarding school where their father had placed them. Scheff helped with that request but denied Bock additional information she had requested regarding another student who claimed to have been sexually abused at the boarding school. In posts following their altercation, Bock engaged in defamation per se, which is the use of terms that are facially defamatory, such as false accusations of criminal activity, immoral acts, professional incompetence, or possession of a communicable disease. In states that recognize defamation per se, plaintiffs are not required to prove damages because harm is assumed. Bock did not attend the trial and a jury granted Scheff a default judgment of $6.3 million in compensatory and $5 million in punitive damages (*Scheff v. Bock*, 2006). With no hope of paying the judgment, Bock appealed, but a Florida appellate court upheld the award (*Bock v. Scheff*, 2008).

The previous cases have been related to Web sites and blogs, but the rise in social networking has also precipitated libel suits related to posts on Twitter, MySpace, Instagram, Pinterest, and Craigslist (Michels, 2008; Kearn, 2013).

Courtney Love has been sued for libel three times in connection with social media posts. The first suit followed a 2009 Twitter and MySpace diatribe in which Love alleged that her fashion designer, Dawn Simorangkir, who had just submitted a $4,000 bill, was involved in theft, prostitution, and drug use. The case settled out of court with Love agreeing to pay Simorangkir $430,000 (Associated Press, 2011). The second suit resulted from a tweet posted in 2010, in which Love alleged that a former attorney, who refused to work with her again, had been "bought off" (*Complaint, Gordon & Holmes v. Love*, 2011). The third suit, filed by Simorangkir again, claims Love libeled the designer on Pinterest and the Howard Stern Show by alleging that Simorangkir stole clothing and fashion designs from Love, and that the theft was captured on closed circuit video (*Complaint, Simorangkir v. Love*, 2013). The second and third cases are still pending.

In the United Kingdom, courts have issued judgments for Twitter defamation. When a BBC news program suggested that a "senior Conservative from the Thatcher era" had committed child abuse, Twitter users speculated that it might be Lord Robert Alistair McAlpine, a former Deputy Chairman of the Conservative Party. Before it became clear that McAlpine had nothing to do with the accusation, Sally Bercow, the wife of the Speaker of the House of Commons, tweeted: "Why is Lord McAlpine trending? *Innocent face.*" Lord McAlpine sued her. The UK High Court of Justice concluded that the use of *innocent face* to suggest sarcasm turned the question into an allegation of guilt that was defamatory (*Between the Lord McAlpine of Green West and Sally Bercow*, 2013).

Although defamation law has long recognized that "republication of libel" can be as serious as committing the libel in the first place, U.S. courts have not recognized retweeting as a form of libel. U.S. courts have also generally refused to consider the act of linking to libelous content a separate act of libel (*Salyer v. Southern Poverty Law Center Inc.*, 2009; *In re: Philadelphia Newspapers v. Vahan H. Gureghian*, 2012). Canada has gone further; its Supreme Court has held that linking is not libelous (*Crookes v. Newton*, 2011).

Crossing Jurisdictions

Posting content on such an accessible medium as the Internet heightens one's exposure to potential lawsuits in other states and even other countries. Before a U.S. court can accept jurisdiction over an out-of-state or foreign defendant, for purposes of a lawsuit or criminal trial, it must have a legitimate connection to the defendant, based on the defendant's minimum contacts with the state in which the court is based (*Keeton v. Hustler Magazine, Inc.*, 1984). Courts that do not follow this guideline violate the defendant's rights of due process under the Fourteenth Amendment to the Constitution (U.S. Const. amend. XIV).

In libel cases, courts generally ensure that connection by following *Calder v. Jones* (1984), which requires the plaintiff alleging libel to demonstrate that the defendant targeted the state with the defamation, knowing that the harm from the claim would result there. The Fifth Circuit affirmed the dismissal of a libel suit that Roger Clemens filed in Texas against his former trainer Brian McNamee, who accused Clemens of using performance-enhancing drugs, for lack of personal jurisdiction (*Clemens v. McNamee*, 2010). McNamee, a resident of New York, was interviewed in New York for a report that was later picked up by major media all over the country. He also spoke to a writer for SI.com, a nationally available Web site. The Court of Appeals concluded that McNamee's comments about Clemens were not aimed at Texas. To meet the standards of due process, Clemens would have to file the suit in a jurisdiction with a connection to the defendant, which would most likely be New York, as Clemens resided there.

In cases that involve commercial Web sites, courts may use a separate test to establish the defendant's minimum contacts with the forum. The Zippo balancing test, from the case *Zippo Manufacturing v. Zippo Dot Com*, asks courts to consider the commercial nature and interactivity of the Web site to which the claim is linked. A commercial site, like Amazon.com, for example, is fully interactive. A site that merely describes a company that has brick and mortar stores is not interactive. Using the *Zippo* test, a court will find it easier to assert jurisdiction over a fully interactive site that likely engages in business with the residents of its state than one that simply puts a Web site online but doesn't actually sell merchandise in the state; for this reason, most fully interactive sites require users to agree to their terms of service specifying where any legal disputes may be adjudicated.

Courts outside the United States do not always require a connection to the defendant before asserting jurisdiction in a case. Some will exercise jurisdiction based on a connection to the claim alone, asserting that the defendant should have foreseen that material placed online would be accessed there. The practice of filing a defamation suit in a foreign jurisdiction where the law favors plaintiffs is called libel tourism. The U.S. Congress and several states, including Louisiana, have passed laws to discourage libel tourism (La. Code of Civ. Proc. Art. 2542, 2012). The federal law is awkwardly called the Securing the Protection of our Enduring and Established Constitutional Heritage Act to achieve the acronym SPEECH Act (28 U.S.C. Sec. 4102, 2012). The law requires U.S. courts to refrain from enforcing foreign libel judgments unless 1) the foreign court provides the same protection for freedom of expression that U.S. courts do under the First Amendment to the U.S. Constitution and state law or 2) regardless of the foreign court's protections for expression, the same judgment would have been rendered by a domestic court applying U.S. speech protections.

The Fifth Circuit applied the SPEECH Act to reject a Canadian libel judgment issued against a Mississippi blogger in *Trout Point Lodge v. Handshoe* (2013). The defendant, Doug Handshoe, operated a blog focused on political and legal issues affecting the Gulf Coast. Handshoe zeroed in on corruption scandal involving Aaron Broussard, the former president of Jefferson Parish, Louisiana, who was convicted in 2012 of accepting bribes for parish contracts. Handshoe's entries suggested that Broussard funneled that money into real estate investments in Nova Scotia, which he tied to Trout Point. Broussard owned property near Trout Point, but had no investment in the resort. Trout Point's owners sued Handshoe for libel and, when he failed to show up to fight the lawsuit, were awarded a $350,000 default judgment against him, which they asked a Mississippi court to enforce. The Fifth Circuit upheld the lower court's judgment that the SPEECH Act prohibited enforcement of the judgment because Nova Scotia law does not provide the same level of protection to libel defendants that the First Amendment or Mississippi state law does. Canadian plaintiffs do not have to prove the falsity of defendants' statements when they are related to matters of public concern; instead, defendants must prove their statements are true. The Court of Appeals noted that although the plaintiffs had asserted that Handshoe's statements connecting their hotel to the Louisiana scandal were defamatory and untrue, they had provided no evidence to "contradict or otherwise undermine the allegedly defamatory statements" (*Trout Point Lodge, Ltd. v. Handshoe*, 2013). Without that, there was insufficient evidence to support a libel claim.

Shielding Service Providers From Libel

Congress has shielded interactive computer services from liability for their users' defamatory posts through Section 230 of the Communications Decency Act (47 U.S.C. Sec. 230, 2012). The law prevents Web sites from being treated as publishers who are responsible for anything their users put online. Because online services bear no responsibility for libelous user-generated content, they are less likely to engage in censorship, precipitating an environment that encourages free expression.

Although specifically intended to shield ISPs from defamation claims, courts have applied Section 230 of the Communications Decency Act to interactive Web sites generally. The statute has also been used to bar claims for invasion of privacy, misappropriation of trade secrets, cyberstalking, and negligence. In 2008, the Fifth Circuit upheld a district court's decision based on Sec. 230 to dismiss negligence claims against MySpace for failing to protect a thirteen-year-old from sexual predators by using age verification software to screen her profile for truthfulness (*Doe v. MySpace*, 2008). By lying about her age, the victim had circumvented a safety feature that would have prevented the public display of her profile. The district court concluded that MySpace was shielded from responsibility because it was the distributor of third-party content, not the content provider.

Section 230 does not, however, shield interactive service providers from liability for users' posts if ISPs ignore criminal acts committed on their sites, such as the solicitation of child pornography, for example. Nor does the law shield ISPs from copyright claims that may result from infringing material posted by subscribers. However, another law discussed later in this chapter does provide ISPs with qualified immunity for their subscribers' infringing posts.

Anonymity Online

Courts protect the right to publish anonymously as an aspect of freedom of expression, particularly when anonymity is used to communicate political speech or it is likely the speaker may suffer from reprisal (*Bates v. City of Little Rock*, 1960; *McIntyre v. Ohio Elections Commission*, 1995). However, courts will waive the right to anonymity when it is used to cloak fraudulent or libelous speech.

Many online services allow their users to post anonymously. Because Internet service providers are spared liability for user posts through Section 230 of the Communications Decency Act, they have little incentive to cooperate with potential plaintiffs in a suit against their users (but see *Jones v. Dirty World Entertainment Recordings*, 2013). This puts plaintiffs in the position of first having to convince a judge to subpoena the name of the original poster from the Internet service provider.

Federal circuits have adopted different tests to determine when it is appropriate to protect John Does who publish on the Internet and when it is appropriate to unmask them. At a minimum, courts ask plaintiffs to demonstrate they have made an effort to notify the anonymous poster of the pending case and provide evidence to show their claim has merit (*Dendrite International v. Doe*, 2001; *Doe v. Cahill*, 2005; *In re: Does 1-10*, 2007). The Fifth Circuit has not yet adopted a test of its own, but a district court in Louisiana developed one to resolve the issue of anonymity in a libel case (*In re: Richard L. Baxter*, 2001). The court concluded that the proper standard should depend on whether the statements alleged to have been libelous involved a matter of public or private concern and whether the potential plaintiff could show "a reasonable probability or a reasonable possibility of recovery on a defamation claim" (*In re: Richard L. Baxter*, 2001). The judge concluded that although a reasonable probability of success was the better standard, it might be too high in cases in which the plaintiff was a public figure or official suing over speech involving a public issue. In such a case, the plaintiff would be required to prove actual malice on the part of the defendant. Without knowing the defendant's identity, the court realized it would be impossible to make an argument regarding the defendant's state of mind.

High-profile cases like the Twitter impersonation of the Dalai Lama (Semuels, 2009), the suicide of a Missouri teen in reaction to a cruel MySpace impersonation (*United States v. Drew*, 2008), and an Illinois case in which a woman fell for a "man" online who was actually a woman using twenty separate characters to carry out the ruse (*Bonhomme v. St. James*, 2012), have prompted states like California, New York, Texas, and Louisiana to pass laws that make it illegal to impersonate someone on the Internet.

In Louisiana, it is a misdemeanor offense to impersonate—with the intent to harm, intimidate, threaten, or defraud—another person online (La. R.S. 14:73.10, 2013). Opening an email or social media account in another's person's name, or posting or sending messages on behalf of another person, without his or her consent, can result in a fine of $250-$1,000 or incarceration of up to six months. Some interactive sites, like Facebook, already prohibit impersonation, regardless of purpose. Others, like Twitter, allow it for purposes of parody, provided there is no likelihood of confusion.

Occasionally anonymous posters become the targets of other Internet users determined to reveal their identify. The practice of scouring the Internet for personal data—usually with the intention of publishing it, to unmask someone posting under an alias or to retaliate by revealing information that leaves the person vulnerable—is called doxing (Doxing[Def. 1], 2011). Derived from the words document tracing, doxing is not illegal, if the information is publicly available. But hacking into a private database violates the Computer Fraud and Abuse Act (18 U.S.C. Sec. 1030, 2012). The statute prohibits *accessing* a computer without authorization, *transmitting* "a program, information, code, or command" that intentionally causes damage to a protected computer, or "*trafficking* in any password or similar information through which a computer may be accessed without authorization."

PRIVACY

Just as technology has made information more accessible, it has also made personal information more accessible to others. People reveal intimate details about themselves on social networking sites that save that information for years and may share it with advertisers and third-party software developers. Internet service providers and search companies track online behavior and file away their search requests. Company Web sites capture the data viewers enter each time they visit their sites to build profiles about them for marketing purposes (Krishnamurthy & Willis, 2009).

The government is also increasingly more active in data collection. Former contractor for the National Security Agency Edward Snowden revealed the breadth of government surveillance activities in 2013 when he disclosed more than 200,000 classified documents to *The Washington Post* and *The Guardian* newspaper in London. The files showed that the National Security Agency had obtained permission from the Foreign Intelligence Surveillance Court to sweep up metadata for all phone calls to preserve the information for future searches done in relation to terrorism investigations (*In re application of the Federal Bureau of Investigation*, n.d.). Metadata refers to phone numbers called and received and the length of phone conversations. The leaked documents also described a program called PRISM, through which the NSA has partnered with Microsoft, Yahoo, Google, Facebook, PalTalk, AOL, Skype, YouTube, and Apple to collect data for intelligence purposes. The FISA Amendments Act of 2008 immunized telecommunications companies that cooperated voluntarily with U.S. intelligence agencies from lawsuits (FISA Amendments Act of 2008). In exchange for that immunity, the companies must accept a "directive" from the attorney general and director of national intelligence to open their servers (Gellman & Poitras, 2013). NSA analysts use search terms designed to target communications by non-U.S. persons with fifty-one percent accuracy, but also do "contact" chaining, which means they screen the files of people their targets have contacted, as well as files belonging to anyone these secondary people may have contacted (PRISM Collection Manager S35333, 2013). Screeners are allowed two hops, increasing their reach to three degrees of separation and, with it, the probability of reviewing U.S. citizens' communications.

Since 2010, the Department of Homeland Security has monitored the publicly accessible sections of social media sites like Facebook, Twitter, and YouTube for purposes of "situational awareness" (Department of Homeland Security, 2012). In 2012, the FBI even put out a "Request for Information" on the federal business opportunities Web site, seeking a software application that would "provide an automatic search and scrape capability of both social networking sites and open source news sites" (Federal Bureau of Investigation, 2012).

Law enforcement uses global positioning systems and cell phones to gather location data in criminal investigations. In *United States v. Jones* (2012), the Supreme Court admonished the government for leaving a GPS tracking device on a car for twenty-eight days without a warrant. The Court held that use of the device constituted a warrantless search under the Fourth Amendment. The focus of the case, however, was really the government's action of attaching the device to a person's property. The Court refused to take the next step to conclude whether the government could have subpoenaed the GPS data from the defendant's phone company or a satellite service like OnStar.

The U.S. Court of Appeals for the Fifth Circuit has held that authorities do not need a warrant to obtain cell phone location data (*In re: Application of the U.S. for Historical Cell Site Data*, 2013). The decision came in response to a lower court's refusal to grant a subpoena to authorities who wanted access to sixty days of cell site data from mobile providers in relation to several criminal investigations. The lower court concluded that subscribers had a Fourth Amendment privacy interest in data stored with their mobile providers and that the authorities needed a warrant rather than a subpoena to access the information. To obtain a warrant, authorities must show that the evidence to be gathered is needed for on ongoing criminal investigation. A subpoena merely requires them to show that the information sought may be useful to an investigation. The Court of Appeals disagreed that a warrant was needed, basing the determination on what has come to be known as the "third party doctrine." The doctrine, developed by the Supreme Court in *Katz v. United States* (1967), asserts that the government does not need a warrant to access information a person has voluntarily shared with third parties, such as a bank or mobile phone provider, even if the person never had any intention of sharing that information with anyone else.

The Fifth Circuit does recognize that individuals have a privacy interest in the information stored on their cell phones. Access to those data requires a warrant. However, the court found the warrantless search of a cell phone lawful in conjunction with an arrest (*United States v. Finley*, 2007).

Statutory protections for privacy in the digital world leave much to be desired. The predominant source of data protection is the Electronic Communications Privacy Act (ECPA), which has three components: the Federal Wiretap Act (18 U.S.C. Secs. 2510-2522, 2012), the Pen Register Statute (18 U.S.C. Secs. 3132 (a)(1), 2012), and the Stored Communications Act (18 U.S.C. Secs. 2701-11, 2012), described in the next three paragraphs.

The Wiretap Act makes it illegal to intercept electronic communications in transit or to disclose them. In doing so, it protects phone calls, emails, or file transfers in progress. Law enforcement may only access this information with a warrant.

The Pen Register Statute protects dialing information for phone calls and routing information for email messages. Because this information is assumed to be less private than the message itself, authorities may access it with a subpoena. The government's mass collection of telephone metadata is accomplished under a court order, based on a broad interpretation of Sec. 215 of the PATRIOT Act, which gives the government access to "business records" if there are reasonable grounds to believe the records sought are relevant to an investigation (50 U.S.C. Sec. 1861 (b)(2)(A)).

The Stored Communications Act protects emails and files that are stored by an Internet Service Provider or, in the case of phone mail or texts, by a telecommunications provider. Government authorities require a warrant to gain access to stored files that are less than six months old. After that, a subpoena will do in most jurisdictions (but see *United States v. Warshak*, 2010). In 1986, when the Stored Communications Act was passed, Congress did not anticipate the Web, much less cloud computing. They assumed that messages stored after six months were simply abandoned. Consequently, under current law, files stored remotely receive less protection than files stored at home.

Exceptions to the Electronic Communications Privacy Act weaken its privacy protection in other respects. First, both the Wiretap Act and Stored Communications Act allow users and the entity providing service to the user to access the user's data (18 U.S.C. Sec. 2701(c)(1)). This means an ISP has access to all of the data it transmits and stores and can mine those data for marketing purposes (Bogatin, 2006; Tate, 2011). Google, for example, scans its users' emails for key words it then uses to target advertising to them. Because Gmail subscribers exchange emails with users of other email services, their messages may incorporate content from individuals who have not agreed to Google's terms of service. In a court filing intended to ward off a class action lawsuit from nonsubscribers whose emails are scanned, the company stated that people sending communications to any of Google's 425 million Gmail users have no "reasonable expectation" of privacy (Rushe, 2013). The SCA's exemption for provider access also allows employers who supply their employees with Internet access or phone service to examine their files and voice messages without the employee's permission.

Second, both the Wiretap Act and Stored Communications Act allow users of interactive services to authorize a third party's access to their personal data (18 U.S.C. Sec. 2701(c)(2)). This exception has been interpreted oddly to allow Web sites to authorize third parties to collect data from people who visit their Web sites through the use of cookies (small text files which are downloaded to a user's computer and that store information about user page activities and browsing habits) and web bugs (a form of spyware that is embedded in Web sites and emails as a clear GIF and used to monitor online actions; it is activated when a user's browser requests information from a Web site). A federal district court in New York held in *In re DoubleClick, Inc. Privacy Litigation* (2001) that Google's Internet marketing company, DoubleClick, did not violate the Electronic Communications Privacy Act by placing cookies on people's computers without their permission. DoubleClick places a cookie with a unique identifier on computers that access any of the thousands of Web sites in its network. These bits of code help the company track consumers across Web sites in its network so it can build profiles based on their purchasing habits and later target them with personalized ads. Consumers who discovered the practice sued DoubleClick for violating the Wiretap and Stored Communications Acts. The federal court reviewing the case thought the behavior fell under the statutes' exemptions. The court reasoned that the Web sites were equal partners with their users in an online communication. As a party to the exchange, the Web sites could authorize a third party—DoubleClick—to intercept data on their behalf (*In re DoubleClick Inc. Privacy Litigation*, 2001).

Although online data aggregators can collect and sell practically any data they wish from adult Internet users in the United States, the same liberties do not apply to children who venture online. The Children's Online Privacy Protection Act authorizes the Federal Trade Commission to regulate sites that collect personal information from children under thirteen (15 U.S.C. Secs. 6501-6506, 2012). Companies that operate such sites must get viable consent from a parent or a legal guardian to collect information such as the child's name, home address, email address, telephone number, Social Security number, or any other personal identifiers, including geolocation information or data collected through cookies. COPPA also prevents third-party marketers from collecting personal information for behavioral advertising purposes without parental consent.

Adults have no real protections against the use of their electronic data for marketing purposes other than the guarantees provided in the terms of service of the Web sites they visit. These agreements that require users to click OK before proceeding are enforceable contracts and companies are expected to honor them. The Federal Trade Commission uses its power to punish unfair and deceptive advertising as a way to take action against companies that violate their privacy policies. In years past, the FTC has issued consent orders against Google, Facebook, MySpace, and Twitter for violating their promises to protect subscribers' privacy (see *In the Matter of Google, Inc.*, 2011; Angwin, 2012). The agency fined Google $22.5 million after it discovered that the company was bypassing the "do not track" privacy settings function on the Safari browser. Facebook was penalized for changing its privacy settings without first informing its users. MySpace was found to be sharing identifiable information about its users with its advertisers. Twitter paid for lax security of its users' passwords (Kravets, 2012).

INTELLECTUAL PROPERTY

Intellectual property law includes copyright, patent, trademark, and trade secret protection. All are applicable to digital media, but copyright and trademark are most pertinent to media producers. State protections for the right of publicity are also increasingly relevant.

It is a common misconception that copyright laws do not apply online. They do, even when the work has not been officially registered and carries no copyright symbol, because protection is automatic as long as the work is original, fixed in a tangible medium of expression and based on a modicum of creativity (17 U.S.C. Sec. 102(a), 2012). Copyright applies to works that are literary (including software), musical, dramatic, choreographic, graphic, pictorial, sculptural, audiovisual, and architectural (17 U.S.C. Sec. 106, 2012). Copyright law also protects derivative versions of works, which means that copying an image or a music file and digitally changing it or using part of it may violate the original copyright holder's rights as well.

Because it is so easy to copy and upload digital files, Internet users commit copyright infringement on a regular basis. Depending on the circumstances, the fair use doctrine may protect an unauthorized use of a copyrighted work, particularly for purposes of criticism, commentary, news reporting, teaching, scholarship, or research (17 U.S.C. Sec. 107). The protection is more likely to apply when the use of a work is limited and transformative. So, while downloading an unauthorized copy of *World War Z* from a file-sharing site for personal use would violate copyright law, incorporating a clip from the film into a documentary about zombies would likely be protected. Fair use is also more likely to apply when the copyrighted work is nonfictional and its use is not for profit, although neither is an essential criterion (*Campbell v. Acuff-Rose Music, Inc.*, 1994).

Courts have been less willing to recognize the unauthorized use of music as fair. In *Bridgeport Music, Inc., et al v. UMG Recordings, Inc., et al.* (2009), the Sixth Circuit affirmed a lower court's decision that Public Announcement infringed upon George Clinton's copyright in "Atomic Dog" by using the phrase "Bow wow wow, yippie yo, yippie yea," in its song, "D.O.G. in Me" (see also *Bridgeport Music, Inc. v. Dimension Films*, 2005; *Bridgeport Music, Inc. v. UMG Recordings, Inc.*, 2009). In contrast, the Beastie Boys got away with a *de minimis* use of a six-second, three-note segment of James Newton's jazz composition (*Newton v. Diamond*, 2003). Significantly, they had licensed use of the sound recording from EMC Records, but had failed to license use of the composition from Newton as well. So the court was operating from the question of whether someone would have recognized three notes from the sheet music rather than the recorded version.

Trade groups such as the American Society of Composers, Authors, and Publishers (ASCAP), Broadcast Music, Inc. (BMI), and the Society of European Stage Authors and Composers (SESAC) license the performance of compositions. Licenses to use a sound recording are negotiated with the record companies that produce the music. Obtaining a license can be arduous and expensive. The Creative Commons, a nonprofit organization that helps artists to license uses of their work that they find acceptable, generally for free, provides an alternative source of music and imagery (*Creative Commons*, n.d.).

The Digital Millennium Copyright Act prevents users of digital music, films, and games from circumventing the digital rights management software embedded in CDs and DVDs to prevent copying. Circumventing DRM software on a protected work or trafficking in any technology, product, or service used to circumvent technological measures controlling access to such works may result in civil or criminal penalties, depending on the extent of the violation (17 U.S.C. Secs. 1201 (a)(b), 2012). Congress gave the Librarian of Congress the power to grant exemptions in three-year increments to circumvention activities it deemed a fair use (17 U.S.C. Secs. 1201 (a)(1)(c), 2012). The most recent exemption allows users to disable software used to protect DVDs or motion pictures online to copy short segments for inclusion in nonprofit videos or documentary films, or for educational use (65260 Fed. Reg. 77, 2012). Consumers are also allowed to "jailbreak" protection devices on their mobile phones in order to add additional software and applications, but this privilege does not apply to tablets or gaming devices.

The Digital Millennium Copyright Act also protects Internet service providers from liability for their users' copyright infringements. DMCA protection applies as long as service providers take no part in editing the material, have no actual knowledge of the infringement or awareness of "facts and circumstances from which infringing activity is apparent," and gain no financial benefit from the infringing activity (17 U.S.C. Sec. 512 (c)(1)(A)(ii)). Once the provider is notified that infringing material is present on the site, the provider is obligated to disable public access to it. This provision in the law has been dubbed the "notice and take-down procedure." The provider is then required to inform the poster that someone has asserted ownership of the material. If the poster submits a counter notification disputing the claim, the service provider will send the counter claim to the person who submitted the original notification and restore access to the work. At that point, responsibility shifts to the person who submitted the take-down notice to seek a court order restraining the poster from further infringement of the work. Issuing a false takedown notice is a violation of the Act, and a person or company caught misrepresenting a claim may be held liable for damages and attorney's fees (17 U.S.C. Sec. 512(f)).

Trademark law, another area of intellectual property, is intended to protect consumers against confusion caused by misleading packaging and advertising. Trademark infringement claims must show that the use of the trademark is likely to confuse consumers regarding the source of a product or service (15 U.S.C. Sec. 1114(1)). Trademark dilution, which applies only to famous marks, must show that the commercial use of the mark diluted it by blurring its distinctiveness or tarnishing it through a negative association (15 U.S.C. Sec. 1125(c)).

To earn protection a trademark must be distinctive, like Google, or acquire a secondary meaning that triggers the company first in consumers' minds, like Dell. The distinctive characteristics associated with a brand, other than its registered mark, such as its packaging, color scheme or unique shape, may be protected as "trade dress" (15 U.S.C. Sec. 1125(a)(3)). At least two courts, including one in Louisiana, have concluded that trade dress may protect the look and feel of a Web site's design.

In a trade dress case brought by Conference Companion against its former partner-turned-competitor Sound Images, the U.S. District Court for the Western District of Pennsylvania held that trade dress applies to Web sites, explaining:

> Like the famed Coca-Cola classic dynamic ribbon, or the iconic Apple logo, on the Internet, the appearance of a web site is essential to a firm's standing in the market. The simple layout of Google's home page, the listing of tweets on Twitter.com, or the organization of photographs and status updates on Facebook.com are all integral to the recognition of their brands, and consequently the firm's reputation (*Conference Archives, Inc. v. Sound Images, Inc.*, 2010).

The court said that the determination would be based on similarities in visual design and interface design. In a similar case filed in Louisiana, Express Lien, a seller of legal self-help materials, sued National Association of Credit Management for infringing on its copyrights and trade dress by publishing similar information on its Web site, along with choices of color, font, links, and other content (*Express Lien, Inc. v. National Association of Credit Management, Inc.*, 2013). NACM moved to dismiss the suit, arguing that the government documents it duplicated on Express Lien's site were not protected by copyright law and that, although there were similarities in the Web site's look, there were also differences that protected it from claims of trademark infringement. A federal district court in Louisiana allowed the case to go forward. It noted that copyright law protects compilations of unprotected works if they are selected and arranged in an original way, which Express Lien claimed to have done by incorporating answers to frequently asked questions among the resources (15 U.S.C. Sec. 1125(a)(3), 2012). To meet the Fifth Circuit's test for trade dress, the plaintiff would have to demonstrate the Web site's distinctiveness. This would be established if consumers automatically recognized the brand by seeing some aspect of its presentation (e.g., color or familiar design) even without viewing the name (*Allied Marketing Group, Inc. v. CDL Marketing, Inc.*, 1989).

Trademark law is not meant to be used to stifle criticism about companies. The use of someone else's trademark is protected in parodies, criticism, and commentary, including news reports (15 U.S.C. Sec. 1125 (c) (4)). It is also safe to use a competitor's trademark in comparative advertising, as long as the advertisement is true. The purchase of trademarks as search engine keywords to summon advertisements from competitors has generated a number of suits in federal circuits but has not been considered a trademark infringement in the Fifth Circuit (*College Network, Inc. v. Moore Educational Publishers, Inc.*, 2010). In *College Network, Inc. v. Moore Educational Publishers, Inc.* (2010), the U.S. Court of Appeals for the Fifth Circuit upheld a jury's decision that an advertiser's purchase of its competitor's trademark, "The College Network," from Google and Yahoo to summon its own sponsored link advertising was not likely to confuse consumers about the source of the ad.

The use of another party's trademark in the domain name of a Web site to trick consumers into believing it is the trademark holder's site, or to ransom the domain name back to the trademark owner, is considered cybersquatting. The Anti-Cybersquatting Consumer Protection Act imposes liability on anyone who registers a domain name that is identical or confusingly similar to a protected trademark "in bad faith" (15 U.S.C. Sec.

1125(d)(1)(A), 2012). In contrast, the use of another's trademark in the domain name of a non-commercial site for commentary, criticism, or parody is protected. In *TMI, Inc. v. Maxwell* (2004), the Fifth Circuit held that the use of the domain trendmakerhomes.com in a gripe site to criticize a company by the same name was not a violation of trademark law or the Anti-Cybersquatting Consumer Protection Act. Significant was the fact that the defendants did not try to sell, advertise, or link to any other products or services.

Right of publicity, an offshoot of privacy law that is characteristically similar to intellectual property protection, protects publicly known persons against the unauthorized commercial exploitation of their identity. Courts have recognized right of publicity claims in cases in which a company has used an identifiable characteristic of a famous person (such as a name, voice, look, or trademarked slogan) to evoke the celebrity in an advertisement or entertainment product like a comic book or song (*Carson v. Here's Johnny Portable Toilets*, 1983; *Onassis v. Christian Dior*, 1984; *Midler v. Ford Motor Co.*, 1988; *Abdul Jabbar v. General Motors*, 1996; *Doe v. TCI Cablevision, a/k/a Tony Twist v. TCI Cablevision*, 2003; *Parks v. LaFace Records*, 2003). But courts have also balanced right of publicity claims against freedom of expression to prevent celebrities from using it to stifle criticism and commentary. In *Taylor v. NBC* (1994), for example, a California court refused to allow Elizabeth Taylor to use her right of publicity to stop a documentary about her life. In *C.B.C. Distribution & Marketing, Inc. v. Major League Baseball Advanced Media, L.P.* (2007), the Eighth Circuit concluded that, although the unauthorized use of major league baseball players' identities for online fantasy baseball games implicated their rights of publicity, the appellant's First Amendment rights in offering fantasy baseball products held greater weight. The court reasoned that the public value of information about "the national pastime" deserved substantial protection. It also noted that the statistical information at issue was already available in the public domain.

Manufacturers of electronic games that have attempted to evoke realism by including images of real people in their games have found themselves defending right of publicity suits. In *Hart et al. v. Electronic Arts, Inc.* (2013), the U.S. Court of Appeals for the Third Circuit held that fair use may protect the incorporation of someone's likeness in a reality game, but only if the use of the likeness is transformative. Ryan Hart, the plaintiff in the case, is a former Rutgers University quarterback who filed suit against Electronic Arts for appropriating his likeness, biographical information and statistics into its *NCAA Football* game without permission. A federal district court granted Electronic Arts summary judgment in the case, observing that the company's right to free expression outweighed the player's right of publicity (*Hart v. Electronic Arts, Inc.*, 2011). The First Amendment protects video games as a form of expression (*Brown v. Entertainment Merchants Association*, 2011). However, the Third Circuit reversed, finding EA's use of the player's identity was not sufficiently transformative because the representation was too literal. The transformative use test asks "whether the product containing a celebrity's likeness is so transformed that is has become primarily the defendant's own expression rather than the celebrity's likeness" (*Comedy III Productions v. Gary Saderup, Inc.*, 2001). The appellate court compared the *Hart* case to another involving the video game Band Hero, in which musicians from the band No Doubt were used as avatars (*No Doubt v. Activision Publishing, Inc.*, 2011). Although the scenes and music changed, the depictions didn't; the musicians were virtually doing exactly what they did in real life. The same was true of Hart's representation. Demanding a change in the avatar is a strict interpretation of the transformative use test, which was originally intended to determine whether the product containing the likeness was transformed, not whether the likeness itself was transformed. In a similar case, the Ninth Circuit held that Electronic Arts could not use former Arizona State quarterback Sam Keller's likenesses without consent or compensation (*Keller v. Electronic Arts*, 2013).

Conclusion

Digital media are consistently evolving and pushing the law to evolve with them. In the past twenty years, a body of law has emerged in reaction to technology that has both widened and narrowed freedom of expression and privacy protection.

Protections for digital media expanded when the Supreme Court held that the Internet and video games were fully protected under the First Amendment (*Reno v. ACLU*, 1997; *Brown v. Entertainment Merchants Association*, 2011). By requiring proof of a speaker's specific intent to communicate a threat, the Court also opened more space for heated expression online (*Virginia v. Black*, 2003). Through passage of the Communications Decency Act and the Digital Millennium Copyright Act, Congress shielded Internet service providers from liability for user posts that are defamatory or infringing (17 U.S.C. Sec. 512 (c)(1)(A)(B); 47 U.S.C. Sec. 230, 2012). In doing so, it allowed online services to create an environment that encouraged more freedom of expression. Passage of the SPEECH Act ensured that U.S. writers who operate within First Amendment constraints would not be subjected to foreign libel judgments from jurisdictions with fewer protections (28 U.S.C. Sec. 4102, 2012). Congress passed the Children's Online Privacy Protection Act to prevent marketers from gathering personally identifying information from children (15 U.S.C. Secs. 6501-6506).

In other respects, protections have narrowed. Courts have imposed disproportionately high libel judgments on individuals who have committed defamation online (*Scheff v. Bock*, 2006; *Orix Capital v. Super Future Equities*, 2009; *Obsidian Finance Group, LLC v. Cox*, 2011). In response to the ease with which digital products can be reproduced and distributed, Congress and the courts have increased protections for intellectual property, limiting the rights of copyright users. Congressional passage of the Copyright Term Extension Act lengthened copyright protection by twenty years, both prospectively and retrospectively, keeping millions of works out of the public domain (Pub. L. No. 105-298, 1998). Passage of the Digital Millennium Copyright Act effectively created a new right for intellectual property owners to control access to digital works by criminalizing efforts to bypass digital rights management software (15 U.S.C. Sec. 512; see also Sharp, 2002). Meanwhile courts have applied stricter interpretations of the fair use doctrine. In order to deem a use fair, courts are more likely to demand that copyright users demonstrate they have transformed the work into something new (Gold, 2006; *No Doubt v. Activision Publishing, Inc.*, 2011; *Hart v. Electronic Arts, Inc.*, 2013; *Keller v. Electronic Arts, Inc.*, 2013; see also Kimbrough, 2012). The transformation test is also more frequently applied to right of publicity cases, with greater expectations of what constitutes "transformation." Online privacy for adults is minimal. It is clear that not only marketers but also government agencies are gathering extraordinary amounts of data surreptitiously (Ball & Ackerman, 2013; Savage, 2013).

It takes time for courts and legislatures to assess the implications of their decisions. When negative policy implications emerge, lawmakers do move to right them. For example, the increase in libel decisions prompted at least twenty-seven states including Louisiana to pass anti-SLAPP statutes that empower courts to dismiss libel suits intended to chill protected expression (Packard, 2012). Congress passed safe harbor protections for Internet service providers in reaction to court decisions that held service providers potentially liable for their users' defamatory and infringing posts (*Playboy Enterprises v. Frena*, 1993; *Religious Technology Center v. Netcom*, 1995; *Stratton Oakmont v. Prodigy Services, Inc.*, 1995). When the Federal Trade Commission realized that marketers were tracking children's online behavior through cookies and unique identifiers on their computers, the agency classified data gathered by those methods as "personally identifying information." The new administrative rule enabled the FTC to strengthen its enforcement of the Children's Online Privacy Protection Act. Congressional bills are under consideration to require authorities to obtain a warrant to access information stored by an Internet service provider, no matter how old it is, as well as location data stored by geolocation or wireless communication services (Communications Electronic Privacy Act Amendments Act, 2013; Geolocational Privacy and Surveillance Act, 2013).

REFERENCES

Access to certain business records for foreign intelligence and international terrorism investigations, 50 U.S.C. Sec. 1866(b)(2)(A).

Angwin, J. (2012, July 10). Google, FTC near settlement on privacy. *The Wall Street Journal*, p. A1.

Associated Press. (2011, March 5). Tweets can be costly, just ask Courtney Love. First Amendment Center. Retrieved from http://www.firstamendmentcenter.org

Associated Press. (2012, Nov. 9). Obama threat gets Turlock woman fired, reports Secret Service. San Jose Mercury News. Retrieved from: http://www.mercurynews.com/top-stories/ci_21969395/obama-threat-gets-turlock-woman-fired-reported-secret

Ball, J. & Ackerman, S. (2013, Aug. 9). NSA loophole allows warrantless search for U.S. citizens' emails and phone calls. The Guardian. Retrieved from: http://www.theguardian.com/world/2013/aug/09/nsa-loophole-warrantless-searches-email-calls

Between the Lord McAlpine of Green West and Sally Bercow, EWHC 1142 (QB) (2013). Retrieved from: http://www.bailii.org/ew/cases/EWHC/QB/2013/1342.html

Bogatin, D. (2006, Sept. 10). Free Google Gmail: The high price you pay. ZDNet. Retrieved from: http://www.zdnet.com/blog/micro-markets/free-google-gmail-the-high-price-you-pay/428

Children's Online Privacy Protection Act, Pub. L. 105-277, 15 U.S.C. 6501-6506 (2012).

Circumvention of copyright protecting systems, 17 U.S.C. Sec. 1201(a)(b).

Communications Electronic Privacy Act Amendments Act, H.R. 1847, 113th Cong. (2013).

Copyright Term Extension Act, Pub. L. No. 105-298, 112 Stat. 2827 (1998).

Creative Commons (n.d.). Retrieved from http://www.creativecommons.org

Department of Homeland Security. (2012, Nov. 8). Privacy compliance review of the NOC publicly available social media monitoring and situated awareness initiative (Rep.) Retrieved from: http://www.dhs.gov

Design Technology Group, LLC d/b/a Bettie Page Clothing, 359 NLRB No. 96 (2013).

Doxing [Def. 1]. (2011, Dec. 29). Urban Dictionary. Retrieved from http://www.urbandictionary.com

Exclusive rights in copyright works, 17 U.S.C. Sec. 106.

Federal Bureau of Investigation. (2012, Jan. 19). FedBizOpps.gov (Request for Information: Social media application). Retrieved from http://www.fbo.gov

Federal Wiretap Act, 18 U.S.C. 2510-2522 (2012).

FISA Amendments of 2008, Pub. L. No. 110-261, 122 Stat. 2436, codified in relevant part at 50 U.S.C. Sec. 1885 (a)(4)(b).

Fraud and related activity in connection with computers, 18 U.S.C. Sec. 1030.

Gellman, B. & Poitras, L. (2013, June 6). U.S., British intelligence mining data from nine U.S. Internet companies in broad secret program. *The Washington Post*. Retrieved from: http://www.washingtonpost.com

Geolocational Privacy and Surveillance Act, H.R. 1312, 113th Cong. (2013).

Gold, P. (2006). Fair use and the First Amendment compromise control of copyright is stifling documentary-making and thwarting the aims of the First Amendment. *University of Baltimore Intellectual Property Law Journal*(15), 1.

Greenhouse, S. (2013, Jan. 21). Even if it enrages your boss, social net speech is protected. *The New York Times*. Retrieved from http://www.nytimes.com

Hispanics United of Buffalo, National Labor Relations Board Decision, 359 NLRB 037 (2012).

Ho, V. (2004, July 29). Cyberstalker enters guilty plea. Seattle Post Intelligencer, p. B1.

In the matter of Facebook, Inc., FTC File No. 0923184 (2012). Retrieved from: http://www.ftc.gov/opa/2012/08/facebook.shtm

In the matter of Google, Inc., FTC Docket No. C-4336 (2011). Retrieved from: http://www.ftc.gov/05/caselist/1023136/index.shtm

In re: Application of the Federal Bureau of Investigation for an order requiring the production of tangible things from Verizon Business Network, Inc., No. BR-13-109, U.S. FISA Court. Retrieved from: http://www.uscourts.gov/uscourts/courts/fisc/br13-09-primary-order.pdf

In re: Application of the U.S. for historical cell site data, 2013 U.S. App. LEXIS 15510 (2013).

In re: Does 1-10, 242 S.W.3d 805 (Tex. Ct. App. 2007).

In re: DoubleClick Inc. Privacy Litigation, 154 F.Supp.2d 497 (S.D.N.Y. 2001).

In re: Richard L. Baxter, 2001 U.S. Dist. LEXIS 26001 (W.D. La. 2001).

In re: Philadelphia Newspapers v. Vahon H. Gureghian, 11-3257, 2012 WL 3038578 (3rd Cir. 2012).

Importation or transportation of obscene matter, 18 U.S.C. 1462.

Interstate communications, 18 U.S.C. Sec. 875(c).

Kearn, R. (2013, July 26). Woman claims rapper's lie ruined her life. *Courthouse News Service*.

Kimbrough, A. (2012). Transformative use v. market impact: Why the fourth fair use factor should not be supplanted by transformative use as the most important element in fair use analysis. *Alabama Law Review, 60*, 625.

Kravets, D. (2012, July 10). Google, FTC near settlement on privacy. *Wall Street Journal*, p. A1.

Krishnamurthy, B. & Willis, C. (2009). On the leakage of personally identifiable information via online social networks (Rep.). *AT&T Labs & Worcester Polytechnic Institute*. Retrieved from: http://web.cs.wpi.edu/wcew/papers/wasn09.pdf

Lanham Act, Pub. L. No. 79-489, 15 U.S.C. Sec. 1114(1).

Lanham Act, Pub. L. No. 79-489, 15 U.S.C. Sec. 1125(a).

Lanham Act, Pub. L. No. 79-489, 15 U.S.C. Sec. 1125(c).

La. Code of Civ. Proc. Art. 971.

La. Code of Civ. Proc. Art. 2542 (2012).

La. R.S. 14:40.3.

La. R.S. 14:47 (2013).

La. R.S. 14:73.10 (2013).

La. R.S. 14:91.5 (2013).

La. R.S. 15:542.1 (D) (1) (2013).

Limitations on exclusive rights: Fair use, 17 U.S.C. Sec. 107.

Limitations on liability relating to material online, 17 U.S.C. Sec. 512(f).

Mailing obscene or crime-inciting matter, 18 U.S.C. Sec. 1461.

Michels, S. (2008, Dec. 2). Craigslist rant ends in rare criminal charges. *ABC News*. Retrieved from: http://abcnews.go.com

MLRC actions against online speech (n.d.). *Media Law Resource Center*. Retrieved Oct. 25, 2013, from http://mlrcblogsuits.blogspot.com

Muhl, C. (2001, January). The employment at-will doctrine: Three major exceptions. *Monthly Labor Review*. Retrieved from: http://www.bls.gov/opub/mlr/2001/01/art-1full.pdf

New York Party Shuttle, LLC, 359 NLRB No. 112 (2013).

Obscene or harassing telephone calls in the District of Columbia or in interstate or foreign communications, 47 U.S.C. Sec. 223(a)(1)(c).

Obscene visual representations of the sexual abuse of children, 18 U.S.C. Sec. 1466A.

Packard, A. R. (2012). *Digital Media Law* (2nd Ed.). West Sussex, UK: John Wiley & Sons.

Padgett, E. (2010, June 22). *Los Angeles Times* suspends Presstime blogger [Web log post]. Retrieved from: http://edpadgett.blogspot.com/2010/66/los-angeles-times-suspends-pressman.html

PRISM Collection Manager 535333 (2003, April). PRISM/US-984 XV overview on The SIGAD used most in NSA reporting overview [PowerPoint slides 1-11]. Reprinted in *The Guardian*, NSA file, part 3. Retrieved from http://www.theguardian.com

Production and transportation of obscene matters for sale or distribution, 18 U.S.C. 1465.

Recognition of foreign defamation judgments, 28 U.S.C. 4102 (2012).

Right of employees as to organization, collective bargaining, etc., 29 U.S.C. Sec. 157.

Rusle, D. (2013, Aug. 14). Google: Don't expect privacy when sending to Gmail. *The Guardian*. Retrieved from: http://www.theguardian.com/technology/2013/aug/14/google-gmail-users-privacy-email-lawsuit

Savage, C. (2013, Aug. 8). Broader sifting of message done by N.S.A. is seen. *The New York Times*, p. A1.

Section 230 of the Communications Decency Act, 47 U.S.C. 230.

Semuels, A. (2009, Feb. 9). Dalai Lama impostor escorted from Twitter. *The Los Angeles Times*. Retrieved from: http://latimesblogs.latimes.com/technology/2009/02/twitter-dalai-l.html

Sharp, J. (2002). Coming soon to pay-per-view: How the Digital Millennium Copyright Act enables digital content owners to circumvent educational fair use. *American Business Law Journal*, 40, 1.

Springer, D. (2011, Dec. 12). A $2.5 million libel judgment brings the question: Are bloggers journalists? *Fox.com*. Retrieved from: http://www.foxnews.com/us/2011/12/22/bloggers-not-journalists

Stalking, 18 U.S.C. Sec. 2261A (2012).

Stored Communications Act, 18 U.S.C. Secs. 2701-11 (2012).

Subject matter in copyright, 17 U.S.C. Sec. 102(a).

Tate, R. (2011, May 11). How Google spies on your Gmail account and how to stop it. *Gawker*. Retrieved from http://www.gawker.com/5800868

Unlawful access to stored communication, 18 U.S.C. Sec. 2701 (a)(1).

U.S. Const. Amend. XIV.

CASES CITED

Abdul-Jabbar v. General Motors, 75 F.3d 1391 (9th Cir. 1996).
ACLU v. Ashcroft, 322 F.3d 240 (3rd Cir. Pa. 2003).
Allied Marketing Group, Inc. v. CBL Marketing, Inc., 878 F.2d 806 (5th Cir. 1989).
Bates v. City of Little Rock, 316 U.S. 516 (1960).
Baxter v. Scott, 2003 La. App. LEXIS 2080 (La. App.2 Cir. 2003).
Baxter v. Scott, 2003 La. LEXIS 3240 (La. 2003).
Beussink v. Woodland R-IV School District, 30 F.Supp.2d 1175 (E.D. Mo. 1998).
Bland v. Roberts, No. 12-1671 (4th Cir. 2013).
Board of County Commissioners, Wabaunsee County v. Umbehr, 518 U.S. 668 (1995).
Bock v. Scheff, 991 So. 2d 1043 (Fla. 4th Dist. 2008).
Bonhomme v. St. James, 970 N.E.2d 1, 2012 IL 112393 (2012).
Branti v. Finkel, 445 U.S. 507 (1980).
Bridgeport Music, Inc. v. Dimension Films, 410 F.3d 792 (6th Cir. 2005).
Bridgeport Music, Inc. v. UMG Recordings, Inc., 585 F.3d 267 (6th Cir. 2009).
Brown v. Entertainment Merchants Association, 131 S.Ct. 2729 (2011).
CBC Distribution & Marketing, Inc. v. Major League Baseball Advanced Media, L.P., 505 F.3d 818 (8th Cir. 2007).
Calder v. Jones, 465 U.S. 763 (1984).
Campbell v. Acuff-Rose Music, Inc., 510 U.S. 569 (1994).
Carson v. Here's Johnny Portable Toilets, 698 F.2d 831 (6th Cir. 1983).
Clemens v. McNamee, 615 F.3d 774 (5th Cir. 2010).
College Network, Inc. v. Moore Educational Publishers, Inc., 2012 WL 1923763 (5th Cir. 2010).
Comedy III Productions, Inc. v. Gary Saberus, Inc., 25 Cal.4th 387 (2001).
Complaint, Gordon & Holmes v. Love, No. BC-462438 (Cal. Super. Ct. 2011).

Complaint, Simorangkir v. Love, No. BC-521565 (Cal. Super. Ct. 2013).
Conference Archives, Inc. v. Sound Images, Inc., Civ. No. 3: 2006-76, 2010 WL 1626072 (W.D. Pa. 2010).
Connick v. Myers, 461 U.S. 138 (1983).
Dendrite International v. Doe, 775 A.2d 756 (N.J. App.Div. 2001).
Doe v. Cahill, 884 A.2d 451 (Del. 2005).
Doe v. Jindal, 853 F.Supp.2d 596, 2012 U.S. Dist. LEXIS 19841 (M.D. La. 2012).
Doe v. MySpace, 528 F.3d 413 (5th Cir. 2008).
Doe v. Prosecutor, Marion County, No. 12-2512 (7th Cir. 2013).
Doe v. State of Nebraska, No. 8:09 CV 456 (D. Neb. 2012).
Doe v. TCI Cablevision, a/k/a Tony Twist v. TCI Cablevision, No. 5C 84856 (Mo. 2003).
Doninger v. Niehoff, 527 F.3d 41 (2nd Cir. 2008).
Elrod v. Burns, 427 U.S. 347 (1976).
Estavillo v. Sony Computer Entertainment, 2009 WL 3072887 (N.D. Cal. 2009).
Express Lien, Inc. v. National Association of Credit Management, Inc., Civ. No. 13-3323 (E.D. La. 2013).
Gertz v. Robert Welch, 418 U.S. 323 (1974).
Harrell v. Southern Oregon University, Civ. 08-3037-CL (D. Ore. 2009).
Harrell v. Southern Oregon University (9th Cir. 2012) [unpublished case].
Hart v. Electronic Arts, Inc., 809 F. Supp.2d 757 (D.N.J. 2011).
Hart v. Electronic Arts, Inc., 717 F.3d 141 (3rd Cir. 2013).
Jones v. Dirty World Entertainment Recordings, Civ. No. 09-219-WOB (E.D. Ky. 2013).
J.S. v. Bethlehem Area School District, 569 Pa. 638, 807 A.2d 847 (Pa. 2002).
J.S. v. Blue Mountain School District, 650 F.3d 205 (3rd Cir. 2011).
Katz v. United States, 389 U.S. 347 (1967).
Keeton v. Hustler Magazine, Inc., 465 U.S. 770 (1984).
Keller v. Electronic Arts, No. 10-15387 (9th Cir. 2013).
Kowalski v. Berkeley County Schools, 652 F.3d 565 (4th Cir. 2011).
Layshock v. Hermitage School District, 650 F.3d 205 (3rd Cir. 2011).
McIntyre v. Ohio Elections Commission, 514 U.S. 334 (1995).
Midler v. Ford Motor Co., 849 F.2d 460 (9th Cir. 1988).
Milkovich v. Lorain Journal Co., 497 U.S. 2 (1990).
New York Times v. Sullivan, 376 U.S. 254 (1964).
Newton v. Diamond, 388 F.3d 1189 (2003).
No Doubt v. Activision Publishing, Inc., 122 Cal. Rptr. 3d 397 (Cal. Ct. App. 2011).
Obsidian Finance Group, LLC v. Cox, 2011 WL 2745849 (D. Or. 2011).
Onassis v. Christian Dior, Inc., 472 N.Y.S.2d 254 (1984).
Orix Capital v. Super Future Equities, 3:06-CV-0271-B (N.D. Tex. 2009).
Parks v. LaFace Records, 329 F.3d 437 (6th Cir. 2003).
Pickering v. Board of Education, 391 U.S. 563 (1968).
Playboy Enterprises v. Frena, 839 F.Supp. 1552 (M.D. Fla. 1993).
Religious Technology Center v. Netcom, 907 F.Supp. 1361 (N.D. Cal. 1995).
Reno v. ACLU, 521 U.S. 844 (1997).
Richardson v. Becker, 337 Fed. Appx. 637 (9th Cir. 2009).
Rutan v. Republican Party, 497 U.S. 62 (1990).
Salyer v. Southern Poverty Law Center, Inc., 701 F.Supp. 912 (W.D. Ky. 2009).
Scheff v. Bock, No. CACE03022837 (Fla. Cir. Ct. 2006).
Snead v. Redland Aggregates Ltd., 998 F.2d 1325 (5th Cir. 1993).
Stratton Oakmont v. Prodigy Services, Inc., 1995 WL 323710 (N.Y. Sup. Ct. 1995).
Super Future Equities v. Wells Fargo, 553 F.Supp.2d 680, 2008 U.S. Dist. LEXIS 21501 (N.D. Tex. 2008).
Tatro v. University of Minnesota, 816 N.W.2d 509 (Minn. 2012).
Taylor v. NBC, No. BC 110922 (Cal. Super. Ct. 1994).
Tinker v. Des Moines Independent School District, 518 U.S. 668 (1969).

Trout Point Lodge, Ltd. v. Handshoe, 729 F.3d 481 (5th Cir. 2013).
United States v. Bagdasarian, 652 F.3d 1113 (9th Cir. 2011).
United States v. Drew, Crim. No. 08-00582 (C.D. Cal. 2008).
United States v. Finley, 477 F.3d 250 (5th Cir. 2007).
United States v. Grob, 625 F.3d 2009 (9th Cir. 2009).
United States v. Jeffries, 10-CR-100 (E.D. Tenn. 2010).
United States v. Jones, 132 S.Ct. 945 (2012).
United States v. Morales, 272 F.3d 284 (5th Cir. 2009).
United States v. National Treasury Employees Union, 513 U.S. 454 (1995).
United States v. O'Dwyer, 2011 WL 4448739 (C.A.5. La. 2011).
United States v. O'Dwyer, 443 Fed. Appx. 18 (5th Cir. 2011).
United States v. Warshak, 631 F.3d 266 (6th Cir. 2010).
Virginia v. Black, 538 U.S. 343 (2003).
Watts v. United States, 394 U.S. 705 (1969).

Glossary

Acquittal: Legally binding conclusion to a trial indicating that the accused person(s) is not guilty of the charges set against them.

Actual Damages: Civil trial award of monetary compensation designed to remedy losses suffered by the plaintiff; also referred to as *compensatory damages*.

Actual Malice: Standard of fault used in certain libel trials showing defamatory statements were made with knowledge of their falseness or with reckless disregard for the truth.

Administrative Law: Judicial code that derives its authority from the regulations set forth by executive agencies of government.

Admonition Order: from judge to trial participants, especially jury members to avoid exposure to media coverage of litigation, or personal discussions, until case has been deliberated and decided.

Affidavit: Written document where the signer swears under oath before a notary or other public official that the statements in the document are true. A declaration under penalty of perjury not requiring any oath before a notary also can be the equivalent of an affidavit.

Answer: Written response from the defendant in a complaint addressing each issue in a civil lawsuit. This pleading can either admit or deny separate claims in the civil action, or be stated as a general denial to all of the pending allegations.

Amicus Curiae: Latin for a "friend of the court" used in reference to briefs, opinions, or other records submitted from third parties not directly involved in a lawsuit, but who wish to comment on a matter of law, usually at the appellate level.

Appeal Petition: to a court for judicial review of a lower court's decision based on the belief that there was a procedural or substantive error in a matter of law.

Appellant: First one named in a dispute (eg. Black in Black v. White) indicating the losing party appealing to a higher court in order to reverse a lower court's decision.

Appellate Court: Judicial body holding jurisdiction over lower court's rulings and authorized to review those decisions and take further action.

Appellee; Second party named in an appellate case (eg. White in Black v. White) indicating the one seeking to affirm the lower's court decision. Appellee usually submits the responsive brief challenging the arguments and claims advanced by the appellant's brief.

Arraignment: Court hearing where formal charges are read against a criminal defendant and the defendant is asked to enter a plea.

Arrest: Apprehension and restraint of a suspect by a law enforcement agent in connection with a crime or other offense that may be based on a court-ordered warrant, an indictment, or suspicious activity.

Assault: Real or threatened act of force or violence inflicted upon a person against their will. In criminal terms, it relates to battery that involves physical contact, however, assault can also mean in legal terms a communicated threat of violence that holds civil liability.

Bar: Multi-definitional term that applies either to the legal profession, the examination required for admission to the professional practice of law, or the physical division in the courtroom separating the public's seating area and the working space for the jury, judge and attorneys to present arguments and examine evidence.

Beyond a Reasonable Doubt: Standard of evidence in criminal trials that requires the state to prove guilt to the extent that the juror cannot harbor serious and substantive disbelief that the accused was guilty of the crimes charged against him or her. The standard of belief for criminal conviction is less than absolute certainty but greater than probably guilty.

Bill Ignoramus: When a grand jury does not find enough evidence to charge a crime, it returns a no bill, or bill ignoramus, instead of a true bill.

Bill of Particulars: Written statement of charges or claims by either the plaintiff in civil complaint or prosecutor in a criminal case that details the nature and grounds of the offense. No longer required by most states that use the discovery phase for those findings.

Bill of Rights: First ten amendments to the U.S. Constitution offered to protect individual freedoms and state rights from federal usurpation. Considered by some historians to be a political necessity in order to ensure the charter's full acceptance throughout the nation.

Breach of Contract: Failure of a party to perform services or supply goods according to the terms of a contract that gives rise to a lawsuit seeking the reward of damages resulting from a broken agreement.

Brief: Legal document submitted by attorneys in a dispute that form the basis of their arguments for why their side should prevail in the case; briefs include those arguments filed at pre-trial, trial, appellate, and merit briefs among others.

Burden of Proof: Legal requirement of the measure of evidence necessary for a party to meet in order to resolve a legal matter in dispute.

Cause of Action: Statement of the offense alleged in a complaint based on the facts and legal grounds that justify the lawsuit to obtain damages or enforcement of particular rights.

Capitalism: Economic system based on rights of individual ownership including rights to buy, to sell, or to otherwise dispose of personal property.

Certiorari (or Cert): Writ of a higher court to a lower court to send all case documents so that the higher court can review the lower court's decision. Taken from Latin term meaning to be fully informed. The U.S. Supreme Court grants certiorari to decide what cases are ready for hearing.

Challenge for Cause: Attorney's right to object to the seating of a potential juror for reasons such as prejudice, prior knowledge, or other connections to the case that would prevent them rendering an impartial opinion.

Glossary

Complaint: Legal document that sets out the facts and reasons a plaintiff is seeking either damages or equitable action by the court as a remedy for the cause of action.

Circuit Court: Judicial bench overseeing a particular region or district that has mobile capacity for maintaining judicial sessions at different locations during set periods of time.

Civil Code: Collection of statutes and laws concerning torts and claims of liability.

Civil Law: System of legal principles that prefers codification of articles as primary source of law, and considers common law based on landmark precedents to be secondary to statutory law, and the code's judicial interpretation.

Civil Suit: Action involved in petition for monetary damages as the result of a personal wrong or injury. It differs from criminal actions of law enforcement that seek justice for crimes against society.

Class Action: Lawsuit where a group sue together as plaintiffs in claims for damages.

Common Law: Traditional judge-made law dating back to ancient Britain, based on case rulings and customs that were compiled in commentaries on the law.

Compulsory Licensing: A statutory arrangement under which permission is not required before using someone else's intellectual property, provided that a fee is paid.

Concurring Opinion: When justices agree with the result reached by the majority, but they think the majority's rationale is wrong, the justice may author a concurrence which agrees with the result but offers a different rationale.

Contempt of Court: Citations issued for the purposes of either preventing undesirable behavior in court (direct contempt), such as acts of defiance to a judge's orders, or to encourage a positive response from witnesses (indirect contempt), such as a contempt citation issued to journalists in order to compel them to reveal their confidential sources or other secret items of information.

Continuance: Postponement of legal proceedings until a later date.

Contract: Agreement of a party to perform services or supply goods based on consideration and acceptance of terms. Breach of contract can give rise to a civil lawsuit seeking a reward of damages resulting from the broken agreement.

Contract of Silence: An agreement where one party agrees not to disclose certain items of information about another party.

Conditional Acceptance: Qualified receipt of a contractual offer that relies upon further stipulations or changes in terms of the original offer.

Counter-offer: Conditional response to an offer that changes the terms of the original offer, and therefore requires a new acceptance.

Consideration: Exchange of a thing or service of value to the mutual satisfaction of both parties involved in a contract. Money, goods, or services are typical forms of consideration.

Copyright: Exclusive rights granted to the author of a creative work such as book, movie, song, painting, photograph, design, computer software, or architecture.

Corroborating Evidence: Legally acceptable confirmation of a legal proposition in proof that supports the claim offered in initial evidence directed toward a finding favoring one party in a case: defendant, plaintiff, or prosecution.

Court of Record: Trial court that records all proceedings, which serves as the written record of the trial and can be used as the basis for an appeal to a higher court by either party.

Crime: An act or offense thought serious enough to cause harm not just to individuals, but also to society at large, and is therefore subject to punishment by fine and/or imprisonment.

Criminal Law: Body of law that defines and prohibits activities deemed to be a threat to the community at large, and therefore requires punishment by the state.

Culpability: Extent to which a person should be held legally accountable for a particular tort or criminal offense.

Cyberstalking: Harassment or pursuit of a person on the Internet often by means of social media.

Damages: Monetary compensation a person receives for injury to their property or rights because of the willful act or negligence of another.

De Novo: From the Latin phrase to mean to begin anew and refers to issues or cases that are decided again without regard to the prior holdings or conclusions.

Declaratory Judgment: Court decision that usually comes preceding a trial that is used to determine the rights of parties in dispute without ordering any further action be taken such as the awarding of damages.

Defamation: Intentional false communication, either written or spoken, that harms a person's reputation; lowers their social esteem and public regard, which can deny them friendly relations and engenders hostility and disagreeable contacts.

Defendant: Person who is subject of either a legal or civil action. The accused in a criminal legal proceeding, or responding party in a civil proceeding initiated by complaint; defendant must answer the charges in criminal court or the plaintiff's complaint in civil cases.

De facto: Latin phrase meaning in fact, but is used to indicate a condition that is accepted for practical purposes even though it actually stands in variance with the law.

De Minimis: Latin phrase indicating that it is a small matter, and therefore the law will not consider it because it is of minimal importance.

Demurrer: A motion that challenges the legal sufficiency of a claim set forth in a filing by an opposing party.

De Novo: Latin term meaning "from the beginning," which is used when the appellate court reviews a non-jury trial record. It may conduct a review de novo, or call for a trial de novo if there are errors in the judge's findings of fact, as well as matters of law.

Derivative Work: In copyright, a new creative work based upon an existing work, such as a translation of a book, or a movie based from a novel.

Deposition: Sworn witness accounts and oral testimony that is transcribed outside the courtroom for inclusion in the trial record before the case comes to trial.

Dicta: Judicial assertions found in appellate court rulings that serve as either individual pronouncements or arguable conclusions but do not serve as binding principles of law.

Discovery: Pre-trial procedure in civil lawsuits that serve as the means to obtain evidence from the opposing side, including witness depositions, public records and documents, and the answers to interrogatories.

Dissent: Written opinion following the judgment of a case from one or more judges that stands in disagreement with the position taken by the majority opinion.

Docket: Schedule of proceedings in a pending lawsuit, or reference to an agenda of trials pending in a court of law.

Double Jeopardy: Prohibited action of putting someone on trial a second time for an offense for which he/she has been acquitted by an earlier court judgment.

En banc: French for "in the bench," meaning judicial consideration by a full court of magistrates overseeing a jurisdiction where more than three judges have been seated.

Enjoin: Court order to either take action or cease some activity; usually a hearing is held but prior the presentation of evidence and arguments, the judge may grant a temporary restraining order before deciding whether or not to grant a writ of injunction. The object of an injunction is often to prevent harm from occurring to one or more individuals.

Equity Law: A court-ordered remedy that requires disputing parties to either perform, or refrain from, certain actions rather than requiring the payment of damages. Modern U.S. courts exercise both equitable remedies and decisions based on black letter law.

Evidentiary Hearing: Legal proceeding where evidence is reviewed and judgment is made whether to admit it into trial or suppress it; sometimes called suppression hearing.

Execute: Legal act of completing or performing as required by law the obligations under a court order or contract.

Exhibit: Item of evidence brought to trial for inspection by jury and other parties. May be a record, photograph, contract or other document needed as proof.

Exoneration: Act or expression removing all guilt or responsibility from the accused person.

Fair Comment: A traditional defense in libel or slander suits dating back to the common law.

Fair Use: Legal limitation for others to use copyrighted materials without the owner's consent and excuses unauthorized uses of a work especially for a transformative purpose such as research, scholarship, parody, criticism, or journalism.

False Light: Privacy claim stemming from a publication or graphic communication that contains elements of fact but somehow distorts or exaggerates the truth and to an offensive degree. Liability requires a showing of actual malice – knowledge of falsity or reckless disregard for the truth.

Felony: Serious crimes such as rape or murder that carry heavier penalties than misdemeanors, including incarceration.

Fiduciary: Legal relationship based on a financial trust between two or more people. Also used to describe a person who has financial responsibility for another's monetary assets.

Fine: Amount of money prescribed as the punishment for violating a law or defying legal authority.

Fraud: Intentional misrepresentation of facts or deceit used to deny someone their lawful rights or their use of property or money.

Freedom of Contract: The freedom of groups and individuals to form contracts without interference from the government.

Gag Order: Colloquial term used to describe a judge's order that restrains or forbids trial participants from speaking with news media of and concerning pending litigation.

Grand Jury: Group of citizens empanelled to hear testimony and evidence regarding alleged crimes in order to determine if charges should be brought against particular individual(s).

Habeus Corpus: Latin term meaning you have the body, and commands a law enforcement officer or government official to bring a prisoner forward so that the court can determine if the person's custody is legal or not, and if that individual should be released.

Harmless Error: Mistake made during a trial that is not serious or substantive enough to reverse or modify the original verdict. Discrepancies that either have no bearing on the result, or were somehow corrected prior to the trial verdict would be considered as such.

Hold Harmless Clause: Provision in a contract where one party agrees not to hold the other party responsible for any damages. This is a unilateral indemnification of one party by another, but it can be reciprocal among multiple parties.

Implied Consent: Form of approval that is not evident in explicit statements, but is inferred from other actions or agreements.

Implied Acceptance: Receipt of an offer that is evident by individual context rather than an explicit statement of recipient to the offer.

In Camera: Latin term meaning in chambers used to describe a hearing held before the judge away from the courtroom in a private office to the exclusion of witnesses or jurors.

Incarceration: Court-imposed confinement in a jail or prison.

Incorporeal: Without tangible existence but used for the purposes of property rights and financial liability.

Glossary

Indict: Formal charges brought against an individual suspected of a crime; often handed down by grand jury.

Infringement: Violation or breach of a legal right, contract, or statute, or unauthorized use of a patent, copyright, or trademark.

Indemnify: Agreement to compensate a party for any loss or damage that occurs through the execution of a contractual agreement.

Information: Formal criminal charge that a state prosecutor issues directly to a defendant rather than seeking a grand jury indictment.

Injunctive Relief: Legal form of remedy in equity law that enjoins parties from acting and commands the cessation of a certain activity.

Instruction: Rules given to the jury to serve the administration of impartial justice that directs their deliberations on how to correctly apply the law to a given set of facts.

Intent: An attitudinal state deemed necessary to hold an individual accountable for a crime; once a person foresees and desires to cause a certain unlawful act to occur and then proceeds with the necessary activity to facilitate it, criminal intent is established.

Interlocutory: Temporary or provisional ruling that addresses a question considered to be a subordinate issue, and which does not serve to resolve a larger legal dispute.

Intervention: Court procedure to allow an outside party referred to as an intervener to participate in ongoing litigation in order to represent interests that are affected directly or indirectly by the outcome; intervention provides the legal right to be heard.

Intrusion: Privacy claim in which the plaintiff's private affairs, concerns or personal space used for solitude or seclusion has been subjected to unwanted invasion or inspection.

Judgment: Closing resolution to a court case that decides which side prevails and what will be the remedies assessed in terms of damages and other forms of relief, such as an injunction.

Judicial Review: Doctrine under which the judiciary is the final interpreter of the constitutionality of executive and legislative actions and laws. First established in Marbury v. Madison (1803).

Jurisdiction: Oversight or control of a legal issue bounded by subject matter or location.

Jurisprudence: State of judicial norms and practices, including the study of law and legal issues based on Latin term, juris prudentia, suggesting legal philosophy.

Jurisprudence Constante: Civilian law doctrine that differs from stare decisis that looks to single landmark rulings for precedent-setting guidance. This doctrine instead asks the court to look for a series of repeated decisions to establish a particular rule of law.
Jury (grand and petit) Two types of juries empanelled in criminal law. The grand jury decides whether or not to indict or charge an individual with a crime, while the petit jury is assigned the task of determining the defendant's guilt following a trial.

Landmark Ruling: Opinion handed down by an appellate court that establishes a principle binding future judicial decisions dealing with the same or similar issues.

Liability: Being or potentially being subject to legal obligation.

Libel: Cause of action under tort law designed to remediate false and harmful expressions offending a person's reputation that is deserving of an award of damages. If it is an obvious libel, it is called libel per se, but if it injures by implication, it is libel per quod.

Limited Liability Entity: Legal structure that blends elements of the partnership and corporation structures while providing limited liability to its owners.

Limitations, Statute: Law that establishes the maximum period a person has from the date of a supposed offense that they have to file a lawsuit. In criminal law, it is the time period that prosecutors have to charge a person with a crime starting at the date of the alleged act.

Magistrate: Generic term to define any judicial officer, although often used to describe justices of the peace or police judges who serve in inferior courts below the district level.

Mandamus, writ of: Court order for a public agency or governmental body to perform an act required by law, which it has neglected or refused to do.

Mens rea: Latin term suggesting a purposeful or intentional attitude; used to indicate the state of mind of a defendant suspected of performing a harmful act or expression. Extracted from the Latin phrase, actus reus non facit reum nisi men's sit rea, which means the person who

Miranda Rule: Arresting officer's duty to inform suspect at the point of arrest of their legal rights prior to interrogation as established the 1966 landmark case of Miranda v. Arizona.

Misdemeanor: Criminal offense considered less serious than a felony and therefore is to be punished by a fine, service activity, or in some cases jail time, but not in a state prison.

Mistrial: Court case brought to a conclusion without a verdict or final disposition, often for reasons of a deadlocked jury, or for improper conduct by participants in the case.

Mitigating Circumstances: Evidence that establishes a defendant's wrongful actions or words although still considered legally an offense were motivated by reasons that would lessen their level of culpability or guilt.

Moot: A dispute or issue no longer posing any unsettled question or debate; hypothetical or theoretical in purpose without real substance.

Morals Clause: Provision in a contract that prohibits specific behavior or expression engaged in the private life of one of the contractual parties.

Motion to Dismiss: Request by a participant in a trial to dismiss the case for a variety of reasons including failure to state a valid claim or a lack of jurisdiction in the matter.

Motion to Quash: Official request by a participant involved in a legal dispute to set aside or nullify an action such as a summons or an indictment for legal reasons, such as a failure to follow due process.

Glossary

Negligence: Breach of a duty that results in reasonably foreseeable harm.

Nolo Contendere: Latin term for "I will not contest," which is used in a criminal proceedings as the defendant's pleading that he or she claims neither guilt nor innocence.

Non-Compete Clause: Provision in a contract that prevents a person or company from competing in a market, often an employee who has learned trade secrets or adopted useful skills after employment terminates that would give the competing entity an advantage.

Objection: Formal protest by an attorney who asks that the judge prohibit an opposing lawyer's question, witness' answer, or evidence from admission into the record. The judge can sustain (accept) the objection; overrule (deny) it, or ask for grounds of the objection.

Parole: Early and conditional release of a prisoner prior to the completion of the sentence. Derived from French term for spoken word meaning the inmate agrees to comply with the terms of the parole supervision for the remainder of the sentence.

Per Curiam: A decision rendered with an opinion, but not signed; a type of ruling is "by the Court" as a whole.

Peremptory Challenge: A challenge to a potential juror during the voire dire that is given without cause. Rival attorneys are usually given one or more "strikes" without having to specify the reason(s) for striking their names.

Plagiarism: Attempt to present someone else's original expression or creative ideas as one's own.

Plaintiff: Party filing a civil complaint that seeks either to resolve an issue or recover damages for the harm done by a defendant.

Pleadings: First stage in a civil lawsuit in which formal documents are submitted to the court containing the disputed claims and defenses from the opposing sides.

Precedent: Decision serving as the authority for subsequent cases in a specific area of law.

Preponderance of Evidence: Standard of proof required in civil cases that is a lesser requirement than the criminal standard of beyond a reasonable doubt.

Presumptive Right of Access: Legal premise of openness in criminal trials including pretrial hearings that holds they are presumptively open to the public based on the ruling in Richmond Newspapers, In. v. Virginia (1980): "presumption of openness inheres in the very nature of a criminal trial under our system of justice."

Preliminary Hearing: Judicial hearing prior to a trial to determine if there is sufficient evidence to prosecute an individual who was not subject to a grand jury indictment, but is subject to the prosecutor's evidence and criminal charges.

Presumption of Innocence: Principle of law emphasizing the burden of proof is not to be placed on the accused but on the accuser who must show guilt beyond a reasonable doubt.

Prima Facie Case: First appearance indicating that a wrong has occurred and is observable; used in civil cases to show that sufficient proof has been established to support the claim of tortuous harm.

Privilege: A benefit, immunity, or exemption extended to specific persons or people based on their circumstance under law. In journalism, personal immunity from being forced to reveal confidential sources is protected by shield laws.

Prior Restraint: An act of censorship that occurs when the state or governing body is able to stop communication before it happens as opposed to punishing a communicator afterward.

Pro forma: Latin term for "as a matter of form" used in reference to court rulings merely intended to facilitate the legal process.

Promissory Estoppel: Implicit agreement that is recognized by the court as a promise from one party to another that was relied upon by the receiving party to their detriment and requires no written agreement. See § 90 The Restatement (Second) of Contracts.

Probable Cause: Constitutional requirement that law enforcement officers have a valid reason above mere suspicion before making an arrest, searching private property, or seizing items in the context of a criminal investigation.

Probate: Legal document and process to administer the estate of someone who has died and holds property that is subject to claims by debtors and/or heirs.

Probation: Alternative punishment to incarceration where a person convicted of a crime is released from serving time in prison, but remains under some form of legal supervision.

Prurient Interest: Shameful or morbid interest in sexual activities, expressions, or imagery as opposed to a healthy desire or attraction. Taken from the Latin term prurio, which means an itching sensation.

Punitive Damages: Compensation awarded in a lawsuit designed to set an example

Remand: Action taken by a higher appellate court that chooses to send back, or remand, a case to a lower court for subsequent action.

Respondent: The responding party in a legal proceeding, particularly in appellate proceedings or proceedings initiated by petition.

Respond eat: Superior Common-law principle holding an employer accountable for damage done by their employees if the offense occurred within the scope of their employment.

Reversible Error: Discrepancy in the trial's procedures or substance that sufficiently invalidates the decision that an appellate court finds it necessary to call for a reversal.

Scienter: From Latin term for "having knowledge," used in the legal sense to indicate the guilty knowledge that an individual possesses by knowing their activity is unlawful.

Search Warrant: Court order requiring a lawful search by officers of a location, person or vehicle for the collection of evidence suspected of use in the commission of a crime.

Not used for the collection of evidence in a civil complaint.

Seditious Libel: Written expressions, signs, symbols or utterances intended to challenge or overthrow the government, its policies, and/or office holders; advocacy of the overthrow of government by force that potentially incites citizens to take violent action.

Sentence: Punishment handed down in response to the conviction of a crime that can consist of both a monetary fine and time in jail or prison.

Sequestration: The process of keeping jurors secluded so that information pertinent to the trial is not shared with others outside of court.

Shield Laws: Acts adopted by a majority of the United States that afford privilege to journalists who wish to withhold information including the names of confidential sources along with particular notes or other records obtained during newsgathering activities.

Slander: False and defamatory message usually offered through verbal communication that harms an individual's reputation and social relations.

Soliciting: Generally refers to either offering or attempting to purchase goods or services.

Stare Decisis: Latin term meaning to let the decision stand, which is the common law policy of abiding by the legal principles established by a precedent-setting ruling preceding the present case.

Statute or Statutory Law: Enactments that are created as rules by a legislative body as distinguished from common or judge-made law.

Statutory Damages: Predetermined payments established by law to compensate for certain injuries and liabilities.

Stay: Court order calling for the suspension of a judicial proceeding or action. In federal law a stay of execution is required for ten days after a verdict is reached in civil trial. The judge issues a stay either by request or stay sua ponte based on his or her judgment.

Strict Liability: Legal presumption of fault assigned to the defendant in a civil lawsuit without any required showing of negligence or intent.

Strict Scrutiny: Highest standard of judicial review used to scrutinize a law that may be in conflict with constitutional rights. Requires the government to demonstrate a compelling obligation to enforce the rule, and how that it regulates no more speech than is absolutely necessary to achieve that specific end.

Subpoena Writ: issued by a court or governmental agency requiring the testimony of a witness or submission of evidence subject to punishment for failure to comply.

Substantive Law: Codified record of written offenses covering criminal acts and corresponding penalties, in addition to personal obligations and liabilities in civil law.

Summary Judgment: Court ruling in response to a motion that contends all necessary factual issues are accepted and the outcome can be determined without further trial.

Summons: Document served on an individual either to announce that a legal action has been initiated against that person, or their name has been included in a proceeding either as a participant or as a witness in a legal dispute.

Tort: French term meaning a broken or wrongful act, intentional or accidental, causing injury to occur to another; it gives rise to a legal complaint seeking recovery of damages in compensation.

True Bill: Criminal indictment rendered in writing by a grand jury following the prosecution's presentation of evidence that indicates it has heard sufficient evidence and considers it likely the person of interest should be brought to trial for the commission of a crime.

Venue, Change of: Court-ordered relocation of a trial usually to avoid prejudicial publicity.

Venire, Change of: Court order to bring prospective jurors in from a distant location holding no prior knowledge of the case to weigh evidence in a trial.

Verdict: Decision reached by a court or jury at trial following the presentation of evidence and arguments addressing questions of guilt or liability in connection with crimes or torts. In jury trials, the verdict is reported to the presiding judge who can accept it or set it aside.
Voir Dire Pre-trial process used for jury selection, from French term meaning to see to speak.

Waiver: Voluntary decision to relinquish or surrender a legal right or privilege.

Warrant: Writ issued by a court to be executed by a law enforcement officer usually for the purpose of searching and seizing articles of evidence or the arrest of suspects in connection with a crime.
Writ Written order by a judge requiring legal action from the party to whom the writ is directed.

Index of Court Cases

44 Liquormart, Inc., v. Rhode Island (1996), 32

Abdul Jabbar v. General Motors (1996), 255
Abington Township v. Schempp (1963), 48-49, 59
Abrams v. U.S. (1926), 26
ACLU v. Ashcroft (2003), 244
Adamson-James v. Florida (2013), 223
Adderly v. Florida (1966), 34
Airport Commissioners v. Jews for Jesus (1987), 35
Allen v. Thompson Newspapers (2005), 66
Allied Marketing Group, Inc. v. CDL Marketing, Inc. (1989), 254
Ardoin v. Hartford (1980), 14

Bad Frog Brewery, Inc. v. New York State Liquor Authority (1998), 219
Bates v. City of Little Rock, 248
Baxter v. Scott (2003), 245
Bethel v. Fraser, 112
Beussink v. Woodland R-IV School District (1998), 242
Bigelow v. Virginia (1975), 217
Bivens v. Albuquerque Schools (1995), 115
Bland v. Roberts (2013), 242
Board of Airport Commissioners v. Jews for Jesus (1982), 47
Board of County Commissioners, Wabaunsee County v. Umbehr (1996), 242
Board of Supervisors of La. State Univ. v. Lewark (1973), 117
Bock v. Scheff (2008), 246
Bolger v. Youngs Drug Products Corp. (1983), 219
Bolton v. City of Dallas (2006), 223
Bonhomme v. St. James, 249
Boone v. Reese Services, Inc. (2004), 63
Bowman v. Parma Board of Education (1988), 228
Boy Scouts of America v. Dale (2000), 35
Brandenburg v. Ohio (1969), 33, 115
Branti v. Finkel (1980), 242
Branzburg v. Hayes (1972), 229
Bridgeport Music, Inc. v. Dimension Films (2005), 253
Bridgeport Music, Inc. v. UMG Recordings, Inc. (2009), 253
Brown v. Entertainment Merchants Association (2011), 33, 255-56
Brown v. Louisiana (1966), 34
Buck's Run Enterprises, Inc. v. Mapp Const., Inc. (2001), 229
Bujol v. Ward (2001), 65
Burnside v. Byars (1966), 114

Calder v. Jones (1984), 247
Campbell v. Acuff-Rose Music, 253
Camp, Dresser & McKee, Inc. v. Steimle and Associates (1995), 100
Canady v. Bossier Parish School Board (2001), 115

Cantwell v. Connecticut (1940), 30, 47
Capdeboscq v. Francis (2004), 95
Carr v. City of New Orleans (1993), 225
Carson v. Here's Johnny Portable Toilets (1983), 255
Catfish Cabin of Monroe, Inc., v. State Farm Fire and Cas. Co. (2002), 65
C.B.C. Distribution & Marketing, Inc. v. Major League Baseball AdCBS, 50
Central Hudson Gas & Electric Corporation v. Public Service Commission of New York (1980), 216, 218-219
Chaplinsky v. New Hampshire (1942), 33
Church of Lukumi Babalu Aye v. City of Hialeah (1993), 47
Ciecierski v. Avondale Shipyards, 80
Cintas Corp. v. NLRB (2007), 223
Citizens United v. Federal Election Commission (2010), 222
City of Boerne v. Flores (1997), 53
City of Ladue v. Gilleo (1994), 217
Clemens v. McNamee, 247
Cloutier v. Costco Wholesale Corp. (2004), 227
Cohen v. California (1971), 35
Cohen v. Cowles Media Co. (1991), 126, 227, 230, 234
College Network, Inc. v. Moore Educational Publishers, Inc. (2010), 254
Columbia Broadcasting System, Inc. v. Democratic Nat. Committee (1973), 229
Comedy III Productions v. Gary Saderup, 255
Communications Workers of America v. Ector County Hospital District (2006), 223
Conference Archives, Inc. v. Sound Images, Inc. (2010), 254
Connick v. Myers (1983), 223, 241
Corley v. Louisiana ex re. Division of Administration, Office of Risk Management (2011), 224
Costello v. Hardy (2004), 38, 65-66, 76, 99
County of Allegheny v. ACLU (1989), 51
Cox v. Louisiana (1965), 34, 105
Crawford v. U.S. Dept. of Homeland Security (2007), 224
Crookes v. Newton, 247
Cummings v. Washington Mut. (2011), 225
Curtis Publishing Co. v. Butts and Associated Press v. Walker (1967), 71

DeJonge v. Oregon (1937), 30
Delcarpio v. St. Tammany Parish School Board (1994), 232
Dixon v. Coburg Dairy, Inc. (2004), 226
Doerr v. Mobil Oil Corp (2000), 40
Doe v. Cahill, 249
Doe v. Jindal (2012), 244
Doe v. Michigan (1989), 117
Doe v. MySpace, 248
Doe v. Prosecutor (2013), 244
Doe v. State of Nebraska (2012), 244
Doe v. TCI Cablevision, a/k/a Tony Twist v. TCI Cablevision (2003), 255
Doninger v. Niehoff (2008), 242
Duke v. North Texas State University (1972), 223
Dun & Bradstreet, Inc. v. Greenmoss Builders, Inc., 74, 82

East Bank Consolidated Special Service Fire Protection Dist. v. Crossen (2004), 224, 225
Easter Seal Society for Crippled Children and Adults of Louisiana., Inc. v. Playboy Enterprises., Inc.

(1988), 99
Eastwood v. Superior Court (1983), 231
Economy Carpets Manufacturers and Distributors, Inc. v. Better Business Bureau of Baton Rouge Area, Inc. (1976), 232
Edenfield v. Fane (1993), 218-19
Edwards v. Aguillard (1987), 49
Edwards v. South Carolina (1963), 30
E.E.O.C. v. Sunbelt Rentals, Inc. (2008), 226
Elmer v. Coplin (1986), 75
Elrod v. Burns (1976), 242
Employment Division v. Smith (1990), 46, 52, 55
Engel v. Vitale (1962), 48
Epperson v. Arkansas (1968), 49
Erznoznil v. City of Jacksonville (1975), 221
Estavillo v. Sony Computer Entertainment (2009), 240
Everson v. Board of Education (1947), 30, 47
Express Lien, Inc. v. National Association of Credit Management, Inc. (2013), 254

Faculty Rights Coalition v. Shahrokhi (2006), 223
FCC v. Pacifica (1978), 35
Films, Inc. v. Dimension, 253
Finkelstein v. Barthelemy (1990), 36
Fitzgerald v. Tucker (1999), 67
Fluker Community Church v. Hitchens (1982), 55
Frisby v. Schultz (1988), 33, 221
Frudden v. Pilling (2014), 115

Gambino v. Fairfax, 111, 119
Garcetti v. Ceballos (2006), 35
Garner v. Louisiana (1961), 34
Garrison v. Louisiana (1964), 68, 71
Gertz v. Robert Welch, Inc. (1974), 33, 42, 72-73, 245
Gitlow v. New York (1925), 30
Gonzales v. O Centro Espirita Beneficente Uniao do Vegetal (2006), 52
Good News Club v. Milford Central School (2001), 33
Gordon & Holmes v. Love, 246
Gorman v. Swaggart, 64
Greater New Orleans Broadcasting v. U.S. (1999), 216
Green v. Chicago Tribune Co. (1996), 89
Greer v. Spock (1976), 34
Gregory v. Louisiana Board of Chiropractic Examiners (1992), 216
Gregory v. The Louisiana Board of Chiropractic Examiners (1992), 220
Gugliuzza v. K.C.M.C. (1992), 69
Guillory v. St. Landry Parish Police Jury (1986), 222
Gureghian, Philadelphia Newspapers v. Vahan H., 247

Hamilton v. Lumbermen's Mutual Casualty Co. (1955), 90-91
Harper and Row Publishers, Inc. v. Nation Enterprises (1985), 230
Harper v. Poway (2007), 113
Hart et al. v. Electronic Arts, Inc. (2013), 255-56
Hayes v. Muller (1963), 227

Hazelwood School District v. Kuhlmeier (1988), 35, 112-14, 118-19
Healy v. James, 111, 119
Henley v. Dillard Department Stores, 88
Hero Lands Co., Inc. v. Texaco, Inc. (1975), 232
Hicks v. Casablanca Records (1978), 231
Hosty v. Carter (2005), 114
Hustler Magazine, Inc. v. Falwell (1988), 232-33

ISKCON v. Lee (1992), 34

Jaubert v. Crowley Post-Signal, Inc. (1979), 39, 42, 90-92, 94-98, 102, 225, 236
Jenkins v. Louisiana State Board of Education (1975), 106
JetPay Merchant Services, LLC v. Tepoorten (2009), 228, 236
Johnson v. KTBS, 64
Johnson v. St. Paul Mercury Insurance Co. (1970), 15
Jones v. Chevalier (1991), 229
Jones v. Dirty World Entertainment Recordings, 249
Joseph v. U.S. Civil Service Commission (1977), 226
J. S. v. Bethlehem Area School District (2002), 242
J. S. v. Blue Mountain School District (2011), 242

Kadlec Medical Center v. Lakeview Anesthesia Associates (2008), 232-33
Kaiser Aetna v. U.S. (1979), 230
Karraker v. Rent-A-Center, Inc. (2005), 225
Kasky v. Nike, Inc. (2002), 216
Katz v. United States (1967), 98, 250
Keeton v. Hustler Magazine, 247
Keller v. Aymond (1998), 39
Keller v. Electronic Arts, Inc. (2013), 255-56
Kennedy v. Sheriff of East Baton Rouge (2006), 76
Kent v. Cobb (2002), 232
Kidder v. Anderson (1978), 72
Kincaid v. Gibson (2001), 114
King v. Phelps Dunbar, L.L.P. (1999), 232
Kohn v. Southwest Regional Council of Carpenters (2003), 231
Kowalski v. Berkeley County Schools (2011), 242

Lambert v. Dow Chemical Company (1968), 224
Lamb's Chapel v. Center Moriches Union Free School District (1993), 33
Lander v. Seaver (1859), 109
Landrum v. Board of Commissioners of the Orleans Levee Dist. (1996), 225
Lane v. Sabine Parish School Board, 50
Langford v. Lane (1991), 225
Layshock v. Hermitage School District (2011), 242
Lee v. Weisman (1992), 49
Lehman v. City of Shaker Heights (1974), 34
Lemon v. Kurtzman (1971), 48, 51
Lewis v. Liberty Industrial Life Ins. Co. (1936), 227
Lewis v. Meredith Corp. (2008), 232
Lloyd Corp. v. Tanner (1972), 231
Longview Outdoor Advertising Co., LLC v. City of Winter Garden, Fla. (2006), 217

Index

Lorillard Tobacco Co. v. Reilly (2001), 218
Louisiana Federation of Teachers v. State of Louisiana (2013), 57
Louisiana, Inc. v. Covenant Broadcasting Corporation of, 64
Louisiana Smokes Products, Inc. v. Savoie's Sausage and Food Products, Inc. (1997), 227
Love v. Southern Bell Telephone & Telegraph Co. (1972), 224
Ltd. v. Handshoe, 248
Lynch v. Donnelly (1984), 49

Marsh v. Chambers (1983), 52
Martin v. Markley, 66
Mashburn v. Collin, 64, 77
Matthews v. Military Dept. ex rel. State (2007), 224
McAndrews v. Roy, 92
McBeth v. United Press International, 64
McConathy v. Ungar (2000), 64
McCreary County v. ACLU (2005), 51-52, 59
McIntyre v. Ohio Elections Commission, 248
Metromedia, Inc. v. City of San Diego (1981), 216
Midler v. Ford Motor Co. (1988), 255
Milkovich v. Lorain Journal (1990), 77, 246, 261
Miller v. California (1973), 33, 176
Milliner v. Turner (1983), 111-12, 119
Minersville, Pa. v. Gobitis (1940), 109
Mix v. University of New Orleans (1992), 222
Moore v. Big Picture Co. (1987), 225
Moore v. Cabiniss, 92
Morse v. Frederick (2007), 113
Mulina v. Item Co., 64

Naihaus v. Louisiana Weekly Publishing Co., 64
National Aeronautics and Space Administration v. Nelson (2011), 225
National Ass'n of Mfrs. v. N.L.R.B. (2013), 221
NCH Corp. v. Broyles (1985), 228
Near v. Minnesota (1931), 29-30
Neuberger, Coerver & Goins v. The Times Picayune Pub. Co. (1992), 73
Newton v. Diamond, 253
New York Times v. Sullivan (1964), 29, 33, 68-69, 71, 73, 229-30, 232, 238, 245
New York Times v. U.S. (1971), 28-29
New York v. Ferber (1982), 33
N.L.R.B. v. Gissel Packing Co. (1969), 223
N.L.R.B. v. Magnavox Co. of Tennessee (1974), 222
No Doubt v. Activision Publishing, Inc. (2011), 255-56
Noyes v. Kelly Services (2007), 226

Obsidian Finance Group, LLC v. Cox (2011), 256, 261
Ohralik v. Ohio State Bar Association (1978), 218
Ollman v. Evans, 77
Onassis v. Christian Dior (1984), 255
Orix Capital v. Super Future Equities (2009), 245, 256

Papish v. Board of Curators, 111, 119

Parish Nat. Bank v. Lane, 92
Parish National Bank v. Lane (1981), 91
Parks v. LaFace Records (2003), 255
Passaic Daily News v. Blair (1973), 226
People v. Bush (1976), 231
Perere v. Louisiana Television Broadcasting Corp. (1988), 99
Petermann v. International Brotherhood of Teamsters, Chauffeurs, Warehousemen, and Helpers of America, Local 396 (1959), 222
Philadelphia Newspapers v. Hepps (1986), 73
Phillips v. Smalley Maintenance Services, Inc. (1983), 224, 225
Pickering v. Board of Education (1968), 223, 238, 241, 261
Porter v. Ascension Parish Sch. Bd. (2004), 116
Powell v. Yellow Book USA, Inc. (2006), 227
Prince v. Out Pub. Inc. (2002), 95
Prudhomme v. Procter & Gamble Co. (1992), 93
Public Citizen, Inc. v. Louisiana Attorney General Disciplinary Board (2011), 220
Puig v. Greater New Orleans Expressway Commission (2000), 224

Rankin v. McPherson (1987), 223
R. A. V. v. City of St. Paul (2003), 33
Religious Technology Center v. Netcom (1995), 256
Reno v. ACLU (1997), 35, 240, 244, 256
Renton v. Playtime Theatres (1986), 34
Reynolds v. U.S. (1878), 46
Richardson v. Beckon (2009), 241
Richmond Newspapers v. Virginia (1980), 35
Riley v. National Federation of the Blind of North Carolina, Inc. (1988), 216, 221, 227
Roberson v. Rochester Folding Box Co. (1902), 86
Robbins v. Pruneyard Shopping Center (1980), 36, 55
Roppolo v. Moore (1994), 54, 60
Rosenberger v. Rector and Visitors of the University of Virginia (1995), 33
Rosenblatt v. Baer (1966), 70
Rosenbloom v. Metromedia, Inc. (1971), 71
Roshto v. Hebert (1983), 92, 96-97
Rowan v. U.S. Post Office Dept. (1970), 221
Ruffin v. Wal-Mart Stores, Inc. (2002), 232
Rutan v. Republican Party (1990), 242

Salyer v. Southern Poverty Law Center Inc., 247
San Francisco Arts & Athletics, Inc. v. U.S. Olympic Committee (1987), 231
Santa Fe Independent School District v. Doe (2000), 27, 49
Sassone v. Elder (1993), 67
Scheff v. Bock (2006), 246, 256
SDT Industries, Inc. v. Leeper (2001), 220, 228
Sharrif v. American Broadcasting Co. (1993), 85, 99
Sherbert v. Verner (1963), 46-47
Simmons v. Mamou, 70
Simorangkir v. Love, 246
Simpson v. Perry (2004), 98
Singletary v. Fridley (2000), 225
Slocum v. Sears Roebuck & Co. (1989), 91, 103

Index

Smith v. Arkansas Louisiana Gas Co. (1994), 99
Smith v. Superior Court (1996), 228
Snead v. Redland Aggregates Ltd. (1993), 245
Snepp v. U.S. (1980), 230
Snyder v. Phelps (2011), 231
Society of Professional Journalists, Headliners Chapter v. Briggs (1988), 228
Soileau v. Smith True Value and Rental (2013), 228
Sonnier v. Crain (2010), 117
St. Amant v. Thompson (1968), 68-69
State of Louisiana v. Morice (1994), 106
State University of New York v. Fox (1989), 217
Stern v. Doe (2001), 90, 99
Stewart v. Courtyard Management Corp. (2005), 225, 232, 239
Stone v. Graham (1980), 49
Stratton Oakmont v. Prodigy Services, Inc. (1995), 256, 261
Super Future Equities v. Wells Fargo (2008), 245-46
Sweezy v. New Hampshire, 110, 119

Tate v. Bradley, 66
Tate v. Woman's Hospital Foundation, 92
Tatro v. University of Minnesota (2012), 243
Tatum v. New Orleans Aviation Board, 93
Taylor v. Louisiana (1962), 34
Taylor v. NBC (1994), 255
Texas Beef Group v. Winfrey (1998), 78, 220
Texas v. Johnson (1989), 32-33
The Florida Bar v. Catarcio (1998), 220
Thomas v. City of Monroe, 76
Thompson v. Western States Medical Center (2002), 218
Tiernan v. Charleston Area Med. Ctr., Inc. (1998), 222
Time, Inc. v. Hill (1967), 224, 233
Tinker v. Des Moines (1969), 32, 43, 110-15, 117-18, 120, 242, 261
Title Research Corp. v. Rausch (1984), 92
TMI, Inc. v. Maxwell (2004), 255
Tooley v. Canal Motors, 93-94
Toomer v. Breaux (1962), 75
Town of Newton v. Rumery (1987), 229
Trans World Airlines v. Hardison (1977), 53
Trentecosta v. Beck, 75
Trout Point Lodge v. Handshoe (2013), 247
Trustees of Dartmouth College v. Woodward (1819), 222
Turner v. Safley (1987), 35

UAW Labor Employment and Training Corp. v. Chao (2003), 221
United Group of National Paper Distributors, Inc. v. Vinson (1996), 220, 231
United States v. Bagdasarian (2011), 243
United States v. Drew, 249
United States v. Finley (2007), 251
United States v. Grob (2009), 244
United States v. Jeffries (2011), 243
United States v. Jones (2012), 250

United States v. Morales (2001), 243
United States v. National Treasury Employees Union (1995), 242
United States v. Warshak (2010), 251
U.S. v. Eichman, 216
U.S. v. Grace, 216
U.S. v. O'Brien (1968), 33
U.S. v. O'Dwyer (2011), 243
U.S. v. Phillip Morris USA, Inc. (2009), 227
U.S. v. Stevens (2010), 33
U.S. v. Ziegler (2007), 225

Valentine v. Chrestensen (1942), 217
Van Orden v. Perry (2005), 51
Virginia State Board of Pharmacy v. Virginia Citizens Consumer Council, Inc. (1976), 216-218
Virginia v. Black (2003), 33, 243, 256

Wallace v. Jaffree (1985), 49
Watkins v. General Refractories Co. (1992), 225
Watts v. United States (1969), 243
West Virginia State Board of Education v. Barnette (1942), 27, 47, 109
White v. Monsanto (1991), 39, 232
Widmar v. Vincent (1981), 33
Winn v. New Orleans City (2013), 225
Wisconsin v. Yoder (1972), 46
Wood v. Del Giorno (2007), 78
Worden v. SunTrust Banks, Inc. (2008), 225

Yoeckel v. Samonig, 86

Zacchini v. Scripps-Howard Broadcasting Co. (1977), 231
Zaffuto v. Hammond, 98
Zaunderer v. Office of Disciplinary Counsel of Supreme Court of Ohio (1985), 219
Zelman v. Simmons-Harris (2002), 48, 52, 57, 60
Zippo Manufacturing v. Zippo Dot Com, 247

Index

A.M.E. Church, see African Methodist Episcopal Church
ABC, see American Broadcasting Company
Abington Township, 48
Abington, 48-49, 59
ACLU, 35, 43, 50-52, 59, 115, 119-20, 184-85, 189, 240, 244, 256, 260-61
Act for Establishing Religious Freedom, 45
Activision Publishing, Inc., 255-56
Acuff-Rose Music, 253
AFL-CIO, 223
African Methodist Episcopal Church, 55
Aiello, Thomas, 105
Alabama, 12, 67-68, 71, 259
Albuquerque, N.M., 115
Alcaldes, 15
Alexandria, La., 16, 171, 173, 180, 200, 225, 235
Allied Marketing Group, Inc., 254
Amazon.com, 247
America's Funniest Home Videos, 84
American Broadcasting Company, 84-85, 99, 101, 141, 142, 196, 259
American Civil Liberties Union, see ACLU
American Opinion, 72
Anderson, Bob, 72
Anglican Church, 45
Anti-Cybersquatting Consumer Protection Act, 254, 255
AOL, 250
Apple, 209, 210, 250, 254
Aquinas, Thomas, 45
Arizona Daily Star, 241
Arizona State University, 255
Arkansas Louisiana Gas Co., 99
Arkansas, 113
ASCAP, 194, 201, 253
Ascension Parish, La., 10, 116, 119
Ashcroft, John, 244
Assemblies of God, 64
Associated Press, 71, 138, 202-03, 212, 241, 246, 258
Assumption Parish, La., 10
Avondale Shipyards, 80

Bad Frog Brewery, 219, 234
Bagdasarian, Walter, 243

Band Hero, 255
Baptists, 45
Barnette, 47, 60, 109, 110, 119
Baton Rouge Advocate, 6
Baton Rouge, La. 6, 10, 20, 25, 37, 42, 69, 72, 76, 82, 105, 119, 124, 127, 130, 131, 136, 137, 166, 173, 177, 200, 203, 205, 213, 232, 235
Baxter, Richard, 245, 249
BBC, 246
Beastie Boys, 253
Beef Corral, 66
Berkeley County Schools, 242
Bethel, 112, 115, 118-19
Bethlehem Area School District, 242
Better Business Bureau of Baton Rouge Area, Inc., 232
Bettie Page Clothing, 223, 235, 241, 258
Big Picture Co., 1987, 225
Bill of Rights, 23, 29-30, 35, 36, 46, 193, 264
Black, Hugo, 28, 30-31, 68
Blades, Lawrence, 216
Blue Mountain School District, 242
BMI, 194, 201, 253
Bock, Carey, 246
Boggs, Lindy, 80
Booker T. Washington High School, 114
Bossier City, La., 115, 119
Boston Massacre, 77
Boston Newsletter, 107
Bourbon Street, 95, 131
Boy Scouts of America, 35, 42, 115
Brandeis, Louis, 85
Brennan, William, 68
Breyer, Stephen, 51, 222
Broadcast Music, Inc., see BMI
Broussard, Aaron, 248
Brown, John, 12
Bryant, Paul "Bear," 71
Buck's Run Enterprises, Inc., 229
Burnett, George, 71
Burnside, Margaret, 114
Bush, George W., 17, 221
Butts, Wally, 71

C.B.C. Distribution & Marketing, Inc., 255

California, 23, 33, 35-36, 42-43, 86, 88-89, 95, 113, 122-23, 125-26, 134, 137-38, 141-42, 158, 176-77, 179, 184-86, 189, 223, 235, 237, 240, 249, 255
Calvin, John, 45
Camp, Dresser & McKee, Inc., 100
Canal Ford Motor, 93-94, 103
Canal Street, 68
Candy the Stripper, 100
Canterbury, 62
Captive Voices, 111
Casablanca Records, 1978, 231
Catfish Cabin, 65
CBS, see Columbia Broadcasting System, Inc.
CDL Marketing, Inc., 25
Center Moriches Union Free School District, 33
Central Hudson Gas & Electric Corporation, 216, 218-19, 233-34
Central Intelligence Agency (CIA), 124, 230
Certiorari, 19, 264
Chalmette, La., 75
Charleston Area Med. Ctr., Inc., 222
Chicago Tribune, 24, 89, 102, 138, 142
Chicago, Il., 24, 72, 82, 89, 102, 122, 138, 142, 195, 213
Children's Online Privacy Protection Act, 252, 256, 258
Chrestensen, F.J., 217
Christian Dior, 255
Church of England, 45, 62
Church of Lukumi Babalu Aye, 47, 59
CIA, see Central Intelligence Agency
Cintas Corp., 223
Citizens United, 222
City of Shaker Heights, 34
Civil Rights Act of 1964, 53, 226, 239
Civil Rights Movement, 34
Civil War, 36, 169
Claiborne, William, 16
Clemens, Roger, 247
Cleveland, Grover, 85
Clinton, George, 253
Clinton, Hillary, 6
Coburg Dairy, Inc., 226
Coca-Cola, 254
Code Noir, 15
Code O'Reilly, 15
Code of 1825 (Louisiana), 12
Code of 1870 (Louisiana), 12, 13
Code of Practice of 1805 (Louisiana), 12

Code of Practice of 1825 (Louisiana), 12
Cohe, Andrew, 50
Cold Stone Creamery, 241
College Network, Inc., 254
Colorado, 68, 113, 115, 135-36, 141
Columbia Broadcasting System, Inc., 50, 229
Columbine, Colorado, 115
Comedy III Productions, 255
Communication Workers of America, 223
Communication: Journalism Education Today, 113
Communications Decency Act, 185, 188, 248, 256, 260
Communications Electronic Privacy Act Amendments Act, 257-58
Confederate States of America, 36
Conference Archives, Inc., 254
Confucius, 215, 233, 234
Connecticut, 46
Connick, Harry, 241
Constitution of 1845 (Louisiana), 16
Constitution of 1852 (Louisiana), 16
Constitution of 1879 (Louisiana), 16, 20
Constitution of 1898 (Louisiana), 20
Consumer Product Safety Improvement Act of 2008, 224, 234
Copyright Act, 192-93, 195, 197, 199, 212, 230-31, 253, 256, 260
Cosby, William, 62
Costco Wholesale Corp., 227
Costello, Josephine, 66
Court of Pleas, 16
Courtyard Management Corp., 225, 232, 239
Covenant Broadcasting Corporation, 64
Covington, La., 6
Cowles Media Co.,, 126, 227, 230, 234
Cox, B. Elton, 34, 105
Craigslist, 246, 259
Creationism, 49
Creative Commons, 191, 195, 201, 211-12, 253, 258
Crowley Post-Signal, 39, 42, 90-92, 94-98, 102, 225, 236
Curtis Publishing Co., 71, 82, 230, 235
Custom of Paris, 11

Dalai Lama, 249
Dallas, Tex., 223
Dartmouth College, 222, 239
Darwin, Charles, 49

De Libellis Famosis, 62
De Scandalis Magnatum, 62
Dean-O's Pizza, 6
Declaration of Independence, 26
Deists, 45
Dell Computers, 209, 213, 254
Democratic National Committee, 229
Dendrite International, 249
Dennis, James, 15
Derbigny, Pierre, 13
Des Moines, Iowa, 32, 43, 110-15, 117-18, 120, 242, 261
Design Technology Group, LLC, 241
Digest of the Criminal Law, 62, 82
Digital Millennium Copyright Act, 253, 256, 260
Dillard's Department Store, 88
DirectTV Holdings, LLC, 223
Dirty World Entertainment Recordings, 249
Dish Network Corporation, 223
DMCA, 253
Donaldsonville, La., 16, 116
DoubleClick, 251, 252, 259
Douglas, William O., 30-31
Dow Chemical Company, 1968, 224
Dun & Bradstreet, Inc., 74, 82
Dupuis, Greg, 70

East Ascension High School, 116
East Bank Consolidated Special Service Fire Protection District, 224-25
East Baton Rouge Parish, La., 10, 37, 42, 76, 82
East Feliciana Parish, La., 10
Easter Seal Society for Crippled Children and Adults of Louisiana., Inc., 99
Eastern Kentucky University, 114
Ebarb, Sara, 50
Economy Carpets Manufacturers and Distributors, Inc., 232
EEOC (Equal Employment Opportunity Commission), 57, 226
Elder, Bill, 67
Electronic Arts, Inc., 2013, 255-56
Electronic Communications Privacy Act (ECPA), 225, 235, 251
Emerson, Ralph Waldo, 105
Emerson, Thomas, 27
England, 26, 38, 44-45, 62, 70, 202
Entertainment Merchants Association, 2011, 33, 255, 256
Equal Access Act of 1984, 117
Equal Employment Opportunity Commission, see EEOC
Establishment Clause, 30, 47-52, 57, 58
Express Lien, Inc., 254

Facebook, 108, 139-40, 223, 241-43, 249-50, 252, 254, 258
Faculty Rights Coalition, 223
Falwell, Jerry, 232, 233
FBI, 98, 124, 127, 134, 250
FCC (Federal Communications Commission), 35, 42, 117, 185, 205
Federal Communications Commission, see FCC
Federal Securities and Exchange Commission, 220
Federal Trade Commission, 220, 252, 256
Federal Wiretap Act, 251, 258
Filmer, Robert, 44
FISA Amendments Act of 2008, 250
Florida, 12, 34, 42, 47, 121-23, 125-27, 129, 131, 134-35, 137-39, 141-42, 165, 171, 199, 217-18, 220, 223, 234-35, 246
Fluker Community Church, 55, 59
Foote, Elizabeth Enry, 70
Ford Motor Co., 255
Foundation for Individual Rights in Education, 117, 120
Fournet, John, 19
Fourteenth Amendment, 30, 110, 247
France, 10-11, 15, 38, 169
Frankish law, 61
Free Assembly Clause, 30
Free Exercise Clause, 30, 46-47, 52, 55-57
Free Press Clause, 29-30
Free Press Underground, 111
Free Speech and its Relation to Self-Government, 27
Free Speech, 27-28, 30, 47, 67, 184, 188, 223-24, 226, 230-31
Freedom of Expression, 26
French Quarter, 68

Garrison, James, 68, 71
Gay Olympics, 231
General Motors, 228, 255
General Refractories Co., 225
Genesis (book of), 49
Geolocational Privacy and Surveillance Act, 257-58
Georgia, 12, 71, 122, 126-29, 141-42, 176-77, 182, 189, 234
Gertz, Elmer, 33, 42, 72-73, 77, 80, 82, 245,

261
Gilleo, Margaret, 217
Giorno, Bob Del, 78
Girls Gone Wild, 95-96
Gissel Packing Co., 223
Gmail, 251, 258, 260
Gobitis, 109, 119
Goddess of Justice, 111
Goldstein, Adam, 110
Gonzales, La., 52, 116
Good News Club, 33
Google, 140, 250-52, 254, 258-60
Gorman, Marvin, 64
Governor's State University, 114
Grambling State University, 105-06, 114, 117, 119
Gramblinite, 114
Great Britain, 61, 193
Greater New Orleans Broadcasting, 216
Greater New Orleans Expressway Commission, 224
Greenmoss Builders, Inc., 74, 82
Greenmoss, 74, 82
Gretna, La., 20, 205
Guardian, 250

Hamilton, Andrew, 62
Hammond, La., 98
Handshoe, Doug, 248
Hannukah, 52
Hardy, Ashton, 66
Harper and Row Publishers, Inc., 230
Hart, Ryan, 255-56
Harvard Law Review, 85
Haynes, Charles, 50
Hazelwood East High School, 35, 42, 112-14, 118-19
Hebrews, 61
Henley, Don, 88, 93
Here's Johnny Portable Toilets,, 255
Hermitage School District, 242
Hero Lands Co., Inc., 232
Hialeah, Florida, 47
Hiestand, Michael, 110
Hispanics United of Buffalo, 241
Holmes, Oliver Wendell, 26, 110
Homeland Security (United States Department of), 224, 250, 258
Houston, Texas, 245
Hustler Magazine, 232-33, 247

Iberville, 10, 96, 97
incorporation doctrine, 30
Indiana, 124, 138, 244
Instagram, 246
Institutes on the Christian Religion, 45
International Association of Machinists and Aerospace Workers, 223
International Brotherhood of Teamsters, Chauffeurs, Warehousemen, and Helpers of America, 59, 222
Iowa, 113
ISKCON, 34
Item Co., 64

Jack in the Box, 76
Jacksonville, Fl., 1975, 221
James (book of), 61
Jefferson Parish, La., 65, 248
Jefferson, Thomas, 16, 26, 45-48
Jehovah's Witnesses, 47, 109
JetPay Merchant Services, LLC, 228, 236
Jews for Jesus, 35, 47
Jindal, Bobby, 6, 244
John Minor Wisdom United States Court of Appeals Building, 12
Johnson, Bernette J., 18
Journalism and Mass Communication Educator, 113
Journalism and Mass Communication Quarterly, 113
Journalism Student Protection Act of 2006, 113
Journalism Teacher Protection Act of 2008, 113

K.C.M.C., 69
Kadlec Medical Center, 232, 233
Kaiser Aetna, 230
Kansas, 113
Katz, Charles, 98, 250
Keller, Sam, 255
Kelly Services, 226
Kentucky, 16, 49, 114, 125, 158, 175
Kidder, Howard, 72
Kimball, "Kitty," 18
KTBS, 64

Labbe, Ron, 19
LaFace Records, 255
Lafayette, La., 66
Lafourche Parish, La., 10

Lake Charles, La., 5, 20, 129, 131, 203
Lakeview Anesthesia Associates, 232-33
Lamb's Chapel, 33
Lane, Scott, 50
Lane, Sharon, 50
Langton, Stephen, 61
Laussat, Pierre de, 15
Law Institute's Restatement (Second) of Torts, 61
Law of the Student Press, 111, 119
Laws of the Indies, 15
Legislative Council of the Territory of Orleans, 11
Lemon Test, 48-49, 51, 59
Letter Concerning Toleration, 44-45, 59
Letter to the Danbury Baptists, 46, 59
Liberty Industrial Life Ins. Co., 227
Lion's Roar, 106
Lislet, L. Moreau, 13
Little Rock, Ark. 248
Livingston Parish, La., 10
Livingston, Edward, 13
Lloyd Corp., 231
Locke, John, 26, 31, 42, 44-46, 59
lockstep doctrine, 36, 40, 41, 44, 54
LoMonte, Frank, 110
Long, Huey P., 105
Longview Outdoor Advertising Co., LLC, 217
Lorain Journal, 77, 246, 261
Lord's Prayer, 48
Lorillard Tobacco Co., 218, 237
Los Angeles International Airport, 47
Los Angeles Times, 213, 241, 259-60
Los Angeles, Calf., 47, 98, 123, 135, 170, 171, 189, 213, 241, 259-60
Louisiana Appellate Court Districts, 19
Louisiana Attorney General Disciplinary Board, 220
Louisiana Board of Chiropractic Examiners, 216, 220
Louisiana Civil Code, 10, 12-13, 25, 38-40, 90, 100, 102, 222, 229
Louisiana Constitution, 11, 19, 23-24, 36-39, 41, 54, 63, 79, 90, 92, 102, 143, 154, 193, 215, 222, 232
Louisiana Court of Appeals, 20, 37, 39
Louisiana Employment Discrimination Law, 57, 226, 237
Louisiana Federation of Teachers, 57
Louisiana Human Rights Commission, 57
Louisiana Legislature, 19, 49, 55, 165-66, 188
Louisiana Office of Attorney General, 220
Louisiana Preservation of Religious Freedom Act, 55-56
Louisiana Public Records Act, 92, 143
Louisiana Science Education Act, 56, 58
Louisiana Smokes Products, Inc., 227
Louisiana State Board of Education, 105-06, 119
Louisiana State Employees Retirement System, 66
Louisiana State Police, 105
Louisiana State University, 6, 7, 25, 105, 106, 117, 119, 156, 166, 203, 213
Louisiana Supreme Court Districts, 17
Louisiana Television Broadcasting Corp., 99
Louisiana Uniform Trade Secret Act, 231, 237
Louisiana Weekly, 64, 83
Loup, Ty, 94
Love, Courtney, 246
LSU, see Louisiana State University
Lumbermen's Mutual Casualty Co., 90, 91
Luther, Martin, 45
Lynch, Bill, 49, 51, 59, 66-67

Madison, James, 31, 45, 46
Magnavox Co., 222
Maison de Mashburn, 77
Major League Baseball Advanced Media, L.P., 255
Mamou, La., 70
Mapp Const., Inc., 229
Marshall, John, 222
Martyn, Larry, 84
Marvin Gorman Ministries, 64
Massachusetts, 46, 113, 126-27, 139, 158, 171, 189, 218
McAlpine, Lord Robert Alistair, 246
McCreary County, Ken., 51, 52, 59
McMahon, Henry, 15
McNamee, Brian, 247
MCPC, Inc., 223
Media Law Resource Center, 82, 244, 259
Meiklejohn, Alexander, 27, 42, 146
Memorial and Remonstrance against Religious Assessments, 45
Meredith Corp., 232
Methodists, 45
Metromedia, Inc., 71, 216
Microsoft, 139, 250
Mill, John Stuart, 26, 27

Milton, John, 26
Minersville, Pa., 109
Mississippi, 12, 71, 114, 127, 130, 149, 166-67, 247-48
Missouri, 33, 106, 111, 119, 249
Mobil Oil Corp, 40
Monroe, La., 16, 65, 76, 82-83, 105, 238, 245
Montana, 244
Montgomery, Alabama, 67
Moore Educational Publishers, Inc., 254
Mormons, 46
Morris, Vanessa, 223
MySpace, 242, 246, 248, 249, 252, 261

NAACP, 18
Naihaus, Carl, 64
Napoleon, 15
Natchitoches, La., 16
Nation Enterprises, 230
National Aeronautics and Space Administration, 225
National Association of Credit Management, Inc., 254
National Association of Manufacturers, 221
National Broadcasting Company (NBC), 255
National Drinking Age Act, 112
National Federation of the Blind of North Carolina, Inc., 216, 221, 227
National Football League, 206, 228
National Labor Relations Act, 221-23
National Labor Relations Board, 221, 223, 235, 237, 241, 258-59
National Security Agency, 250
National Treasury Employees Union, 242
NBC, see National Broadcasting Company
NCH Corp., 228
Nebraska, 127-28, 134, 142, 244, 261
Negreet High School, 50
Netcom, 256
New Hampshire, 33, 42, 46, 70, 110, 119, 127
New Orleans, La., 4, 12, 15-16, 20, 56, 64, 66-67, 73, 77-78, 93-94, 99-100, 103, 106, 112, 117, 120-21, 123-24, 130-37, 139, 141-42, 144, 173-75, 179-81, 191, 195, 199, 202, 205-07, 216, 222, 224-25, 234, 236-39, 243
New Orleans Aviation Board, 93
New Orleans Clothing Store, 64
New Orleans States-Item, 66, 77
New Testament, 48, 61

New York Board of Regents, 48
New York City, 62, 175, 217
New York Party Shuttle, 2013, 241
New York State Liquor Authority, 219, 234
New York Times, 7, 24, 28-29, 33, 43, 67-68, 69, 71-74, 76, 126, 133, 138, 199, 229, 230, 232, 238, 245, 258, 260-61
New York, 7, 24, 28-30, 33, 42-43, 48, 62, 67-74, 76, 82, 86, 88, 102, 110, 122, 125-26, 133, 137-38, 142, 149, 165-70, 172, 175, 178, 182, 185, 189-90, 199, 212, 216-19, 229-30, 232-35, 237-39, 241, 245, 247, 249, 251, 258-61
New-York Weekly Journal, 62
Newton, James, 253
Newtown, Connecticut, 115
Nike, Inc., 216
NLRA, see National Labor Relations Act
NLRB, see National Labor Relations Board
No Doubt, 255-56
Nobel-Prize, 56
North Texas State University, 223

O'Connor, Sandra Day, 73
O'Dwyer, Ashton, 243
O'Reilly, Don Alejandro, 11, 15
Obama, Barack, 210, 241, 243, 258
Obsidian Finance Group, LLC, 256, 261
Ohio Elections Commission, 248
Ohio State Bar Association, 218
On Liberty, 26
OnStar, 250
Opelousas, La., 16
Oregon, 113
Orix Capital, 245-46, 256, 261
Orleans Levee District, 1996, 225
Orleans Parish, La., 10, 56, 68, 133, 142, 146, 166, 241
Out Pub. Inc., 95

PalTalk, 250
Pap's A. M., 33
Paradise Lost, 26
Parish Nat. Bank, 92
Parkway High School, 115
Passaic Daily News, 226
PBS, see Public Broadcasting Service
Pen Register Statute, 251
Penn, William, 45
Pennsylvania, 45, 121, 184, 188, 242, 254
Petition Clause, 30
Phelps Dunbar, L.L.P., 232

Index

Philadelphia Inquirer, 73
Philadelphia, Mississippi, 114
Philadelphia, Penn., 247
Phillip Morris USA, Inc., 227
Pinterest, 246
Plaquemines Parish, La., 10, 135, 143, 152, 165
Playboy, 99, 100, 102, 256, 261
Playtime Theatres, 34
Pledge of Allegiance, 47, 109
Pointe Coupee, La., 10, 16
Powell, Lewis, 72
Practice Act of 1805, 13
Presbyterians, 45
Prior Restraint, 107
Procter & Gamble Co., 93
Prodigy Services, Inc., 256, 261
Prosser, William, 86-87, 89, 91-92, 102
Proverbs (book of), 61
Prudhomme, Paul, 93
Pruneyard Shopping Center, 36, 55
Psalms (book of), 61
Public Broadcasting Service (PBS), 99-100
Public Citizen, Inc., 220
Publick Occurrences, 107

R.A.V., 2003, 33
Rapides Parish, La., 16, 152, 166, 173, 180
Reagan, Ronald, 32, 223
Red Guild, 72
Reddit, 241
Redland Aggregates Ltd., 245
Reese Services, Inc., 63
Rehnquist, William, 159, 218, 233
Religious Freedom Restoration Act, 46, 52, 53, 238
Religious Land Use and Institutionalized Persons Act, 53
Religious Liberty, 5, 31, 44, 54, 55
Religious Technology Center, 256
Rent-A-Center, Inc., 225
Republican National Convention, 32
"Reveille Seven," 106, 109
Reveille, 105
Revolutionary Communist Youth, 117
Reynolds, George, 46
Rhode Island, 32, 43, 45, 127, 149, 234
Rives, Richard, 12
RLUIPA, 53
Robert Welch, Inc., 26, 33, 42, 72-73, 77, 80, 82, 245

Rochester Folding Box Co., 86
Roe, Jennifer, 115
Rome, Italy, 11
Rousseau, Jean-Jacques, 46
Rutgers University, 255

Sabine Parish, La., 21, 50
Saderup, Gary, 255
Salic law, 61
San Diego, Calf., 71, 216
Santa Fe Independent School District, 27, 49
Saturday Evening Post, 71
Savoie's Sausage and Food Products, Inc., 227
Scalia, Antonin, 52
Schaefer, Jr., Roy B. 66
Scheff, Sue, 246, 256
Scopes Monkey Trial, 49
Scripps-Howard Broadcasting Co., 231
SDT Industries, Inc., 220, 228
Sears Roebuck & Co., 91, 103
Second Restatement of Torts (1977), 87
Second Treatise on Government, 26, 31, 44, 59
Securing the Protection of our Enduring and Established Constitutional Heritage Act, 247
SESAC, 253
Seventh-Day Adventist, 46
Sharrif, Umar, 84, 85, 99, 101
Sherbert, Adell, 46-47
Shreveport, La., 18, 20, 69, 177, 189, 202-03
SICB, 56
Siete Partidas, 15
Simmons, Bobby, 70
Simmons, Jack, 94
Simorangkir, Dawn, 246
Skype, 250
SLAPP, see Strategic Lawsuit Against Public Participation
Slidell Memorial Hospital, 73
Smalley Maintenance Services, Inc., 224, 225
Smith True Value and Rental, 228
Smith, James Monroe, 105
Snowden, Edward, 250
Society for Integrative and Comparative Biology, 56
Society of European Stage Authors and Composers (SESAC), 253
Society of Professional Journalists, 8, 228
Sony, 240, 261

Sound Images, Inc., 254, 261
South Carolina, 30, 42, 46, 140
Southeast Journalism Conference, 106
Southeastern Louisiana University, 5, 104, 106, 117
Southern Bell Telephone & Telegraph Co., 224
Southern Oregon University, 243, 261
Southern Poverty Law Center Inc., 247
Southern University, 105, 111
Southern University at New Orleans (SUNO), 112
Southwest Regional Council of Carpenters, 231
Spain, 10-11, 15, 151-52, 166
Spectrum, 112
SPLC, 111, 120
St. Bernard Parish, La., 10, 75, 175
St. Charles Parish, La., 10
St. Helena Parish, La., 10
St. James Parish, La., 10
St. John the Baptist Parish, La., 10
St. Landry Parish, La., 222
St. Paul Mercury Insurance Co., 15
St. Tammany Parish, La., 10, 138, 232, 235
Star Chamber, 61
State Farm Fire and Cas. Co., 65
State University of New York, 217
Statue of Liberty, 111
Steimle and Associates, 100
Stern, Howard, 246
Stevens, John Paul, 222
Stored Communications Act, 251, 260
Strategic Lawsuit Against Public Participation (SLAPP), 79, 245, 256
Student Press Law Center, 106, 110-11, 113, 119-20
Submarine case, 217, 233
Sulllivan, L. B., 67
Sunbelt Rentals, Inc., 226
SUNO, see Southern University at New Orleans
SunTrust Banks, Inc., 225
Super Future Equities , 245-46, 256, 261
Superior Council, 15
Supremacy Clause (of U.S. Constitution), 9
Sutton, Eric Sutton, 223
Swaggart, Jimmy, 64

Tangipahoa Parish, La., 10, 119, 175
Taylor, Elizabeth, 255
TCI Cablevision, 255
Ten Commandments, 49, 51-52
Tennessee, 49, 222
Tepoorten, 228, 236
Terrebonne Parish, La., 10
Territory of Orleans, 11
Texaco, Inc., 232
Texas Beef Group, 78, 220
Texas Food Disparagement Law, 220
Texas, 12, 23, 32-33, 43, 71, 78, 88, 124, 127, 130, 133, 138, 141, 220, 223, 235, 239, 245-47, 249
Thompson Newspapers, 66
Thundervision, LLC, 100
Time Magazine, 224, 233
Times-Picayune, 73, 83, 212
Title Research Corp., 92
Title VII, 53, 54, 57, 226, 239
Titus (book of), 61
TMI, Inc., 255
Tooley, John, 93, 94, 103
"Toward a General Theory of the First Amendment," 27
Trans World Airlines, 53
Transportation Security Administration, 115
Trentecosta, Gordon "Tiny," 75
Trout Point Lodge, 247
Tucson, Arizona, 241
Tuttle, Elbert, 12
Twibel, 63, 83
Twitter, 63, 139-40, 241, 246, 249-50, 252, 254, 260

U. S. Army, 71
U. S. House of Representatives, 31
U.S. Civil Service Commission, 226
U.S. Justice Department, 18
U.S. Olympic Committee, 231, 238
U.S. Post Office Dept., 221
UAW Labor Employment and Training Corp., 221
UMG Recordings, 253
United Group of National Paper Distributors, Inc., 220, 231
United Press International, 64
United States Army, 226
United States Bankruptcy Court, 100
United States Census, 17
United States Voting Rights Act, 17
University of Alabama, 71
University of Georgia, 71
University of Louisiana-Monroe, 245

Index

University of Minnesota, 243, 261
University of Mississippi, 71
University of Missouri at Kansas City, 33
University of Missouri, 33, 106, 111, 119
University of New Orleans, 111, 117, 222, 237
University of Virginia, 33
Utah, 46, 239

Veggie Libel, 78
Ventress, La., 18
Victory, Jeffrey P., 18
Vietnam War, 105, 110, 242
Ville Platte Gazette, 70
Virginia, 27, 31, 33, 35, 43, 45-47, 60, 109-10, 119, 125, 127-28, 131, 135, 142, 148-49, 166, 171, 216-18, 234, 239, 242-43, 256, 262, 271
Virginia Citizens Consumer Council, 216, 218
Virginia Declaration of Rights, 31
Virginia State Board of Pharmacy, 216-18
Virginia Statute for Religious Freedom, 45, 46
Voting Rights Act, 9, 17, 25

Wal-Mart Stores, Inc., 232
Walker, Edwin, 71
Warren, Earl, 110
Warren, Samuel, 85
Washington Parish, La., 64
Washington Post, 250
Washington, D.C., 10, 111, 130-31, 182
Wells Fargo, 245, 246
West Baton Rouge Parish, La., 10
West Feliciana Parish, La., 10
West Virginia, 27, 43, 47, 60, 109-10, 119, 127, 149, 242
Western States Medical Center, 218
Whistleblower Protection Act, 224
Williams, Roger, 45
Winfrey, Oprah, 78, 220
Winter Garden, Fla., 217
Wiretap Act, 251, 258
Wisconsin, 46, 60, 86, 102, 149, 153, 165
Wisdom, John Minor, 12
Woman's Hospital Foundation, 92
Wood, Pinckney, 78
Woodland R-IV School District, 242
World War Z, 252

Yahoo, 243, 250, 254

Yale Law Journal, 27
Yellow Book USA, Inc., 227
Youngs Drug Products Corp., 219
YouTube, 210, 243, 250

Zacchini, Hugo, 231
Zaffuto, Terry, 98
Zenger, John Peter, 62, 82
Zippo Dot Com, 247
Zippo Manufacturing, 247